If I say *If*

This book is available as a free fully-searchable PDF from
www.adelaide.edu.au/press

If I Say If

The Poems and Short Stories of Boris Vian

Translations by

Maria Freij and Peter Hodges

Edited by

Alistair Rolls
School of Humanities and Social Science, The University of Newcastle

John West-Sooby and Jean Fornasiero
School of Humanities, The University of Adelaide

UNIVERSITY OF
ADELAIDE PRESS

Published in Adelaide by

University of Adelaide Press
The University of Adelaide
Level 1, 254 North Terrace
South Australia 5005
press@adelaide.edu.au
www.adelaide.edu.au/press

The University of Adelaide Press publishes externally refereed scholarly books by staff of the University of Adelaide. It aims to maximise access to the University's best research by publishing works through the internet as free downloads and for sale as high quality printed volumes.

For the full Cataloguing-in-Publication data please contact the National Library of Australia: cip@nla.gov.au

ISBN (paperback) 978-1-922064-60-8
ISBN (ebook: pdf) 978-1-922064-62-2
ISBN (ebook: epub) 978-1-922064-71-4
ISBN (ebook: mobi) 978-1-922064-72-1

Book design: Zoë Stokes
Book illustrations: © 2014 Lucy West-Sooby
Cover design: Emma Spoehr
Cover illustrations: © 2014 Tom Jellett
Additional support: Celia Jellett
Paperback printed by Griffin Press, South Australia

CONTENTS

FOREWORD

The collective endeavour behind this book is not only praiseworthy, it is historical as well. No anthology collecting so many poems and short stories by Boris Vian in English translation has ever been published before. The reader will find here all of the poems from the collection *Je voudrais pas crever* (*I wouldn't wanna die*) as well as the 28 short stories which appeared posthumously in two previous books in French, *Le Loup-garou* (*The Werewolf*) and *Le Ratichon baigneur* (translated here as *The Swimming Priest*). Vian's first collection of short stories (*Les Fourmis*, 1949) was translated by Julia Older and published in 1992 under the title *Blues for a Black Cat and Other Stories*. As the late Noël Arnaud wrote in his preface to *Le Ratichon baigneur*, it is safe to say that today all of Vian's short stories are available, but now we are able to add: in English. Arnaud not only insists that the short story genre is a difficult one, but also hints at the fact that Vian is one of the rare French writers of his time to be so prolific in it. Notoriously, Vian cultivated a strong affinity for short texts, be they fictional, journalistic or satirical (even his novels, except *Autumn in Peking*, are relatively short). The short story offers a format that suits his tastes particularly well. He can indulge profusely in his sweet and sour humour, deconstruct language and directly hit out at his favourite targets, all of which wear uniforms: the church, the military, cops and even bus drivers. He can easily flip the world around: in his universe, a werewolf is a real gentleman and a heart of gold is literally worth stealing. Vian's unique style blends irony and tenderness, acidity and affection. One never knows for sure where one is being led in his stories, which almost all the time end up with an unexpected or irreverent "chute" — an ultimate line which provides the whole narrative with an indispensible and powerful punch.

Boris Vian's reputation holds a paradoxical status which is slowly evolving to the point, hopefully, of being radically altered. First and foremost, despite his huge popularity in France, he is still largely snubbed by French academics, who condescendingly view him as an insignificant, at best marginal, author, a jack-of-all-trades, or even sometimes a novelist for grade twelve students. Furthermore, despite his public popularity in the Hexagon, he is still relatively unknown in the English-speaking world, most notably in North America (with the exception of French-speaking Quebec, where he is quite adulated). There is hope that the present book will shake off this uncomfortable status for good. True, TamTam Books (California) has diligently published half a dozen Vian titles, starting with the novel *I Spit on Your Graves* in 1998; but, despite positive reviews in *The New Yorker*, *The Believer* and the *Los Angeles Times*, it is still too early to assess the impact these publications are having on a potential readership. That said, it is not surprising to find that *Foam of the Daze* is TamTam's bestselling novel, along with the aforementioned hard-boiled thriller, *I Spit on your Graves*, the original version of which was published in France in 1946 under the pseudonym Vernon Sullivan. This illustrates that there is at least some coherence between the French and English readerships.

Translating Boris Vian, the prose writer and the poet, is no small feat. It would measure up to something like translating Swift or Joyce into French (which has been done, however, and quite successfully so). The problem here lies in Vian's unique way of treating, or rather mistreating, the French idiom. Add to this a cutting type of humour and a constant use of slang that are in part firmly anchored in the post-war period, and you have all the ingredients to make the task of translating those texts rather daunting. In addition, many characters that populate these short stories really existed in Vian's entourage, or are only slight subversions of them.[1] The good news is simple to assert: the texts you are about to discover have been handled by people who have dutifully done their homework. They know Boris Vian very well, and they are obviously familiar with his novels and the rest of his short stories already published in English. Indeed, the translators Maria Freij and Peter Hodges were well equipped to perform a task that demanded time, effort and relentless patience. With regard to Boris Vian's short stories in English, it is less known that Vian had himself translated into English seven of the eleven short stories

1 For that, the reader is advised to consult the endnotes, or peruse Vian's *Manuel de Saint-Germain-des-Prés*, available in translation from TamTam Books.

collected in *Les Fourmis*. However, for lack of evidence, we do not know what he hoped for in doing so.[2] In a sense, therefore, this book closes the loop he had opened himself in the mid 1940s.

Specialists of the life and works of Boris Vian do not roam in abundance around this planet. In fact, they are generally so scarce that they can easily gather in one single conference, as happened at the Sorbonne in June 2007, or pile up in one volume. Such is practically the case here, where you have the essence of Vianism both in French and English academia, with articles by Alistair Rolls, Christelle Gonzalo, François Roulmann and Audrey Camus, not to mention the technical notes of the translators and editors of this volume. What a treat! Not only will you, dear reader, relish discovering this truly gripping poetry and astonishing short fiction, but as a bonus you will get the elevated comments that do not usually accompany works of such nature. Bon voyage!

Marc Lapprand

---

[2] Cf. *Œuvres romanesques complètes* (Paris: Gallimard, Bibliothèque de la Pléiade, 2 vols, 2010), vol. II, p. 1214.

BORIS VIAN: A LIFE IN PARADOX

Alistair Rolls, John West-Sooby and Jean Fornasiero

Introducing Boris Vian to an Anglo-Saxon audience presents something of a challenge, principally because he is so well known in his native France that it is difficult to imagine how he could have escaped the attention of the rest of the world. And yet, Vian remains almost unknown outside academic circles in countries such as Great Britain and the United States, where so many other prominent figures of the French cultural and intellectual landscape of the 1940s and 1950s — most of whom Vian frequented and counted as his friends — remain a subject of enduring fascination.[1] Whereas other figures of that heady period such as Georges Perec, Albert Camus, Jean-Paul Sartre and Simone de Beauvoir have long been granted a place in the pantheon of world literature, Vian remains obstinately in the shadows. In terms of public impact, then, we might say that Boris Vian is one of France's most surprising export failures.

Why surprising? Because Vian's involvement in the Parisian intellectual life of the post-war period and the eclectic nature of his artistic pursuits — which ranged from hard-boiled crime writing to science fiction and jazz — give him the kind of profile that would seem tailor-made to appeal to a wider public, and particularly to the English-speaking world. It is nevertheless the case that his life and work have not yet found that broader resonance. British

[1] Interestingly, he has achieved recognition in some other parts of the world. His books are quite widely read in translation in Hungary, for example, and he has a certain following in Japan.

crime-fiction readers will know Georges Simenon but not have heard of Boris Vian; generations of American feminists will know Simone de Beauvoir but not this man she used to meet at parties and in the cafés of Saint-Germain-des-Prés, and of whom she was quite fond; Sci-Fi fans throughout the Anglo-Saxon world are familiar with Jules Verne but not with France's translator of A.E. van Vogt; and soul-searching teenagers around the world work through their angst or at times discover it in the works of Jean-Paul Sartre, but will never know the man with whom he shared so much.

It should be noted that, even in France, Boris Vian's work has not acquired the kind of status enjoyed by several of his contemporaries, whose works feature routinely on the curriculum in French universities and are the subject of on-going scholarly analysis. Apart from the few pioneering doctoral theses, Vian's work has remained outside the ivory towers of French academia, and is to some degree still frowned upon by scholars.[2] As far as the French education system is concerned, he appears to warrant discussion only in high schools, and even then he is treated in little more than a cursory manner. This state of affairs is all the more perverse when we consider that Vian became one of France's most widely read and cherished authors following his death in 1959, and especially following the events of May 1968. His anti-establishment attitude and his image as the "eternal adolescent" made him a much-loved figure for the younger generation in the sixties and seventies. A sign of his enduring popular appeal is the fact that he has been the subject of any number of biographies; indeed, they seem to appear with some regularity, rarely varying much in content or in the packaging of the myth.[3]

Boris Vian thus occupies a paradoxical position: on the one hand, he is a popular and well-read author who can be counted among the most important figures of twentieth-century French literature in terms of the quality of his work, the depth and breadth of his thinking, the enormity of his commercial success and the impact of his vision (on the French peace movement, to give

---

2 It is still the case that students in France who wish to do postgraduate research on Vian are warned off or offered other, more "suitable", choices.

3 The following is a selection: Jean Clouzet, *Boris Vian* (Paris: Seghers, 1966); Françoise Renaudot, *Il était une fois Boris Vian* (Paris: Seghers, 1973); Philippe Boggio, *Boris Vian* (Paris: Flammarion, 1993); Frédéric Richaud, *Boris Vian. C'est joli de vivre* (Paris: Éditions du Chêne, 1999); Claire Julliard, *Boris Vian* (Paris: Gallimard, 2007).

but one example); but at the same time, he is neglected by scholarship and frequently dismissed as an author for young people — not a compliment in France. If we are to describe the man (and the myth with which he has now merged), it is important to keep in mind this fundamental binary opposition, for many others follow from it. It is Vian's frivolous side, for example, rather more than his serious other side, that is largely responsible for the revered position he has acquired in the French popular imaginary. There is further irony in the fact that it is outside France that the scholarly study of Boris Vian has flourished.

It is indeed as an exported commodity that Vian's work has been reconfigured over the decades as something worthy of academic scholarship. Despite his almost non-existent public reputation in the English-speaking world, it is in the Anglo-Saxon system — and most especially in the universities of North America, where some of the great names of Vian studies have worked (we might think of Gilbert Pestureau, Michel Rybalka and Marc Lapprand) — that the most influential work has emerged.[4] Thanks to the efforts of these and other scholars, for whom Vian's less-than-serious side has been seen not as an impediment to our understanding of his writing but as one of the keys to it, his work has taken on new stature, and new markets are beginning to emerge in various parts of the world. In 2004, Marc Lapprand was thus able to write in a special edition of France's most famous literary journal, the *Magazine littéraire*, that, as far as Vian was concerned, "the most interesting

4 Michel Rybalka was Professor of Romance Languages at Washington University, St Louis. He is the author of one of the earliest scholarly studies of Vian, entitled *Boris Vian: Essai d'interprétation et de documentation* (Paris: Minard, 1969). A graduate of the Sorbonne, Gilbert Pestureau ended his career at Loyola University Chicago, having previously taught in various other parts of the world, including the University of Nantes, in France. He was a member of the team that produced the first edition of Vian's complete works with Fayard in 1999-2003. He is also the author of *Boris Vian, les Amerlauds et les Godons* (Paris: UGE, 10/18, 1978) and of the *Dictionnaire des personnages de Vian* (Paris: Bourgois, 1985). Marc Lapprand has taught in the Department of French at the University of Victoria in British Columbia since 1989. He was a member of the editorial team responsible for Vian's complete works, and also led the team that prepared Vian's prose works for publication in Gallimard's Pléaide series in 2010. He is the author of the influential study *Boris Vian: La vie contre* (Ottawa: Presses de l'Université d'Ottawa, 1993).

contemporary phenomenon [was happening] overseas".[5] In support of this claim, he noted that, in addition to the new editions of Vian's work being published in Japan, Romania and Spain, the Californian case of Tosh Berman's TamTam press, which has produced English versions of a number of Vian's longer prose works, has led something of a renaissance for Vian in America.

There are, promisingly, some signs that the literary milieu in France has likewise begun to take Vian more seriously of late. Already in 1999, a project to publish his complete works was undertaken by the reputable publishing house Fayard. More recently, in 2010, Gallimard published Vian's collected prose writings in its prestigious "Pléiade" series — the ultimate consecration for an author in France and, in Vian's case, a belated recognition of one of the country's cultural miracles.[6] This may be the catalyst for his work to be taken more seriously in academic circles in France. And conversely, given the paradoxes that seem to characterise the man and his work, it is entirely possible that the new-found prestige conferred upon him by this editorial canonisation in his native land might also lead to a larger public profile elsewhere, and in particular in the Anglo-Saxon world. That, at least, is the mission to which this present volume aims to contribute.

***

It may surprise those readers who are already familiar with his work that Vian needs to be transported to the Anglo-Saxon world at all. For, in a great many of his texts, his characters famously visit, and often never set foot outside, the United States. He also passed himself off for some time as the translator of a Black American author by the name of Vernon Sullivan, though he himself

---

5 Marc Lapprand, "Lire Boris Vian", *Magazine littéraire*, 6, 2004-2005, pp. 97-98 (p. 97) (our translation). This special number was the first of the new *Collections* series, a sort of best-of album designed to bring together previously published academic material along with work by the current leading specialists. That Vian was chosen for this inaugural number is testament to his stature among the reading public in France.

6 Boris Vian, *Œuvres romanesques complètes*, edited by Marc Lapprand, with Christelle Gonzalo and François Roulmann (Paris: Gallimard, Bibliothèque de la Pléiade, 2 vols, 2010).

never crossed the Atlantic.[7] This is yet another of the paradoxes with which Vian has become synonymous. The foreign has a strangely familiar quality in much of his work. In Vian's second major novel signed under his own name, for instance, *L'Automne à Pékin* (*Autumn in Peking*), his characters are all catapulted from Paris onto the desert sands of the imaginary land of Exopotamia; but this turns out to be a journey into mythical space, and Exopotamia a thinly veiled allegory of Paris itself. In some ways, the more exotic he appeared, in fact and fiction, the more Parisian he turned out to be. As he notes himself in his song "L'Âme slave" ("The Slavic Soul"):

> J'ai jamais été plus loin que la barrière de Pantin
> Tout c'que j'ai d'russe en moi c'est le prénom
> Mais ça suffit bien
> [I've never been further than the barrière de Pantin (in Paris)
> The only thing Russian about me is my name
> But that's quite enough][8]

This contrast between his real self and his imagined other was learned in childhood. Born in 1920 at Ville d'Avray, on the western edge of Paris, he was raised in a world of imagination, fuelled by literature and society games (including chess with childhood friends and neighbours such as the child prodigy Yehudi Menuhin and François Rostand, the only son of the well-known writer and free thinker Jean Rostand). His early life was carefree and comfortable. His parents were well-off, and the villa where they lived was not far from the Parc de Saint Cloud, where Boris, his sister Ninon and his brothers Lélio and Alain would go to catch frogs at the request of their neighbour Jean Rostand. This easy existence was destined to be short-lived, however. The stock market crash put an end to the Vian fortune in 1929, forcing Boris's parents to move the family to the caretaker's cottage in order to let the main house out

---

7 Vian not only wrote a tetralogy of novels under this pseudonym, but he also had far more success with novels such as *J'irai cracher sur vos tombes* (*I Spit on Your Graves*) (1946) than he did with those that he produced under his own name. This was painfully true in the case of his first major novel *L'Écume des jours* (*Foam of the Daze*) (1947), for which he famously did not win the *Prix de la Pléiade*. Indeed, Vian's only real literary success in his own lifetime, especially popularly but also critically, was as Vernon Sullivan.

8 "L'Âme slave" (1954), in Boris Vian, *Chansons* (Paris: Bourgois, 1994), pp. 58-59 (p. 59) (our translation).

for rent (to the Menuhins). Then, at the age of twelve, a heart problem, which was diagnosed early and which would be a constant, ticking reminder of his mortality until his early death at the age of 39, consigned the young Boris to his bedroom and to the care of an overly controlling mother. The perverse, but understandable, result of this condition was the unbridled imagination seen in evidence above, along with an enormous lust for life.

Despite the regular interruptions to his education caused by the effects of his heart condition, Boris succeeded in obtaining his baccalaureate and in 1939 gained entry to the prestigious engineering school known as the *École centrale de Paris*. The outbreak of war forced the school to relocate to Angoulême, in south-west France, where Boris continued his studies, obtaining his engineering qualification in 1942. He spent the war years largely on the fringe, detached from these dramatic events, a spectator rather than a participant. As he would later observe, "I did not fight, I was not deported, I did not collaborate, I remained for four years just one of many other under-fed imbeciles."[9]

Following his studies, he financed his rich "other" existence — as a writer of novels, plays, short stories, poems and songs, as a jazz impresario, critic and trumpeter, as an inventor, intellectual and socialite — by working long hours at a series of day jobs, beginning with that most French of French bureaucratic organisations, the mind-numbing office of standardisation (AFNOR: *Association Française de Normalisation*). Unsurprisingly, he left that office as soon as he could and tried his hand at a variety of occupations. He worked as a translator of lengthy memoirs, wrote for jazz journals and eventually found employment with Philips Records, where he was put in charge of the jazz section. In his spare time, he could be found in the trendy hot spots of Saint-Germain-des-Prés, rubbing shoulders and exchanging ideas with the likes of Sartre, Beauvoir, Raymond Queneau, Juliette Greco and Anne-Marie Cazalis, or simply playing his trumpet. He also found the wherewithal to write, producing a prodigious number of novels, short stories, poems, plays, songs… in what would prove to be a limited space of time. In short, he "lived" himself quite literally to death, forcing his body to grab back every one of his limited hours on earth, almost tempting fate. Offices, jazz

---

[9] Quoted in Richaud, *Boris Vian: C'est joli de vivre*, p. 31 (our translation).

cellars and cafés framed his Parisian adventures, and tiny flats were his home. Only summer vacations, spent at Landemer in Normandy during his youth, and later, as an adult, in Saint-Tropez, took him away from Paris.

When Boris Vian died, it was with a sense of poetry and irony that only he could get away with. The story is, like much of Vian's life and legacy, so fabulous that it appears more myth than reality. On 23 June 1959 Boris went into the Petit Marbeuf cinema just off the Champs-Élysées to attend a private screening of a film adaptation of his novel, *J'irai cracher sur vos tombes* (*I Spit on Your Graves*), a film that he had disapproved of from the outset, believing that it betrayed the spirit of his book. No sooner had the opening credits rolled past than, to the great consternation of those gathered in the small theatre, his head slumped back. He would never get to see any more of the film he had publicly denounced and whose production he had fought. A short time later, at the Laennec hospital where he was transported, Boris Vian was pronounced dead from a heart attack.

***

Vian's extreme wanderlust of the imagination is certainly in part explained by his medical condition and by his family and working life in Paris. The sense of confinement — of himself in small rooms, in the same city, and of his imagination beating irregularly and too loudly inside his chest — found its natural safety valve in literary outpourings that reached far beyond the particular metropolis to which he was bound. He was quintessentially Parisian, but this did not prevent the rest of the country from also identifying strongly with him. Vian is certainly owned by Parisians and non-Parisians alike. He is synonymous with Paris, its literary avant-garde and its Liberation euphoria (frenetic dancing in cellars, zazous and bobby-soxers, black American jazz musicians, and so on). On the other hand, he is also renowned, and owned, throughout France as a representative of French culture more generally. Few are those who have not heard his songs, especially his famous song about avoiding conscription, "Le Déserteur", which brought him a rare moment of international acclaim. Most people you meet in France are also likely to have read one of his novels — generally *L'Écume des jours* (*Foam of the Daze*) or

J'irai cracher sur vos tombes (*I Spit on Your Graves*). The release in April 2013 of a new film version of *L'Écume des jours* (English title: *Mood Indigo*) starring Romain Duris, Audrey Tautou, Gad Elmaleh and Omar Sy is likely to win him a new generation of aficionados.[10] He is well known for his tendency to populate his novels and short stories with characters based on his own family members, friends and, quite often, enemies, to the point that much academic work has found it hard to go beyond "biographical interpretation" of his work.[11] And yet, the intertextuality on which his work is equally predicated attests to a vast erudition, and especially an extensive knowledge of French literature. He was a voracious and eclectic reader. He is famous, in fact, for having "read everything".[12] He was thus a repository of France's literary culture and a catalyst in many ways for its rediscovery and reinvention by subsequent generations.

***

Vian began his career as an author of fiction just as the Second World War was drawing to a close. His early novels are attuned to the Zeitgeist. The move from prelapsarian bliss to entropy in *L'Écume des jours* is one way of capturing the duality of the Liberation mood with its heady mix of euphoria and recrimination; another is the translation hoax that is *J'irai cracher sur vos tombes*, which appears to parody the famous translated thrillers of Marcel Duhamel's *Série Noire*, but which in fact *translates* their allegorical staging

---

10 An earlier film version was produced in 1968 (English title: *Spray of the Days*).

11 Marc Lapprand has played a pioneering role in refocusing Boris Vian studies on the text rather than the man. In his opening article for the above-mentioned issue of the *Magazine littéraire*, "Sept mots clés pour expliquer sa postérité" (pp. 7-12), he moves swiftly on from the Vernon Sullivan case and Vian's sudden death to a discussion of the seven key features of his works that have given him an enduring legacy as an author. These are: humour, eccentricity, eclecticism, jazz (although here Lapprand is forced to discuss Vian's musicianship in addition to the influence of this musical genre on his writing), sensuality, professionalism and freedom.

12 Nicole Bertolt of the Vian Foundation, who arguably knows the man behind the myth better than anyone, will point for evidence to the groaning bookshelves in his flat in Cité Véron, whose balcony overlooks the roof of the Moulin Rouge, and then remind you that much less literature was published annually in Vian's lifetime than today. She adds this disclaimer not to belittle his achievement but to emphasise that the claim is meant quite literally in Vian's case.

of the post-war mood with great precision.[13] Across his range of writings, therefore, Vian played a foundational role in French cultural production under the Fourth Republic, a time during which the influence of American culture could be seen everywhere. To be French, throughout Vian's adult life, meant to define oneself, consciously or otherwise, in terms of one's love or hatred for the new trans-Atlantic superpower. Vian's ambivalent attitude towards the United States is well recorded.[14] His feelings towards the British were equally mixed.[15] Nevertheless, translation into "English" was part of Vian's psyche as much as it was an inescapable part of French post-war literature.

That post-war ambience and Vian's ambivalent attitude towards American culture are certainly in evidence in the poems and stories presented here — as indeed are all of his personal obsessions (his love of jazz and cars, for instance) along with his cultural and literary influences, surrealism and existentialism prominent among them. What is also striking in these texts is his fascination with language itself — a fascination that pre-dates his involvement with the seriously facetious "College of 'Pataphysics", but that was no doubt nurtured by it.[16] Vian's constant recourse to word play and his experimentation with the sounds and syntax of French often appear as almost a reflex reaction on his part, an automatic response to the question of how to represent the world as he perceived it. They are certainly one of the well-springs of his literary creativity.

This creative use of language of course presents a particular challenge for the translator. Some might indeed argue that translating Vian is a highly

---

[13] For more on Vian's work in this context, see Alistair Rolls and Deborah Walker, *French and American Noir: Dark Crossings* (Houndmills: Palgrave Macmillan, 2009).

[14] See, for example, Christopher Jones, *Boris Vian Transatlantic: Sources, Myths, and Dreams* (New York/Bern: Peter Lang, 1998).

[15] While the poem "If I say *if*" (as translated in the present volume) stages a stereotypical Anglophobia, Vian at the same time had what might be considered a rather British sense of irony. P.G. Wodehouse's work was among his influences. For more on his British and American influences, see Gilbert Pestureau, *Boris Vian, les Amerlauds et les Godons.*

[16] Founded in 1948, the "Collège de 'Pataphysique" is a society that has as its motto *Eadem mutata resurgo* ("I rise again the same though changed"). It was here that, in the 1950s, Vian frequented such luminaries as Marcel Duchamp, Max Ernst, Raymond Queneau, Eugène Ionesco, René Clair and Joan Miró, among others.

utopian undertaking. For David Bellos, however, there is no such thing as an untranslatable text, only texts demanding greater or lesser degrees of translatorly acrobatics.[17] Furthermore, instances where meaning or even that "certain poetic something" become lost in translation are, to Bellos's mind, greatly exaggerated. He would certainly take issue with the notion that Vian is untranslatable. After all, he himself has translated Georges Perec, as has Gilbert Adair, while Barbara Wright is renowned for her translations of Raymond Queneau. These authors are just as difficult to translate as Vian, not least because of their association with the Oulipo movement, which was built on a series of word plays and formal constraints.[18]

But of course, successfully translating puns is only one aspect of the task facing the literary translator. In the case of Vian, as Sophie de Nodrest has argued, the two early English translations of *L'Écume des jours* — Stanley Chapman's *Froth on the Daydream* and John Sturrock's *Mood Indigo* — could both be defended as good translations from that perspective.[19] And yet, both somehow fail to convey the poignancy of the love story that is at the heart of the novel. It was with the avowed purpose of recapturing the spirit of the original manuscript that Brian Harper retranslated the novel in 2003, with the title *Foam of the Daze*. This is spelled out in Tosh Berman's editor's note, which precedes the translator's introduction to the text. As Berman makes clear, fidelity to the "inherent qualities of the author" was a driving factor

---

[17] David Bellos, *Is That a Fish in Your Ear? Translation and the Meaning of Everything* (London: Penguin, 2011).

[18] "Oulipo" (or "OuLiPo") is an abbreviation of "Ouvroir de littérature potentielle", which translates roughly as "Workshop of potential literature". The movement, which sought to foster the creation of literary works using constrained writing techniques (such as writing a novel without using the letter "e"), was founded in 1960 by Raymond Queneau and François Le Lionnais. It counted among its members mathematicians, poets and novelists, including Georges Perec and Italo Calvino.

[19] See her Masters thesis, entitled Re-Creation of a Recreation: A Comparative Study of Two English Translations of "*L'Écume des jours,*" in which she bases much of her praise for the work of Stanley Chapman and John Sturrock on their ability to recreate, with linguistic exactitude, Vian's humour and puns. The thesis can be found at the following website: http://rob.toadshow.com.au/01_cms/details.asp?ID=339 (accessed 8 February 2012). *Froth on the Daydream* was published in London by Rapp & Carroll in 1967; *Mood Indigo* appeared the following year through New York's Grove Press.

behind this new edition of the novel; the other was Vian's evolving status in the French popular imaginary.[20]

To translate a novel by Boris Vian is therefore not just difficult because it is full of jokes with culturally specific points of reference both to French literature or history and to the world of his own personal entourage; it is challenging because the playful allusions and often quasi-adolescent humour are frequently combined with deep pathos. In this respect, Vian's writing at first appears quintessentially bathetic: at one moment sublime and the next ridiculous. And yet, present in bathos is the idea of a marked descent from the one to the other. And it is precisely this movement between states that is absent from Vian's fiction: the shift from farce to pathos always works in both directions and simultaneously. This duality or coexistence of tones presents particular challenges to the translator. To render a dextrous French play on words with an equally clever one in English is possible, and it is to this type of gymnastics that Bellos justifiably pays homage. In Vian's case, however, pathos is grafted onto the punch-lines. Vian's translators therefore have to work that much harder in order to make the jokes work in English without losing that sense of pathos.

The texts translated here pose their own particular problems and specificities. The poems give voice to an "I" that is uncharacteristic in Vian's *œuvre*. There is a sense in which his guard appears to be dropped and a feeling of wholeness restored or daring to show itself for the first time.[21] Perversely, though, this reunion of Boris Vian and his inner self ends up fragmenting his poetic persona as much as it restores unity. And in this fragmentation more than anywhere else we have bathos. There is a genuine shift from one register to another, from highs to lows, from death to life. And while these opposites vie for space in the poems, with one element evidently flowing from the other,

---

20 Boris Vian, *Foam of the Daze*, translated by Brian Harper (California: TamTam Books, 2003).

21 In his famous essay, "Edgar Poe, sa vie et ses œuvres", Baudelaire notes a comparable change in mood in Poe's poetry: "There is never any love in Poe's short stories. [...] Perhaps he thought that prose was not a suitable vehicle for this bizarre and almost untranslatable sentiment, because his poems, on the other hand, are utterly saturated with it." Charles Baudelaire, *Œuvres complètes*, edited by Claude Pichois (Paris: Gallimard, Bibliothèque de la Pléiade, 2 vols, 1976), vol. II, p. 312 (our translation).

the sincerity of these pieces, where the humour is less guarded, the smile more forthright, lies in the deployment of separate spaces for the two aspects of Vian's personality. Easier to translate than the novels, then, one might think, because there is only one voice at a time to render, a lover's discourse between Vian and his Other with inevitable slippage into an erotics of reading in which it is the reader who feels the force of this double seduction. And such a discourse lends itself to music, a music that must not be "lost in translation". To this end, that is to retain this poetic voice with its musicality, tempo and rhyme scheme, the translator must be also, and above all, a poet. As Barbara Folkart has put it: "Only by re-enacting — or better, re-inventing — the 'ratio difficilis' invented by the source-language poet can the translator — the target-language writer — produce a text that not only resonates with the original but is capable of functioning as a freestanding poem".[22] A lofty ambition indeed!

The short stories exhibit the same tensions, though the voice is different. In fact, given the time-span covered by the stories presented here, we are dealing with not one but a variety of voices. The task of the translator is therefore not just to capture the tensions to be found in individual stories between humour and pathos, between that confident sense of self and the discreet but insistent sense of anxiety and even alienation that so often lurks in Vian's prose; it is also to capture the shift in stance and tone that can be detected as we move from the early, playful stories to the more genuinely troubling tales of his later years. By presenting these short stories chronologically, therefore, we hope the reader will be able to gain an appreciation of that evolution in Vian's writing.

The poetry and prose works translated here offer Vian at both ends of his broad spectrum. They have fuelled the arguments of those who believe him to be underrated as well as those who have judged him overrated. If the circle of those engaged in this debate can be widened thanks to this volume, the labour of love it has taken to prepare it will not have been in vain.

---

[22] Barbara Folkart, *Second Finding: A Poetics of Translation* (Ottawa: University of Ottawa Press, 2007), p. xi.

NOTE ON THE TEXTS

Boris Vian's collected poetry was published in 1962, three years after his death, by Jean-Jacques Pauvert, in a volume entitled *Je voudrais pas crever* (*I wouldn't wanna die*). This title, which was not chosen by Vian, was taken from the first poem in the collection. It is those twenty-three poems that are translated here.

A significant number of Vian's short stories were published during his lifetime in magazines and reviews. The majority were subsequently incorporated into three collections: *Les Fourmis* (published in 1949 by Éditions du Scorpion), *Le Loup-garou* (published posthumously in 1970 by Christian Bourgois under the 10/18 label) and *Le Ratichon baigneur* (likewise published under the 10/18 label by Christian Bourgois, in 1981). All of these stories were included in the edition of Vian's complete prose works published in 2010 by Marc Lapprand and his collaborators Christelle Gonzalo and François Roulmann in Gallimard's prestigious Pléiade collection (*Œuvres romanesques complètes*, 2 volumes).

The stories in *Les Fourmis* were translated into English by Julia Older and published under the title *Blues for a Black Cat and Other Stories* (Lincoln: University of Nebraska Press, 1992). One of the stories from *Le Ratichon baigneur* — "Méfie-toi de l'orchestre" — was translated into English by Peter Hodges and published in the March 2010 edition of *The AALITRA Review* with the title "Don't Trust the Band". One of the stories from *Le Loup-garou*, "Les Pas vernis", was likewise translated into English by Peter Hodges and published in the September 2008 number of *The AALITRA Review* with the title "The Slip-up". The remainder of the short stories in the two posthumous collections are published here in English translation for the first time.[1]

[1] This includes a slightly reworked version of Peter Hodges's translations of "Don't Trust the Band" and "The Slip-up".

It is worth noting that the editors of the Pléiade edition of Vian's prose works have reproduced the texts of the short stories as they were published in reviews and other outlets, whereas the versions given in Christian Bourgois's 10/18 volumes are based on the manuscript sources. While in most cases the stories are essentially the same, there are some important differences between the two versions in a number of the later stories. It is the Pléiade edition of the short stories that has served as the basis for the translations given here.

PART I

THE POETRY OF BORIS VIAN

Translated by Maria Freij

I WOULDN'T WANNA DIE

I wouldn't wanna die
Before I've had the chance to know
Those black dogs of Mexico
Who asleep do dreamlessly lie
The bare-arsed monkeys
Devourers of the tropics
The silver spiders
Their nests full of bubbles
I wouldn't wanna die
Without knowing if the moon
Which poses as a doubloon
Has a pointy side
If the sun is cold
If the four seasons
Are really only four
Without having tried
To appear in a frock
On a Paris boulevard
Without having eyed
The eye of the sewer
Without having put my cock
In any old place bizarre
I wouldn't want it to end
Without having leprosy
Or the seven diseases
You catch over there
Neither good nor bad
Would cause me woe
If if if I only knew
That I'd be first to go
And there is too as well
All that I know
All that is swell

That I know to be so
The green depths of the sea
Where strands of seaweed waltz
Over the rippled sand
The parched grass of June
The crunch of the soil
The smell of the pine
And the kisses so fine
Of what's her name — ah
This beauty — voilà
My bear cub, Ursula
I wouldn't wanna die
Before I'd consumed
Her mouth with my mouth
Her body with my hands
The rest with my eyes
I'd best say no more
Some respect'd be wise
I wouldn't wanna die
Before the invention
Of eternal roses
The two-hour day
The sea on the mountain
The mountain in the sea
The end of all distress
Colour-printing in the press
The children all happy
And so much more stuff
That slumbers in the heads of
Ingenious engineers
Amused arborists
Solicitous socialists
Urban urbanists
And thoughtful thinkers
So many things to remark

To see and contemplate
What a wait to await
When fumbling in the dark

And I can see the end
Catching up on me fast
With its great ugly face
And its wobbly frog arms
Op'ning up in embrace

I wouldn't wanna die
No sir, no ma'am
Having seen the chance fly by
To sample the torturous taste
The taste that's the strongest of all
I wouldn't wanna die
Without having first got to try
The flavour of death…

WHY DO I LIVE

Why do I live
Why do I live
For the golden leg
Of a leggy blonde
Leaning against the wall
Under the basking sun
For the rounded sail
Of a port bound cutter
For the shade of the blind
The iced coffee
You drink from a tube
To touch the sand
See the watery depths
That become so blue
That plunge so far
With the fish
The calm fish
They graze the bottom
Fly above
The seaweed hair
Like slow-moving birds
Like blue-moving birds
Why do I live
For the beauty it gives.

LIFE IS LIKE A TOOTH

Life is like a tooth
You don't consider it at first
You satisfy your hunger and thirst
And suddenly pain starts to emit
It hurts you and you cling to it
You care for it and worry too
And to be cured there's naught to do
But simply pull life out of you.

THERE WAS A BRASS LAMP

There was a brass lamp
That had been burning for many a year
An enchanted mirror was hanging there
In which you saw the face
The face that you'd have
On your golden deathbed
There was a blue leather book
Holding heaven and earth's histories
Water, fire, the thirteen mysteries
The hourglass needle of dust
Let time out in measured quantities
And there was a weighty lock
Embedded as in solid rock
In the tower's oaken door
Closing it for evermore
On the round room, the table
The whitewashed vault, the window
With panes encased in lead
Rats climbed in the ivy that had grown
And wound around the tower's stone
Which the sun no longer reached

It was really dreadfully romantic.

WHEN THE WIND'S BLOWING THROUGH MY SKULL

When the wind's blowing through my skull
When my bones are green with moss
You may think that you see a smile though dull
But then you'll be gravely at a loss
Because I will have shed
My surrounding plastic
Plastic tick tick
On which the rats have fed
My playthings, the pair
My calves, my kneecaps bare
My thighs my derrière
On which I rested true
My fistulas my hair
My eyes cerulean fair
My jawbones strong and square
With which I smothered you
My considerable nose
My heart my liver back — all those
Impressive nothings that compose
The fame my name has made
With dukes and duchesses
With popes and popesses
With abbots and she-asses
And people in the trade
No more would I possess
This slight soft phosphorus
This brain that served me
By warning life would flee
The green bones, the wind in this mould
Oh how hard I find it to grow old.

I'M NO LONGER AT EASE

I'm no longer at ease
Composing poetries
If it were like before
I'd churn out many more
But I feel senescentious
I'm feeling very serious
I'm feeling conscientious
I'm feeling indolentious.

IF I WERE A POET-O

If I were a poet-o
I would be a drunk-o
I'd have a red nose-o
And a big box-o
Where I would collect
A hundred or more sonnects
Where I would collect
My œuvre complect.

I BOUGHT SOME BREAD, STALE AND ALL

I bought some bread, stale and all
To place upon the garden wall
By old man Thyme's beard
Not a single hen appeared
I was quite sure, Mummy
I was quite sure.

THERE IS SUNSHINE IN THE STREET

There is sunshine in the street
I like sunshine but not the street
So I stay at home
Waiting for the world to arrive
With its golden towers
And its white waterfalls
With its voices filled with tears
And the songs of those who are happy
Or of people who are paid to sing
And in the evening comes a moment
When the street becomes something else
And vanishes neath the wings
Of night full of may-be
And of dreams of the dead
So I go out into the street
That stretches all the way to dawn
Smoke rises nearby
And I walk awash with dry water
In the harsh water of the fresh night
The sun will soon return.

A STARK NAKED MAN WAS WALKING

A stark naked man was walking
His gear in his hand
His gear in his hand
It might be a little bland
But it makes me laugh
His gear in his hand
His gear in his hand
A-ha ha ha ha ha ha
A stark naked man
A stark naked man
Walking the land
His suit in his hand.

MY RAPIER HURTS

My rapier hurts
But I'll never tell
My chisel hurts
But I'll never tell
My couplings hurt
My lubricators hurt
My ball-bearings hurt
My tool bag hurts
But I'll never tell, so there
I'll never tell.

THEY ARE BREAKING THE WORLD

They are breaking the world
Into little bits
They are breaking the world
With hammer hits
But I don't care
I really don't care
There remains enough for me
There remains enough
I need just to love
A feather shimmering blue
A sandy path
A frightened bird or two
I need just to love
A slender strand of grass
A drop of dew
A wood cricket
They can break the world
Into little bits
There remains enough for me
There remains enough
I will always have some air
A trickle of life's course
In my eyes a little glare
The wind in the gorse
Even if, even if
They send me to jail
There remains enough for me
There remains enough
I need just to love
This corroded stone
These iron hooks
Where a spot of blood lingers
I love, I love

The worn boards of my bed
The mattress and the bedstead
The dust dancing in the sun
I love the peephole that opens
The men who have come for me
Who step in, take me with them
Back to the world
Back to life and its colour
I love these two tall posts
This triangular blade
These men dressed in black
It's my party and I'm proud
I love, I love
This basket of straw
In which I'll rest my head
Oh, I love it for evermore
I need just to love
A strand of grass tinted blue
A single drop of dew
A lovely frightened bird or two
They are breaking the world
With weighty hammers
There remains enough for me,
My love enough remains.

YET ANOTHER

Yet another
One you don't need
But since the others
Ask themselves the questions of others
And answer them in the words of others
What else is there to do
But write, like the others
And hesitate
Reiterate
And extricate
Investigate
Then not locate
And get irate
And tell yourself it's pointless
It would be better to earn a living
But my life, I do have it
I don't need to earn it
It's not a problem at all
It's the one thing that isn't
Everything else, that's the problem
But it's long been in contention
They've all asked the question
On all the subjects you could mention
So what remains for me
They've taken all the easy words
The noble and expressive terms
The foaming, the steamy, the gross
The heavens, the stars, the lanterns
And these waves limp and crude
Rage ravage the red rocks
It's full of cries and darkness
It's full of blood and full of sex
Full of rubies and of leeches

So what remains for me
Must I wonder in all discreetness
And without writing and without sleeping
Must I search for myself
Without saying a word, not even to the concierge
To the midget running under my floor
To the sodomite in my pocket
Nor to the clergyman in my drawer
Do I, do I have to probe
All alone without a nun at the gate
Who grabs you by the dick
And stabs you like a policeman
With a vaseline spear
Do I, do I have to stick
A swab up my nose to contain
The uremia affecting my brain
And see my words go down the drain
They've all asked the question
I've lost the right to speak
They've taken all the lovely shiny words
They've put them on a pedestal
Where the poets have their place
With pedal lyres
With steam lyres
With eight-cylinder lyres
And jet Pegasuses
The slightest subject is denied me
I have but the dullest words
The dumbest and the wimpy
I have but me myself it them
I have but whose who what is it
What is, him and her, I have but they we you nor
How do you expect me to write
A poem using but this lot?
Oh well, whatever, I will not.

I SHOULD LIKE

I should like
I should like
To be a poet greatly read
And people
Would put
Lots of laurel on my head
But there
I don't care
Enough for books as such
And I ponder life too much
And I think about people in excess
To find eternal happiness
Writing air and emptiness.

IF I SAY *IF*

If I say *if*
That's yew for you
From *triage*
A tree is born
Playing pontoon, the bridge opens up,
Swallowing the canons, the soldiers
Culled, sacked, down to the bottom
Of the red river
Oh yes, the French are truly dangerous.

A POET

A poet
Is someone heaven sent
You can meet any time
Who thinks only in rhyme
Writes with musical bent
On most any paradigm
Be it crude or sublime
But always magnificent.

IF POETS WEREN'T SUCH FOOLS

If poets weren't such fools
And if they weren't so indolent
They would make everyone content
So that they could attend in peace
To their literary suffering
They would build yellow houses
With large gardens out front
And trees full of birds
Of nasal flutes and lizirds
Of chickadeels and warblerings
Of featherigars and peckasites
And little red ravens
Who would tell fortunes
There would be large fountains
With lights in them
There would be two hundred fishes
From crustoceans to antlishes
From lampdragoons to pepaflies
From needlefish to rare curuleyes
And from bowsprats to poodlefishes
There would be fresh new air
Perfumed with the smell of leaves
You would eat when you wanted
And work at your leisure
Constructing stairways
Of shapes ne'er before seen
From wood veined with mauve
Smooth as she to your touch

But poets are such fools
They write to begin
Instead of getting stuck in
And hence they feel a great remorse

They keep until they've run their course
Delighted to have suffered so
Great speeches sing their praise then they
Are forgotten in a single day
But if they weren't so indolent
It would take two — that's evident.

IT WOULD BE THERE, SO HEAVY

It would be there, so heavy
With its iron belly
And its brass flounces
Its feverish waterpipes
It would run on its tracks
Like death runs to war
And shadow falls upon the eyes
There's so much work to do
So much grinding down
So much suffering and distress
So much anger and eagerness
So many years are whiled
So many visions filed
So much willpower compiled
And injuries and pride
Metal torn from the soil
Tormented by the flames
Folded, tortured, wrecked
Contorted into dreams
The sweat of the ages
Is sealed in these cages
Ten and a hundred thousand years of waiting
And of gaucheness overcome
If there remained
A bird
And a locomotive
And me alone in the desert
With the bird and the whatsit
And if they said choose
What would I do, what would I do
It would have a slender beak
As befits a coniroster
Two beaming buttons for eyes

A plump little tummy
I would hold it in my hand
And its heart would beat so quickly…
All around, the end of the world
In two hundred and twelve episodes
It would have grey feathers
A tad of rust on its breast
And its fine dry feet
Needles sheathed in skin
Come on, what would you keep
For everything must perish
But for your loyal services
You will be allowed to keep
Only one out of the two
The birdie or the choo-choo
All will need to start anew
All weighty secrets lost from view
All of science to re-do
If I don't choose the machine
But its wings are so fine
And its heart would beat so quickly
That I would keep the bird.

THERE ARE THOSE WHO HAVE DEAR LITTLE TRUMPETS

There are those who have dear little trumpets
And bugles
And wooden serpents
There are those who have clarinets
And ophicleides of giant form
There are those with large drums
Pa rum pum pum pums
And rat a tat tat
But I have only a kazoo
And I kazoom
From nightfall until break of day
I have but a kazoo
But I don't care as long as I can play my way.

So, tell me, do you like the way I play?

I WANT A LIFE SHAPED LIKE A FISHBONE

I want a life shaped like a fishbone
On a blue plate
I want a life shaped like an object
On the bottom of a lone thingy
I want a life shaped like sand in hand
In the shape of green bread or a pitcher
In the shape of a floppy old shoe
In the shape of tralala
Of a chimney sweep or a lilac
Of stony ground
Of a wild barber or crazy eiderdown
I want a life shaped like you
And that I have, but it is still not enough for me
I am never satisfied.

ONE DAY

One day
There will be something other than the day
A more honest thing that you will call the Yodel
Yet another, translucent like resin
That you'll set in your eye most elegantly
There will be the goldenear, more cruel
The spirelf, more unravelled
The last straw, less everlasting
The hot impro, always snow-covered
There will be the chalamonder
The drunkaninny, the heroi-baroque
And a whole plantation of anahologies
The hours will be different
Dissimilar, inconclusive
No point settling now
On the exact details of the how
One certitude subsists: one day
There will be something other than the day.

EVERYTHING HAS BEEN SAID A HUNDRED TIMES

Everything has been said a hundred times
And a lot better than in my rhymes
And when I'm writing poetry
Then it's 'cos it amuses me
Then it's 'cos it amuses me
Then it's 'cos it amuses me and I don't give a shit about you.

I SHALL DIE OF A CANCER OF THE SPINE

I shall die of a cancer of the spine
It will be on an awful night
Clear, hot, fragrant, sensual
I shall die of a decay
Of certain little known cells
I shall die of a leg torn off
By a giant rat springing out of a giant hole
I shall die of a hundred cuts
The sky will have fallen in on me
Shattering like a heavy pane of glass
I shall die of a vocal burst
Splitting my ears
I shall die of silent wounds
Inflicted at two in the morning
By killers indecisive and bald
I shall die without noticing
That I'm dying, I shall die
Buried under the dry ruins
Of a thousand metres of collapsing cotton
I shall die drowned in motor oil
Trampled by the feet of indifferent beasts
And, directly after, by different beasts
I shall die naked, or clad in red cloth
Or sown into a bag with razor blades
I shall perhaps die without a worry
Nail polish on my toenails
And handfuls of tears
And handfuls of tears
I shall die when they pry open
My eyelids under a raging sun
When people slowly whisper
Spiteful things in my ear
I shall die from watching children tortured

And men surprised and pale
I shall die eaten alive
By worms, I shall die with
My hands fastened under a waterfall
I shall die burning in a sad fire
I shall die a little, a lot,
Without passion, but with interest
And then when all is done
I shall die.

REREADING VIAN: A POETICS OF PARTIAL DISCLOSURE

Alistair Rolls

Periodically a call is issued from academic circles to reread the works of Boris Vian, whose name has become synonymous both with the exuberance of youth and the haunting menace of death. This call to reread Boris Vian is due in no small part to the way in which his untimely and yet long foreseen death has singularly failed to curb his *joie de vivre*. To say that Vian was born again in death is, however, something of a misrepresentation: as an author, his success, in his own name at least, has been almost entirely posthumous.[1] As a man, working without respite to assuage an overweening drive to create, and thereby consigning himself to an even earlier death than might otherwise have been his lot, and as an author, determined to "coincide" with his published works, Vian exemplifies the conflation of Eros and Thanatos.[2] Our aim here is

1 Testament to this are academic studies such as Michel Fauré's *Les Vies posthumes de Boris Vian* (Paris: UGE, 1975) and, as noted in the introductory essay here, the biographies that have been published with metronomic regularity over the last few decades, including Philippe Boggio, *Boris Vian* (Paris: Flammarion, 1993); Emma Baus, *Boris Vian: 'Un jour il y aura autre chose que le jour'* (Paris: L'Esprit frappeur, 2002) and Claire Julliard, *Boris Vian* (Paris: Gallimard, 2007).

2 The pseudonymous works that constitute Vian's Vernon Sullivan project appear at first glance to contradict this coincidence of biography and fiction. However, real life dramatically impinged on the distance and objectivity of these transatlantic, and trans-ethnic, pseudo-translations in the form of a very real murder carried out in Paris in the spring of 1947 and apparently inspired by a strangulation scene from *J'irai cracher sur vos tombes*. While this event

to reread the interplay of these two apparently mutually exclusive drives in the poems most commonly known by the title under which they were originally, and — as so often in Vian's case — posthumously, published: *Je voudrais pas crever* (*I wouldn't wanna die*). In so doing, it is our wish to offer a critical accompaniment to Maria Freij's translations, thereby presenting readers with the various aspects of rereading that form the basis of Vian scholarship.

Our title, "Rereading Vian", is itself a partial translation of Marc Lapprand's "Relire Vian aujourd'hui", in which he analyses the intersection of man and work that has shaped Boris Vian and that continues both to define and be defined by the popular desire to reread him.[3] One of Lapprand's key objectives, not merely in that particular article but throughout his career as a *vianiste*, is to account for, and indeed to challenge, the over-determining role of biography in Vian studies in the hope of encouraging a new, critical engagement with the *œuvre*. With this as his goal, he locates the need to reread Vian within a context of opportunity and hindrance; for, while serious academic critique has waxed and waned over the years since the author's death, popular interest (albeit among an audience made up of predominantly adolescent readers) has continued to grow.[4] (Anecdotally, one would be hard-

---

could not have been foreseen by Vian, the project seems nonetheless to have contained a built-in failure mechanism, almost as if he always intended the truth of his authorship of these works to come out. Such a commercial and personal death wish by proxy may have formed part of a desire on Vian's part to become more completely himself through the eventual exposure of his pseudonymous alter ego. This is, of course, the purest of speculation, but there are resonances in the anthology of poems under study here of something akin to a quest for salvation by exposure and death, and by self-othering via a literary, and non-coinciding, "I".

[3] Marc Lapprand, "Relire Vian aujourd'hui", *Europe*, 967-968, 2009, pp. 38-49.

[4] Lapprand's essay is especially timely since it was published to mark the fiftieth anniversary of Boris Vian's death in 1959. His analysis also sums up the sentiment of the 2007 conference, *Le Cas Vian*, convened at the Sorbonne by Audrey Camus. Furthermore, it stands as an apologia for a critical engagement with the Pléiade edition, which Lapprand oversaw and which was released in October 2010. No-one, I should argue, has articulated this need to reread Vian more elegantly or more intelligently than Lapprand, who notes that his own initial desire to engage with the text alone was confronted from the outset by the shadow of the man, in a way that has always, as much now as then, proven a source both of frustration and inspiration to him. Lapprand's work is all the more powerful for this perversity: his defence of Vian the text is predicated on an understanding of Vian the man that few of the author's biographers can hope to have rivalled.

pressed to meet a current or former undergraduate student in France who has not read a novel by Vian, more often than not *L'Écume des jours*, or who does not know the words to his song "Le Déserteur".) In discussing whether Vian has finally become a classic, Lapprand simultaneously raises the question of whether such a canonisation is likely to prove a catalyst for the kind of critical reread that the author's stature undoubtedly warrants.

Reading and Rereading

It is in this distinction between the critical and uncritical reread that our problematisation of the life and death drives in Vian's poetic persona finds its parallel. For, if the surfeit of life that is Vian's hallmark, and that has been concentrated via his own early death into his works, is responsible for the reading public's desire to engage with his works, either for the first time or in the form of a reread after a long pause (perhaps prompted by the nostalgia that tends to come when people surpass the age Vian himself attained at the time of his death), it leads usually, if not necessarily, to the kind of reread that delimits the text; or rather, this is a reading praxis that marks the text as limited, complete... in other words, as dead. This is how Roland Barthes sums up the work of literature in *S/Z*.[5] Literature, he suggests, differs from a more hermeneutically challenging text type such as a crossword puzzle or an advertisement inasmuch as its meaning is transparent; the reader can, therefore, be content to digest the story. Barthes calls this the "readerly" text (*le texte lisible*). Its opposite, this difficult text, which forces the reader into a collaborative act of meaning-making, he refers to as the "writerly" text (*le texte scriptible*). The latter comes to life as one reads. As one reads Barthes's account of the reader's active production of living text — from the dead mass of the extant, printed work — one becomes aware of the irony intended in his earlier definition of the literary classic. No act of reading — not even the most cursory and unimaginative — can be entirely readerly as there is no single true meaning (what deconstructionism refers to as the metaphysical reading) into which the reader can simply tap.

---

5 Roland Barthes, *S/Z* (Paris: Seuil, 1973). For the English version, see Richard Miller's translation, published as *S/Z* (Oxford: Blackwell, 1990).

The demands are not only made by the text, however. Readers, too, make demands, not only of the text but also of themselves as their own identity becomes (re)forged alongside that of the writerly reading. Thus, the demands of reading are made by the reader as much as they are by the work, for the reader demands to be "made", to be made different via the construction — and not the absorption — of meaning. Indeed, in accordance with his own essay on the death of the author,[6] Barthes's writerly text produces life in both the text and the reader (who actively produces it). This is, however, only possible because of the break made from the work's "original" progenitor. To reread, in the sense of making the work come alive, is thus necessarily, in this poststructuralist framework, to circumscribe the life of the author.

Clearly, this goes against the desire of the Vian aficionado. As if it had not been bad enough to lose the man so early once before, it is surely now nothing less than an act of cruelty to use his own works to "kill" him again, and forever. Yet Boris Vian can be seen to have himself predicted this cruel posthumous literary death in a number of his works. In light of this, the poem "I wouldn't wanna die", which lends its name to the collective volume of Vian's poetry, published for the first time here in English translation, can be read as both an acknowledgement of his mortality and the expression of a profound attachment to life. And this paradoxical combination takes on particular poignancy because of the force of the first person singular, which is so atypical of Vian-the-author. The reflexivity of the poem in question suggests that the desire to savour death, which is expressed in its concluding lines, contains a desire to be made again, that is to say to be reread, by the reader.[7]

---

6 The English version of this essay "The Death of the Author" is available in Roland Barthes, *Image, Music, Text*, translated by Stephen Heath (New York: Hill and Wang, 1978), pp. 142-148. ("La Mort de l'auteur" first appeared in 1968 and is available in French in *Le Bruissement de la langue*, published in Paris by Seuil in 1984.)

7 I have demonstrated elsewhere how the self-referentiality of the parodic classic *J'irai cracher sur vos tombes* operates simultaneously as a death wish, to the extent that it constitutes a victory of bad taste and commercial success (and as such parallels the bloody vengeance of its own storyline), and as an intertextual rebirth (of protagonist, work and, vicariously, the author himself). See Alistair Rolls, "C'est en se déguisant qu'on devient Boris Vian: *J'irai cracher sur vos tombes* et la 'bonne littérature érotique latine'", *Europe*, 967-968, 2009, pp. 50-60. I have also previously analysed the reflexivity of the poem under study here in another call to reread Vian. See Alistair Rolls, "Prière de relire *Je voudrais pas crever*", *Poésie*, 96, 2003, pp. 35-41.

And so, perhaps in accordance with the wishes of Boris Vian himself, or at least in a desire to pay tribute to him, accompanied by a parallel desire to do justice to the writings left behind, we find ourselves joining with Lapprand in his request to reread Vian's works in both senses of the term — by treating them as both readerly and writerly texts. Public and scholars alike, we are called upon to read *de nouveau*, or again, in discovery of our childhood selves, and also *à nouveau*, or anew, with fresh eyes.

Rereading and Recreation

Clearly, this double meaning at the heart of the notion of rereading parallels the double objective of the present book, which is to reproduce a number of Vian's works for an English-speaking audience, thereby making accessible texts that would have remained impenetrable in the original French, and to (re) produce meaning in the "original" versions by reflecting back that meaning — which is to say, both conveying it as a faithful duplication of itself and diverting it from coincidence with itself — and generating new discourse. This is the strength of the prefix *re-*, which can signify a simple repetition (to "read again") or a transfer of ownership resulting from the generation of new and personalised meaning (to "read differently" from other readers... and from the writer). In this second sense, the reader is reclaiming the text, taking it back from the author (in Barthes's poststructuralist account) or from the "meaning" that is widely attributed to it.

Rereading, then, works in two ways. On the one hand, it enables the reader to produce difference in sameness: from one work, a quasi-infinite number of virtual meanings can be actualised into any number of rereads. On the other hand, and this is Barthes's warning to the faint-hearted reader, it can also be synonymous with the passive type of reading which leaves both the work and the reader "unchanged". The problem with this undifferentiating type of reading is that it is infectious: it tends to get passed on to all works read by this "same" reader, until all end up being reduced to parts, albeit recognisably autonomous at the surface level of words on the page, of an undifferentiated whole.[8] This is, of course, very different from the singularity

[8] In Barthes's opinion, this process of uncritical reading of different works amounts to reading the same text everywhere, which is the very opposite of the textual production that he

of Julia Kristeva's "Intertext",[9] whose universality is based on differentiation effected everywhere (but always at the local level) and not homogenisation imposed universally. Hence Barthes's preference for readers to reread the same work, as opposed to reading many different ones: the critical reflection encouraged by this reread not only accentuates the work's critical difference (from itself rather than from other works), but it also produces fundamental change in the reader. In the reread, then, one does not "lose oneself in a good book"; instead, one recreates oneself in it and, at the same time, recreates the book as a text. This is the erotic call of the work itself, which seduces us into reading its virtual possibilities and, effectively, rewriting it according to its own inchoate desire for differentiation. Given the reflexivity of Vian's collected poetry (and especially of its eponymous poem), and given the way in which the author both includes and excludes himself from the narrative (in the form of the highly fictionalised use of the first person singular pronoun), we can see that the text is savouring, or rereading, itself — which is, of course, a form of auto-eroticism.

Pleasure

If the call to read — that is to say, the call exerted by the work of literature itself rather than by academia or the reading public — can be justifiably considered a form of seduction, an act more "erotic" than "scholarly" or "leisurely", it is because the risks associated with reading are also a powerful source of pleasure. The pleasure of the text is located at that magical, convulsive place where two opposing currents meet.[10] If we translate these troubled waters onto our call to "reread" Vian (in the active rather than the passive sense), we

---

urges (in the form of the writerly text). For an excellent account of this process, see Barbara Johnson, "The Critical Difference", in Diana Knight (ed.), *Critical Essays on Roland Barthes* (New York: G.K. Hall and Co., 2000), pp. 174-182.

9 Kristeva defines this concept in *Séméiotikè. Recherches pour une sémanalyse* (Paris: Seuil, 1978).

10 This image is taken from *L'Écume des jours*. It is an enigmatically unspecific analogy, which describes the play of light on water in the eddies where a river runs into the sea. The passage can be found in volume one of Boris Vian's *Œuvres romanesques complètes*, edited by Marc Lapprand, Christelle Gonzalo and François Roulmann (Paris: Gallimard, 2010), p. 420. The most recent English translation is Brian Harper's *Foam of the Daze*, published by Tosh Berman (California: TamTam Books, 2003), and the reference is located on page 108.

discover that pleasure is a tension: it is derived from the opposition between the critical and the submissive approaches to rereading. Strictly speaking, the latter, with all that it implies in terms of a leisurely loss of self in the text, is the *pleasurable* experience from the reader's perspective. Indeed, it is in this passive consumption of the written word that Barthes locates *le plaisir*.[11] Of course, to "lose oneself in a good book" is only to put oneself temporarily aside and to emerge later unchanged by the reading experience. This momentary loss is really more a retention of a limited identity, and not the positive loss of Jean-Paul Sartre's "loser wins" (*qui perd gagne*), whereby to accept loss of a fixed identity is to embrace responsibility for self and, ultimately, to be free. The critical reread, for its part, requires the reader to take responsibility for the meaning that is brought out of the literary work. From the author's perspective, this release of the control of meaning is a *blissful* act (referred to by Barthes as *la jouissance*, and generally opposed to *le plaisir*). Finally, from the perspective of the text, pleasure must embrace both these perspectives. This is erotic, passionate, an act of violent collision and not of smooth synthesis. As a living thing, an actualisation of the work's potential for meaning, the text encompasses both *le plaisir* and *la jouissance*.[12]

What a reflexive poem like "I wouldn't wanna die" reminds us, of course, is that the power of pleasure is derived from the complexity of the currents at play. The bliss is not just release on the author's part, for the reader is seduced by the words on the page and is made to take responsibility for their meaning. In this most intimate and collaborative production of meaning, the reader's identity must be put on the line, at least partially. And, perhaps

---

11 Roland Barthes, *Le Plaisir du texte* (Paris: Seuil, 1973). It is translated as *The Pleasure of the Text* by Richard Miller (New York: Hill and Wang, 1975).

12 We should note that Barthes's preference for the blissful, writerly text over the pleasurable, readerly one does not at first appear to be borne out in his choice of the term *plaisir* for his overarching title, *Le Plaisir du texte*. Our suggestion here is that the pleasure of Barthes's title is that associated with the text, which does not belong to the reader any more than it does to the author; rather, the text is a virtual entity, an interface at which meaning is (re)created. Our argument in terms of Vian's poem "I wouldn't wanna die" is that the author is aligning himself quite deliberately with this liminal, shared pleasure. His bliss is thus pre-read as the text's pleasure, which, perversely, both strengthens the authorial dominance of the text and weakens the narrative subject's coincidence with him, as Vian occupies this virtual, textual space. Hence, the idea of his "partial" disclosure of himself in the poem.

more importantly, it is not only the reader who experiences the pleasure of savouring the words, of enjoying the other's control: Vian, too, savours the results of his own abandonment of power proleptically. From this perspective, the anthology *I wouldn't wanna die* might be considered a highly complex, and erotic, example of a "pre-posthumous" poetics. By so forcefully bringing together cathexis and anticathexis, or *pleasure* and *unpleasure*, Vian himself urges us to reconsider *le plaisir* and *la jouissance* and, ultimately, to reread pleasure itself.

The Desiring Subject

In the case of *I wouldn't wanna die*, there is a strong sense that the poetic voice, which can perhaps be conflated with that of the author himself, operates this same problematisation of pleasure. This title phrase can be seen as an expression of the poet's (and the poetry's) fear that the collection will become a congealed work of literature. At the same time, inherent in this plaintive cry is the aspiration to live on as (writerly) text through the complicity of the reader, who becomes the direct recipient of the text's desire. And yet, the closing lines of the title poem itself reveal the pleasure to be had in savouring death, which suggests on the author's part a desire to coincide — in death — with himself, or in this case, with the sum total of his previously written, if posthumously published, parts. This is the very bad faith of which Roquentin, the protagonist of Sartre's own classic work of 1938 *La Nausée* (*Nausea*), can be considered guilty when he longs for salvation through the eternal life granted to an author who will become known for, and ultimately one with, the novel that he has created. This is the novel as self-founding object (from the existentialist perspective) and as readerly text with one single metaphysical meaning (from the poststructuralist-deconstructionist perspective). The pleasure for the "I" of Vian's poem exists, therefore, in the tension between the bliss of abandonment of authorial meaning to the reader and the vicarious pleasure the author takes in the reader's digestion of him (and his work) as transparently meaningful and thus dead. The poem concludes with the enjoyment of death, which inevitably brings death to life, making it, like pleasure, a tense mixture of itself (death) and its opposite (life). From the perspective of the tragically disappointed poet, this is a clever ploy, a trap to generate another self in which he will manage not only to live on forever as himself (as the author of *I wouldn't wanna die* and especially of his own beloved novel, *Foam of the Daze*, for which he contentiously did not win the accolades that he and others believed were his due) but also in an infinity of virtual rebirths.[13]

Intertextual Predecessors 1: "Le Dormeur du Val"

While Boris Vian proleptically savours his own posthumous publication and recreation, projecting himself forwards in time and text, he also casts himself back into previous poetic deaths. One such intertextual reference in "I wouldn't wanna die" is Arthur Rimbaud's poem, "Le Dormeur du val" ("The Sleeper in the Valley", 1870), which famously paints the picture of a young soldier sleeping peacefully in a lush, green valley. The reason why this poem is so well known, of course, is that the soldier turns out not to be asleep but dead. As one rereads the poem with the benefit of this hindsight, one soon realises that the valley was not entirely green even at the beginning. That is to say that the poem's linear progression — from sleep to death — is already checked and turned back on itself by the continual use of oxymorons, all of which stand metonymically for the poem itself. In this way, the grass is dressed oxymoronically in silver rags and the pride of the mountain is contradicted by the smallness of the valley. The vernal exuberance of the poem's beginning is thus inoculated by death even in its opening words: "C'est un trou de verdure" ("It's a green hole").[14] "It" — Rimbaud's poem — announces itself as a space

[13] His failure to win the *Prix de la Pléiade* in 1946 for *L'Écume des jours* has entered Vian folklore. It also entered his subsequent novels in the form of various, and variously unflattering, allusions to the winner of the prize (Jean Grosjean) and to those who voted for him (especially Jean Paulhan), all of which has contributed to the delimiting idea that his works can be reduced to such biographical references.

[14] Arthur Rimbaud, "Le Dormeur du val", in *Rimbaud. Complete Works, Selected Letters*, translated by Wallace Fowlie (Chicago/London: The University of Chicago Press, 1966), p. 56. We refer our readers to this text as it includes both the French and the English versions of the poem. Fowlie's translation of this line does not lend itself to our analysis, however, as he opts for a more poetic term than "hole" to render the French *trou*. His term "hollow" loses the baseness of *trou*, which establishes the oxymoron of the "green hole", and which becomes the expression of the whole poem. The opening pronoun *ce* ('it') pushes forward into this intial oxymoron and thus defines what "it" (the poem) is — namely, a paradox: itself and its own other.

of tension where life is constantly morphing into death and, logically, where death is always brought (back) to life. The poem ('it') is therefore both itself and a denial of itself, and as such it sows within its lines the substance of its own reread.

Intertextual Predecessors 2: "Rue de Seine"

If the paradoxical duality of Rimbaud's "Le Dormeur du val" itself evokes poetry past (for example, Baudelaire's prose poetry of a decade or so earlier), it also has resonances with poetry to come. Jacques Prévert's prosaic poem "Rue de Seine" (1946), published in an anthology of poetry entitled *Paroles*, would have been familiar to Boris Vian — not only because *Paroles* profoundly marked the Parisian literary landscape of the period immediately following the Second World War, but also because Jacques Prévert was his next-door neighbour![15] Prévert's "Rue de Seine" is, like so many of the pieces in *Paroles*, a paradoxical poem of intersection and failed intersection. As a selection of poetic expressions of the prosaic, and vice versa, *Paroles* articulates with maximum simplicity simple acts of language (French in spoken rather than versified form) and, often, language "unacted" (instances of miscommunication).[16] In the famous "Déjeuner du matin" ("Breakfast"), for example, the poem speaks of a couple's failure to speak; its beauty is thus composed of a repetition of mundane and markedly non-poetic, unbeautiful gestures. In "Rue de Seine", a further level of reflexivity is introduced as the poem is seen to take the form of the non-

---

[15] From their terraces in Cité Véron, just off Place Blanche, they could talk to each other as they looked out across the roof of the Moulin Rouge. Vian and Prévert moved into their adjoining apartments in 1953 and 1954, respectively.

[16] My translation. There has been some debate among Prévert scholars as to whether the poems of *Paroles* should be read as (prosaic) poetry or (poetic) prose. For his part, Jacques Poujol, having himself hesitated in categorising this "poésie nouvelle qui se moque de la poésie" ("new poetry which mocks poetry"), finally averred in 1958 that "les écrits de Prévert sont de la poésie et non de la prose" ("Prévert's writings are poetry and not prose"). Jacques Poujol, "Jacques Prévert ou le langage en procès", *French Review*, 31, 5, 1958, pp. 391-392. This careful weighing up of options rather misses the point, however, since Prévert's poems are both at once. Prose poetry after all — and this is why Baudelaire creates it as the perfect expression of his alienation in the face of the duality of Parisian modernity — is oxymoronic and, as such, can abide no synthesis. In this way, *Paroles* can be shown to function as a prose poetics in terms of its basic dynamics and not merely because of its motifs and settings.

writing of a poem. As an anthology of the self and the self's opposite, *Paroles* forms part of a poetic tradition stretching, once more, back to Baudelaire himself.

The reflexivity of "Rue de Seine" has particular relevance for Vian's "I wouldn't wanna die". In the case of "Rue de Seine", the first person singular does not mark the poem's beginning; it is, however, no less powerful when it bursts into life:

> Pierre dis-moi la vérité
> Pierre dis-moi la vérité
> je veux tout savoir
> [Pierre tell me the truth
> Pierre tell me the truth
> I want to know all][17]

The power of this pronoun lies arguably in the contrast that it strikes with its predecessors in the poem. Both the masculine and feminine forms of the third person singular have already been used, each time referring initially to a "person" — a stumbling man and a woman shaking him out of his lethargy — but soon becoming paralleled and, to a degree, subsumed by their respective metonyms, a hat for him (*un* chapeau) and a voice for her (*une* voix). Thus, when the personal pronoun "I" ("je") finally makes its appearance, it does not stand in the poem for a previously introduced "person"; rather, it fleshes out the second person singular imperative that demands that Pierre tell the truth.

In "Rue de Seine", therefore, the depersonalising effect of personal pronouns rather gives the lie to the romantic idyll. In fact, this poem undermines the myth of the City of Lights, or perhaps underscores its mythological nature. We note in passing that it also contradicts the central idea of Thomas Shapcott's contemporary poem "Georges Perec in Brisbane". In Brisbane, or so the poem goes, "Humans are peripheral [...] / Whereas they are all that matters in Paris."[18] The absence of sub-tropical fruit and fauna in the Paris cityscape tends to put

---

17 Jacques Prévert, "Rue de Seine", in *Paroles* (Paris: Gallimard, 1949), p. 61. The parallel translation offered here is by Lawrence Ferlinghetti and is taken from Jacques Prévert, *Selections from 'Paroles'* (London: Penguin, 1965), p. 23.

18 Thomas Shapcott, "Georges Perec in Brisbane", published in the review section of *The Weekend Australian*, August 14-15 2010, p. 22.

people centre stage. The opposite appears to be true in Prévert's vision, where beauty is "convulsive", in accordance with the wish expressed by André Breton in his Surrealist manifesto, and emerges at the meeting point between failed human interaction and the failure of grammatically predicated, or conscious, poetry writing. In "Rue de Seine", "I" is the voice of the unconscious, oneiric desire "to become poem" desperately trying to surface in the real world, in the waking moment of the poetry-writing process.

It certainly becomes difficult to read "Rue de Seine" as a straightforward story of failed or hesitating romance between two people. Even at the reflexive level of textual erotics and reading pleasure, there is nothing simple at play in this poem. Both "he" ("il") and "she" ("elle") are double: they are simultaneously characters in and products of a poem. They are also both expressions of the production process, with her grammatical femininity seeming to function as the abstract voice of *la Poésie* to his masculine, existent *poème*, in all its processes and techniques. And so, when this pair of third-person-singular pronouns, depersonalised and reduced to their simplest terms — as the linguistic building blocks of a love poem — are finally joined by the raw emotion of the first person pronoun, this voice is already allotted its place within the structure of this poetry-writing process, which will, in the very instance of its failure to become actualised, finally become a poem (about process).[19]

The "I" of Prévert's "I want to know all" is thus comparable to that of Vian's "I wouldn't wanna die": both assume the voice of the reader from within a reflexive poem where they are associated with the poet himself. This is the desire to know everything as a plea to "be known"; it is the poetics of the pre-posthumous, in which the desire to be voiced, to be brought to life —

[19] Given Prévert's links to Surrealism one might be tempted to interpret this union of poem and non-poem as an expression of André Breton's "supreme point". And yet, this abolition of all binaries (exemplified in the merging of the dream and the waking moment in instances of objective chance) that inspired all the endeavours of the Surrealist movement is a synthesis, however fleeting and fatal. Convulsive beauty and Love itself immediately usher in their opposite: death. Prévert's collision of life and death, on the other hand, functions as a double motion, an oscillation across the dichotomy, and not as a synthesis. By producing its own reread (poem out of non-poem), "Rue de Seine" already moves us on, away from the coincidence of self and other, and into the other side of the opposition. This is very much "poetry in motion": it is, continuously, life moving towards decay and death ceding to renewal. It is therefore far too frenetic and too balanced to admit even that most ephemeral stasis of the supreme point.

expressed in "Rue de Seine" as "une furieuse envie de vivre" ("a furious desire to live")[20] — is built into the mechanics of the poem as already completed and dead. Hence the importance of Prévert's conclusion when the reader realises that the poem is only complete once the poet-in-the-poem has finished failing to write it(self).

Incompletion is, of course, only ever a spin on the endless possibility of the virtual space that is the writerly text. This same space also has another name: Paris.[21] For people are not all that matters in Paris, contrary to what Shapcott imagines; instead, we are able to experience a life that is essentially double precisely because we are in Paris, because Paris itself is all that matters, which is to say that Paris, as representation and as a real and present metropolis, is both itself and other than itself.[22] This capacity to encompass two mutually exclusive spaces at any given time, which is the very stuff of Baudelaire's oxymoronic, prose-poetic Paris, is announced right from the opening lines of "Rue de Seine":

> Rue de Seine dix heures et demie
> le soir
> au coin d'une autre rue
> [Rue de Seine half past ten
> at night
> on the corner of another street][23]

As both here and somewhere else, "Rue de Seine" offers itself as a mobile space, a double movement between the Rue de Seine and the corner of another street. This is an auto-differentiating technique directly comparable

---

20 "Rue de Seine", p. 60 (English translation: p. 21).

21 For an excellent analysis of Paris as prose poem, and vice versa, along the lines of presentation and representation/re-presentation, see Michel Covin, *L'Homme de la rue: Essai sur la poétique baudelairienne* (Paris: L'Harmattan, 2000).

22 I have written elsewhere at greater length on Paris as capital of Modernity and on its tendency to be both itself and other than itself. See, for example, Alistair Rolls, "L'Élégante de la rue Lepic: A New Look for *Une Passante*", *Contemporary French Civilization*, 34, 2, 2010, pp. 91-114. For an excellent account of the way in which the *flâneur* is haunted by the city of his imaginings, and/or the past, as he confronts the modern cityscape in the present moment, see Ross Chambers, *Loiterature* (Lincoln/London: University of Nebraska Press, 1999).

23 "Rue de Seine", p. 60. (English translation: p. 21).

to the "it" ("ce") of Rimbaud's "C'est un trou de verdure" ("It's a green hole"). Furthermore, if the poem is predicated on a tension between the Rue de Seine and another street, it is because this is the identity of the Rue de Seine itself. This is a double street because it is both offered (by the poet and poem) and read (by the reader); for reading itself operates the same defamiliarisation as walking in Paris.[24] And so too Vian's poem announces the critical double space of modernity, the poet's desire to transport himself to unfamiliar places being ultimately the expression of his Parisian self. The source of meaning in "I wouldn't wanna die" as in "Rue de Seine" is not an in-between space: it is *both here and there.*

I, It, Boris Vian

This pre-posthumous recuperation by the author of the reader's erotic encounter with the text evokes all the currents and counter-currents of pleasure. With a slight change of perspective, Boris Vian's poetics of partial disclosure can be summed up rather neatly by the following quotation from Richard Machin and Christopher Norris:

> The source of meaning always used to be an author. But it might be the reader (just another author), language (the medium as the message), or ideology (a mixture of all three). We do always require a source, a centre around which we can coordinate strategies to "make sense" of a piece of writing — much as we require the subject for a verb. (In this sense, "It's great", said of a poem, is akin to "It's raining", said of the weather.) Within the ensuing discourse a new subjectivity emerges, which the text then claims and reproduces as its own. Since, without enlisting the help of powerful rhetoric, we can't attribute will to an (often departed) author, and since we get the feeling that, no matter how partisan we are, significance within the text is not solely our own responsibility, on many occasions the text's usurpation of a strictly human capacity to make meaning takes place by default. There is certainly a sort of floating

[24] As Chambers suggests, "reading a text is a matter of activating the split between 'saying' and 'meaning'" (*Loiterature*, p. 217). I should agree with him that there is no difference between the double encounter of the urban experience, in which streets summon ghosts (of the past and of expectations) to accompany their bricks and mortar, and the dynamics of critical reading, which produces meaning that both matches and deconstructs the words on the page.

> subjectivity around when we talk about literature, an “it” waiting to seize its chance to become an “I”.[25]

The “it is” of Rimbaud’s poem is made personal, or “I”, in Prévert’s Parisan *Paroles*, only for this personal touch to be revealed as the desiring voice of poetry itself (or the muse of poetry willing itself to live as text, to be concretised as poem). This is the personal as essentially depersonalised. It is this same “I” of the poem that is seized by Vian, and this time its furious desire to live (or not to die) is immediately counterbalanced by a simultaneous summoning of the great death of elsewhere. Intertextually and prose-poetically, the desire to live death *vicariously oneself* is a partial disclosure of the author because it is an “I” tired of waiting, which has seized its chance to become an “it” and which is living that chance as fully as only Boris Vian ever could.

---

[25] Richard Machin and Christopher Norris (eds), *Post-structuralist Readings of English Poetry* (Cambridge: Cambridge University Press, 1987). This quotation is taken from the editors’ Introduction, p. 4.

PART II

THE SHORT STORIES OF BORIS VIAN

Translated by Peter Hodges

MARTIN CALLED...

I

Martin called at five o'clock. I was at my desk writing something. I can't remember what. Most likely something pointless. I didn't have too much trouble understanding him. He speaks English with an accent that's a mixture of American and Dutch. He might be Jewish as well. It makes for an overall effect that is a little unusual, but on my phone, it's okay. I had to be at his hotel in rue Notoire-du-Vidame at seven-thirty, and wait. He was short a drummer. I said to him, "*Stay here, I will call Doddy right now.*" And he said, "*Good, Roby, I stay.*" Doddy wasn't at his desk. I asked for him to call me back. There were seven hundred and fifty francs to be made by playing a gig in the suburbs from eight till midnight. I called Martin back and he said to me, "*Your brother can't play?*" And I said, "*Too far. I must go back home now, and eat something before I go to your hotel.*" And he said, "*So! Good, Roby, don't bother, I'll go and look for a drummer. Just remember you must be at my hotel at seven-thirty.*" Miqueut wasn't there, so I took off at quarter to six. Half an hour to kill. I went back home to get my trumpet. I had a shave. When you play for the Red Cross, you never know; if you're playing for officers, it's embarrassing to be dirty. At the very least your face should be clean. Can't do anything about the clothes, though they wouldn't know anyway. My face was red raw. I can't shave two days in a row. It hurts too much. Still, it's better than nothing. I didn't have time to eat a proper dinner. I had a bowl of soup, said goodnight and left. The weather was mild. I was still heading towards my office. I work in rue Notoire-du-Vidame as well. Martin said to me, "We'll be paid right after we've finished playing." I liked that better. Usually with the Red Cross, they make you wait weeks before they pay you, and then you have to go to rue Caumartin, which doesn't suit Miqueut. I didn't like the idea of playing with Martin again. When he plays the piano, he drowns out everyone. He's a professional and he complains when we don't play well. If he didn't want me, he wouldn't have called. Heinz Neuman was sure to be there as well. Martin Romberg, Heinz Neuman. Both Dutch. Heinz spoke some French. "*Je voudrais vous reverrer? C'est comme ça qu'on dit?*" That's what he asked me last time at the Normandie Bar. That's where that faggot, Freddy, was during the war. He would lock himself away to use the phone that was hidden in a large wardrobe and he would say, "Yes, yes, yes, yes, yes, yes…" in that very high-pitched voice the Germans have, with that vague laugh of his that seemed quite contrived. It's awful, the Normandie, with its false exposed beams made of compressed cork. Even so, I had pinched a copy of the 28 August edition of *New Yorker* and the September edition of *Photography* from there. That's the one where you can see the mug of citizen Weegee, the guy who gets his kicks by taking photos of New York from all different angles, especially shots from high up. During heatwaves, it's of people in the heavily populated areas sleeping on the landings of fire stairs, sometimes five or six kids and half-naked sixteen and seventeen year-old girls. Maybe in his book you can see even more. It's called *Naked City*, and you probably won't find it in France. I arrived at rue de Trévise. It's dark. It's a drag, this way every day. Then I went past my office. It's at the top of rue Notoire-du-Vidame, and right at the other end is Martin's hotel. He wasn't there. Nobody was there. Neither was the truck. I poked my head through the door of the hotel… to the left, there was a man and a woman at a cane table with something in front of them, deep in conversation. Through an open door at the back you could see the table where the manager, or the owner, was having dinner with his family. I didn't go in. Martin would have been waiting there for me. I stood my trumpet case upright on the footpath and sat down on it while I waited for the truck, Heinz and Martin. The phone rang in the hotel foyer and I got to my feet. It was bound to be Martin. The boss came out, "Is Mr Roby…" "That's me." I grabbed the receiver. That phone didn't work as well as the one in the office. It had a higher pitch and I had to get him to repeat everything. He was near Doddy's, but Doddy wasn't there and we had to go around and get him at Marcel's place, 73 rue Lamarck, *seventy-three*. Okay, so he's been around there having dinner. Too lazy to go back to his hotel. The truck should be able to drop by and pick him up. I tried to phone Temsey to at least have a guitar. OK by Martin. No Temsey. That's allright. We'll play trumpet, clarinet and piano, but it's not as mellow… and all the lights are out in the street. A blackout. I sat down on my trumpet case, leaned against the wall to the right of the hotel and waited. A young girl ran out of the hotel. She jumped to the side when she saw me, and when she came back she kept her distance. It was very dark in the street. A fat woman with a shopping bag walked past. I had seen her when I arrived. Dressed in black, she looked like one of those old women from the country. No, she's walking the street. That's funny, because this is not an area with a lot of passing trade. There were headlights at the end of the street. Yellow ones. It wasn't the truck. American ones are white. A black 11 for a change. Then a lorry, but a French one. Twenty to the hour, at the very least. Then the right one. It pulled up, half on the footpath, and the driver turned off his lights, just so he could take a piss against the wall. Signs of acknowledgement. We had a chat. Are the others going to turn up? There is only one other — Heinz. Already five to eight. The guy, a former driver for TCRP, dressed in an American uniform. I didn't know what to say to him. He seemed quite nice. I asked him if the truck was clean inside. Last time, in the one belonging to the showboat, I sat in some oil and grubbied my raincoat. No, this one is clean. I hopped into the back and dangled my legs over the side. We were waiting for Heinz. The guy couldn't be kept waiting too long. His American colonel was expecting him at quarter past nine and he had to pick up his car from the garage. I asked him if he drove around everywhere in the truck and if he would be much better off using his car. "Not really… it's not an American car. It's an Opel." I heard footsteps. It still wasn't Heinz. The lights suddenly came back on, and the driver said to me: "We can't wait any longer. I have to make a call so the guy at the garage can get a jeep ready for you, while I go and pick up my colonel. You speak English?" "Yes." "You'll explain to them…" Good. Heinz turned up. He started complaining as soon as he found out we had to go and get Martin. He bitches about him all the time, but when they are together, they spend all their time joking around in Dutch and taking the piss out of the rest of the band. Anyway,

I know what I am talking about, because I understand some of what they say. It's like German. Dutchmen, they are all bastards, half Krauts, even bigger arse-lickers when they want something from you. And tight, like you have no idea. And I don't like the way they suck up to the customers for cigarettes. After all, at least we have a bit of class. They are manipulative, and that makes me… Yes, I am an engineer, which, put simply, really is the most stupid job in the world. But it brings you respect and the feeling that you are doing something worthwhile. But if all it took was to push the button. Bang!… No more Martin. No more Heinz. Goodbye. Just because they are musicians is not a reason. Professionals are all bastards. The driver came back and we climbed back in. Heinz thought he had a drummer lined up for nine o'clock. But where were we going? The driver had to take us to 7 Place Vendôme. That's all he knew. There wasn't much time. So we took off along rue de Rivoli towards rue de Berri. He was complaining because army trucks can't go any faster than twenty miles an hour. He turned sharply to avoid going up a one-way street. Damn reruns. What was that we just passed? Oh, yes. The Park Club at Ambassadeurs. I haven't played there yet, but I have played the Colombia. That day it was full of pretty girls. It's a shame to see them with the Americans, but then, that's their business. The prettier they are, the more stupid they are. I couldn't care less. I don't want to screw them. I'm too tired. I just want to look at them. There is nothing I like more than looking at pretty girls. Yes there is… burying your nose in their hair when they are wearing perfume. There's nothing wrong with that. He jammed on the brakes. We were at the garage. A tall guy dressed in an American uniform. French? American? Maybe Jewish as well. He had the Stars and Stripes emblazoned on his shoulder. It's the garage that belongs to the newspaper. Heinz asked if he could use the phone to call his drummer. I explained what was going on to some guy who didn't give a damn. He wasn't going to move. Heinz came back. No drummer. "Okay, so will we all fit into a jeep?" "Yes, but we don't have a driver." Enough of this shit. I'll let them sort it out. I am sick of talking to them, and besides, you pick up that disgusting accent, and then the English look down their noses at you. And bugger it, they all give me the shits. They sorted it out. The driver had worked it out. "We're going to take the Opel, pick up Martin and then he'll take us to Place Vendôme." The Opel was grey. It'd do. He brought it around the front and parked it across the driveway. We squeezed in next to Heinz. It's better than the truck, at least. Heinz was having a good old laugh. But it's a heap of shit. It was shaking and rattling, and the idling was appalling. I remember the Delage. You could put a glass of water on the mudguard, not a ripple. Its six-cylinder engine can be more finely tuned than any other. The driver didn't get in. They were making him wait for his exit pass. We were already twenty minutes late. I didn't care. After all, it's Martin who's boss. He will sort it out with them. A jeep with a trailer pulled up at the garage. The guys inside look like something from the 1900s, in their leather goatskins, sitting on split seats, their lanky legs and knees tucked up under their chins. We were blocking their way. One of them jumped into the Opel and reversed it a couple of metres. After the jeep had gone past, he put it back in the same spot. What a dickhead. I was starting to lose it. The driver finally got his pass. We took off. Heap of shit. It almost made you throw up the way it handled corners. Everything was sloppy, suspension, steering. That figures. I had learned about that. A certain phase value makes you seasick. The Germans must surely know this too, but maybe a different phase value makes them seasick. Outside Saint-Lazare, we almost collided with a Matford. The guy crossed the intersection without looking. We went up rue Amsterdam, along the outer boulevards, to rue Lamarck. Number 73, it's on the right, I told him. I got out in front of Marcel's place. Martin was sitting at a table, watching the door, when he saw me. That's what it is. Bastard. Too damn lazy to go back to rue Notoire-du-Vidame, and he's even had a feed. The sign he made through the door as he approached was very gangsterish. He and Heinz started jabbering away in Dutch. There they go, they are at it again. Heinz wasn't abusing him at all, that's for sure. We roll around another corner. "It's like being on a swing!" the driver said. Number 7 Place Vendôme, Air Transport Command. There weren't many lights on. "Goodbye!" the driver said to me, as we shook hands. "I'm off to get the colonel." There is nobody here. "This isn't it," I said. "If you can't find anyone, call Elysée 07-05," he said. "It's the garage. They are the ones who told me to bring you here. But obviously, it's quarter to nine, which makes you three quarters of an hour late." He left. "*Go and ask, Roby,*" Martin said to me. "Go and ask yourself. You're the boss!" We went inside. Definitely not here. Nobody knew anything. It was eerie. You would have thought you were in a post office. So we went back out. "*Where's this driver?*" Martin asked. A girl wearing some sort of white sheepskin thing, and an American saw us. "*That's the band!*" "*Yes,*" Martin said, "*we've been waiting for half an hour.*" He's got some cheek, but I got a good laugh out of it anyway. The brunette, not a bad body. We'll soon see. We followed them. Finally, a half-decent car. A black 1939 Packard with driver. The driver was complaining, "I can't take them all! It will blow the tyres." You have got to be joking! You obviously know nothing about Packards! Three in the back: two girls and a Yank. On the fold-out seats: Martin, Heinz and me. In the front: the driver and two more Yanks. Rue de la Paix, Champs-Elysées, rue Balzac. First stop, Hôtel Celtique. The two in the front got out. We waited. Opposite, there was the sky-blue Chrysler belonging to the US Navy. I have already seen it go past a few times in Paris. I wonder if it is the fluid drive model, with oil-lubricated gear change. They were jabbering away inside the car, Heinz and Martin in Dutch, the driver in French. Oh! They're a pain. One of them climbed back in the front seat. He passed something between Heinz and me to the guy behind. "*There's a gift from Captain,*" whatever it was. "*Thank you Terry,*" the guy in the back said as he unwrapped it. It was the size of a packet of cigarette papers. He handed it back. We took off. A navy officer and two women climbed into the Chrysler and followed us. We immediately turned off to the right. Now this is a car! Even so, the driver was complaining about Bernard or O'Hara. One and the same. And eight in the car were too many. I wasn't listening to what they were saying in the back. Before we got to the Bois de Boulogne, we had to go through Garches and Saint-Cloud. There was a blonde with big breasts in the middle. To her left was the brunette, and to her right an American. Hollywood… "I heard Santa Monica *is nice,*" the girl in the middle said to nobody in particular. Of course you'd say something like that, bimbo. You're bloody hopeless and I don't like the look of you, it serves you right. The other one, the brunette, she was better. She can't be American. They are all saddle-backed, except for those two I saw one night on the showboat. Wearing pants, with tiny little waists and well rounded backsides. You would have thought they were blow-up dolls that had been squeezed tightly around the middle to make their chests and bums stick out. It was awful. "*What's the name of that friend of yours, Chris…*" the American guy asks the brunette. "Christiane," she answers. "*Nice name, and she's nice too.*" "*Yes,*" she replies, "*but she's got a strange voice*" — what a good friend! — "*and when she's on the stage, she makes such an awful noise... yes... but she's nice. Maybe we'll go to New York in February,*" she adds, "*and where do you come from?*" — "*New York,*" the guy says. "*It would be wonderful to see you again, and this other friend of yours, Florence?*" "*Yes,*" she says, "*she's got a nice face, but the rest is bad.*" What a nice thing to say about your friends! "*And who will come too? All the chorus girls?*" That's when I realised that she was from the Fête Foraine, but maybe I was wrong. It was wearing me down listening to Heinz and Martin speaking Dutch beside me. "*I think you're the best,*" the guy said. She didn't answer. Maybe it was true, even though he didn't say it as a compliment. We arrived at the Suresnes Bridge, which was full of potholes and poorly maintained. They had started to build a new one next to it in 1940, but now, five years later, it was in a right state, it had to have some rust in it. On the climb to Suresnes, the tyres on the big car make a sweet smooth humming sound on the paving. We dropped down a gear and climbed the hill. Eight in a Packard too many? What an idiot! All drivers are idiots. They are a rotten bunch. Screw them, I am an engineer. They are all on a first name basis with the musicians, and it makes them feel good. There is no difference between us. We both grovel. That's all right. I'll get my revenge later with a Colt. I'll take them all out. But I don't want to risk anything, because my skin is worth more than theirs. It would be crazy to do time for guys like that. I ask myself why I wouldn't do it for real. Go find a guy like Maxence Van der Meersch, and say to him, "You don't like pimps and nightclub owners. Well, neither do I. We form a secret pact and, one night, let's say we do a drive by in a black Citroën, and mow down all the guys from Toulouse." "Why stop there?" Van der Meersch says to me. "We have to kill them all." "In that case," I say, "I have another idea. We organise a big meeting of all the syndicates, and then we, do away with them. All it would take is some good planning." "What if we get caught?" Van der Meersch asks. "It doesn't matter," I say to him. "We'll have had a good laugh. But the next day others will come along and take their place." "In that case," he says, "we'll come up with another plan." "Okay. Goodbye, Maxence." The car pulled up. Golf Club. This was it. We get out and go inside. Tiled floor, exposed beams. I have seen places like this before. We got changed in a small room. Obviously, another pretty good requisition. Down a passageway. To the left, a large auditorium with a piano. This is it.

II

It was surprisingly hot at first. I was wrong to wear my sweatshirt, and I'll have to watch out for the hole in my pants. But my jacket is quite long, so they won't see it. It doesn't matter anyway. They are nothing but a bunch of whores and guys I don't give a damn about. The heaters are on, and the three of us sit down. Martin obviously thinks this is not the place to play swing. Heinz picks up his violin instead of his clarinet and they play some gypsy thing. While this is happening, I take it easy. I blow into my trumpet to warm it up a little. I unscrew the second valve, which sticks when it has been oiled. I put a bit of spit on it. Too sloppy. Spit everywhere. Even Buescher Slide Oil doesn't free it up. I tried paraffin once, and next time I had the taste in my mouth for hours. There are exposed beams painted in old red, golden yellow and faded royal blue. Very old-fashioned. A huge ornamental chimney with a torch fixed to a spiral pike on each side. Old pennants hanging from crossbeams that support a ten-metre-high ceiling. That's a high ceiling. All sorts of animal heads mounted on walls. Old Arab weapons. Just opposite me, an Aubusson rug, some sort of stork and exotic greenery. It's quite a nice colour scheme, with yellows and greens through to turquoise. A huge cathedral chandelier in the middle of the room, with at least a hundred electric light bulbs twisted into the shape of candles. Funny. They look like real flames. Just before Martin and Heinz start, some guy turns off the radio, which was hidden in the library behind a set of shelves full of false book spines used as a trompe-l'œil. I check out the legs of the brunette facing me. She is wearing a rather nice bluish-grey woollen dress with a small pocket on the sleeve. An olive green handkerchief is tucked inside. But when I see her from behind, the back of her dress is badly cut, the top is too big and the zipper pokes out a little. She is wearing platform shoes. She has good legs, slender at the knees and ankles. She doesn't have a stomach, and I am sure her backside would be nice and firm. Perfect. I am also guessing she has the eyes of a hooker. The other girl from the car is there too. She has a terrible complexion. It's too pale. She's the dumb one. She has big breasts. I have already mentioned that, but lousy legs and an awful brown and beige checked dress. Uninteresting. A French captain, the type of officer who is tall, bald, who distinguished himself in the First World War… Why is he having that effect on me?… It must be because of the books by Mac Orlan. He is talking to the dumb one. There are also two or three Americans, including one who is a captain, but one with no class. They all must have plenty of money if they pay so little attention to their appearance. A kind of bar to my left on the other side of the piano near the entrance. A barman behind, but I can only see the top of his head. The guys are starting to hoe into the whisky in orangeade glasses. The atmosphere is terrible. Heinz and Martin have finished their thing. No response. We are going to play Johnny Mercer's *Dream*. I take my trumpet, Heinz his clarinet. One couple get up to dance, along with the brunette, and a few others follow suit. Not many. There must be other rooms out back. It's crazy how hot it is in here with the heaters on. After *Dream*, something to wake them up, *Margie*. I am using a mute. There's hardly anyone dancing, and yes, it does sound better with the clarinet. I tune the trumpet slightly because it was too sharp. Usually it's the piano that's too sharp, but this one is flat because of the heat. We are not overdoing it, and there's not much enthusiasm in the dancing. Some guy comes in wearing a black trimmed jacket, a shirt with a starched collar and striped pants. My guess is that he's a steward. That's probably what he is. He signals to the waiter, who brings us over three cocktails. Gin and orange, or something like that. I like Coca-Cola better. It doesn't mess with my liver. He comes back over when the song has finished and asks what he can bring us. Very obliging. He has a thin face, a red nose, a mark on the side and an unusual complexion. He looks sad, poor fellow. Someone in the family must have had yellow fever. He goes away and comes back with two plates. One with four huge slices of apple tart. On the other, a pile of sandwiches, some with corned pork, and butter, with foie gras on the rest. Damn, how good is this! In trying not to show it, Martin has this silly look on his face, and his nose almost touches his chin. The guy tells us, "You only have to ask if you would like some more." After a sandwich, we start playing again. The good-looking brunette is clowning around and shaking her firm backside with the American. They are dancing, knees bent, heads down, as if they're doing a hammed up version of a 1900s gallopade. I already saw it being done the other day. It must be the new craze. It started over there in Auteuil again, with the *zazous*. Just behind me, there are two stags' heads, labelled Dittishausen 1916 and Unadingen 21 June 1928. I think they really only have a limited appeal. They are mounted on polished blocks of wood cut from the log on a slightly angled cross-section. They are oval or, to be more precise, elliptical in shape. A Major enters. No. A silver star. A colonel with a good-looking girl in tow. “Good-looking” is perhaps a bit of an overstatement. She has pale pink skin and rounded features, as if she had just been carved out of ice which is starting to melt. The ones with no blemishes, with no lumps, bumps or dimples, have something slightly off-putting about them. They are inevitably trying to hide something. They remind me of an anus after an enema, squeaky clean and disinfected. The guy is fairly nondescript. A big nose and grey hair. He gives her a squeeze and she rubs up against him. You are disgusting, both of you. Go and do it in a corner somewhere, and then come back, if that’s what you have in mind. It’s stupid all this canoodling. It’s like a cat with diarrhoea shitting in kitty litter. Yuk! You disgust me. I am betting that she is clean and a little moist between her thighs. There’s another sandy-haired girl. You saw photos of girls like her in 1910. She has a red ribbon around her head. American Beauty. Nothing has changed. Still the girl who’s squeaky clean, that one. What’s more, she doesn’t have a very good body, and with her bow legs, she looks like the “Alice in Wonderland” type. The women must all be American or English. The brunette is still dancing. We stop playing. She comes up to the piano and asks Martin to play *Laura*. He doesn’t know it. What about *Sentimental Journey?* Good. I get to play the sixth note. They are all dancing. What a bunch of jerks! Are they dancing for the music, to get the girls, or just for the sake of it? The colonel is still rubbing up against her. Some girl told me the other day that she can’t stand American officers. They are always talking politics, they can’t dance and they are a pain in the arse into the bargain. (They are not worth the effort. Make do with the rest.) I have to agree with her. I like the ordinary soldiers better. The officers are even more full of themselves than the young French cadets. And they are enough to push the needle of the dickheadmeter off the scale, with those little sticks they use to stick up horses’ bums. I am sitting on a rustic, hand-stitched chair from the Middle Ages that is damned hard on the backside. If I stand up, I have to watch out for the hole in my pants. The brunette comes back over. Another discussion with Martin. Dirty old bastard. You’d feel her up too, wouldn’t you. I know why. It’s warm, and that normally perks us up. Usually, on the showboat, it’s cold as buggery, which takes the fun out of playing. Time is going slowly tonight. It’s harder to play when there are only three of you. And this music is a drag. We play another two songs and take a short break. We gobble down the tart, and then an American, Bernard or O'Hara, the guy the driver was talking to outside the Celtique, comes over. "*If you want some coffee, you can get a cup now. Come on.*" "*Thanks!*" Martin says. And off we go. We go back across the foyer. We turn left. A small sitting room. Wall-to-wall Aubusson carpet. Hung with Aubusson tapestries. Oak panelling. On the couch are the colonel and his fondling female. She is wearing a black suit and sheer stockings that are a little too pink. She is blonde and her mouth is moist. We go past without looking at them. It wouldn't bother them anyway. They are not doing anything, just expressing their feelings. We go through another room, a bar, and a dining room. More Aubusson — it's an obsession — and a stylish rug on the carpet. Mountains of cakes. Two dozen or so people of both sexes, about a quarter of them women, smoking and drinking white coffee. There are plates and more plates. We make for it, trying not to be too obvious, but make for it we do. Currant buns filled with peanut butter, I love them. Little currant biscuits, I love them too. Apple tart with a two-centimetre layer of marmalade cream under the apples, and mouth-watering pastry. The evening won't have been a total waste. I eat until there is no room left, and then I eat some more, just to be sure I have no regrets later. I down my cup of white coffee, about half a litre of it, and a few more cakes. Martin and Heinz both take an apple. Not me. It bothers me taking things while those idiots are watching. But the Dutch are like dogs. They have no sense of decency. About the only thing they are sensitive to is a kick up the backside. We hang around for a while. I have my back to the wall because of the hole. We go back into the main auditorium. I undo two buttons because it's hard to blow a trumpet after having just eaten. We start up again. The brunette is there. She wants *I Dream of You*. Ah! I know that one! But Martin doesn't. It doesn't matter. He suggests *Dream*, but we have already played it. He launches into *Here, I've Said It Again*. I rather like that one because of the middle part, where you make a lovely change of key from F major to B flat, without making it obvious. And so we play, and we stop, and we play again, and we have a bit of a snooze. Two new girls have turned up. They are filthy. Must be French. Huge heads of hair. They both look like something of a cross between an intellectual typist and a maid. They immediately feel this need to come over and ask us to play a musette. To give them something to complain about, we play *Le Petit Vin blanc* in swing. They don't even recognise the tune.

What idiots. Yes they do, right at the end, and then they pull a face. The Americans don't give a damn. They like anything lousy. I think things are winding down. It's after midnight. We've played heaps of old rubbish. I pour a Coca-Cola into a large glass. Martin has just been handed our pay in a thick envelope. He looked at it and said, "*Nice people, Roby. They have paid for four musicians, though we were only three.*" That's what he said, the idiot. That means there are three thousand francs in the envelope. Martin goes and takes a piss, and when he comes back, puts out his hand for a packet of Chesterfields. "*Thank you, sir. Thanks a lot!*" What a flunkey! A tall red-headed guy comes over and asks me something about a set of drums. He wants one for tomorrow. I give him two addresses, and then another guy comes over and explains things better. He wanted to hire a set of drums. I don't have any addresses for what he wants, so I can't help. He offers a cigarette as well. We keep on playing, and somehow it ends up being one o'clock. We close with *Good Night Sweetheart*. That's enough. Time to get out of here. Just one more... We play *Sentimental Journey* again. They are upset this is the last one. They're feeling mellow. Now we have to think about leaving. We go and get changed. It's cold in the hallway and foyer. I put on my raincoat. Martin signals to me. He is with Heinz. Good. He slips me seven hundred francs. I get it. You're going to pocket the rest, you bastard. It would give me great pleasure to punch you in the face. But why the hell would I care? I am not as dumb as you are, and you are fifty years old. I hope you drop dead. He doesn't pay Heinz in front of me. You are really sly, both of you. I give him my share of the cigarettes, just to hear him say, "*We thank you very much, Roby.*" We are waiting for a car. The floor in the hallway is tiled. There are two red buckets full of water and a fire extinguisher, and signs everywhere — "*Beware of Fire*", "*Don't put your ashes*", etc. I would really like to know whose house this is. Heinz and I go into raptures. He really likes it too. We go back into the foyer. Martin goes and takes a piss. He has pinched a copy of *Yank* from somewhere and gives it to me to look after. We are near the phone. Martin comes back, and says to me, "*Can you call my hotel, Roby, I wonder if my wife's arrived.*" His wife was due to arrive today. So I phone the hotel on behalf of Mr Romberg to find out if his key is hanging on the board. Yes, it's there, but your wife isn't. You can always go and get off in front of a pin-up girl. We go back into the lobby, then over to the Packard. The driver doesn't want to take all three of us. He's pissed off. "Go without us. We'll manage." We go back into the foyer. I sit down. Heinz is sounding off, in gibberish, just for a change. Martin is deep in conversation with Doublemetre. He's an American guy. Really nice. He finds us a car, but Martin has to take a shit, so we wait. I go back into the lobby. After all that, Heinz has just given twenty francs to one of the stewards. He's rather nice. "Whose house is this?" "It belongs to some English guy. He's a government official in South Africa, and he has another house near London. It's a good house, and during the Occupation the Germans didn't damage it at all. They were here, of course." The English guy lost his wife three years ago and has just remarried. The servant hasn't met the new lady of the house yet. It's sad when you lose someone. He had a friend, someone he had known for six years, and he lost him. Yes, it leaves a void that can't be filled. I condole and we shake hands. Goodbye. Thank you. Heinz and Martin finally arrive. We go outside. The car is in a laneway. It's a Chrysler. No, better still, it's the other one, a Lincoln. I take a piss against a tree. The two maid-typists and an American turn up. He's the driver. The three of us are in the back. He's in the front with the two girls. They complain because they are too squashed. I really don't give a damn. I have plenty of room. They turn on the radio. The engine starts. The car lurches forward. We are following another car. The music helps pass the time. It's white jazz. It doesn't have much swing, but it hangs pretty well together. We are going along in the car and I say to Heinz, "I could easily drive around like this all night." He would prefer to go home to bed. Paris, Concorde, Rue Royale, Boulevards, Vivienne, Bourse, stop… Martin gets out. I am next. Heinz is furious. We have done the grand tour. We are at Gare du Nord and he has to go back to Neuilly. Let him sort it out with the driver. Goodbye, kids. I shake the driver's hand. "*Thanks a lot. Good night.*" I am finally at home in the sack. And just before I fall asleep, I turn over and let out an almighty quack.

THE SWIMMING PRIEST

All of this is Pauwels' fault. If it wasn't for his article, I never would have been at Deligny Baths and nothing would have happened. I wanted to check out the women and, to tell the truth, I had a good chance of getting by unnoticed. I may not be the toughest guy around, and I might be a bit of a clod, but I do have dark skin (it's my liver) and all my limbs. It was pleasant out on the timber deck. I didn't dare go for a swim. Pauwels, he scared me off about the bleach. And then there were women to see. But luck must have been against me, nothing but ugly ones. I lay down on my back, closed my eyes and waited to turn black all over. And then, just as I was going to have to roll over to hide the tent pole, along comes some guy who trips right over the top of me. He was reading while walking, and he was reading a prayer book. That's right, he was a priest. "So they do bathe, then!" I say to myself, and then I remember that only women's body parts are denied water by the Seminarist Code.

Now that the ice had been broken, I was going to kill him, but I change my mind.

"For *La Rue*, Father, an interview?" I say to him.

"Yes, my son," the priest says. "That is the least I can do for a lost sheep."

I try to make him understand that I am a man, and so that makes me more of a ram than a sheep. But, blow me down, no more tent pole. No more man. No more anything. Good, I think, it's because of the priest. It will come back when he's gone. Anyway, too bad, I am going to begin.

"Father," I ask, "are you a Marxist?"

"No, my son," the priest says. "Who is Marx?"

"A poor sinner, Father."

"So let us pray for him, my child."

He begins to pray. Like a sucker, I was about to follow suit, and I start to join my hands together, but a bra strap snaps right under my nose, and I can feel it coming back. It is putting me back on track.

"Father," I continue, "do you visit b…?"

"No, my son," he says. "What are they?"

"You don't… with yourself?"

"No, my son," he says, "I read my prayer book."

"But what about things of the flesh?"

"Oh!" the priest says, "they don't count."

"Are you an existentialist, Father?" I continue. "Have you won the Pléiade Prize? Are you an anarcho-masochist, social democrat, barrister, member of the Constituent Assembly, Israelite, big landowner, or trafficker of religious artefacts?"

"No, my son," he says to me. "I pray, and I also read *Pilgrim*. Sometimes *Christian Witness*, although it does tend to promote immorality."

I don't give up.

"Do you have a degree in philosophy? Are you a champion sprinter or a pelota player? Do you like Picasso? Do you give lectures on religious sentiment in the works of Rimbaud? Are you one of those people who, like Kierkegaard, believe that the way you look at things depends on your situation? Have you published a critical edition of the *Hundred and Twenty Days of Sodom?*"

"No, my son," the priest says. "I go to Deligny, and I live in the peace of the Lord. I repaint my church every two years, and I hear the confessions of my parishioners."

"But you will never amount to anything, you silly fool!" I say to him. (I was starting to lose my temper.) "Come on! How long are you planning to keep this up? You lead a ridiculous existence! No social life? No Cremona Violin or Géricault Trumpet? No hidden vices? No black masses? No satanic rituals?"

"No."

"Oh, Father! You are too much."

"I swear to you before God," the priest says.

"But Father, you do realise that if you don't try all these things, you can't exist as a priest?"

"Alas, my son," the priest says.

"Do you believe in God?"

"That is not up for discussion."

"Not even that?" (I was throwing him a lifeline.)

"I have faith," the priest says.

"You don't exist, Father. You don't exist. It's not possible."

"It is true, my son. You may be right."

He seemed to be a broken man. I watched him turn pale, and his skin became transparent.

"What is wrong with you, Father? Take hold of yourself! You still have time to write a volume of verse!"

"Too late," he whispered in a distant voice. "What do you expect? I believe in God, and that is all there is to it."

"But a priest like you doesn't exist." (I was whispering too.)

He was becoming more and more transparent, and then he disappeared into thin air. Gee, I was uncomfortable. No more priest. I took the prayer book as a keepsake. I read it a little every night. I found his address inside. From time to time, I go to the place in the presbytery where he used to live. It's becoming a habit. His maid has overcome her grief, and she likes me now. And sometimes I hear the confessions of girls, young girls… I drink altar wine… When it's all said and done, it's not so bad being a priest.

Reverend Boris Vian
Member of the NSCJ
National Society of the Company of Jesus

ANOTHER DAY IN MARSEILLE

I

It was another day in Marseille. The butcher's boy raised the olive green steel shutter that concealed the top half of the shop front. Metal grated against metal, but the terrible noise it made was not loud enough to drown out his whistling. He was whistling *The Palavas Palace Is Not the Office of the House of Havas*, a catchy little tune that he had heard on the radio. He couldn't get it out of his head because they kept on playing it over and over again, all day long.

Next, he lifted the three-tiered metal grille that sealed off the bottom half of the shop and folded it into place. Once this task had been completed, he swept into a pile the sawdust that had been scattered over the floor at the end of the previous shift and stood there twiddling his thumbs.

The sound of the butcher's footsteps in the corridor reminded him of something he had forgotten to do. He had just bought a beautiful brand new knife the day before. He raced over to where he had left it and feverishly set to work putting an edge on the blade with a sharpening steel.

In the meantime, his boss was approaching, clearing his throat in the same disgusting way he did every morning. He was a tall, dark-haired man, as strong as an ox, and a little frightening. And yet he came from Nogent.

"So, how's that knife coming along?"

"It's getting there," the boy answered, slightly flushed. His short blonde hair and pug nose made him look like a little pig.

"Show me."

The boy held out the blade for his boss to examine. The butcher took the knife, and ran the cutting edge across his fingernail to test it.

"Shi…," he swore. "Where did you learn to sharpen a knife? There's no way you could slit a North Korean's throat with that thing."

He made that comment to wind up his apprentice, because he was well aware of the boy's radical views.

"Oh! I bet you I could!" the boy protested.

He had spoken too soon. The butcher gave him an ominous look.

"Go on, then!" he said.

The boy, feeling a bit confused, timidly tried to get back on the front foot.

"A male or a female…" he suggested.

"Okay!" the butcher said with a sneer.

He cleared his throat one last time. The young boy couldn't stomach the noise any longer and threw up in the pile of sawdust.

II

Mr Mackinley, deep in thought, struck a match on the leather sole of his left shoe. He had both feet on his desk, and had to lean a long way forward, which reactivated his old Iwo Jima lumbago pains.

In actual fact, Mr Mackinley was not his real name, and this export company served as a cover for one of the most active agents of ASS, the American Secret Service. The wrinkles etched deep in his animated face made it quite clear that Mr Mackinley was able to make the tough decisions when he had to.

His hand hit a buzzer, and a secretary appeared.

"Have Mrs Eskubova come in." He spoke English without the slightest trace of any accent.

"Yes sir," she said. Mr Mackinley winced every time he heard that grating voice which reminded him of Brooklyn. Nevertheless, he managed to maintain enough self-control to keep himself in check, just like Emperor Hirohito.

Shortly afterwards a woman entered the office. There was an air of mystery about her. She was buxom and had a certain mystique; she had blue eyes and brown hair; her curvaceous body was enticing; she was the perfect agent for a delicate mission.

"Hello, Pelagia," Mr Mackinley said briefly. She answered him in the same language. What follows is a transcript of their conversation.

"I have a confidential assignment for you," Mackinley said, getting straight to the point, as Americans do.

"What is it?" Pelagia asked, firing straight back at him.

"Now, this is what we've got," Mackinley whispered. He had lowered his voice. "We have learned from a very reliable source that a well-known French political figure, Mr Jules M., has in his possession certain information that is of the utmost importance to us. It has to do with the Gromiline Report."

Pelagia turned pale, but remained silent.

"Um," said Mackinley, ill at ease. "Well then, to put it simply, you are the only one who can obtain this information."

"And how am I supposed to do that?" she asked, drawing a breath.

"My dear lady," Mackinley said with exquisite courtesy, "your well-known charm..."

Pelagia's silver cigarette case struck his left eyebrow, causing a few drops of blood to appear. Mackinley was still smiling, but his jaws suddenly clenched. He picked up the cigarette case and handed it back to Pelagia.

"You take me for a whore," she said. "I am not Marthe Richard. Don't forget that, Mackinley."

"My dear," he said, "It's either yes or..."

He drew his finger threateningly across his Adam's apple. She exploded into a fit of rage.

"I refuse," she said. "He is revolting. When you engaged my services, it was agreed that my loyalty to Georges would not be compromised in any way."

"Ha!" Mackinley sneered. "So what do you have to say about that little blonde-haired fellow with rosy cheeks, a butcher's boy from Montpellier, I believe… the one you go riding around with in taxis."

On this occasion, she knew he had gotten the better of her.

"You monster! So you know everything then," she said drawing a breath.

He bowed gallantly.

"I would like to know more," he said, "and that is why I took the liberty of asking for your cooperation."

"Sleep with Jules M.… How awful!" she said under her breath.

She shuddered and stood up.

"I don't think we have anything more to say to each other," Mackinley concluded. "In a few days, our agent, F-5, will contact you in Montpellier. You will be given a complete set of identity papers and, naturally, some spending money…"

"How much?" she asked in a muffled voice.

"H'm…" Mackinley said. "You will be given five hundred thousand francs in cash, and another five thousand dollars will be deposited into your account, if the mission is successful. The department would like to be seen as being rather generous on this occasion. You see, my dear Pelagia, the Gromiline Report is extremely important to the President…"

III

The taxi slowly pulled away from the kerb. It was an old Vivaquatre whose driver was half-deaf.

On the cushions in the back seat, Pelagia was stroking the butcher boy's short hair affectionately.

"My darling," she said in Russian, "when I was very young, I had a little pink pig, a baby pig. His name was Pulaski. You remind me of him."

A cloud passed over her face. The butcher's boy, who was not the brightest, was quietly allowing himself to be petted.

"Listen to me!" Pelagia muttered to herself. "I sound like one of those damn American women on a trip down memory lane."

The taxi was approaching the hotel where they went for their trysts.

"Listen," Pelagia said, mustering her best French, "you... come... you, my little pigeon, take knife... cut my throat."

"I can't bring myself to sleep with that guy," she added in Russian. Reverting to French, she said, "Listen, Goloubtchik, if you love me, you must do this."

"Are you North Korean?" the butcher's boy asked bluntly.

"Oh..." Pelagia said. "From Harbin, not far."

"That's all right then," he said. "It's agreed. I will be happy to."

Pelagia gave a shudder.

"I would rather it be you, my pink pig," she added very quickly. "At Palavas, where we first met."

She gave him a long passionate kiss, and the driver, who was watching in the rear-view mirror, almost ran into the back of a truck.

"We will do it tomorrow," the butcher's boy said. "I will sharpen the thing later tonight when I go back. I will meet you on the beach at nine o'clock."

It was the third of September.

IV

"Still not great," the butcher observed. "Obviously you don't know how to sharpen a knife."

"We'll see about that," the boy boasted.

"I'm still waiting for that North Korean," the butcher said teasingly.

"Patience," the boy said.

He grabbed the sharpening steel and began enthusiastically to run the blade back and forth across the surface. The tip of his tongue protruded from between his lips. The butcher sniggered, then spat in the pile of sawdust, right on top of a big green fly.

V

"Stop here," Pelagia said, tapping the driver on the shoulder. He did as he was told. She threw two one-thousand-franc notes in his direction and got out of the car. She was wearing a black skirt and a white blouse with a plunging neckline.

The driver clicked his tongue as he watched her disappear.

"For that sort of money, I would gladly have her every night of the week," he commented with disgusting vulgarity.

She strode towards the beach. It was almost eight o'clock. She occasionally looked back over her shoulder. Two men stopped when they saw her walk past.

"Hmm!" one said.

"Oh, yes!" added the other.

Night was falling quickly. Pelagia was walking on Palavas beach. She was now alone. She was almost at the meeting point. She was early. She dropped down onto the sand and waited.

From out of the shadows, he suddenly loomed up behind her. She became aware of his presence.

"My pink pig," she sighed.

He was agitated.

"I have a problem," he said. "I looked on a map for Harbin, and it's not in North Korea at all. It's in China."

"What does it matter?" Pelagia sighed again. "Anything is better than sleeping with that guy. Get it over with, Goloubtchik."

He remembered how the paratroopers did it in the movies. At the same time his natural love of cleanliness gave him an idea.

"Go into the water," he said. "That way, we won't make a mess."

She did as she was told. He turned her around roughly, stuck his thumb under her nose and tilted her head back. He plunged the knife into her throat. Once.

"Gosh," he said as he removed the knife. "The boss won't be able to say that it wasn't sharp enough this time."

Blood was coming from the lifeless body floating in the dark water at his feet.

"A job well done. I kept my word," he said to himself.

A heavy object struck him on the side of the head, causing him to collapse in a heap.

Agent F-5 whistled softly. A dinghy approached.

"Put him in," he said. "This bloke saved me from a most unpleasant task."

The other man loaded the body of the butcher's boy on board the boat.

"Give him a shot of NRF* and we'll take him back to his place.

He searched the body. The wound was no longer bleeding. He picked up the knife and hurled it out to sea. The wallet and belt, he would dispose of later. He dragged the body towards the beach. He needed to be sure that the body was found. F-5 knew that he needed to cover his tracks when dealing with Mackinley.

The motor of the small dinghy was ticking over quietly. F-5 climbed in. The flimsy hull sank lower in the water under the extra weight.

"Let's go. There is still work to be done," he said. The silhouette of the boat disappeared into the dark of night.

---

* Non Remember Fluid. Amnesia Serum developed by the American Secret Service during the war.

DOGS, DEATH AND DESIRE

They got me. I am going to the chair tomorrow. But I am going to write this anyway, because I want to explain. The jury didn't understand. And now, since Slacks's death, it has been difficult to talk about it, knowing that no-one would believe me. If only Slacks had been able to pull herself from the car. If only she had been able to come and tell everyone what happened. Let's not talk about that any more. Nothing can be done about it. Nothing on earth.

The trouble with being a cab driver is that you get yourself into routines. You spend all day driving around, so you end up knowing all the different neighbourhoods. There are some you prefer to others. I know drivers, for example, who would sooner let themselves be slashed with a knife than take a fare to Brooklyn. Me, I am happy to. I mean I was happy to, because now I won't be doing it any more. It's one of those routines I got myself into. Almost every night around one o'clock, I would drive past the Three Deuces. One time, I dropped a customer there. He was as drunk as a skunk and he wanted me to go in with him. When I came back out, I knew what kind of girls you could find inside. Ever since, it's crazy, you'll see for yourself.

Every night around five to one, five past one, I would drive by. She was just leaving. They often had singers at Deuces, and I knew who she was. "Slacks," they called her, because she was almost always in pants. They also said in the papers that she was a lesbian. She hung out a lot with the same two guys — her piano player and bass player — and you would see them driving around in the piano player's car. They would play a gig somewhere else and then come back to Deuces to finish off the night. I found that out later.

I never stayed there long. I couldn't keep my cab out of service all the time, or leave it parked for too long either, because there were always more customers in that neighbourhood than anywhere else.

But on the night I'm talking about, they had an argument, something serious. She punched the piano player in the face. That girl could pack a mean punch. She knocked him down like a real pro. He was plastered, but even if he'd been sober, I still think he would have gone down. The only thing was, because he was so drunk, he stayed down. The other guy tried bringing him around by slapping him hard enough to knock his block off. I didn't see the end, because she came over, opened the door of the cab and climbed into the seat next to me. Then she lit a cigarette lighter and had a close look at me.

"Would you like me to turn on the light?"

She said no and put out her lighter. I drove off. Not far down the road, after having turned into York Avenue, I asked her where she wanted to go, because I finally realised that she hadn't said anything.

"Straight ahead."

Hey, it made no difference to me. The meter was ticking. So I kept driving straight ahead. At that time of night, there are always people in the nightclub district, but as soon as you leave the centre, that's it. The streets are deserted. You wouldn't believe it, but once one o'clock comes around, it's worse than the suburbs. A few cars, and every now and then some guy by himself.

Since she had the idea of sitting next to me in the front of the cab, I didn't expect much about that girl to be normal. I looked across at her. She had black hair down to her shoulders and a complexion that was so pale it made her look unhealthy. The lipstick she was wearing was almost black and it made her mouth look like a dark hole. We were still driving. She decided to speak.

"Swap places."

I stopped the car. I decided not to object. I had seen the way she had just flattened her partner and I wasn't too keen to pick a fight with a girl of that calibre. I was about to get out of the car, when she grabbed my arm.

"Don't bother. I'll slide across. Move over."

She sat on my knee and slid into place on my left. Her body was as firm as a chunk of frozen meat, only not the same temperature.

She realised that something had stirred in me and started to laugh, but not in a nasty sort of way. She almost seemed happy. When she started up my old heap, I thought the gearbox was going to blow up. When she took off, the sudden jolt pushed us right back in our seats.

After crossing the Harlem River, we arrived in the Bronx. She was driving like a maniac. When I was called up, I saw the way they drive in France. Now, they know how to knock a car around, but they couldn't do half as much damage as that broad in pants. The French are simply dangerous. She was a complete disaster. Still, I said nothing.

Oh, so you think this is funny! You think that with my size and strength, I should have been able to bring a woman under control, don't you? You wouldn't have tried to either, if you'd seen that girl's mouth and the look on her face in that car. Deathly white, and that black hole… I gave her a sideways glance and said nothing. All the while, I was keeping a look out. I didn't want the cops to pull us over because there were two of us in the front.

You wouldn't think that in a city like New York there could be so few people around in the wee hours. But you can take my word for it. She kept turning down streets. You could go for whole blocks without seeing a soul. Then you'd see one or two people. A bum, sometimes a woman, people returning home from work. There are shops that don't close until one or two in the morning. Some don't even close at all. Every time she saw someone on the sidewalk on the passenger's side, she would swerve and drive alongside them as close as possible. She would slow down a little and then hit the accelerator as soon as she passed them. I still didn't say anything, but after the fourth time I asked her why she did it.

"I suppose I get a kick out of it," she said.

I didn't answer. She looked at me. I didn't like the fact that she was looking at me while she was driving and, in spite of myself, I found that my hand had grabbed hold of the steering wheel. She punched me hard on the back of the hand with her right fist, without missing a beat. It felt as if a horse had kicked me. I swore and she laughed again.

"It's hilarious how they jump when they first hear the sound of the motor…"

She must have seen the dog crossing the street. I was looking around for something to hang on to, for when she hit the brakes. But instead of slowing down, she accelerated and I heard a thud against the front of the car. I felt the sudden impact.

"Damn!" I said. "You were going flat out. A dog that size must have done some damage to the car…"

"Shut up!"

She seemed to be in a daze. She had a vague look in her eyes. The car was veering all over the road. Two blocks later, she pulled over to the kerb.

I wanted to get out to see if the front grille had been smashed in, but she grabbed my arm. Her breathing sounded like the snorting of a horse.

The look on her face just then… I'll never forget the look on her face. To see a woman in that state when you've put her in that state, that's OK, that's fine… but when that's the last thing on your mind and you see her like that all of a sudden… She was sitting motionless, squeezing my wrist as tight as she could. Dribble was running down her chin. The corners of her mouth were moist.

I looked outside. I didn't know where we were. There wasn't a soul around. One tug of the zipper and her pants were off. When you do it in a car, you're usually left with the feeling that there should have been more to it. But even so, that is one time I will never forget. Not even after they've shaved my head tomorrow morning.

***

A little later, I made her move back over to the passenger's seat and I took the wheel again. Almost immediately, she asked me to stop the car. She had straightened herself up best as she could, swearing like a trooper. She got out and sat in the back. Then she handed me the address of a nightclub where she had to go and sing. I tried to work out where we were. I was disorientated, like when you come out of a month in rehab. But I managed all the same not to fall over when my turn came to get out of the car. I wanted to check the front of the car. Nothing. Just a bloodstain that had spread over the right fender because of the speed the car had been travelling. It could have been any old stain.

The quickest way out of there was to turn the car around and go back the same way.

I could see her in the rear-view mirror. She was looking out the window. When I spotted the body of the animal, a black mass on the sidewalk, I heard her. Once again, her breathing became heavier. The dog was still moving a little. The impact of the car must have broken its back and it had dragged itself off to the side. I wanted to vomit. I felt weak. She started laughing behind me. She could see that I felt sick and she began to insult me under her breath. She said some terrible things, and I could have taken her right there and then and done it all over again in the street.

I don't know what the rest of you guys are made of, but when I took her back to that nightclub where she had to knock out a number, I couldn't stay outside and wait. I took off straight away. I had to go home. I had to lie down. It's not funny living by yourself all the time, but man, I was glad to be alone that night. I didn't even get undressed. I had a few slugs of something I found and lay down. I was drained. I was that damned drained…

The next night, there I was again waiting for her right out front. I lowered the flag and got out to stretch my legs. The place was buzzing. I couldn't stay, but I waited anyway. She came out, once again at the same time. Like clockwork, that girl. She saw me and recognised me straight away. The two guys were following her like they always did. She laughed in her usual way. I don't know how to explain it, but seeing her like that, it felt as though I no longer had both feet firmly planted on the ground. She opened the door of the cab and the three of them climbed in. I felt suffocated. I wasn't expecting that. "Idiot," I said to myself. You don't understand that with a girl like that, everything she does is on the spur of the moment. One night, everything is sweet and the next you're just a cab driver. You're a nobody.

A nobody! You've got to be joking! I was driving like an idiot and I almost ran up the backside of a big car in front of me. Sure, I was fuming. I was pissed off and all. In the back, the three of them were having a good old time. She was telling stories in her man's voice, that grating voice that sounded like someone talking at you when you've had too much to drink.

As soon as we arrived, she was first out. The two guys didn't even try to insist on paying. They knew what she was like too... They went inside and she leaned through the window to stroke my cheek, as if I were a baby. I took her money. I didn't want to have any issues with her. I was going to say something, but I didn't know what. She spoke first.

"You wait for me?" she asked.

"Where?"

"Here. I'll be back in fifteen minutes."

"Alone?"

Man, I was full of myself. I wanted to take that back, but there was no way I could take anything back. She grabbed my cheek with her fingernails.

"See that?" she said.

She laughed again. I didn't realise what she'd done. She let go of me almost straight away. I touched my cheek. It was bleeding.

"That's nothing!" she said. "It will have stopped bleeding by the time I come back. Wait for me, all right? Here."

She went into the nightclub. I tried to take a look in the rear-view mirror. On my cheek there were three curved marks. There was also a fourth, deeper scratch made by her thumb. It wasn't bleeding badly and I didn't feel anything.

So, I waited. That night, we didn't kill anything. I didn't get any either.

***

I don't think she'd been playing that game for very long. She didn't talk much and I knew nothing about her. I was now just killing time during the day, waiting, so I could go and pick her up at night in my old cab. She didn't sit next to me any more. It would have been really stupid to get yourself thrown in the slammer for that. I would get out and she would take my place behind the wheel. We managed to score a few dogs and cats, at least two or three times a week.

After we'd been seeing each other for about a month, I got the impression that she wanted something more. It wasn't having the same effect on her as it did the first few times, and I think she got the idea in her head to go after more substantial game. I can't tell you anything else. I found that natural. She was no longer reacting the way she used to, and I wanted her to be like she was before. I know you'll think I'm a monster, but you didn't know that girl. A dog or some kid. It made no difference to me. I would have killed anything for that girl. So we killed a fifteen-year-old girl. She was taking a stroll with her friend, a sailor. She was on her way home from the amusement park. But let me tell you the whole story.

Slacks was terrifying that night. As soon as she got in, I could see that she was after something. And I knew that, even if it meant we had to drive around all night, we'd have to find that something.

Man, things got off to a bad start! I headed straight onto Queensborough Bridge and from there out onto the ring road. Never before had I seen so many cars and so few pedestrians. That's to be expected on a motorway, you might say. But that night, I didn't think so. I had other things on my mind. We drove for miles, doing the full circuit, and ended up right in the middle of Coney Island. Slacks had already been behind the wheel for a while and I was in the back, holding on tight around the corners. She looked like she was out of control. I was waiting. As usual. I'm telling you, I was on standby. I switched on the moment she climbed into the back seat with me. Man! It doesn't bear thinking about.

There was nothing to it. She began zigzagging from West 24th to 23rd, and then she saw them. They were enjoying themselves. He was walking on the sidewalk, and she was next to him on the road, giving the impression that she was even smaller than she was. He was a tall young man, a handsome young man. From the back, the girl looked quite young, with blonde hair and a short dress. It was hard to see. I saw Slacks's hands on the steering wheel. The bitch. She could drive. She drove straight into them, and hit the girl from the side. That's when I felt as though I was dying. I managed to turn around. She was lying on the ground, a lifeless mass, and the guy was yelling and running after us. Then I saw a green car appear out of nowhere, one of the old model police cars.

"Faster!" I screamed.

She looked at me for a second and we almost ran up onto the sidewalk.

"Go! Go!"

I know that, at that moment, there was something I missed out on seeing. I know. I couldn't see anything except her back, but now I can picture everything. You see, that's why I don't give a damn. That's why tomorrow morning they can damn well come and shave my head. Or they can cut my hair into a fringe so they can get a laugh out of it. Or they can paint me green like the police car. You see, I don't care.

Slacks was hammering it. She somehow managed to get us onto Surf Avenue. That old heap was making one hell of a racket. Behind us, the police car must have started giving chase.

Then we got onto an approach ramp to the motorway. No more red lights. Man, I wished I had a different car! Everything was a blur. The other car was in pursuit. It felt like we were crawling along at a snail's pace. It was enough to make you want to chew your fingernails down to the bone.

Slacks was giving it everything. I could still see her back and I knew what she wanted, because I wanted it as much as her. "Go!" I screamed again. She kept going and then she turned around for a second. Another car was coming off a ramp, about to join the motorway. She didn't see him. He was coming up on our right, doing at least seventy-five. I saw the tree and tucked myself into a ball, but she didn't move. When they got me out of there, I was screaming like a madman. Slacks still wasn't moving. The steering wheel had crushed her chest. It was a difficult job to free her, and in the end they pulled her out by the hands, hands that were as white as her face. Dribble was still running down her chin. Her eyes were open. I couldn't move either because of my leg, which was bent around the wrong way. I asked them to bring her over to me. I saw her eyes, and then I saw her. Blood was streaming from her. There was blood everywhere, except for on her face.

They opened her fur coat and they saw that she was wearing nothing underneath, except for her slacks. The pale skin of her hips appeared dull and lifeless under the glow of the sodium vapour reflector lamps that lit up the road. When we'd hit the tree, her zipper was already undone.

DON'T TRUST THE BAND

Nightclub patrons, don't trust the band!

You arrive there, feeling good, well dressed, smelling nice, and happy with life because you have had a delightful meal. You sit yourself down at a comfortable table, a mouth-watering cocktail in front of you. You have taken off your expensive warm overcoat. You carelessly spread out your jewellery, furs and other bits and pieces. You smile. You start to relax... You look at your neighbour's corsage and think that, while you are dancing, you might move in on her... you ask her to dance... and that's when your troubles begin.

Of course you have noticed those six guys in white jackets producing the rhythm on stage. At first the music doesn't have any effect on you, but then gradually it enters your body through the pores of your skin, reaches the eighteenth nerve centre of the fourth cerebral convolution at the top on the left which, as everyone knows since the work of Broca and Captain Pamphile, is where the centre of pleasure born from the detection of harmonious sounds is located.

Six guys in white jackets. Six flunkeys. As a general rule, staff only had eyes to avoid knocking over your glass when handing you the menu and ears designed specifically for taking your order or for hearing the discreet tap of your finger on the crystal. You allow yourself to jump to conclusions about those six guys, because of their white jackets.

Oh, friends! Don't let them fool you!

(Please don't be annoyed if I am talking to you like this, man to man, and please don't be offended if I emphasise the dazzling cut of your neckline with a bold stroke of the pen. Friends, you should all be aware that you are hermaphroditic.)

But just as you are about to ask your neighbour to dance... Oh, friends! Woe betide you!

For one of those guys in white jackets, one of those guys blowing in tubes or tapping on skins or keys or plucking strings, one of them has spotted you. What do you expect? Even though he is wearing a white jacket, he is still a man!... And your neighbour, the one you have just asked to dance, she is a woman!... No mistake about that!... She is careful not to come here wrapped in the vulgar trappings of the suit, slacks and heavy-soled shoes which, were you to meet her on the Avenue du Bois in the fading light, could make you take her for the teenager she was not, oh, that was doubly evident!...

Doubly evident indeed, for that is what, more than anything, strikes the guy in the white jacket, whose elevated position allows him to scan the crowd, a technique made fashionable by certain great people in the world — Charles de Gaulle, known as Double-Master, and Yvon Pétra known as Double-Metre, to name but two — whose lofty station was only matched by their great height.)

And friends, that is when you cease to be hermaphroditic.

You split in two: a horrible man, a red-faced over-indulger, the king of gluttony, a coke dealer, a dirty politician; and a ravishing woman, whose tight-lipped smile bears witness to the harshness of the times that forces her to dance with such a clod.

What does it matter, you horrible man, if in reality you are twenty-five years old with the body of Apollo, if your charming smile reveals a perfect set of teeth, if the dashing cut of your suit emphasises the broadness of your shoulders?

You will never win. You are a peasant, a miser, a misfit. You have a father who is an arms dealer, a mother who has been around, a brother on drugs and a manic sister.

She begs to be noticed... she is ravishing, I am telling you.

Her dress... with that neckline! Square, or round, or heart-shaped, or plunging, or to the side, or no neckline at all if the dress is off the shoulder

… And that figure!… You know it's easy to tell whether or not she is wearing anything under her dress… there are faint raised lines around the top of her thighs…

(But they are only there if she has anything on underneath. Usually, if there are no raised lines, the guy on the trumpet hits a false note that you probably wouldn't notice, because you generously put it down as being what you would expect from hot jazz.)

And her smile!… Her perfectly shaped red lips that surely taste like raspberries… And you!… You dance like an elephant. You are sure to crush her delicate feet.

And then you return to your seats. Finally she can catch her breath. She sits back down next to you.

Now what?

Her hand… Her slender fingers with silver nail polish… on your country bumpkin shoulder?… And she is smiling at you?…

Oh!… The bitch!… All the same!…

And then the guys in white jackets launch into the next number…

RAMPARTS OF THE SOUTH

I

The Major, up to his ears in debt like almost never before, decided to buy a car so that his holidays would be more enjoyable.

The first step was to draw on the funds that were readily available to him. By this, he meant hitting his usual three friends for a loan so he could go and get thoroughly pissed. This was because his glass eye was turning indigo blue, which was a sign that he needed a drink. All up, this cost him three thousand francs, but he had not the slightest regret in spending it, since he had no intention of repaying it.

So, after having thus made things more interesting, he tried his best to complicate the operation further in order to turn it into something of a pagan miracle and he treated himself to another bender with the money raised from the sale of his all-leather, clove-studded, medieval chastity belt, so highly embossed that no-one had come near it.

He didn't have much to his name, but even so, it was still too much. He paid his rent with his watch, swapped his trousers for a pair of shorts and his shirt for a Lacoste T-shirt and, raring to go, set off in search of a way to spend his remaining money.

(During his search, he had the misfortune of inheriting some money but, fortunately, quickly learned that he could not touch it for months, which gave him more than enough time.)

The Major still had eleven francs and some food left over. He could not leave under these circumstances, so he threw a middle-sized party at his house.

The party was a success, and at its conclusion there was only a single hundred-gram packet of slightly stale curry powder left over that nobody had been able to finish. Contrary to all of the Major's expectations, the celery salt, which had proven to be very popular, was indeed the base for most of the last cocktails that were served, because nobody had liked the curry mix that he had specially prepared for that purpose.

(The remarkable misfortune that seemed to follow the Major continued because, as fate would have it, one of his guests left her handbag, containing five hundred francs, at his house. Everything seemed to be starting all over again when the Major, inspired by one of those flashes of brilliance for which he was famous, came up with the idea of going on holidays, with a permit for the use of a motor vehicle obtained through official government channels. It must be immediately pointed out that it was this plan that eventually saved him.)

II

The Major burst in on his friend Bison, just as Bison was sitting down at the table with his wife and Little Bison. Their jaws were smacking, because for once Mrs Bison had seen fit to spend ten minutes preparing a meal of pasta that was now simmering away, and the whole family was thrilled at the prospect of the ensuing feast.

"I'm having lunch with you!" the Major exclaimed, shaking with excitement when he saw the noodles on the stove.

"Pig!" Bison said. "You could smell them cooking a mile off, couldn't you?"

"Absolutely!" the Major said, helping himself to a big slug of wine taken from their allocation and put aside especially for him. It had been allowed to turn a little sour, which added a little more complexity to the original flavour. This is without doubt extremely effective, as everyone knows.

Bison took an extra plate from the sideboard and placed it on the table in front of the Major. The Major allowed himself to be served without feeling any resentment towards those serving him.

"Now this is what I've come to see you about," the Major said. "Where do you plan on spending your vacation?"

"By the sea. I want to see it before I die," Bison declared.

"Very well," the Major said. "I'm buying a car and taking you to Saint-Jean-de-Luz."

"Just a minute!" Bison said. "Do you have any cash?"

"I most certainly do," the Major replied. "There's no need to worry about that."

"Do you have a place to stay?"

"I most certainly do," the Major answered. "My grandmother, who's dead, had an apartment there, and my father wouldn't let go."

Bison, although not hearing the Major clearly, still realised that he meant that his father had kept the apartment, and not the grandmother.

The noodles were continuing to swell as they absorbed the simmering water and Mrs Bison had already taken the garbage bin out three times to empty those that had spilled out of the pot.

"Good, let's take that as read," Bison said. "You have fuel, I suppose. Because it's handy to have fuel when you have a car."

"That will take care of itself," the Major assured him. "If we have a valid permit, we get petrol coupons."

"Perfect!" Bison said. "Do you know somebody at the prefecture who can help you to obtain a permit?"

"No," the Major replied, "but what about the two of you? Don't you know anyone?"

"So that's what you're up to!"

Bison looked down at him disapprovingly.

"I'm warning you," his wife interrupted, "that if you don't hurry up and eat these noodles, we'll have to move to another room, because we're not going to be able to stay in this one for much longer."

All four of them pounced on the bowl of noodles, taking great delight in thinking about the faces the Germans used to pull when they sat down to Normandy butter and fatty sausages.

The Major was drinking one glass of rough red after another, and because he didn't want to waste a single drop, his one good eye was forced to do all it could to help him see double.

Dessert consisted of slices of bread that had been carefully allowed to turn stale, arranged between sheets of pink gelatine scented with Cheramy Oregano, prepared in the style of Jules Gouffé. After the Major had a third helping, there was none left.

"Wouldn't Annie be able to pull a few strings for us at the prefect's office, through her newspaper?" Mrs Bison asked. "Because there's no way I'm going with you if you don't have a permit."

"Excellent idea!" the Major said. "Don't worry. I don't like the police any more than you do. The sight of a police officer ties my stomach in knots."

"Well, perhaps we'd better hurry up," Bison remarked. "My holidays begin in three weeks."

"Perfect!" the Major said, thinking he would have time to dispose of the five hundred francs he had just acquired.

He had one final slug of red, took a cigarette from Mrs Bison's packet, let out an enormous belch and stood up.

"I'm going to look at cars," he said, as he walked out the door.

III

"Listen," Annie said, "I'm going to put you in touch with Pistoletti, the guy at the prefect's office who handles the permits for the newspaper. You'll find that it's quite straightforward. He's very helpful."

"All right," the Major said. "I think that if I speak to him, everything will be fine. It will all work out just fine. Pistoletti is a wonderful man."

Seated on the terrace of the *Café Duflor*, they were waiting for Mrs Bison and her son, who were running a little late.

"I think," the Major said, "that she's going to be bringing along a doctor's certificate for the child. That will help us to obtain the permit. She must have been having it done today."

"Oh?" Annie said. "What is the certificate going to say?"

"That the child is not well enough to travel by train," the Major replied, polishing his foggy monocle.

"There they are!" Annie said.

Mrs Bison was running after Little Bison, who had just let go of her hand. He had taken off like a shot and was now fifteen metres away remonstrating with a round table at the Deux Mâghos which had a marble top one moment and was in pieces the next.

The Major stood up and tried to separate the child from the table. A waiter arrived on the scene and started to remonstrate.

"Allow me," the Major said. "I saw everything. The table started it. Don't argue, or I'll have you arrested."

He produced his fake police ID and the waiter fainted. The Major then took his watch and, grabbing the child by the hand, dragged him over to where Annie and Mrs Bison were standing.

"You should keep an eye on your son," he said.

"You get on my nerves. I have the certificate. The child has rickets and is not well enough to travel by train."

Just as she was saying this, she gave her son a great wallop, which sent him into hysterics.

"That's lucky for the SNCF," muttered the Major.

"I suppose you're going to tell me that you've never broken a table in a café," she said, starting to get her back up.

"Not at that age!" the Major said.

"Of course not! You're backward!"

"That's enough!" the Major said. "Let's not get started. Give me that certificate."

"Show me," Annie said.

"There was no problem with the doctor," Mrs Bison said. "Anyone can see that the child has rickets. Will you let go of that chair!..."

Little Bison had just grabbed hold of the back of a chair belonging to the person seated next to them. The customer ended up on the floor along with a few glasses, producing a tremendous racket.

The Major disappeared behind a tree, pretending he needed to pee, while Annie stood there, acting as if she didn't know anyone.

"Who's responsible for this?" the waiter asked.

"It was the Major," Little Bison said.

"Oh?" the waiter said sceptically. "It wasn't the child then, madam?"

"Don't be ridiculous," she said. "He's three and a half years old."

"Mauriac is a doddering old man," Little Bison stated.

"Now that is quite true," the waiter said, and sat down at the table to discuss literature.

Feeling somewhat reassured, the Major returned and resumed his position between the two women.

"So," Annie said, "You're going to see Pistoletti..."

"And so, what do you think about Duhamel?" the waiter said.

"Do you think it will work?" the Major said.

"Duhamel is highly overrated," Little Bison said.

"Of course," Annie said, "with the letter from the newspaper..."

"All right then, I'll go tomorrow," the Major said.

"I'll send you a copy of my manuscript — let me know what you think," the waiter said. "The story takes place in a ductile mine, but I think you'll like it because our taste in literature is very similar."

"Waiter, how much do we owe you?" Annie asked.

"No," Mrs Bison said, "It's my turn."

"Allow me," the Major said.

Since he didn't have any cash, the waiter lent him some money to pay the bill. The Major left a generous tip and then absent-mindedly pocketed the change.

IV

"I'm going to open it," Little Bison screamed.

"You're getting on my nerves," his father answered. "You know quite well that you're too short to reach the lock."

Throwing a tantrum, Little Bison launched himself at the door feet first, pouncing like a cat. He seemed surprised to find himself on his backside, as something big and green flashed past.

It was the Major. He looked the same as usual, except that his flat-topped hat had a strange uneven glow. He had eaten some turkey.

"Well?" Bison said.

"I have the car! It's a 1927 Renault two-door sedan with rear boot."

"And a bonnet that lifts up from the front?" Bison enquired anxiously.

"Yes…" the Major conceded regretfully. "It also has magneto ignition, with an intricate braking system fitted to the exhaust pipe."

"That's an old system," Bison observed.

"I'm well aware of that," the Major said.

"How much?"

"Twenty thousand."

"That's not expensive," Bison judged. "But then again, it's not cheap either."

"No, and in fact you're going to have to lend me five thousand francs so I can finish paying for it."

"When will you pay me back?"

Bison seemed to have a few misgivings.

"Monday night, without fail," the Major said, trying to reassure him.

"Hum!" Bison said. "I've heard that before."

"I understand," the Major said, as he took the five thousand francs, without so much as a thank you.

"Have you been to the prefecture yet?"

"I'm going there now. I'm always a little reluctant to go and see those disgusting and stubborn officious types."

"Well, try to get over it," Bison said, pushing him out onto the landing. "And do try to get a move on."

"Goodbye!" the Major shouted from the floor below.

He returned two hours later.

"Well old friend," he said, "it still hasn't been sorted out. You have to sign a declaration, stating that you already have all the fuel you need."

"You give me the shits!" Bison said. "I'm fed up with all these delays. I've already been on holidays for a week and I'm not in the slightest bit amused that I'm still here. You'd be much better off taking the train with us."

"Look, it's far more enjoyable to travel by car and it will be easier to get supplies once we're there."

"Obviously," Bison said. "But as soon as I get there I'll have to leave, because my holiday will be over. And besides, we'll get thrown in the slammer along the way."

"It's all going to take care of itself now," the Major guaranteed. "Get that document ready and everything will be in order. If it's not, I'll take the train with you."

"I'm going to come with you," Bison said. "I'll drop by my office and have my secretary type it up."

This was done. They entered the prefecture three quarters of an hour later and, after winding their way through a maze of corridors, arrived at Pistoletti's office.

Pistoletti, an affable, slightly abrupt man in his fifties, only made them wait for five minutes. After some preliminary discussions, he stood up and asked them to follow him. He took with him the forms and justification documents that had been provided by the Major and Bison.

They passed through a narrow passageway that served as a covered bridge linking two adjacent buildings. The Major's stomach was churning and growling like a Nuremberg spinning top. In a vaulted gallery, long lines of people were waiting outside office doors. Most of them were grumbling, while others were preparing to die. The latter would be left where they fell, their bodies to be collected in the evening.

Pistoletti walked to the head of one of the queues. He stopped and seemed put out at not finding himself standing before the person he was expecting to see.

"Hello, Mr Pistoletti," the man opposite him said.

"Good day, sir," Pistoletti said. "Here, I would like you to stamp this application. Everything is in order."

The man examined the bundle of papers.

"Well!" he said, "it states here that you have all the fuel you require. Therefore, there is no need to allocate you any."

"Hum…" Pistoletti said. "I asked Mr Major here to fill out this declaration that you… that your predecessor had suggested… to get some fuel, basically…"

"Oh?" the man said.

He wrote on the document: "No allocation. Applicant claims to have requisite fuel."

"Thank you!" Pistoletti said. He took the papers and left.

Out in the corridor, Pistoletti scratched his head and left bleeding strips of skin on the floor. An official who was passing slipped on them and almost fell. The Major sniggered, but he soon became serious again when he saw the look on Pistoletti's face.

"Things not going well?" Bison asked.

"Well…" Pistoletti said. "Now we'll go and have a chat with Ciabricot. This is bothering me. The official we've just seen must be new, because the first one I saw told me something completely different. Anyway, things can still be sorted out. But the first one said that with that one piece of paper everything would take care of itself."

"Let's go and see Ciabricot all the same," Bison said.

Pistoletti, followed by the two acolytes, reached the end of the corridor, and once again they made their way to the head of the queue. The Major and his friend sat down on a circular bench that surrounded the base of one of the arch supports. To help pass the time, they counted up to one thousand, in multiples of four and a half. Fifteen minutes later, Pistoletti came out of the office. He wore a look of resignation.

"There you have it," he said to them. "He wrote 'granted' on the request. He wrote the date. He said 'good'. He asked 'where do they want to go?' So I told him, or rather he looked on the form. He placed his hand on his liver and said 'that's way too far!', and he crossed out everything he'd just written. His liver is in a bad way."

"So it's been refused?" Bison asked.

"Yes," Pistoletti said.

"And do you think that if we slipped ten thousand francs to this friend of yours, Ciabricot, he might not give us the permit?" Bison said, as a thick cloud of steam started to rise from his shoes.

"And now a child who's too ill to travel by train can't even be moved by car!" the Major chimed in.

"What is it exactly that we're asking for?" Bison continued. "Nothing! Not for petrol, since we're saying we already have it. All we want is a signature at the bottom of a piece of paper so we can take our car out on the road, it being understood that we'll manage to get fuel on the black market. So?"

"So I think they're all a pain in the arse," the Major said.

"Listen," said Pistoletti.

"They're bastards!" Bison said.

"You could start all over again this afternoon..." Pistoletti suggested, starting to feel a little intimidated.

"Oh, no!" Bison said. "We understand! We're leaving!"

"I'm sorry," Pistoletti said.

"We don't bear you the slightest grudge," the Major said. "It's not your fault if Ciabricot suffers with his liver."

They took advantage of a turn in the corridor to perform a pincer movement on Pistoletti, whose body they left slumped in a corner.

"What are we going to do?" Bison asked, as they left the building.

"I don't give a damn," the Major said. "I'm leaving without the permit."

"You can't do that," Bison said. "I'm going to the train station to buy some tickets. I don't like cops."

"Wait until tonight. I have something in mind. I don't like them either. They scare the daylights out of me," the Major said.

"Right," Bison said. "Give me a call."

V

"It's done!" the Major's voice said into the receiver.

"Really? Do you have it?" Bison asked.

He could hardly believe it.

"No, but I will. I went back to the prefecture this afternoon with a girl, one of Verge's friends. He's the guy you saw around at my place. This girl knew some people in the prefect's office. She dropped in on Ciabricot, and that was all it took. They've promised me..."

"When will you have it?"

"Five o'clock, Wednesday!"

"Right!" Bison concluded. "We'll see..."

VI

On Wednesday at five o'clock, the Major was told that the following day at eleven o'clock would be a good time. On Thursday at eleven o'clock, it was suggested that he drop by in the afternoon. In the afternoon, he was told that only fifteen permits were issued each day and he was the sixteenth, and since he didn't want to part with any money, he didn't get the permit.

Friends and acquaintances of employees were constantly arriving and there were scarcely enough employees to cope with the necessary preferential treatment; they asked the Major to help them fill in their forms. He refused and moved off, leaving behind on a desk a hand grenade with the pin pulled. As he was going out of the building, the explosion he heard warmed the cockles of his heart.

Bison, his wife and Little Bison bought their tickets for Saint-Jean-de-Luz. They would have to wait until the following Monday to leave because all the trains were full. On Saturday night, the Major set off in his Renault from his lavish studio in the Rue Cœur-de-Lion. It was expected that he would be in Saint-Jean first and that he would have the apartment ready for the arrival of his friends. Seated next to him was Jean Verge, and the Major already owed him three thousand francs. In the back seat was Joséphine, a friend of the Major's. He had just spent half of the money she had had in her purse on another good old-fashioned binge.

There was also some luggage in the car. There were ten kilos of sugar that Verge was dropping off at his mother's place in Biarritz, a lemonade maker with blue handles that the Major was planning to introduce into the Basque Country, two bird cages containing toads, and a fire extinguisher filled with lavender scent, because carbon tetrachloride doesn't have a very nice smell.

VII

In order to avoid running into those two-legged creatures dressed in dark blue and who, hitched together, go by the name of police officers, the Major, when he left the capital, took a shortcut ceremoniously named the N306. Despite this, he was still packing it.

The Major was following the directions that Verge was giving him. Verge had a Michelin map spread out on his knees, but it was the first time in his life he had attempted anything like this.

And it so happened that at five o'clock the following morning, after having driven for eight hours at an average speed of fifty kilometres per hour, the Major spotted the Montlhéry Tower in the distance. He immediately turned the car around, because if he'd kept going, he would have found himself back in Paris, at the Porte d'Orléans.

At nine o'clock, they entered the town of Orléans. There was only one litre of petrol left in the tank and the Major was feeling happy. They had not seen a single cop's cap.

Verge still had two thousand five hundred francs left that they used to buy twenty litres of petrol and five kilos of potatoes because, given the age of the car, pieces of potato needed to be added to the petrol in the ratio of one to four.

The tyres seemed to be coping. At the end of the brief fuel stop, the Major pulled the cord that regulated the valve of the gearbox, blew the whistle twice, reverse steamed, and the Renault took off.

Leaving the N152, they crossed the Loire over a minor bridge and took the less travelled N751.

The devastation caused by the Occupation had resulted in the growth of thick, lush vegetation in ruts and around puddles. St John's wort was waving about everywhere, while tiger-beetles added a touch of mauve to the pearlescent splash made by the skinflints.

A farmhouse here and there broke the monotony of the journey, each time producing a pleasant sensation that felt something like the tingling in your crotch when you bounce across a small humpback bridge. As they headed off towards Blois, more and more chickens began to appear.

They were pecking away along the network of ditches that had been carefully put in place by the road workers. The next day, sunflower seeds were planted in each of the small holes made by their beaks.

The Major suddenly felt like some chicken. He began pulling sharply on the steering wheel, at the same time adjusting the regulator on the exhaust pipe. This reduced the speed of the car causing it to slow down to the pace of a man walking through a bee-farm.

A nice, plump Houdan chicken, with its backside stuck in the air, was looking the other way. The Major sneakily accelerated, but the chicken turned around unexpectedly and stared at him defiantly. The Major acted as though it didn't matter, but in reality was quite struck by the situation as he spun the steering wheel ninety degrees, and they had to call upon the local postman, whom they met along the way, to help extricate the car from the hundred-year-old oak tree that had been snapped in two as a result of the Major's sound reflexes.

Once the damage had been repaired, the Renault wouldn't start again. So Verge had to get out, go around behind it and say, "boo!" This continued for five kilometres until they persuaded it to go and it grudgingly stopped to let him get back in.

Unperturbed, the Major passed through Cléry, reached Blois and shot off to the south on the N764 towards Pontlevoy. Still no police. His confidence grew.

He was whistling a marching tune, rounding off the end of each bar with an energetic tap of the heel. He was unable to finish his song, however, because his foot went through the floor. If he continued, he ran the risk of totally wrecking the gearbox, which already had two stripped gears from when the tree had landed on the car.

At Montrichard they bought some bread and raced through Le Liège before the car came to a screaming halt at the intersection of the N764 and the D10.

Joséphine woke up.

"What's happening?" she asked.

"Nothing," the Major said. "We bought some bread and now we're stopping to eat it."

The Major was concerned. You can arrive at an intersection from four different directions, and you can also be seen from four different directions.

They climbed out of the car and sat by the side of the road. A white chicken, tucked away in a ditch, became bolder and raised its permed crest up over the level of the road surface. The Major stopped still, not daring to breathe.

He grabbed hold of the two-kilo loaf of bread, raised it, turned around and, looking at the loaf against the light, suddenly struck the chicken with it.

Unfortunately for the Major, the farm of Da Rui, the well-known goalkeeper, was not far from there. The chicken came from that farm and had made the most of his coaching. With a deft header, it cushioned the blow, sent the loaf of bread flying five metres away and, running flat out, regathered it before it had time to hit the ground.

The chicken disappeared into the distance in a cloud of dust, the bread tucked under its wing.

Verge had stood up and was giving chase.

"Jean!" the Major shouted. "Don't worry about it. It doesn't matter. The police will hear you."

"Bitch!" Jean said, puffing, as he continued to give chase.

"Don't worry about it!" the Major yelled. Jean came back. He was seething. "It doesn't matter," the Major explained. "I had a bread roll at the bakery."

"A fat lot of use that is to me!" Verge said, furious.

"Anyway, now that the loaf of bread has been tucked up under its wing, it's going to taste foul," the Major said disgustedly.

"Thanks a lot," Jean concluded. "Let's go back and buy another loaf of bread. From now on, please try to remember that, next time you go hunting chickens, use a weapon that can't be eaten."

"I can do that for you," the Major said. "I'm going to get a spanner. Let's take a little look at what's wrong with the car."

"Didn't you stop the car on purpose?" Joséphine asked, surprised.

"Er… no," the Major said.

VIII

The Major grabbed his breakdown analysis detector, a converted stethoscope, and wiggled his way under the car. Two hours later, he woke up, well rested.

Verge and Joséphine were feasting on unripened apples in a neighbouring field.

The Major took a rubber hose and siphoned three quarters of the remaining fuel into a ditch to lighten the weight in the front of the car. He then slid the jack under the left-hand side, raised the car forty centimetres and opened the bonnet.

He listened to the engine with the stethoscope and discovered that that was not the source of the problem. There was nothing wrong with the fan. The radiator was getting hot, so it was working. That left only the oil filter and magneto.

He switched the magneto and oil filter around and ran a test. That didn't work.

He switched them back to their original positions and ran another test. That worked.

"Right," the Major concluded. "It's the magneto. Just as I suspected. We have to find a garage."

He called out for Verge and Joséphine to come over and push the car. He forgot to remove the jack and, as they started to push, the vehicle began to rock back and forth. The front right-hand wheel landed on Verge's foot and the tyre exploded.

"Idiot!" the Major said, cutting short Verge's protests. "You punctured it! Now you fix it!"

"By the way," he noted shortly afterwards, "it was a stupid idea to try to push the car. Joséphine is going to look for a mechanic."

She headed off down the road and the Major settled down in the shade for a snooze. He was eating a second bread roll pinched from the bakery.

"Bring back some more bread if you're hungry!" he shouted at Joséphine, as she disappeared around a bend in the road.

IX

After he had finished his bread, the Major decided to take a short stroll while he waited for Joséphine to return. Suddenly, in the distance, he spotted two blue caps heading his way.

Off he shot like a rocket. From side on, he looked as if he had five legs. When he reached the car, Verge was leaning against a tree, humming away, staring into space.

"To work!" the Major ordered. "Chop down that tree. Here's a spanner."

Verge slowly came around and mechanically did as he was told.

Once the tree had been felled, he set about cutting it into shorter lengths, according to the Major's instructions.

They buried the leaves in a hole and hid the car under a mound of charcoal. The mound was then covered with the dirt that had been taken from the hole. Verge placed a small piece of glowing charcoal on top, which gave off a sweet harem smelling smoke.

The Major blackened Verge's face and his own with charcoal, and rumpled his clothes.

It was not a moment too soon. The police were coming. The Major was shaking.

"What's all this then?" the fatter one of the two said.

"You working?" his partner added.

"To be sure!" the Major said, adopting the manner of speech of a charcoal burner.

"Smells good, your wood!" the fatter one said.

"What is it?" the other asked. "It smells like a whore," he added with a knowing laugh.

"Camphor and sandalwood," Verge explained.

"For the clap?" the fatter one said.

"That's funny!" laughed the second.

"That's really funny!" laughed Verge and the Major, feeling slightly more at ease.

"Have to let the authorities know you're here, so they can divert traffic," the first policeman concluded. "Cars must be a nuisance."

"Yes, that's what we'll have to do," the second one repeated. "Cars must be a nuisance."

"Thanks for your help!" the Major said.

"Goodbye!" the two policemen called out, as they headed off.

Verge and the Major fired back a hearty farewell and, as soon as they found themselves alone, set to work dismantling the fake mound.

They got a rude shock when they discovered that the car was no longer inside.

"What's going on?" Verge asked.

"I have no idea!" the Major said. "It's a bit of a mystery to me."

"Are you sure it's a Renault?" Verge asked.

"Yes," the Major said. "I've already thought of that. If it were a Ford, you would understand. But it's definitely a Renault."

"But isn't it a 1927 Renault?"

"Yes!" the Major exclaimed.

"That explains everything," Verge said. "Look over there."

They turned around and saw the Renault grazing on the grass at the base of an apple tree.

"How did it get over there?" asked the Major.

"It dug a hole. My father's car used to do the same thing every time he covered it with dirt."

"Did your father cover it with dirt often?"

"Oh, from time to time… not really all that often."

"Is that so?" the Major said suspiciously.

"His car was a Ford," Verge explained.

They left the car to its own devices as they set about clearing the road. They had almost finished when Verge saw the Major drop flat to the ground, staring at something. He signalled for Verge to be quiet.

"A chicken!" he whispered.

All of a sudden, he rolled over and landed full length in the water-filled ditch, on top of the chicken. The chicken duck-dived below the surface, took a few strokes and emerged some distance away. It fled, cackling incessantly. Obviously, Da Rui was also teaching his students to swim underwater.

Just then, the mechanic arrived.

The Major shook the water off himself, extended a wet hand and said, "I'm the Major. You're not a police officer by any chance?"

"Pleased to meet you," he said. "Is it the magneto?"

"How do you know?" the Major asked.

"Because it's the only spare part that I didn't bring with me. That's how," the mechanic said.

"No, it's the oil filter," the Major said.

"In that case, I'll be able to help you with a new magneto," the mechanic said. "I brought along three of them on the chance I needed one. Ha! Ha! I got you there, didn't I?"

"I'll take them," the Major said. "You can give them to me."

"There are two that don't work..."

"That doesn't matter," interrupted the Major.

"And the third is broken..."

"Better still!" the Major said. "But in that case, I'll pay for them..."

"That's fifteen hundred," the mechanic said. "Plus labour..."

"Yes, all right!" the Major said. "Would you like to pay the man, Joséphine?"

She did as she was told. She had a thousand francs left.

"Thank you!" the Major said.

He turned his back on the mechanic and went to look for the car.

He brought it back and opened the bonnet.

The magneto was full of grass, which he removed with the tip of a knife.

"Can you drive me back to the garage?" the mechanic said.

"Gladly!" the Major said. "That will be a thousand francs, payable up front."

"A bargain!" the mechanic said. "There you are."

The Major pocketed the money indifferently.

"Get in!" he said.

They all climbed into the car. The motor got going first time all by itself. They had to go and pick it up and put it back in. And this time the Major did not forget to close the bonnet.

The car came to a screeching halt in front of the garage.

"It has to be the magneto," the mechanic said. "I'll swap it over for one of mine."

He carried out the necessary repairs.

"How much do I owe you?" the Major asked.

"Oh, please! It's not worth worrying about!"

The mechanic was standing in front of the car.

The Major put the car into gear and ran over him before heading off again on the road to Saint-Jean.

X

Still taking minor roads, they headed south through Poitiers, Angoulême, and Châtellerault, and then travelled at a more leisurely pace through the Bordeaux region. The fear of encountering more police caused the Major's normally relaxed features to look strained, and he started to become irritable.

At Montmoreau, they experienced the torment of a police roadblock. Thanks to his telescope, the Major neatly avoided it and veered onto the N709. They ended up at Ribérac without a drop of fuel.

"Do you still have that thousand francs on you?" the Major asked Joséphine.

"Yes," she said.

"Hand them over."

The Major bought ten litres of fuel and, with the thousand francs the mechanic had given him, went and treated himself to a right old nosh-up.

It wasn't far from Ribérac to Chalais. After Martron and Montlieu, they rejoined the N10, which passed through Cavignac, where Jean Verge had a cousin.

XI

Sprawled out on a haystack, the Major, Verge and Joséphine were waiting.

Verge's cousin was supposed to give them a small barrel of wine to deliver to his brother in Biarritz, and the grapes were just in the process of being pressed.

The Major was chewing on a piece of straw thinking about the trip, which was now drawing to an end. Verge was groping Joséphine, and Joséphine was allowing herself to be groped.

The Major was trying to figure out the number of magnetos he now had in his collection. He had lost count, because he had added a few more along the way, in Aubeterre, Martron and Montlieu, in exchange for some of Verge's sugar.

He suddenly buried himself in the haystack on seeing the peak of a soft leather cap appear. But it was the postman. He resurfaced, with two mice in his pocket and his head covered in straw.

There was, in fact, never any chance of the car being spotted by the police, since it was hidden away in the cousin's stable. But this trip had produced some built-in reflex responses.

The Major was enjoying the quiet life on the cousin's farm. In the morning they ate celery, in the evening it was stewed fruit, and, in between, a wide variety of other types of food. And then they slept. Verge was groping Joséphine, and Joséphine was allowing herself to be groped.

This was their routine for three days, until it was finally announced that the wine was ready. Verge was beginning to feel tired but, on the other hand, the Major's morale was soaring. He scarcely gave a thought to a certain Bison family at Saint-Jean-de-Luz, who by now must be sleeping under the stars, awaiting the arrival of the Major and the keys to the apartment.

The Major cleared some space in the boot of the car and slid the barrel neatly into place.

They said their goodbyes to Verge's cousin, after which the Renault bravely made a beeline for Saint-André-de-Cubzac. They took a left turn towards Libourne and then followed a myriad of small roads that led them around Branne, Targon and Langoiran, before ending up in Hostens.

Exactly one week had gone by since leaving the Rue Cœur-de-Lion. At Saint-Jean-de-Luz, the Bison family had been holed up for five days in a room they had found by some miracle. They had gleeful visions of the Major behind the thick bars of a country gaol.

At precisely the same moment, the Major was having visions of that exact same scene. He put his foot on the accelerator, but the Renault rebelled and the magneto exploded.

There was a garage a hundred metres ahead.

"I have a brand new magneto that you can have for three thousand francs, and I can fit it for you." the mechanic declared.

It took him three minutes to swap it over for the old one.

"Wouldn't you prefer to be paid in wine?' the Major asked.

"No thank you! I only drink cognac," the mechanic replied.

"Listen," the Major said, "I'm an honest man. I'll leave you my identity card and my ration card as security, and I'll send you the money from Saint-Jean-de-Luz. I don't have any more on me because I was conned out of everything I had by a bunch of yokels."

The mechanic was charmed by the Major's cultivated manner and agreed.

"I couldn't have a little fuel for my cigarette lighter?" the Major asked.

"Please, help yourself at the pump," the mechanic said.

He went back inside to file the Major's papers.

The Major took only the twenty-five litres he needed and left everything else the way he had found it.

He raised his eyes... over there, behind... two policemen on bicycles.

A storm was brewing.

"Get in, quickly!" he ordered.

The chadburn clicked. The Major cast off slowly and set sail across country, straight for Dax.

In the rear-view mirror, the policemen were little more than specks but, despite the Major's efforts, those specks were not becoming any smaller. A hill suddenly rose up before them. The car took it on at top speed. It was bucketing down and lightning clagged up the sky with gluey luminescence.

The hill became steeper and turned into a mountain.

"We'll have to dump some ballast," Verge said.

"Never! We'll make it!" the Major answered.

But the clutch slipped and a strong smell of burning oil came up through the floor.

As misfortune would have it, the Major spotted a chicken.

He slammed his foot on the brake. The car went arse over turkey and landed right on top of the unfortunate fowl's head, killing it instantly. The car stopped. The Major was revelling in his success. However, he had to pay compensation, in the form of the last three kilos of Verge's sugar, to the owner of the chicken, who was crouching on the side of the road in an *ad hoc* hole, to borrow a phrase from Jules Romains.

The Major left the chicken where it was, because it had shrunk in the rain and was now inedible. He couldn't conceal his anger.

But, above all, the car once again would not start.

The clutch was making a terrible noise and the crankshaft seemed as though it was about to break. The vibration of the mudguards was so strong that the Renault became airborne and, with a hum, flew off to smell a catalpa tree in flower. But it would not move forward.

The specks in the rear-view mirror were becoming larger.

The Major strapped himself to the steering wheel.

"Throw something overboard!" he yelled.

Verge hurled two magnetos out the window.

The car shuddered, but did not move.

"More!" he bellowed. The strain was starting to tell in his voice.

Verge dumped seven more magnetos onto the road in quick succession. The car lurched forward to the terrible noise of the rain, hail and motor, and climbed the hill in one fell swoop.

The police had disappeared. The Major wiped his brow and continued on his way.

Saint-Vincent-de-Tyrosse followed Dax.

At Bayonne, a police roadblock could be seen in the distance. The Major kept his hand on the horn and made the sign of the Red Cross as they passed. Having been raised by a Russian nanny, the Major had made the cross upside down, but the police didn't even seem to notice. And in the back, to add to the effect, Verge had just undressed Joséphine and had wrapped her overalls around her head like a bandage. It was nine o'clock at night. The police waved them through.

The Major cleared the roadblock and passed out. He came around again when the car's bumper was left behind on a roadside distance marker.

La Négresse...

Guéthary...

Saint-Jean-de-Luz...

The grandmother's apartment was number 5 Rue Mazarin.

It was dark.

The Major parked the car at the front door and forced his way inside. They were exhausted and went to bed without even noticing the Bisons' non-presence. In actual fact, the Bisons had not been prepared to have to kick the door down in order to have a roof over their heads. Consequently, they were preparing a warm welcome for the Major in the filthy kitchen-cum-bedroom that someone had generously agreed to rent to them for a thousand francs a day.

The Major woke up at dawn.

He stretched and put on his dressing gown.

In the next room, Verge and Joséphine were beginning to peel apart from one another by pouring hot water over themselves.

The Major went over to the window and opened it.

There were six police officers in front of the house looking at the car.

So the Major swallowed a massive dose of gunpowder and fortunately for him it didn't explode, because after it had been fully digested he found that it was perfectly normal to see police officers standing outside the police station at number 6 Rue Mazarin.

A week later, the Major's car was confiscated in Biarritz, just as he was becoming friendly with a police superintendent, who was really a notorious smuggler with the responsibility for the murder of nine hundred Spanish customs officers weighing on his conscience.

LÉOBILLE'S PARTY

I

From the inside, Folubert Sansonnet's eyelids had a lovely reddish-orange glow, a result of the undulating ray of sunlight that fell directly onto his face through the slats of the shutters, and Folubert was smiling in his sleep. He was walking lightly over the soft, white, warm gravel in the garden of the Hesperides. Beautiful cuddly animals were licking his toes. That's when he woke up. He gently plucked Frédéric the pet snail from his big toe and put him away until the next morning. Frédéric wasn't happy about it, but didn't say anything.

Folubert sat on his bed. He liked to take time every morning to do a day's worth of thinking in order to spare himself the countless problems that clutter the lives of the worried, the finicky and the untidy, for whom the slightest act is the pretext for innumerable distractions, which (sorry about the length of this sentence) are quite often pointless because they are soon forgotten.

Today he had to think about:

1. how he was going to bedeck himself;
2. how he was going to nourish himself;
3. how he was going to entertain himself.

And that's all, because it was Sunday, and what he was going to do for money was one problem already solved.

So Folubert thought about each of these items in turn.

With a great deal of care, he started to get himself ready. He brushed his teeth briskly and blew his nose with his fingers. Then he got dressed. On Sundays, he always started with the tie and finished with the shoes. It was an excellent way to proceed. From his drawer he pulled a pair of striped designer socks that had one blue stripe, one clear stripe, one blue stripe, one clear stripe, and so on. With this style of sock, you could paint your feet whatever colour you wanted, and then that colour would appear in between the blue stripes. Since he was feeling a little shy, he chose a tin of apple green paint.

As for the rest, he put on his everyday clothes — a blue shirt and clean underwear — because he was already thinking about the third item on his list.

For lunch he had herring on stretchers drizzled with sweet oil and bread that was as fresh as a daisy and, like a daisy, fringed in pink.

Finally, he allowed himself to think about how he was going to spend his Sunday.

Today was his friend Léobille's birthday, and there was a lovely party being thrown in his honour.

At the very thought of a party, Folubert went off into his own world. You see, Folubert was extremely shy and he secretly envied the self-assurance of the regular party-goers. He would have liked to possess the smooth style of Grouzniê combined with Doddy's spirit, the smart engaging charm of Rémenfol, the attractive severity of chief Abadibada or the dazzling swashbuckling behaviour of any member from the Lorientais Club.

All the same, Folubert had beautiful horse chestnut-coloured eyes, loosely waved hair and a warm smile thanks to which he won hearts without realising it. But he was never brave enough to exploit his physical advantage and so he always ended up alone while his friends smoothly danced the night away with pretty girls to the swing, the jitterbug and the *barbette gauloise*.

This often made him sad, but at night he would find solace in his dreams, where he would see himself full of confidence, surrounded by beautiful girls, all begging him to agree to just one dance.

Folubert remembered last night's dream. There was a very pretty girl in a dress of lavender blue stretch crepe, with long blonde hair that fell down over her shoulders. She was wearing small blue snakeskin shoes and an unusual bracelet that he could no longer accurately describe. She had liked him a lot in this dream and, at the end, they left the party together.

He must have kissed her, and maybe she had even allowed herself to perform one or two extra little favours for him.

Folubert blushed. He would have plenty of time to think about that on his way to Léobille's. He checked his pockets to make sure he had enough money and went out to buy a bottle of venom liqueur, the cheapest he could find, because he didn't drink.

Just as Folubert was waking up, the Major was being dragged from his sleep by the husky voice of his troubled conscience. Both feet hit the sticky wooden floor of his bedroom at the same time. He had the usual foul taste of plonk in his mouth.

In the shadowy darkness, the sinister glow from his glass eye cast a nasty light on the silk scarf he was painting. The design originally depicted a stupid ass grazing in a field, flanked by the Prévert brothers, but it had assumed the appearance of a Venetian skull and the Major realised that on this particular day he had a rotten deed to perform.

He remembered the party that was being thrown at Léobille's place and gave an evil snigger in D sharp. He hit a wrong note, which proved beyond all doubt his wretched state of mind. Spotting a bottle of cheap red, he swilled down the warm dregs and felt better. Then, standing before the mirror, he did his best to impersonate Sergueï Andrejef Papanine in *Ivan the Terrible*. He didn't quite succeed because he didn't have the beard, but it was nevertheless a reasonable attempt.

The Major sniggered again and retired to his study to plan the sabotage of Léobille's party. He was out for revenge because for several weeks Léobille had been spreading the most vicious rumours about him, going so far as to say that he was turning into a decent human being.

This warranted suitable punishment.

The Major was intent on bringing down anyone who crossed his path. A very bad upbringing was partly responsible, but there was also his natural disposition to be underhanded, as well as his unusually high level of spite.

(While we're at it, let's not forget that horrible little moustache he was perversely cultivating on his top lip to prevent insects from attacking it, covering it with a net during the day so that birds couldn't land.)

Folubert Sansonnet stood trembling before the door to Léobille's apartment. He poked the index finger of his right hand down into the small hole where the door buzzer lay tucked up asleep.

Folubert's sudden action woke the buzzer with a start. It rolled over and bit Folubert savagely on the finger, and he let out a high-pitched scream.

Léobille's sister, who was on the lookout in the entrance foyer, immediately opened the door. As he passed her, she applied a plaster to the wound and quickly relieved him of his bottle.

The sounds from the record player were ringing joyfully throughout the apartment, wrapping the furniture in a light, clear protective layer of music.

Léobille was standing in front of the fireplace, talking to two girls. Folubert became flustered when he saw the second one and, as Léobille came towards him with his hand outstretched, he was obliged to conceal his agitation.

"Hello," Léobille said.

"Hello," Folubert said.

"Let me introduce you," said Léobille. "Azyme (she was the first girl), this is Folubert. Folubert, this is Jennifer."

Folubert acknowledged Azyme with a nod of the head, but lowered his eyes when he held out his hand to greet Jennifer. She was wearing a dress of dull red stretch crepe, red snakeskin shoes and a highly unusual bracelet which he recognised immediately. Her long red hair fell down over her shoulders. She was, in all respects, just like the girl in his dream. Of course, the colours were brighter, but that's to be expected because, after all, dreams take place at night.

Léobille seemed to be quite preoccupied with Azyme, so Folubert, without further ado, asked Jennifer for a dance. He kept his eyes lowered, because right in front of him, unfettered by a low square neckline, were a pair of very interesting items just begging to be noticed.

"Are you an old friend of Léobille's?" Jennifer said.

“I’ve known him for three years,” Folubert explained. “We met each other at judo.”

“You do judo? Have you ever had to fight for your life?”

“Er…” Folubert was embarrassed. “I haven’t had the opportunity… I don’t get to fight very often.”

“Are you afraid?” Jennifer asked with a dose of irony.

Folubert didn’t like the way the conversation was headed and tried to regain the confidence he had had that night in his dream.

“I saw you in a dream…” he ventured.

“I never dream,” Jennifer said. “I think that’s most unlikely. You must have mistaken me for someone else.”

“You were blonde…” Folubert said, on the verge of despair.

Her waist was thin, and up close you could see the twinkle in her eye.

“You see,” Jennifer said. “It wasn’t me… I’m a redhead…”

“It was you…” Folubert mumbled.

“I don’t think so,” Jennifer said. “I don’t like dreams. I prefer the real world.”

She looked him straight in the face, but he lowered his eyes again without realising. He wasn’t holding her too close, because if he did then he wouldn’t be able to take in the view.

Jennifer shrugged her shoulders. She liked sport, and men who were brave and strong.

“I like sport,” she said, “and men who are brave and strong. I don’t like dreams, and I’m as full of life as anyone can be.”

She pulled away from him because the record had come to a screeching halt due to the fact that good old Léobille had cut off the track without warning. Folubert thanked her for the dance. He would have liked to engage her in some captivating and witty conversation, but just as he was about to say something truly captivating, some horrible long lanky fellow edged his way between them and threw his arm around Jennifer’s waist.

Folubert stepped back in horror, but Jennifer had a smile on her face. Devastated, he plonked himself down in a deep goatskin leather armchair.

He was very sad and came to the realisation that this was going to be a party just like all of the others after all, fun and full of pretty girls… but not for him.

Léobille's sister was about to open the door but she stopped, dumbfounded, when she heard a loud explosion. She clutched her racing heart and the door yielded under the force of the Major's boot.

In his hand was a smoking revolver with which he had just shot the buzzer. His mustard-coloured socks were an insult to the entire world.

"I've put an end to that wretched creature once and for all," he said. "Feed it to the vultures."

"But…" Léobille's sister said.

Then she burst into tears, because the buzzer had been with them for so long, it was like part of the family. She ran crying to her room and the Major, with great delight, executed a crepuscular dance move, before putting his gun back in his pocket.

Léobille arrived. He innocently held out his hand to greet the Major.

The Major plonked in his hand something disgusting which he had just collected from outside the front door of the building.

"Out of the way, boy," he said to Léobille. "I want to get past… Anything to drink in this place?"

"Yes," Léobille answered in a trembling voice. "Tell me… you're not going to break anything…"

"I'm going to break EVERYTHING," the Major said coldly through clenched teeth.

He stepped up to Léobille and with that frightening look in his glass eye stared him right in the face.

"So, boy, I hear you've been telling everyone I've got a job? You've been saying I've changed my evil ways? How can you stoop so low?"

He took several deep breaths and in a thundering voice said, "Your party, boy… you could say it's going up in smoke!"

Léobille turned pale. He was still holding the thing the Major had put in his hand, too scared to move.

“I… I didn’t mean to upset you,” he said.

“Shut it boy,” the Major said. “Everything you say from now on will only make it worse for the Ma-jor-i-ty.”

Then he slipped his right foot in behind Léobille’s legs and gave him a shove. Léobille collapsed in a heap on the floor.

The guests didn’t take much notice. They were dancing and drinking and chatting, and couples were disappearing into empty rooms, just like at any other good party.

The Major headed for the bar. Not far away, Folubert was still sitting forlornly in his armchair. The Major grabbed him by the collar of his jacket on the way past and dragged him to his feet.

“Come and drink,” he said. “I never drink alone.”

“But… I don’t drink…” Folubert answered.

He didn’t dare refuse, because he knew what the Major was like.

“Come on,” the Major said. “No nonsense!”

Folubert looked at Jennifer. Fortunately for him, she had her head turned the other way, engaged in lively conversation. Unfortunately for him, it is true, there were three boys standing around her, two others were at her feet, with a sixth admiring her from the top of a wardrobe.

Léobille had quietly picked himself up off the floor and was about to slip out to notify the keepers of the peace, when he thought better of it. If the peace-keepers in question came around to the house and decided to check the bedrooms, then he, Léobille, ran the risk of spending the night at the station.

Besides, he knew the Major and didn’t think he would let him get away as easily as that.

Indeed, the Major had been watching Léobille and gave him a look that nailed him to the floor.

Then, still with Folubert in tow, he drew his gun and, without taking aim, shot the top off a bottle. The guests all turned around in surprise.

“Out,” the Major said. “All the boys out. The girls can stay.”

He handed Folubert a glass.

“Drink up!”

The boys started to file out the door, leaving the girls by themselves. You didn't mess with the Major.

"I don't want to drink," Folubert said.

He took one look at the Major's face and hastily took a drink.

"To your health, boy," the Major said.

Folubert's eyes suddenly fell on Jennifer's face. She was in a corner with the other girls, eyeing him with contempt. Folubert felt his legs give way beneath him.

The Major emptied his glass in one gulp.

Almost all the boys had now left the room. The last one (his name was Jean Berdindin and he was brave) grabbed a heavy ashtray and took aim at the Major's head. The Major caught the missile in mid-flight and, as quick as a flash, was on top of Berdindin.

"You… come over here," he said.

He dragged him into the middle of the room.

"You're going to take one of these girls, whichever one you like, and you're going to undress her, and then you are going to…" (I can't repeat what the Major said, but the girls blushed with horror.)

"I refuse," Berdindin said.

"Be careful, boy," the Major said.

"Anything, but not that," Berdindin said.

Folubert, panic-stricken, poured himself a second drink without thinking and downed it in one go.

The Major didn't say anything. He went up to Berdindin, grabbed an arm and flipped him up in the air. Before he could hit the ground, the Major had whipped off his pants.

"Come on boy," he said, "get ready."

He looked at the girls.

"Any volunteers?" he said with a snigger.

"That's enough," Berdindin said, stumbling around in a daze. He tried to steady himself by clinging onto the Major, but soon regretted it. The Major lifted him off his feet and hurled him to the ground. Berdindin went "thud!" and lay there rubbing his ribs.

"The redhead," the Major said. "Over here."

"Leave me alone," Jennifer said, very pale.

Folubert was onto his fourth drink when the sound of Jennifer's voice struck him like a thunderbolt. He slowly turned around on his heels and looked at her.

The Major went up to her and in the blink of an eye, tore the shoulder strap off her dull red dress (and if the truth be known, the view was really quite pleasant).

"Leave me alone," Jennifer said a second time.

Folubert rubbed his eyes.

"This is all a dream!" he whispered in a husky voice.

"Over here," the Major said to him. "You're going to hold her down while your friend goes to work."

"No!" Berdindin screamed. "I don't want to!... Anything, but not that... Not a woman!"

"Right," the Major said. "I'm a good Major."

Without letting go of Jennifer, he went back over to Folubert.

"Get undressed," he said, "and take care of the guy. I'll take care of her."

"I refuse," Folubert said. "You can nick off to Alfred's. You're a real pain."

The Major let go of Jennifer. He took a deep breath and his chest expanded to at least one hundred and twenty-five centimetres. Jennifer looked at Folubert with surprise, not knowing whether she should pull her dress back up or whether it would be wiser to let Folubert draw strength from the sight of her breasts. She chose the latter.

Folubert looked at Jennifer and snorted. He stomped his feet up and down and charged headlong at the Major. The Major, struck right in the middle of the solar plexus just as he had finished expanding his chest, buckled in two, his body making a horrible crunching noise under the impact. He was back up almost immediately and Folubert took advantage of the situation to deliver an absolutely classical judo move, which involved pulling the opponent's ears down over his eyes while blowing air up his nostrils.

The Major turned bright blue as he started to choke. At that moment, Folubert, whose strength had increased tenfold through love and alcohol, put his head between the Major's legs, lifted him up and hurled him across the table covered with food, through the window of the living room and out onto the street.

Calm was restored to Léobille's living room. Silence reigned. Jennifer, without pulling up the front of her dress, fell into the arms of Folubert, who then collapsed because she was all of sixty kilos. Fortunately, the goatskin leather armchair was behind him.

As for the Major, his body sailed quickly through the air and, thanks to a few well-executed spins, he managed to fall back on his feet; but he had the misfortune of landing in a red and black taxi with an open sunroof which carted him off before he realised what had happened.

When he did realise, he got rid of the driver by threatening him with the ultimate act of malevolence and drove the taxi home to Villa Cœur-de-Lion.

And then, along the way, not wanting to be seen as having been beaten, he deliberately knocked down and killed an old fruit and vegetable merchant, which was fortunate, as he was selling his vegetables without a permit.

Folubert and Jennifer spent the rest of the night stitching together the red dress that she had removed to make the task easier. As a sign of gratitude, Léobille lent them his very own room for the occasion, as well as an electric iron made from Chinese enamel that had been handed down to him from his mother, whose mother had handed it down to her. In fact, his family had been passing it down from one generation of ironers to the next since the time of the First Crusade.

THE SLIP-UP

I

Clams Jorjobert was watching his wife, the lovely Gaviale, breastfeeding the fruit of their loins, a healthy three-month-old baby of the female sect, but none of this has much bearing on the rest of the story.

Clams Jorjobert had eleven francs in his pocket and it was the day before the rent was due. But nothing in the world would make him touch the wads of thousand-franc notes stashed under the mattress on which his eldest son was sleeping. His son was eleven on April twelfth. Clams only ever kept a few notes and some shrapnel up to the value of around ten francs on him, and put the rest aside, which meant that, at that precise moment, Jorjobert considered that all he possessed in the world were those eleven francs and the acute sense of responsibility a newborn baby brings.

"It must be about time that child of mine, whom I acknowledge but who is almost four months old," he said, "started to earn its keep."

"Now listen," his wife, the lovely Gaviale, answered. "Why not wait until she is six (months old)? You can't send children out to work too young, because it can lead to deformities in the spinal column."

"That's a good point," Jorjobert answered. "But there must be a way around this."

"When are you going to buy me that buggy, so I can take her out?" Gaviale replied.

"I'll make you one from an old soapbox and some Packard wheels," Jorjobert said. "That way, it will save us money, but it will still be very smart. In Auteuil, all the kids go out… in… Oh, my God!" he concluded, "I've just had an idea!"

II

The lovely Gaviale tiptoed through the enormous front door of the building located at number one hundred and sixty-ten, as Caroline Lampion, the Belgian star who was well known in Merdozart Avenue, would say. A stairwell decorated with over-wrought iron could be seen down the enormous black and white tiled hallway that stretched off to the left. Parked under the lower part of the spiral staircase, which enclosed a Louis XV lift (an imitation Boulle), were two superb baby carriages, manufactured jointly by Bonnichon Brothers and Mape. They were decorated with white rabbit skin and had been left there waiting for the offspring of the illustrious Bois-Zépais de la Querelle family and of the Marcellin du Congé family, respectively, to come down.

The lengthy description in the last paragraph allowed the lovely Gaviale to hide behind it and to sneak past the concierge's lodge unnoticed. It should also be mentioned that the lovely Gaviale was elegantly dressed in a "new look" long skirt worn over the top of an equally smart lace petticoat from her first communion. In her arms she was tenderly carrying the daughter the Lord had bestowed on her following a moment of skilful interaction with her husband, Clams Jorjobert.

The lovely Gaviale cast a quick glance over the two baby carriages and decided that the one belonging to little Bois-Zépais was in better condition than the one belonging to little Congé. Quite rightly too, because every time a horse crossed his nanny's path, little Congé would piss in his carriage like a dirty old man. It was a strange reaction, because six years later little Congé's father died destitute after losing all of his money on the horses. But let's not get ahead of ourselves…

With a great deal of confidence, she entered the lift, went up to the second floor and came down again by the stairs, making sure she was seen by the concierge. She then approached the baby carriage and gently placed her daughter, named Véronique, whose manner of conception has already been explained, on the rough rabbit skin pillows.

Head held high, she pushed the baby carriage through the huge front door of the building and out onto Merdozart Avenue.

Her husband, Clams Jorjobert, was waiting for her a hundred metres up the street.

"Perfect," he said as he examined the baby carriage. "You'd expect to pay thirty thousand for it in the shops. We should easily be able to get twelve."

"That's twelve thousand for me," Gaviale specified.

"Of course," Clams acknowledged graciously. "It was a trial run and you pulled it off perfectly. I think that's only fair."

III

"So, you'll have it back to me in an hour?" Léon Dodiléon said.

"Of course," Clams guaranteed.

Dodiléon handed Clams a motorcycle helmet. He put it on securely and looked at himself in the mirror.

"Cool!" he said. "It suits me! I look like a real bike rider."

"Off you go," Léon said. "See you here in an hour."

An hour later, Clams pulled up out the front of the building where his old friend Léon lived, on a shiny Norton motorcycle that had mudguards covering half the wheels.

"Not bad," said Léon, who had been standing in front of the building, looking at his watch, waiting for him to return.

"You'd expect to pay two hundred and fifty thousand for it in the shops," Clams said. "But since there are no papers, given that I've stolen it, I wouldn't expect it to fetch much more than a hundred. But nevertheless, it was still worthwhile borrowing your helmet, wasn't it?"

"Sure," Léon Dodiléon said. "Tell me… what if I swap you mine for it? That way, you won't have any problems with the papers."

"Okay," Clams said. "Is yours a Norton too?"

"Yes," Léon Dodiléon said. "But it doesn't have the same smooth tricuspid gear change like this one."

"I'm a man of my word," Clams answered. "Let's shake on it. You're still my friend, even if you're getting the better end of the deal."

IV

Clams sold Dodiléon's bike for a hundred and fifty thousand and, while his friend was rotting away in prison, he bought himself a nice chauffeur's uniform, complete with cap.

"You do understand," he explained to his wife, the lovely Gaviale (who was munching her way through handfuls of Turkish delight while Véronique was sucking on a bottle filled with Heidsieck Vintage Brut Reserve), "that no-one would ever think of stopping a vehicle belonging to the diplomatic corps, especially one with a chauffeur inside."

"Especially one with a chauffeur inside," she answered. "That's right."

"I could just as easily steal a train," Clams Jorjobert explained. "But I'd have to get grease on my hands and soot on my face. Besides, even though I have a good education, it doesn't necessarily mean I could drive a train."

"Oh!" Gaviale said. "I'm sure you'd manage quite nicely."

"I'd prefer not to have to try," Jorjobert said. "Besides, I'm not overly ambitious, so an income of around a hundred thousand francs a day is more than enough for me. Then there's also the inconvenience of being restricted to railway tracks. Travelling on the rail network without authorisation is bound to cause a few problems as well, and I'm sure I'd be noticed if I took the train onto the road."

"You don't have the mettle," the lovely Gaviale replied, "and that's why I love you. Can I ask you something?"

"Whatever you want, my dear," said Clams Jorjobert.

He strutted around like a peacock in his chauffeur's uniform. She pulled him towards her, whispered a few words in his ear, blushed and then buried her face in a high-speed cushion.

Clams burst out laughing.

"I'll convert the embassy's Cadillac into cash and then I'll go and get it for you straight away," he said.

Things with the Cadillac went according to plan. He had no trouble collecting his thirteen hundred thousand francs, because false papers for Cadillacs (which are now mass-produced) had just been put on sale and were now available for purchase at all tobacconists.

Before returning home, Clams paid a visit to a second-hand clothes dealer he knew. A quarter of an hour later, he went back up to see Gaviale. Everything was completed and he was carrying a large parcel.

"Here you are dear," he said. "I have the uniform. It's all there, right down to the axe. The fire truck is all yours whenever you want it."

"Can we take it out on Sundays?"

"Of course."

"Will it have a long ladder?"

"It will have a very long ladder."

"Darling, I love you!"

Véronique was not happy because she thought two children in the family were already enough.

V

In his prison cell, Dodiléon was léonging to be let out. He heard footsteps and stood up to see who it was. The guard stopped in front of his door and the key rattled in the lock. Clams Jorjobert entered.

"Hello," he said.

"Hello, old friend," Dodiléon replied. "It's nice of you to come and keep me company, because I'm léonging to be let out."

They both laughed, even though the word play had just been used.

"What brings you here?" Léon asked.

"It's ridiculous," Jorjobert sighed. "I'd just pinched a fire truck for her, but you can never please women. She decided she wanted a hearse."

"She has to be joking," Dodiléon said sympathetically. His own wife had never wanted anything more than a thirty-five-seater bus.

"Do you know what I had to go through?" Clams continued. "I bought a coffin, I climbed inside and off I went in search of a hearse."

"That should have done it," Dodiléon said.

"Have you ever tried walking around in a coffin?" Clams said. "My feet got tangled up inside and when I slipped over I crushed a small dog. As it belonged to the wife of the governor of the prison, I was in here in no time, as you can imagine."

Léon Dodiléon shook his head.

"Damn," he said. "Some people just don't seem to have any luck!"

FRANKFURT ON TAP

There were three of us in all, not counting Joséphine who was doing all the work, and she was sucking up a fair amount of oil, I might add. Personally, I saw myself a little like a delighted Jason, with Jef and Pralin as the Argonauts. We were on a quest to discover America, looking for doughnuts and Coca-Cola in Frankfurt.

Jef, full of enthusiasm, was asleep. He was the one who had managed to sort out the mission, the finances (ninety Occupation dollars each) and team morale.

He and Pralin had met up with me in Knokke. It was there, while listening to some Belgian jazz, that I asked myself why the Belgian franc was selling for seven of our francs (don't forget that the story of August '48 is an old one) since, taking into account the black market exchange rate, the cost of living was three times higher in Belgium than in France. That made me feel as though I was doing the Belgians a favour, which they don't need. They all drive around in big Cadillacs.

But let's put aside these thoughts on the Bretton Woods Accords and go back on the road. Speaking of which, it was starting to smell of the smoked sausage that gave its name to the big city we were hoping to reach.

Jef extricated himself from a troubled sleep and raised his head. His hair was standing on end, like a porcupine arching its back.

"Where are we?" he said.

"Almost in Frankfurt," Pralin replied, as visions of German women afflicted with steatopygia flashed before his eyes.

"That didn't take long," Jef said.

Jef is that kind of guy. He sleeps non-stop for eight hours, his head nodding gently on your shoulder, his arms and legs getting caught up in the gearstick, almost causing an accident. You can put up with that. You can put up with the wild look in his eye when a roar from Pralin tries to draw his attention to a particularly apposite rear end. You can put up with his soft snoring. You can put up with all of this… And, after eight hours, worn out and exhausted, you shake Jef who wakes up as fresh as a daisy and says to you: "That didn't take long."

I let Jef know what I thought, and he offered to take the wheel while I had a rest, but I had to decline because my dear wife has this terrible weakness of caring for me.

Pralin let out a stifled squeal.

"Hey guys!… That backside!… Look at that backside!… inviting… perfect shape… honest…"

This person on a bicycle had truly muscular thighs.

"An intelligent backside…" Pralin sighed again, almost beside himself.

I passed the subject of our interest and Jef burst out laughing in Pralin's face. It was a man in shorts, and Pralin, terribly disappointed, fell into a disgusted silence. We were on the outskirts of Frankfurt. Jef regained control of the situation.

"That way," he said to me. "Go straight ahead to get there."

You didn't have to be a genius to work that out because there was a road sign three metres high. I followed the arrows and twenty minutes later we were at the Press Club. The Roman orgy was about to begin.

In all honesty, this lifestyle suited me perfectly. I had met up again with Gilbert who was producing a short film on occupied Germany for Sablier en Goguette. He was drinking old-fashioneds and we were on whisky and coke, much to his great horror. We had big rooms, hot baths and some "you want it we've got it" American rubbish from the PX.

But Jef wanted to do business. When he was here a year ago, he had seen people make a fortune out of cigarettes and, according to him, all you had to do was give it a try.

I didn't want to disappoint him but on the road, in the English zone, we had already had trouble getting ten marks to the dollar, and that caused me to have some doubts. I had even more when I noticed that petrol, after official conversion, cost the "krauts" on the black market about half the official price back home. From that point on, I adopted the following approach: don't worry, spend the dollars, go home when there aren't any left and, in the meantime, do some real serious reporting.

On the second night, Jef set out on a nocturnal expedition. Pralin too, but his motives were purely bestial and extramonetary. He took along a cake of soap as a small gift.

At three o'clock in the morning, I was woken suddenly by an excited Jef, who had charged in like Woody Woodpecker.

"Great news," he said. "I've found this guy who'll give us fifteen marks to the dollar. Maybe sixteen."

"Great," I said, in a slightly husky voice.

"Tomorrow night, we'll all be millionaires," Jef said simply.

"Good," I said. "Tomorrow afternoon I'm going to the PX."

"Don't spend it all," Jef said. "We need to keep some for the marks. That's a far more interesting proposition."

"Yeah," I said.

And I slept some more.

The following afternoon, I converted some cash into chocolate. Jef gave me enough to cover what he thought would be the cost of our board and lodging for the next six days, to keep in a safe place. It was around forty dollars. He took a dollar from what remained, that's to say round forty-five dollars, to buy himself an automatic, silver-plated cigarette lighter made in Austria or Moldovalakia, which broke the same night. But let's not get ahead of ourselves.

Pralin, the realist, bought himself a pair of pyjamas and some shaving cream.

I went to bed early that night, as Jef set off into the wild to track down some marks. Pralin went with him, rather excited at the prospect of unhooking the braces of his basic instincts.

At one o'clock in the morning, I struggled to lend a curious ear to the ranting and raving of Jef, who was more outraged than ever.

"The bastard," he said. "A guy I trusted completely. 'Give me the dollars,' he said to me, 'and I'll be back.' I hand them over, he goes inside the café and, an hour later, he still hasn't come back out."

"Stop," I said. "I get it. Besides, I have to tell you, just between you and me, he looked distinctly shady. I happened to catch a glimpse of him this afternoon working as a so-called guide."

"I'm not going to let that happen," Jef said. "I'm going to report it to the MPs."

"They don't give a damn," I said. "If you do that, we're cooked. It's not really very legal to be exchanging dollars for marks."

Through a haze, I heard him curse and swear for another hour, and Morpheus took me back into his furry embrace.

The following three days were spent in pursuit of Jef's forty dollars. This was a change of plan. Originally, we were to go to Stuttgart, and I was very pleased to cut that out. With the price of petrol being what it was, I saw no harm in driving Jef around all day, especially as it gave Pralin a broader insight into the backsides of the capital.

This adventure had, if I may say, put some steel in Jef's head. In the compound, where I bought some crushed mustard seed socks, a shabby cherry red-currant-cordial-coloured jacket and periwinkle blue satin slippers, I would see him cast an envious eye over anything that would help him make an impression on the typists at the paper.

Pralin, the philosopher, was carefully rubbing up the ladies of Frankfurt in the bushes by the river Main. And that is where all of his soap was going, which was not a lot to pay for a little debauchery.

However, on the evening of the fifth day, Jef did his sums. If we wanted to stay any longer, we would have to find a way to support him (and that was out of the question — it would have been immoral).

"When it's all said and done," he said, "for eighty dollars, around nineteen thousand francs, I will bring back a one dollar cigarette lighter."

"Quite right," I said approvingly. "That sums up the situation perfectly. After all, you've survived for six days and you're about to write one of those stories that will balance your budget for a good month."

"That cigarette lighter will have cost me eighteen thousand francs," Jef continued.

"You can count that as being twenty-eight in purchasing power," Pralin pointed out, "because, if you had had the marks and the merchandise you could have bought with them, you would have easily made yourself ten thousand profit."

"That makes thirty thousand then," Jef sighed. "You have here a cigarette lighter that's worth thirty big ones."

"Doesn't look like it," I said, with no particular intent.

"Because it's broken," Jef remarked. "But that's nothing… it just needs a screw. You can pick one up anywhere for next to nothing."

"At least sixty francs," Pralin observed, still optimistic. "At that price, I could get another cake of soap."

"And all the joy it brings," I said, in order to cut short any more Pralinian remarks on the phenomenology of Germanic rumps.

"Pralin," Jef said, "this lighter is worth thirty thousand."

"Less a hundred francs," I said. "Let's round it off."

"Twenty-nine thousand, nine hundred francs," Jef said. "If I sell it to you for twenty thousand, Pralin, you'll make nine thousand, nine hundred, almost ten thousand francs, without lifting a finger."

"Ten thousand francs," I said, "that's almost a hundred and seventy cakes of soap."

"Wow!…" Pralin sighed, intrigued by the numbers. "Six months of sheer ecstasy…"

I looked at Jef. His face, which normally reminds me of Vesuvius on the day of a big eruption, was likewise quivering with excitement.

"Well, Pralin?" Jef asked sweetly.

I looked at my watch. We still had a chance of leaving that day if the deal came off.

"Done," Pralin said.

"Well, guys," I said, "that was one strange piece of business you both did. Let's say we go back to Paris and celebrate?"

"Oh!" Jef said. "We're not in a hurry..."

"Yes we are," Pralin said. "I don't have any more soap..."

And choking with emotion, he lowered his voice and whispered in our ear: "Guys, they're going to do me a special deal if I take the lot for ten thousand francs... They'll let me have them for fifty..."

"As I said..." Jef concluded.

I took my bag and opened it to start packing.

"As I said, you only have to bend over to rake it in..."

A CULTURAL EXPERIENCE

I

The Admiral ran headlong into Charlie just as the latter was leaving Paul Boubal's café, where he could be found almost every day between five o'clock in the afternoon and two o'clock in the morning. So the Admiral was surprised, because it was only half past five.

"You haven't seen the gang? Aren't they there?"

"Yes!" Charlie answered.

"Is Ops there? Is Gréco? What about Anne-Marie?"

"Yes!" Charlie answered.

"I don't understand," the Admiral said.

"You're a bit slow," Charlie answered. "It's Monday."

"Oh!" the Admiral said. "Your movie day..."

"Come with me," Charlie said. "You always say no, but it's very educational. It's a wonderful intellectual experience and it would do you good."

"I'm too young to die of suffocation," the Admiral said. "That would be setting a bad example."

"You shouldn't be so fat then," Charlie remarked. "Come on, I'm counting on you. See you tonight, seven forty-five, out front near the entrance. We need to be early."

"Where are you going now?" the Admiral said, shaking his hand automatically just before going into the café.

"To buy an American tank from army surplus!" Charlie said. "That way, we'll be sure to get a seat!"

II

"You should come with us," the Admiral said. "It's very intellectual and a wonderful educational experience…"

He couldn't remember Charlie's exact words and finished off with an inarticulate grunt of conviction.

"Yes," Ops said, "it should be interesting, but tonight Astruc has promised to take me to see *Gone With the Christmas Spirit,* with Edward G. Robinson in the role of Father Christmas, and I wouldn't want to miss that."

"It's by failing to cultivate one's mind in such ways," the Admiral declared, "that one ends up, to borrow the well-known phrase of…"

"Of…?" Ops asked impatiently, playing with her long blonde locks.

Her hairdresser would spend four hours a week straightening her locks, while Ops ate sticks of liquorice in order to obtain, by imitation, a sufficient degree of capillary rigidity.

"I don't remember!" the Admiral said.

"But what was that well-known phrase?" Ops insisted with a real lack of tact and in a very strong Italian accent.

"It's not important," the Admiral declared, embarrassed.

"You've talked me into it," Ops said. "I'll bring Djean."

"Who's that?" the Admiral asked, alarmed.

"Jeannette. You know her. She's my cousin."

"Charlie reckons all you have to do to get a seat is arrive early," the Admiral said. "Bring Djean along. It will be more fun with the four of us."

III

"Push harder!" Charlie grunted.

"Can't!" the Admiral gasped. "I have to get Ops up off the ground. They're biting her legs."

"They didn't have any tanks at army surplus," Charlie said. "I could only find salicylate chewing gum. Beeman's."

"Try chewing some and then breathe on everyone!" the Admiral said.

They were five metres from the closed doors of the movie theatre. An almost silent surging mass of still living human flesh writhed before them. From time to time a muffled roar would rise, quickly silenced by the sound of tightly rolled newspapers brandished to finish off the poor unfortunate being who was about to faint. The body would then be manhandled back towards the rear to clear the way.

"What's playing?" asked Djean, whose mouth happened to find itself wedged up against Charlie's ear.

"Waterman Apyston's *Blue-Black Angel*, with Marliche Dihêtrenne. But don't tell anyone. There are already enough people here."

They were quite unusual people, what's more, mostly serious young men sporting crew cuts. Behind a Sapphic exterior, the young girls were hiding a total lack of interest in anything to do with sex. Most had a literary review or, better still, an existentialist magazine tucked under their arm. Those who had nothing gradually withdrew, ashamed.

"I say, Charlie," the Admiral said, "what say we go?"

The woman standing next to him, a blonde, no make-up, with braided hair held in place on top of her head by two black bows, and who had thrown a small green bolero over the top of an authentic pair of non-existent breasts with no bra, looked thunderously at him. But, fortunately for the Admiral, his metal watch chain deflected the discharge down towards the ground.

There was an almighty push, accompanied by pandemonium, and the door to the theatre suddenly gave way because, on the other side, Frédéric, the leader of the sultan's guard, had just breathed his last. Through the breach thus formed stormed the first waves. The Admiral was holding Ops out in front of him and she was desperately clinging to his tie. Propelled forward by Charlie and Djean, who themselves had just been subjected to a renewed attack from the rear, they took a tortuous trajectory before coming to land in a seat. With no room to move, the five of them comfortably piled in on top of each other. The film was about to begin. There were people everywhere, grabbing hold of the curtains on stage, stuck high up on the walls like flies, hanging in bunches from the one and only column. Just above the Admiral, Djean and Ops, five people were suspended from the ceiling light, trying to haul themselves up so they could straddle it. The Admiral looked up and that was the last thing he saw, because right at that moment the light fitting came away from the ceiling.

IV

"I brought you some flowers," Charlie said.

Ops, Djean and the Admiral painfully nodded their heads swathed in spotlessly clean bandages. In true Saint-Germain-des-Prés style, the three of them were sharing the same hospital bed.

"Was the film good?" Djean asked.

"I don't know," Charlie said. "At the last minute they showed *Storm Over Oustoupinski* by Krakovine-Brikoustov."

"Oh!... Damn!..." the Admiral said. "So you can't tell us anything about *Blue-Black Angel?*"

The man in the next bed raised his hand to attract their attention. He seemed to be having difficulty speaking.

"I... went... to see it... last night... at a private screening," he whispered.

"Well?" all four asked anxiously.

"There... there was a blackout," the man said, and silently passed away.

The nurse went over and covered his face with the sheet.

"Of course, *you* haven't seen it?" Charlie snarled at her.

"Seen what?"

"*Blue-Black Angel.*"

"Oh, yes I have! I used to be an usherette before becoming a nurse. I've seen *Blue-Black Angel* at least two hundred and fifty times."

"Well?" Charlie asked with bated breath.

"Oh!..." the former usherette said. "I don't remember much about it really. But I do know that it was completely stupid."

THE TEST

It was through coming to Deligny baths that we all got to know each other. First names only, of course, and we never bothered with small talk and pleasantries. The men would give the women a ceremonial slap on the backside before taking a dip, while the women would sit around bitching about the swimsuit, or the legs, or the cellulite of the one (dear friend) who had not yet arrived. On the whole, it was all good fun.

There was Christiane the porpoise, Georges, who would turn up sporting a pair of clodhoppers that would have given his grandmother a seizure (or anybody else's grandmother for that matter), Ops (the less she wore, the stronger her accent), Michel the architect and Michel with the striped bathers, big Yvette with a bottom jaw like a car bumper (according to the architect, who had a gift for making Hellenic comparisons). There was Claude Luter, who only put down his clarinet to do judo or to get naked in the sun, Nicole, Maxime, Roland and Moustache (covered in a thick coat of black hair and an abundant layer of fat)… in short, a real bunch of mafiosos.

One person we hardly ever saw was Christian Castapioche, the heartbreaker. With good reason — if he had come along too often, we would have taken his suntan oil. We used large quantities of it and even went as far as putting it on the tomatoes we pinched from Ops and the handsome Gilles, the real lady-killer of the group (who I didn't mention before because I was jealous).

The best time was a week-day morning, around nine-thirty, ten o'clock. Not too many people, room to spread out in the sun and bake, and clean water.

This one particular day, I'd managed to get out of bed. I turn up, and who do I see on the deck?… My old friend Castapioche, looking as handsome as anything in a mauve and yellow bikini.

"Hi there!" I said to him. "Trying to make up your mind?"

He was pale. Michel and I looked at him with contempt.

"Yes," Castapioche said, sounding as though he was confiding in us. "I've come to take a look around."

"Haven't you ever been here?" Michel asked.

"Never," Castapioche said. "I have to work during the day."

Nobody knew exactly what it was Castapioche did. According to some, he's a night porter at the Macropolis Hotel. According to others, he has a good thing going with a certain Mademoiselle Laurent. Those in the know say he doesn't do a damn thing. As for me, I have no idea.

"Hey," Michel said to me just then, "check out that body."

I check out the body. This is the favourite pastime at Deligny, where there are bodies indeed worthy of attention. When there's a particularly good one, Michel rolls over to get some sun on his back because he's trying to be discreet, but this time he stayed belly up. This was a good body, but nothing special.

"Pretty well built," Little Bison said.

"Hold on, guys," Castapioche said. "Don't waste your time on that. Tomorrow you'll really see something."

We let that comment pass, but he grabs me and takes me aside.

"Listen," he says to me, "you know I don't keep any secrets from you."

"Sure," I answer. "Me neither."

"I might be getting married," he said. "But first I want to bring her along to the pool."

"So, you're engaged?" I say.

"A man should always bring his fiancée along to the pool before taking the plunge," Christian said. "It's the only place where he can see what she's really like."

"So, you're engaged?" I say.

"Hey, hey!" he says. "Maybe."

On that note, he gets up to leave.

"I'm off to work, guys," he says. "See you tomorrow."

Off he goes. He really is quite pale. Never mind, we're going to have a bit of fun tomorrow. I grab Michel and Little Bison.

"Guys," I say to them, "Castapioche is coming back tomorrow with his sweetheart. We have to do something."

"Gilles!" they both say together.

Ops opens one eye. I have to tell you that she is a little tied up with Gilles at the moment and that she reeks so much of peanut oil, it's not funny. We extricate Gilles's ear and stick a beach bag upside down on Ops's head to keep her quiet.

"What?" says Gilles.

"We need your help," I say to him.

That damn Gilles, he really is built like a god. There are some big strapping men at Deligny, with muscles on muscles, who walk around on their hands for fun and who can lift fourteen squawking parrots on their little finger. But really, you're better off being built like Gilles — broad shoulders, narrow hips and well-defined features. And he had a far better tan than Don Byas, the sax player with the handlebar moustache.

"Okay," said Gilles.

"We have to get that bird away from Castapioche," said Little Bison.

"What's she like?" said Gilles.

"We'll soon see," said Michel. "Come on, Gilles. Are you in?"

"In!" said Gilles.

And just as Ops starts to protest, he throws her on her back and empties a bottle of moontan lotion into her nostrils. Thereupon, we go in for a quick dip.

***

The next day, we're all there on time, in combat position. The operation has been well planned.

Here comes my friend Castapioche wearing the dark glasses his cousin brought back for him from America, a not so unattractive brunette on his arm.

They separate and head off to the changing rooms. Christian has seen us and signals to us to keep our distance. Michel splits from the group, goes over and keeps him talking as the bird disappears behind a door.

Michel is perfect. The girl is ready before Christian can get rid of him. From where we're standing, we see Christian introduce Michel, who then leads her towards our group while Christian finally goes in to change.

Here she is.

"Inez," Michel said, "this is the gang. Everyone, this is Inez Barracuda y Alvarez."

We're all that damn nice as we position her between Gilles and Georges. Georges will make her laugh and Gilles will chat her up.

We're on a roll. Even before Christian has come over, Gilles has grabbed Inez and is leading her in the direction of the bar.

Christian arrives on the scene.

"Where's Inez?" he said.

"Oh, she's gone back to her changing room to look for a pin," one of the girls said. "Her swimsuit won't stay up."

"My compliments," Georges said to Christian. "She's adorable."

Christian puffs out his chest with pride.

"As I've told you," he said, "you should always bring a girl along to the pool before committing yourself. That way, you know what to expect."

We tell him lots of stories and, before you know, time has slipped by. Castapioche is a little worried.

"What's she doing?" he says. "I'm going to get her."

"No need," Michel said. "Here she comes."

Gilles is holding her by the waist. Both of them are dripping wet and she doesn't seem to be walking very straight. They're approaching but instead of coming towards us they cut across along the edge of the pool.

She goes back into the changing room.

"I'm going over," Castapioche said.

"Listen, don't be a fool," Michel said. "She's gone to look for her comb."

As for Gilles, he's gone back to get changed, but Castapioche was completely focused on Inez and didn't see him. Gilles, fully dressed, comes out at the same time as Inez and they meet up again outside her change room.

Good Lord! What a smooch he's just given her!

They head off together.

"Oh!..." Christian said. "Oh!... How about that?..."

"Don't be angry," I say to him.

"I don't get it, it's crazy!" Castapioche said. "A girl from an excellent family! Who I was going to marry!"

"I'll explain it to you," I say to him. "Your swimming pool idea is fine. But you should have got yourself a tan and done some training beforehand."

"Why?" Christian said.

"Do you know what she told me?" Michel said.

"No," Christian replied.

"She told me that, before getting married, a girl should always take her fiancé along to the pool, because it's the only place where she can see what he's really like."

A BIG STAR

"So what's the weather like?" the Admiral asked, stretching.

The dog looked out the window.

"I wouldn't take a human out in it," he said. "Better than yesterday. It shouldn't be too cold."

"Good," the Admiral said. "Have you already been outside?"

"Of course," the dog said. "You don't think I get up at the same time as you, do you?"

"Did you go for a walk?" the Admiral asked. "Who did you see? Any dogs I know?"

"Those females are awful!" the dog said wearily. "I met another one this morning… their fixation with perfume… I said hello to her and then I had to sniff her nose in front of everyone. It smelled too much like carnations down the other end."

He sneezed at the thought.

The Admiral commiserated with him and called for Arthur to bring breakfast.

* * *

Arthur had a disapproving look on his face as he brought in a platter of morning nibbles — roast beef in Madeira sauce, lobster mayonnaise, onion tart and a cognac coffee to wash everything down. The Admiral was on a diet.

A long lanky youth was following behind, his protruding Adam's apple and small floppy bowtie revealing his penchant for bebop.

"My word!" the Admiral said. "It's Charlie!"

"I tried to stop him," Arthur said.

"Hi, Admiral!" Charlie said. "Still in the sack! Do you know what time it is?"

The dog muttered something about intruders and skulked off to places less frequented.

"Eleven forty-five," the Admiral said. "It's the usual time. I need a lot of sleep because I often wake up in the afternoon."

"I've come to get you," Charlie said, "to take you to the movies."

"The latest craze," Arthur said.

"What to see?" the Admiral said. "And why so early?"

Charlie turned red. He had a white shirt and blue eyes, so the Admiral stood to attention.

"I've met a charming young lady," Charlie began unexpectedly. "Her name is Louella Bing and she's in the movies. She's a real artiste. A star."

"Never heard of her!" Arthur said.

"Me either," the Admiral said. "But I don't often go to the movies. I read cookbooks instead."

"I'm telling you..." Charlie added, "she has an important part in a major film, *The Hellhole of Calambar.*"

"Is it new?" the Admiral asked.

"Yes," Arthur said. "Pépé Muguet and José Lamouillette are in it."

"It opens this morning to a triply exclusive audience at the Abbaye, the Club des Stars, and Cygne-Écran. We need to be there around twelve-thirty, one o'clock," Charlie added.

"Ah..." the Admiral said warily. "That's quite soon."

"She's waiting for me in the car," Charlie said. "Hurry up."

"Shall I take all this back then?" Arthur said. "What a waste of time!"

The Admiral's beaming face broke into a painful grimace on seeing Arthur disappear with the platter. Remaining polite nevertheless, he threw back the covers and pulled on his red socks.

***

"What part do you play in this film?" the Admiral asked.

The four of them were in Charlie's car. The dog was in the front next to Charlie, with the Admiral and Louella in the back. The Admiral was scratching his thin black moustache with the tip of a well-manicured fingernail.

"It's quite an interesting story line…" Louella said. "It's about a settler in the tropics who, despite all sorts of rivalries, ends up finding a diamond mine. Unfortunately, he falls in love with a treacherous woman he takes away with him to live in his cabin and she betrays him. It's very moving."

Louella had dark skin and her make-up accentuated the sparkle in her eyes. As for the rest of her, she was well developed, and in all the right places.

"It's a great role!" the Admiral said. "What's more, it's a role that has withstood the test of time. It fits you like a glove."

"Yes," Louella said. "But it's Michelle Meringue who landed it. You know… all you have to do is sleep with everyone…"

"What about you?"

"Me?" Louella said. "I bring something different home for lunch. In the film, I play a half-caste servant."

"So it takes place in the tropics?" the Admiral enquired thoughtfully.

"Yes. And it wasn't too hot while we were shooting…"

She laughed a little self-consciously. The Admiral tried to think about something else because he was worried about his blood pressure.

They all got out because Charlie had just pulled up outside the Abbaye.

***

"Do you think we'll get in?" Charlie said.

"I don't know," the Admiral said.

"You look really silly, you three," said the dog, who came bounding back.

He placed his paw on an old man who was standing still and who held out his hand and opened up his umbrella. They had been waiting for fifty minutes. There was one final surge of the queue in front of them and the cashier abruptly pulled down the shutter, which made a squishing sound.

"We're sold out!" he said.

"Oh!" the Admiral said. "What say we go and have some lunch?"

"Quick!..." Charlie said. "Let's dash over to the Club des Stars. Maybe we can get in there..."

Charlie's car took off again, backfiring. Charlie was wearing a pair of lovely yellow gloves and his flat hat made it look like he had an oval halo. Louella seemed impatient. The Admiral was listening to his ravenous stomach churn out a tune and was waving his finger to the beat. The dog put his head between his paws and fell asleep on the cushion.

They queued up at the Club des Stars from two o'clock until four-twenty and didn't get in. Next, it was the roller shutter at Cygne-Écran that came down, at six-forty, severing the hindquarters of a woman scurrying inside.

They went back to the Abbaye. At eight-thirty they were promised three cheap seats for the night session on the proviso they waited. At ten o'clock, exhausted, the two men stumbled to their allocated seats. Louella, ten metres ahead, was becoming more and more nervous. The dog was still asleep in the car. He only woke up at around eleven to look at the clock and snigger, satisfied.

At the end of the first reel, the Admiral dozed off while stroking the fur on the coat of the lady sitting next to him, which began to purr. The hero had only just set out for Ritatitari, the Hellhole of Calambar.

Behind him, Charlie's soft snoring was becoming lost in the sound of the engines of the black boat that was making for the islands...

Three rows in front, Louella hadn't taken her eyes off the screen.

***

"Yes..." the Admiral said into the phone. "Yes... I must have fallen asleep right at the beginning. Why? It was the explosion in the forest at the end that woke me up."

"Me too," Charlie said. "So, you didn't see her scene?"

"I told her it was very good," the Admiral assured him. "But I can't remember what she answered... I was very tired."

"Me too," Charlie said, "I paid her lots of compliments."

He was speaking with great difficulty, as if he had porridge in his mouth.

"What's wrong with you?" the Admiral said.

"Two broken teeth," Charlie said. "Her scene was cut when they edited the film a month ago. You know, she was no more than an extra."

APRIL'S DAUGHTERS

I

On Friday 1st April, Gouzin felt as though he was about to get lucky. That day he had put on his nice suit with the brown oval checks, his tartan tie and his sharp-looking pointy shoes. He left the building where he lived and, fifty metres down the road, he helped a stunning young girl back to her feet after she had tripped on a matchstick that had been thrown on the ground by an evil Arab.

"Thank you," she said with a captivating smile.

"Just a second," the smooth-talking Gouzin said. "I'm going to put on my dark glasses."

"Why?" she asked innocently.

"It's not the sun that's blinding me," Gouzin said. "It's your smile."

"My name is Lisette," she said, flattered.

"Can I buy you a little pick-me-up?" Gouzin suggested.

"Oh!" she said. And she blushed, starting a fire which raced through Gouzin's heart from tip to butt.

He then took her home and they fornicated for the next few days. On Tuesday 5th, she said to him: "Tomorrow is my birthday."

"My darling!" Gouzin said.

The next day he bought her a lovely bottle of perfume worth eighteen francs.

II

On Friday 8th, as Gouzin was going down into the metro, some fellow in a hurry hurt him when he bumped into him. He grabbed the fellow by the scruff of the neck. He tried to get away but Gouzin noticed that he was carrying a lady's handbag and became suspicious. Thereupon, the lady in question suddenly appeared. She was young and very beautiful, and was demanding explanations. A policeman arrested the thief, congratulated Gouzin, handed the bag back to the lady who, overwhelmed with gratitude, said to Gouzin: "Dear sir, that bag is worth more to me than life itself. And I would like to know what I could do to show my appreciation."

"Allow me to look at you for a moment," Gouzin said simply. "That's all I ask."

Just then, he was struck in the back by a suitcase that a surly porter was carrying for a passenger from the Gare de Lyon. He expressed aloud his desire to find somewhere quiet to go to have a friendly drink and the lady accepted. One drink followed another and, as a result of a few too many rounds, the lady lost all her inhibitions. Thereupon, Gouzin drove her to his place and bonked her several times, because Lisette had departed the day before, on friendly terms, leaving him unencumbered of heart and limb. His new flame's name was Josiane and she really knew how to hump.

On Tuesday 11th, she said to Gouzin: "Tomorrow is my birthday."

"My sweetie!" Gouzin said.

The next day he bought her a beautiful little trinket, a small pig made from mother-of-pearl that cost him twenty-nine francs.

III

On Friday 15th, Gouzin, much to his regret, had just separated from Josiane, who had been summoned to the country by an aunt who was cantankerous but generous with her money. He had just hailed a taxi and was about to get in when a charming young redhead, gasping for breath because she had been running, grabbed hold of his arm.

"Sir… sir," she said, "where are you going?"

"Over to Ternes," Gouzin replied after giving her the once-over.

"Oh! Can you take me with you? I'm so late!"

"Get in! Get in!" Gouzin said, as gallant as ever.

She climbed in. In the taxi, Gouzin seemed troubled. He finally asked her: "Your birthday isn't April 19th by any chance?"

"How do you know that?" she asked, surprised.

Gouzin assumed a modest look and slipped a hand under her dress.

"Allow me," he said. "Your stocking isn't straight."

A few moments later, the taxi took off in another direction, and all this culminated in the kind of activity that is forbidden for those under the age of sixteen, who would probably derive great pleasure from it if only someone would show them.

IV

On April 22nd, which just so happened to fall on a Friday, Gouzin went downstairs. On the first floor, he crossed paths with a thin sylph-like creature with fiery eyes who seemed disorientated.

"Excuse me, sir," the siren said to him, "are you Doctor Klupitzick?"

"No," Gouzin said, "he lives on the second floor."

"I've just come from the second floor," she said. "I rang the bell but no-one's there."

"Can I ask you something?" Gouzin said. "Does your birthday fall on the 26th of this month by any chance?"

"Are you psychic?" the young girl said, visibly impressed.

"I have something of a gift," Gouzin said, feeling that his lucky streak wasn't about to end. "I'm also well versed in anatomy. Can I offer you my services?"

"It's just that…" The beautiful girl hesitated. "I can't get undressed on the stairs…"

"I live on the third floor," Gouzin said.

The redhead had left the day before to go back to her husband and Gouzin was available again, which meant that, for the next three hours, he displayed his dexterity in the art of digital manipulation. The pretty blonde found it quite fascinating, so much so that she thought it would be a good idea to spend a few days with Gouzin. Unfortunately, on the following Thursday, she had to leave. On Friday 29th, Gouzin found himself once again all alone in his bed when, at 8 o'clock in the morning, the doorbell rang. He got up and opened the door, and there stood a delightful creature in the springtime of her life.

"I'm bringing you the mail," she said.

Gouzin remembered that the caretaker's niece was coming to replace her aunt for a week.

"Are you Annette?" he asked. "Come on in and let's have a drink to welcome you aboard."

"I'd love to!" she said. "Oh, you're so much nicer than Doctor Klupitzick."

"How could you not be nice to such an adorable person?" Gouzin said ardently.

He took her hand.

Ten minutes later, she had taken off her clothes because the alcohol was so strong it had made her hot. Overwhelmed with passion, Gouzin gazed lustfully upon all of the downy little spots where he could place his lips. He felt as strong as Hercules.

"Of course," he whispered as she sat on his knee, "you were born in April?"

"Why?" she said, surprised. "No… I was born in October… the 17th October."

Gouzin turned pale.

"October!" he said.

And he thought: "I'm done for."

Then, as happens in such cases, pure gold turned to worthless lead and, unable to secure victory with weaponry that was deserting him, Gouzin remained a forlorn, solitary figure on the battlefield. Despairingly, he cast a reproachful glance at his unfaithful servant, as the sound of a nervous pair of heels grew fainter on the hollow staircase.

LOVE IS BLIND

I

On 5th August at eight o'clock, fog enveloped the city. Being a light fog, it didn't hamper breathing in any way. It had a strange impenetrable look and seemed, moreover, to have a deep blue tinge to it.

The fog descended in even layers. At first it rolled around twenty centimetres above the ground and you walked about unable to see your feet. One woman, who lived at number 22 Saint-Dick Street, dropped her key as she was about to go inside her house and couldn't find it again. Six people, including a baby, came to her assistance. In the meantime, a second layer descended and the key was found, but not the baby, who had taken off in a flash under the veil of the weather, impatient to escape the feeding-bottle and to experience the tranquil joys of married life and settling down. That is how thirteen hundred and sixty-two keys and fourteen dogs went missing on the first morning. Tired of not being able to see their floats, fishermen went mad and took up hunting.

The fog collected in quite thick pockets at the bottom of sloping streets and in hollows. It wafted out from the sewers and ventilation shafts in long spires. It flooded the metro, which stopped functioning once the milky stream reached the height of the red signal lights. But at that precise moment, a third layer of fog had just descended and, outside, people were wading around in a pale, knee-high mist.

Those who lived in the more elevated parts of the city thought at first that they would be spared, and made fun of those who lived on the banks of the river. But, after a week, they were all friends again and could all bump into the furniture in their bedrooms in the same fashion, for the fog had engulfed the tallest buildings. And although the pinnacle of the tower was the last to go under, eventually it too disappeared under the irresistible advance of the opaque tidal wave.

II

On 13th August, Orvert Latuile woke up from a sleep that had lasted three hundred hours. He was recovering from a heavy drinking session and thought at first that he was blind. He was really doing justice to all the alcohol that had been placed in front of him. It was dark, but this was a different kind of darkness because, with his eyes wide open, he was experiencing the same sensation you have when the beam from an electric light shines on your closed eyelids. Clumsily, he reached for the dial on the radio. It worked, but what he heard didn't shed much light on the situation.

Paying no attention to the deejay's idle chatter, Orvert Latuile began to think about things. He scratched his navel and, after sniffing his fingernail, discovered that he needed a bath. But the convenience of the fog that had been thrown over everything, like Noah's cloak over Noah, or like misfortune over the poor world, or like Tanit's veil over Salammbô, or like a cat in a violin, led him to the conclusion that taking a bath would be futile. Anyway, this fog had the sweet aroma of tubercular apricot and was sure to kill any body odour. Besides that, sound was carrying well. Wrapped in this protective padding, noises had assumed a curious resonance that was clean and pure, like the voice of a lyric soprano whose smashed palate, sustained from an unfortunate fall on to a plough handle, had been replaced by a prosthetic device forged from silver.

Firstly, Orvert cleared his head and decided to act as if there was nothing wrong. As a result, he found his clothes and got dressed without any problem because everything had been put away in its usual place. This meant that some of his clothes were on chairs, some were under the bed, socks were inside shoes, one of the shoes was inside a vase and the other shoe was under the chamber pot.

"My God," he said to himself, "what a funny thing this fog is."

This most unoriginal comment saved him from panegyric, from straightforward enthusiasm, from sadness and from deep melancholy by categorising the phenomenon as a simple observation. But as he became used to the unusual, he gradually became more adventurous, to the point where he was now considering making human contact.

"I'm going downstairs to visit my landlady and I'm leaving my fly undone," he said. "Then I'll know for sure whether it really is fog or whether it's my eyes playing tricks on me."

This is because the Cartesian way of thinking of the French leads them to doubt the existence of a thick fog, even if that fog is thick enough to obscure all visibility. And they don't leap to strange conclusions just because of something they've heard on the radio, as they're all morons on the radio.

"I'm taking it out," Orvert said, "and that's how I'm going downstairs."

He took it out and that's how he went downstairs. For the first time in his life he noticed the creak of the first step, the cleak of the second, the squeak of the fourth, the munch of the seventh, the clunch of the tenth, the scrunch of the fourteenth, the snap of the seventeenth, the crackle of the twenty-second and the pop of the brass handrail that had lost its last post.

He encountered someone coming up the stairs, holding on to the wall for support.

"Who's that?" he said, stopping.

"Lerond!" Mr Lerond answered. "The neighbour from across the hall."

"Hello," Orvert said. "Latuile here."

Orvert held out his hand and to his surprise encountered something stiff, which he quickly let go of. Lerond let out an embarrassed chuckle.

"I apologise," Lerond said, "but you can't see anything and this fog is devilishly hot."

"That's true," Orvert said.

He thought about his open fly and was annoyed to discover that Lerond had had the same idea.

"Well, goodbye then," Lerond said.

"Goodbye," Orvert said, slily undoing the last three notches of his belt.

His pants fell to the floor. He took them off and hurled them down the stairwell. It is a fact that this fog was as hot as a feverish bug in a rug and, if Lerond was walking around with his kit and caboodle stuck up in the air, then Orvert couldn't stay dressed the way he was, now could he? It was all or nothing. His jacket and shirt took to the heavens, but he kept his shoes on.

Arriving at the bottom of the stairs, he tapped gently on the glass panel of the door to the caretaker's lodge.

"Enter," said the concierge's voice.

"Is there any mail for me?" Orvert asked.

"Oh! Mr Latuile!" the large lady laughed, "as funny as ever… So, I see you slept well? I didn't want to disturb you… but you should have seen the first few days of this fog!… Everyone went crazy. And now… well, we're all getting used to it…"

The powerful perfume that had managed to pierce the milky barrier alerted him to her approach.

"It's only when you're trying to prepare your meals that it's a bit of a nuisance," she said. "But it's a strange thing, this fog… it sustains you in a funny sort of way. Now look, I'm a good eater, but for the last three days a glass of water, a crust of bread and I'm happy."

"You're going to lose weight," Orvert said.

"Ooh! Ooh!" she chuckled with that laugh of hers that sounded like a bag of nuts being dropped from the sixth floor. "Have a feel, Mr Orvert. I've never been in such good shape. Even my stomachs are starting to shrink. Have a feel."

"But… uh…" Orvert said.

"Come on, have a feel."

She groped around for his hand and placed it on one of the stomachs in question.

"Amazing!" Orvert noted.

"And I'm forty-two years old," the landlady said. "You wouldn't think so, would you? Oh, for those like me, a little large to some people's way of thinking, it's to our advantage..."

"But good God!" Orvert said in astonishment. "You're naked!"

"Well," she said, "so are you!"

"That's true," Orvert mumbled. "How silly of me."

"They've said on the wireless," the landlady continued, "that it's a fucoholic aresole."

"Oh!" Orvert said. The landlady was within touching distance, panting, and just for a moment he felt rejuvenated by this cursed fog.

"Listen, please, Mme Panuche," he pleaded. "We're not animals. If this is an aphrodisiac fog, then we'll just have to control ourselves, dammit."

"Oh, oh!" Mme Panuche panted as her hands found their target with pinpoint accuracy.

"I don't care," Orvert said in a very dignified manner. "Manage by yourself. I'm having nothing to do with it."

"Well," muttered the landlady, without losing her composure, "Mr Lerond is more cooperative than you. With you, I have to do all the work."

"Listen," Orvert said, "I've woken up only today... I'm not used to this."

"I'll show you," the landlady said.

Then things happened over which it would be better to throw the cloak of the poor and the misfortunes of Noah and Salammbô and Tanit's veil in a violin.

Orvert left the lodge in very high spirits. Outside, he stopped to listen. That's what was missing — the sound of cars. But countless songs could be heard. Laughter was emanating from all parts.

He made his way along the road, feeling a little light-headed. His ears were not used to such an expanded auditory horizon. He lost himself in it for a moment and noticed that he was thinking out loud.

"My God," he said. "An aphrodisiac fog!"

As you can see, the remarks he made were all in a similar vein. However, you have to put yourself in the position of a man who has been asleep for eleven days, who wakes up in total darkness aggravated by a wide-spread outbreak of licentiousness, who finds that his fat, decrepit landlady has been transformed into a Valkyrie, with fulsome, pointed breasts, desperately seeking a cavern full of unexpected pleasures.

"Well I never!" Orvert said again in order to render his thoughts more clearly.

Suddenly realising that he was standing in the middle of the street, he took fright. He stepped back to the wall and followed its cornice for a hundred metres. This brought him to the bakery. According to applied health science, food should be taken following all forms of strenuous physical activity. So he stepped inside to buy a bread roll.

There was much commotion in the shop. Orvert was a man of few prejudices but when he realised what the baker's wife was demanding from each of the male customers and what the baker was demanding from each of the female customers he felt his hair stand on end.

"If I give you a loaf of bread that weighs two pounds," the baker's wife said, "I'm entitled to expect something of equivalent size, dammit!"

"But madam," protested the high-pitched organ of a little old man, recognised by Orvert as being Mr Curepipe, the old organ player from down by the end of the wharf. "But madam..."

"And you play the pipe organ!..." the baker's wife said.

Mr Curepipe became angry.

"I'll give you my organ!" he said proudly, and he headed for the door. However, Orvert was standing in the way and the collision knocked the wind out of him.

"Next!" the baker's wife barked.

"I'd like some bread," Orvert said with difficulty, rubbing his stomach.

"A four pound loaf of bread for Mr Latuile," the baker's wife screamed.

"No! No!" Orvert moaned. "Something smaller."

"Loser!" the baker's wife said.

And, turning to her husband: "Hey Lucien, you take care of this one. Teach him a lesson."

The hair on Orvert's head stood on end and he took off as fast as he could, straight into the shop window. It stood firm under the impact.

He walked around it and finally left. In the bakery the orgy was continuing. The baker's boy took care of the children.

"Struth!" Orvert muttered once he was out on the footpath. "Can't a man choose for himself? With a face like hers!"

That's when he remembered the pastry shop across the bridge. The waitress was seventeen years old and had a coy smile and a frilly little apron… maybe she was wearing only her little apron…

Orvert hurried off in the direction of the pastry shop. Three times he tripped over entwined bodies. He didn't bother to stop and see who it was or how many people there were, but in one case, at least, there were five.

"Rome!" he whispered to himself. "*Quo vadis! Fabiola! et cum spiritu tuo!* Orgies! Oh!"

He rubbed his head, having harvested quite a substantial pigeon egg as a result of his brush with the shop window, and quickened his pace, for a part of his person which was standing out some length in front of him was urging him to get there as quickly as possible.

Thinking that he was nearing his goal, he stepped back onto the footpath so he could feel his way along the walls of the houses. He recognised the shop window of the antique dealer with its round plywood plaque bolted down, holding in place one of the cracked mirrors. Two more houses until the pastry shop.

He collided full force with a stationary body that had its back turned towards him. He let out a cry.

"Don't push," a voice bellowed, "and would you mind removing that thing from my bum, otherwise you're going to get my fist in your face…"

"But… uh… what do you take me for?" Orvert said.

He stepped to the left to go around him. A second collision.

"What's your game?" another man's voice asked. "Get your arse in line, like everyone else."

There was a great outburst of laughter.

"What?" Orvert said.

"Yes," a third voice said, "of course you're here for Nelly."

"Yes," Orvert stammered.

"Well, shift your arse," the man said. "There are already sixty of us here."

Orvert didn't say anything. He felt deflated.

He set off again without getting to find out whether or not she was wearing her frilly little apron. He took the first street to the left. A woman was coming from the opposite direction. They both ended up on the ground on their backsides.

"I'm sorry," Orvert said.

"It's my fault," the woman said. "You were keeping to the right."

"Can I help you to your feet?" Orvert said. "Are you alone?"

"What about you?" she said. "There aren't five or six of you about to jump on me, are there?"

"You are a woman, aren't you?" Orvert continued.

"See for yourself," she said.

They drew closer and Orvert felt her long silky hair against his cheek. They were kneeling down facing each other.

"Where can we be alone?" he said.

"In the middle of the street," she said.

They stood on the edge of the footpath to get their bearings and stepped down onto the road.

"I want you," Orvert said.

"And I you," said the woman. "My name is…"

Orvert stopped her.

"It doesn't matter," he said. "The only thing I need to know is what my hands and body tell me."

"Take me," the woman said.

"Naturally," Orvert noted, "you're not wearing any clothes."

"Neither are you," she said.

He lay down beside her.

"There's no hurry," she said. "Start with my feet and work your way up."

Orvert was shocked and told her so.

"This way you'll find out," the woman said. "The only means of investigation left to us, you said so yourself, is touch. Don't forget that I'm no longer afraid of your gaze. Your erotic independence has been reduced to nought. Let's be open and frank."

"You sure know how to talk," Orvert said.

"I read *Les Temps modernes*," the woman said. "Come on. Hurry up and let's get on with my sexual initiation."

Which is what Orvert did a number of times and in varying positions. She obviously had natural talent and, when there's no fear of the light being turned on, a whole new world of possibilities opens up. And besides, when it's all said and done, it's not something you get tired of. Two or three not insignificant new tricks that Orvert taught her and the act of symmetrical coupling, repeated several times over, instilled confidence in their relationship.

That was the kind of sweet and simple life that shows how man is created in the image of the god Pan.

III

However, the radio reported that scientists had noticed a progressive decline in the phenomenon and that the layer of fog was becoming lower day by day.

There was much consultation, the threat being considerable. But a solution was quickly found, because man's genius is multi-faceted, and when the fog cleared, which is what the special detectors indicated, life could continue happily, because everyone had gouged out their eyes.

A DOG OF A JOB

"What's that thing for?" Charlie asked.

"To adjust the speed," the Admiral said. "If you push it down, you're shooting at seventy-two frames. It's the slow motion control."

"Strange," Charlie said. "I always thought normal speed was twenty-four frames. Seventy-two, that's three times faster."

"That's what I'm saying," the Admiral replied. "When you go from seventy-two frames to twenty-four, that's slow motion."

"Oh?" Charlie said. "Okay..."

He hadn't understood a single word.

"Anyway," Charlie continued, "it's a great camera. When do we start shooting?"

"This afternoon," the Admiral said. "Nique has brought me a terrific script. It's called *Hearts Ablaze in the Mexican Sun*. We'll be able to use all of her aunt's old tablecloths for costumes."

"Who's in the cast?" Charlie asked.

He had adopted a modest approach, certain of seeing himself handed the leading role.

"Well..." the Admiral said, "I had thought about Nique in the role of Conchita, Alfred can play Alvarez, Zozo can be Pancho, Arthur the innkeeper..."

"Who's Arthur?" Charlie interrupted.

"My valet... I'll play the priest... And Lou and Denis the two servants."

"What about me?" Charlie said.

"You're the only one I feel I can trust with a camera that's worth a hundred and forty-three thousand seven hundred francs," the Admiral said.

"You're too kind!" Charlie said, feeling terribly put out.

"I hope you're not going to put me in a sheepskin again and get me to play the polar bear," the dog said in anticipation of what he felt was coming.

"You're no fun," the Admiral said. "All you're good for is catching flies and eating the extras' props. You'll do what you're told. There's a parrot in the script and I had you in mind for the part."

"Good," the dog said. "Two pieces of steak is my fee."

"Okay," the Admiral said. "You have no class. You others," he continued to his friends, "go and put on your make-up. Charlie, come with me and I'll explain the scene. Alfred isn't here yet. That's a nuisance..."

As consolation for not landing a part, Charlie had dressed up like a real cameraman on set — baggy golf shorts, Lacoste teeshirt and a green plastic sun visor that made him look like a penguin.

"Alfred will be here. He's bringing a friend who must be running late."

"Damn," the Admiral said. "She's bound to be a shocker... like all the others... and anyway, we don't have a part for her. Damn!" he whispered, turning pale.

Alfred had just made his entrance with a stunning brunette on his arm. Her eyes and colouring were enough to set not only hearts ablaze, but also the entire set and the trees in the adjacent garden.

"Have you started?" Alfred said. "I haven't had a chance to explain the script to Carmen yet. Of course there's a part in it for her?"

"Yes," Charlie said. "She can be..."

"Yes," the Admiral said, "she can be Conchita, I'll be Alvarez, and we'll give you the part of the priest, Alfred, because it really suits you."

"But..." Charlie protested, "Alfred was Alvarez."

"Where did you get that idea?" the Admiral said, glaring at him. "I'll explain it to you," he continued. "In the beginning, there's the love between Alvarez and Conchita, with lots of close-ups of some sensational kissing..."

Alfred wiped his forehead with the sleeve of his cassock.

"This is not possible," he said. "I'm too hot."

The "oo" sound he made was three times longer than usual.

At that very moment, the dog slid off his perch and disappeared into the void. His tail feathers remained stuck to the bar and he began to protest with the utmost energy.

"In Mexico…" Carmen said.

"Have you ever been there?" Nique interrupted pointedly.

She had been relegated to the role of third servant and wasn't about to conceal her anger.

The Admiral, dressed in a crimson poncho and a gardening hat trimmed with green velvet ribbon, made peace between the two protagonists in the drama.

"Would sir please explain what he perceives the innkeeper's role to be?" Arthur said. "It's quite a different character from the one I usually play…"

"Listen," the Admiral said, "we're going to go over the four close-up shots at the beginning one more time to make sure everyone knows what they have to do and then we'll shoot them… At least that will be over and done with."

"Oh! Damn!" Charlie said.

"This is the eleventh time you've rehearsed your close-ups," Denise said.

"We understand that it might not be so unpleasant for you," Lou said impatiently, "but the others are fed up."

"Okay," the Admiral said, "the wedding scene then…"

"Oh… sh…" Charlie said. "We've already done that one seven times. The death scene. You won't keep still when you've been stabbed. It won't look good when we start shooting in earnest."

"Let's go!" the Admiral said in a tone of resignation.

He went away, came back, spread his arms, folded them across his chest in a warlike manner and roared: "Where is Señor Pancho, my arch enemy?"

Zozo rushed at him with a long kitchen knife.

"Now then," Charlie said, "we have five minutes left for filming, because after that there won't be any more light..."

"Let's go!" the actors unenthusiastically said as one.

They were exhausted. Their make-up was running down their faces. Carmen was looking anxiously at the disgusting mixture of burnt cork and brownish-yellow pigment that had formed on the Admiral's cheeks. They took their places and Charlie called out those famous words: "Silence! Action!" for no reason, since it was a silent movie. This sent the dog into hysterics, but his last few feathers blew away, leaving him wearing only the glue.

"Cut!" Charlie called.

The actors fell on top of each other in a heap as the Admiral went up to the camera. He opened it, looked inside, looked at Charlie, flung his arms around wildly and collapsed, well and truly still this time. Charlie looked inside the camera and turned lime green.

"What is it?" asked the voice of Alfred, who was just emerging from underneath the pile of lifeless bodies...

"I... I forgot the film..." Charlie said.

THE THINKER

I

On the day he turned eleven, young Urodonal Carrier abruptly became aware of the existence of God. Indeed, Providence suddenly revealed his status as thinker and, if one considers that up to that point he had proven to be completely stupid in all things, it is difficult to believe that the Lord was not somehow responsible for so prompt a transformation.

The cynical citizens of La-Houspignole-sur-Côtés, in typical fashion, will undoubtedly disagree with me about this, preferring to believe that it was because of the knock on the head young Urodonal sustained the previous day when he fell over, together with the nine swift kicks up the backside generously dished out on the morning of his birthday by his good uncle, whom he had caught keeping an eye on the maid to make sure she was changing her underwear every three weeks as his father had asked. But this village is full of atheists, who are maintained in a state of sin by the irresponsible ramblings of an old-school teacher, and the priest gets drunk every Saturday, which gives less weight to his holy word. However, if one is not used to it, one doesn't become a thinker without being tempted to attribute it to the intervention of a higher Power, and the best thing to do in this type of circumstance is to thank God.

It all happened very simply. The priest, who happened to be sober for a change during the retreat which preceded communion, tested Urodonal:

"What was the reason for Adam and Eve's downfall?"

Nobody knew the answer because in the country making love is no longer considered a sin. But Urodonal raised his hand.

"Do you know?" the priest asked.

"Yes sir," Urodonal said. "There was a mistake in Genesis."

The priest felt the wing of the Holy Spirit pass over him and he closed his collar against the draught. He sent the kids on their way and sat down to think. Three months later, still thinking, he left the village to become a hermit.

"There's a lot to what he said," he mused.

II

From that day, Urodonal's reputation as a thinker became firmly established throughout the whole of La-Houspignole. People would hang on his every word. It must be said that the Holy Spirit hardly ever revealed itself again.

One day in a physics class, during a lesson on electric currents, the teacher asked him, "What does it mean when the needle of a galvanometer moves?"

"That there's current…" Urodonal answered.

But that was nothing. He continued: "That there's current, or that the galvanometer's broken. You'll more than likely find a mouse inside."

So at the age of fourteen, young Urodonal was awarded a scholarship, and for the rest of his school days never had another original thought. But everyone knew what he was capable of.

At the end of his schooling, he reaffirmed his reputation in a blaze of glory during a philosophy lecture.

"I'm going to read to you some words from Epictetus," the teacher said. And so he read:

If you want to improve, be content to be thought foolish and stupid with regard to external things.

"And vice versa…" Urodonal said quietly.

The teacher bowed before him.

"My dear child, I have nothing more to teach you," he said.

Urodonal stood up and left the room, leaving the door ajar. In a friendly voice, the teacher called him back.

"Urodonal, remember, a door must be either open or closed…"

"A door must be either open or closed, or taken off its hinges if the lock needs to be repaired in a hurry," said Urodonal.

Then Urodonal walked away and took the train to Paris in a bid to conquer the capital.

III

Urodonal's first impression of Paris was that Montmartre metro station smelled like a country toilet. However, he kept this observation to himself because he didn't think Parisians would be interested in hearing it. Then he tried to find some work.

He thought long and hard before deciding on a career he wanted to pursue. Since he had been part of the town band in La-Houspignole, where he played the role of second extendable bugle, he was leaning towards something in the field of music.

However, he felt he needed to justify his decision and in typically brilliant fashion quickly found a reason.

"Music," he said to himself, "soothes the savage beast. Now, strict behavioural guidelines are indispensable for any respectable man, so it would be wrong to become a musician. But on the other hand, the inhabitants of this Babylon have no morals whatsoever, and consequently music presents no danger to them."

As you can see, Urodonal's capacity for critical analysis had been developed to such an extent through his studies that some found it disturbing. But we are not talking here about just any ordinary man; his body was strong enough to cope with his exceptional brain.

Music provided Urodonal with plenty of free time, so he decided to try his hand at literature.

Several unsuccessful attempts, far from dampening his genius, only served to inspire the following epigram:

"An author's success," he confided to his friends, "depends on the extent of his ability to look, on paper, like an idiot."

In his love life, Urodonal was just as prodigious.

"To say that you don't love me any more," he declared to his jealous girlfriend, Marinouille, "is like saying that I no longer think that you love me. But how can you be sure?"

Thereupon, Marinouille remained silent.

However, the great expanse of Urodonal's brain would not allow him to be satisfied with the mediocre existence he was leading with Marinouille and his bugle.

"Live dangerously," he would sometimes say, with a fiery look in his untamed eye.

And then one day, Marinouille found him dead in bed. He had only just recently become involved in a reprehensible relationship with a young prison escapee of dubious morals who had been serving a three-month sentence for the murder of twelve people.

Yet there was nothing perverse about Urodonal. The explanation for his sad demise was to be found in a collection of unpublished reflections, which contained only one, on the first page. Urodonal had written:

"What could be more dangerous than to get yourself killed?"

And how true it is.

THE KILLER

It was a prison like any other; a small shed with loam walls painted pumpkin yellow, an immodest chimney and a roof made from the leaves of asparagus fern. It was some time in the distant past, and everywhere there were stones and the shells of ammonites, trilobites, stalagpites and salpingites left over from the Ice Age. Inside the prison, you could hear someone snoring in broken Javanese. I went in.

A man was lying on a wooden bed, asleep. He was wearing a small pair of blue underpants and woollen knee protectors. On his left shoulder were tattooed the initials "K. I."

"Heeeey!" I yelled in his ear.

You might well say that I could have called out something else, but he was asleep and couldn't hear anything. Nonetheless, it woke him up.

"Brrr!" he said as he cleared his throat. "Who's the idiot who opened the door?"

"Me," I said.

Obviously, that made him none the wiser, but you shouldn't expect to be either.

"If you confess, it means you're guilty," the fellow surmised.

"But you are too," I said. "Otherwise, you wouldn't be here."

It is rather difficult to argue with my absolutely diabolical dialectic logic. At that moment, to my astonishment, a red and white crow entered the room through the small skylight and flapped around in a circle seven times before flying straight back out again. To this day, ten years on, I am still wondering whether its sudden appearance had any special significance.

The man, subdued, looked at me and shook his head.

"My name is Cain," he said.

"I can read," I answered. "Is that story about the eye true?"

"You have to be kidding!" he replied. "Yvan Audouard made it up."

"Eye-van Audouard?" I asked.

He burst out laughing.

"Hey, that's funny!" he said.

I blushed self-consciously.

"I suppose you've come to ask me about Abel and why I took him out?" Cain continued.

"Dear me!" I said. "Just between you and me, there was something fishy about the newspapers' version of events."

"They're all the same," Cain said. "All a bunch of liars. You tell them something, they don't get it, and what's more they don't check their work properly because they don't give a damn how they write. Add to that the interference from the chief editor and the type-setters and you can see how far it can go."

"Now then," I said, "to the truth of the matter."

"Abel?" Cain asked. "He was a dirty bitch."

"Bitch?" I asked, surprised.

"Exactly," Cain said. "Does that surprise you? Now I suppose you're going to act like Paul Claudel and tell me that, even after having been in regular correspondence with Monsieur Gide for over forty years, you were still not aware of his tendencies?"

"Is that why Gide received the Nabel Prize?" I asked.

"Exactly!" Cain said. "But let me tell you what happened."

"There's no chance of us being disturbed by the guard?" I asked.

"Not likely," Cain said. "He knows quite well that I have no desire to leave. What would I do on the outside? Nothing but queers and faggots everywhere."

"You're quite right there," I said.

"So," Cain resumed, as he settled down on his hard wooden plank, "you know when it happened. Abel and I were more like friends. You can see what I'm like. I'm more the big hairy type..."

Indeed, Cain was covered in a thick black mat of fur, was well built, and was as strong as an ox, like an eighty kilo wrestler.

"The big hairy type..." Cain said. "I had quite a lot of success with the girls and I was never bored on Sundays. My brother wasn't the same..."

"Abel?" I said.

"Abel. In my opinion, he was a half-brother," Cain said. "I've seen photos of the snake... another big queen, that one... Well, that was him all over. It wouldn't surprise me if the old dear hadn't jumped the fence with that cheeky little maggot... Variety is the spice of life, isn't that what they say? So maybe it's not Abel's fault if he was what he was. Anyway, there wasn't much of a family resemblance. Everyone drooled over his blonde locks. He was pale, sweet, likeable, and he stank of perfume, the dirty little bitch, enough to kill a skunk. When we were young, things were okay. We played cops and robbers, that's all. Nothing intellectual, you understand. That comes later. We shared the same room, we slept in the same bed, we ate from the same plate. We didn't leave each other's side. You see, to me, he was more like a little sister. I mollycoddled him. I combed his blonde hair. All in all, we got on very well together."

"I have to tell you..." continued Cain, who had just stopped mid-sentence to let out a loud snort of disgust, "I have to tell you it bothered him, that little swine, when I started chasing the chicks. But he didn't dare say anything. I thought he'd have time to learn, and after suggesting to him a couple of times to go and find himself a girlfriend I stopped when I saw he wasn't interested... He wasn't as developed as me..."

"Exactly," I agreed. "Besides, that's the very thing everyone has been talking about, and that's what they blame you for. You were twice his size."

"Blamed me for!" Cain exploded. "But he was a dirty pig, that little pile of trash!"

"Settle down," I said.

"Okay," Cain said. "But this is what he did. From time to time, I'd say to him, 'Abel, clear off. I've got a chick coming around and I need the bed.' Of course, he'd go away and come back a couple of hours later. You know, I'd only do it at night. I didn't need tongues wagging all around the town. So, he'd piss off into the night and then when the girl had seen him leave the house she'd come inside. Always at night. As easy as that…"

"It was a little annoying for him," I conceded.

"Come off it!" Cain protested. "I would have done the same for him!"

He started to swear.

"What a pile of trash that little pig was!" he concluded. "So, this one night, I said to him, 'Abel, clear off. I've got a girl coming.' He clears off and there I am waiting. The lass comes in. I don't move. She comes over and starts to go to work on me… you get the picture. That impressed me, because she seemed to be the rather clumsy type. So, I light my candle… and I see that it was that filthy brother of mine… Oh!… I was livid!"

"You should have smashed his face in," I said.

"Well, that's exactly what I did," Cain said. "And you can see where it landed me. Maybe I went a bit too far… but what do you expect? Faggots, I can't stand them."

A HEART OF GOLD

I

Aulne was edging his way raspingly across the face of the wall, casting an uneasy glance over his shoulder every few steps. He had just stolen old man Mimile's heart of gold. Of course he had been forced to hack the old fellow open a little, and in particular to open up his chest with a sickle, but when a heart of gold is there for the taking, you do what has to be done.

After he had gone three hundred metres, he conspicuously tore off the thief's cap he was wearing, threw it into a drain and swapped it for a gentleman's floppy hat. His confidence grew. Nevertheless, old Mimile's heart of gold, which was still quite warm, was bothering him because it was beating unpleasantly in his pocket. Furthermore, he would have liked to take a long leisurely look at it because one glimpse of that heart was enough to make you dangerous again.

A couple of hundred metres further on, in a drain larger than the first, Aulne dumped the bludgeon and sickle. These two implements were matted with blood and hair, and since Aulne did things meticulously, there was no doubt that they were also covered in fingerprints. He didn't change his clothes that were sticky with blood, because after all passers-by don't expect a killer to be dressed like everybody else, and appearances must be kept up.

At the taxi rank, he opted for one that was quite flashy and that stood out from the others. It was an old 1923 model Bernazizi with imitation cane seats, pointed rear boot, a driver with only one eye and rear bumper half hanging off. The colourful raspberry red and yellow striped satin top added an unforgettable touch to the overall effect. Aulne got in.

"Where to, boss?" asked the driver, a Ukrainian Russian, judging by his accent.

"Around the block," said Aulne.

"How many times?"

"As many times as it takes to get spotted by the cops."

"Ah, ah!" the driver thought out loud. "Right, well… let's see… since I can't possibly exceed the speed limit, what if I drive on the wrong side of the road? How would that be?"

"Fine," Aulne said.

He put the top down and sat up as straight as he could so that the blood on his clothes was there for everyone to see. This, together with the gentleman's hat he was wearing, would prove that he had something to hide.

They went around the block twelve times, and they passed a pursuit pony with police licence plates. The pony was painted steel grey and the light wicker cart that it was towing bore the coat of arms of the city. The pony sniffed the Bernazizi and neighed.

"That's good," Aulne said, "they're following us. You had better drive on the right side of the road because we don't want to risk running over some kid."

So that the pony could follow without becoming tired, the driver slowed right down. Showing no emotion, Aulne gave him directions, as they approached the well-to-do part of town.

A second pony, it too painted grey, soon joined the first. Just like the other cart, this one also had a cop inside wearing full dress uniform. The two cops conferred with each other from their respective vehicles, whispering and pointing at Aulne, while the ponies trotted side by side, lifting their legs in unison and nodding their heads like little pigeons.

On spotting a suitable building, Aulne told the driver to stop. So as to be sure the cops didn't miss seeing the blood on his clothes, he leaped lithely over the door of the taxi and landed on the footpath.

He then rushed inside the building and went through to the rear staircase.

Taking his time, he climbed up to the top floor where the maids' quarters were situated. The corridor that was laid with hexagonal-shaped terracotta tiles was playing tricks on his eyes. He could go either left or right. Going left took you out onto a small interior courtyard that separated the bathrooms and the sheet-house. That's the direction he took. Suddenly, the light from a rather high skylight beamed down in front of him. A stepladder to heaven stood beneath. Aulne could now hear the footsteps of the cops echoing on the stairs. He scrambled up onto the roof.

Once there, he took a few deep breaths, before the requisite chase. The extra air in his lungs would be beneficial for when he climbed down.

He scurried across the gently sloping mansard roof. When he reached the steeper section, he stopped and turned around, his back to the void. Then he bent down and, using his hands to steady himself, dropped into the gutter, landing on both feet.

He ran along beside the almost vertical zinc slope. Below, the small paved courtyard seemed tiny, with five garbage bins lined up in a row, an old broom that looked like a paintbrush and a box of rubbish.

He would have to climb down the wall and go through one of the bathrooms on the other side of the courtyard in the adjoining building. In order to do this, one made use of the spikes that were hammered into the wall, then grabbed onto the windowsill with both hands and pulled oneself up. A killer's work is not all fun and games. Aulne stepped out onto the rusty bars.

Up on the roof, the cops were running around in circles, making a racket with their boots, so as to comply with the local government ordinance established for the acceptable minimum noise level in the conduct of police pursuits.

II

The door was shut because Brise-Bonbon's parents had just gone out, and the little angel was home alone. When you are six years old, there is no time to be bored in an apartment in which there are glasses to break, curtains to burn, carpets to spill ink on and walls that can be smeared with fingerprints in all sorts of shades, an interesting way of putting so-called harmless colours to the Bertillon test. When there are, in addition, bathrooms, taps, things that float, and his father's razor with a beautiful sharp blade for carving corks...

Hearing cries in the courtyard beneath the bathroom window, Brise-Bonbon opened the shutters wider to take a better look. Right before his very eyes, the two large hands of a man were clinging to the stone window ledge. Aulne's head flushed from all the exertion attracted Brise-Bonbon's interest.

But Aulne had overestimated his gymnastic ability and couldn't haul himself up in one go. His hands were holding firm, so he let his arms support his body weight in order to catch his breath.

Gently, Brise-Bonbon lifted the razor he was still holding, and ran the sharp blade across the strained white knuckles of the killer's hands. The hands were too big.

Old Mimile's heart of gold was dragging Aulne towards the ground for all it was worth. His hands were bleeding. One by one, the tendons snapped like little guitar strings and as each one ruptured, a frail note rang out. On the window ledge, the tips of ten lifeless fingers remained, a few drops of blood trickling from each one. Aulne's body grazed the stone wall, bounced off the first floor cornice and landed in the old box. The only thing to do was to leave the body where it was. The rubbish collectors would take it away the next day.

IMPOTENCE

I

Every evening, a fine young man by the name of Aurèle Verkhoïansk would come into the bookshop at the Club Saint-Germain-des-Prés. He claimed to be an existentialist, which alone told you that he was suffering from a slight inferiority complex. But he hid it rather well under an embroidered cape, and whenever a pretty girl happened to pass by, he never failed to slap her on the backside and laugh along with her in that high-pitched nasal laugh of an authentic invert. Aurèle received a substantial monthly allowance from his parents that gave him the opportunity to pursue his studies almost seriously, while still keeping up appearances in Saint-Germain, where those who don't drink are looked down on. (If truth be known, it is enough to drink Perrier or something as innocuous as fruit juice to earn a reputation as a gentleman, since alcoholism is no longer considered a virtue. The main thing is to be seen drinking something, even if it is only milk.) So Aurèle would spend a lot of time drinking and had struck up a friendship with the barman, Louis Barucq, a most engaging individual whose absence on Sundays was unanimously lamented by the bookshop regulars. But Louis did need to take a break. It should also be added that Louis's sister, a famous hair artiste named Lisette, would sometimes come into the bar and that Aurèle had fallen in love with her. That is perhaps where the story you are about to read began, although Aurèle's silence over the reasons for his unusual behaviour prevents us from drawing this conclusion with any degree of certainty.

So, one evening Aurèle was sitting at the bar in the bookshop, perched on one of the tall green stools that are always broken, talking to Louis. It was eleven o'clock and, with the rush over, Louis and Aurèle were sampling a Strawberry Sutra, which is like a Brandy Alexander, only instead of crème de cacao, you use the same amount of Héritier-Guyot's Strawberry Success. So, one third fresh cream, one third brandy, one third strawberry cream liqueur; shake with ice in a strainer, pour and add pepper to taste. Since fresh cream was hard to come by, Louis used condensed milk, but even so, it was still a delicious beverage. Aurèle had just finished his sixth Strawberry Sutra and was starting to gaze longingly at his neighbour, a stunning brunette with doe-like eyes who was resolutely on to her eleventh brandy and wondering how it would all end, because her two companions were already completely hammered. Seeing the glimmer of passion in Aurèle's eye, Louis stepped in.

"Miss Miranda…"

"Yes?" the beautiful Miranda Chenillet asked.

"Allow me to introduce you to one of my best customers…"

"Come on," Aurèle interrupted. "I'm the one who invented the Strawberry Sutra and you still don't consider me to be a friend!"

"Oh! I do apologise," Louis said. "But Miss Miranda is well aware that I wouldn't introduce her to just anyone."

Aurèle was becoming increasingly disturbed by the plunging neckline of his neighbour, who straightened her shoulders and filled her blouse with no apparent effort.

"Good evening," Miranda said, turning towards Aurèle. "Are you drunk?"

This shocked Aurèle somewhat, because he thought he held his liquor well.

"Does it show?" he asked, slightly annoyed.

"Not at all," said Miranda. That's not what I meant. But they are and it's bothering me. That's what I'm talking about."

She pointed to her friends.

Louis, ever tactful, intervened. "In short, Miss Miranda is asking if you can escort her home."

"Do you have a large bed?" Aurèle asked Miranda.

In Saint-Germain-des-Prés, libertine comments of this kind shock no-one.

"Of course," Miranda answered, joining in the game. "But you know it won't do you any good because I'm completely frigid."

"Well that's lucky," Aurèle said, flashing a cheeky grin. "Because I'm impotent, totally impotent."

Louis was listening to them with a big smile on his face, and seeing that things couldn't be going any better, went off to attend to other customers.

Aurèle studied Miranda's face closely. She had a beautiful smooth complexion, a slightly turned up nose, unfashionable shoulder-length hair and a poorly defined mouth, which is probably what made it so appealing. From having seen her on her feet, he also knew that she was tall and thin. At that moment, he noticed that her slender fingers took nothing away from her otherwise unusual charm. The Strawberry Sutras had made him more daring, so he took hold of Miranda's right hand and brought it to his lips. She made no effort to remove it.

"Do you know how beautiful it is to sleep with someone without doing anything?" he said.

"Of course I do," Miranda said.

"Next to each other…" Aurèle said.

"Completely naked…" Miranda said.

"No touching…" Aurèle said.

"Yes there is… a little touching… and caressing."

"No kissing…" Aurèle said.

"On the contrary!" Miranda protested. "Lots of kissing. Without kissing, what's the point? Just because you're frigid doesn't mean you can't kiss."

"But that's all you do?" Aurèle was making sure.

"That's all," Miranda confirmed.

Aurèle took the last small piece of ice from the bottom of his glass and held it between his fingers. When they were really cold, he wiped them on his handkerchief and looked at Miranda. There was a patch of bare skin between the collar of her jacket and ear lobe. He placed his index finger there. It sent a shiver down her spine and Miranda tilted her head to the side to prevent Aurèle from withdrawing his hand, as seemed to be his intention.

"That's the kind of thing an impotent man loves to do," Aurèle said. "Just think, I could make you feel like that all over."

Miranda tensed. She looked at him. Then she drew him towards her and planted one of those unforgettable kisses on his mouth — a technicoloured, three-dimensional, fragrant, smooth, perfect kiss.

Aurèle had to admit to himself that his innermost reactions were hardly those of an impotent man, but wanting to play fair with such a respectable young lady, he forced himself to think of Paul Claudel and calmed down almost immediately. He was keeping Gide for when things became more difficult.

"Well," he said, "I think that, when it's all said and done, with you being frigid and me impotent, we're on the true path to sensual gratification."

He was not unhappy with his turn of phrase and even less so when he saw Miranda rise to her feet.

"Take me home," she said.

He stood up, helped her with her red coat and followed her to the door, which he held open.

"Goodbye Louis," Aurèle called out.

As the glass door closed, the last thing Aurèle saw was old Tony, sitting alone at his usual small table with a big smile on his face, shaking his head with great conviction, telling himself stories destined for his ears only.

II

"This is it," Miranda said.

The taxi stopped. Aurèle paid, left a generous tip and joined the brunette as she was starting to go up the stairs.

"I live on the third floor," she said.

"Excellent," Aurèle said.

"Are you sure you're really impotent?"

"I guarantee it," Aurèle said.

It was his intention to remain true to his word. And besides, Paul Claudel had never let him down.

He followed Miranda into her bedroom where it was nice and warm. She took off her coat and shoes.

"Would you like something to drink? Some coffee?"

"It keeps me awake," Aurèle said, "and sometimes it makes me a little edgy."

"Take off your clothes and get into bed," Miranda said. "I'll be back."

Aurèle untied his shoes and placed them under the bed. He removed his jacket, tie and pants, which he placed carefully over the back of a chair, and then he put on top of these his jacket, tie, shirt, socks and underpants with the extra support. He felt quite undressed. By turning his thoughts away from Miranda, he managed to remain decent despite being well-endowed.

Miranda called out from the bathroom.

"Are you in bed?"

"Yes," Aurèle said, climbing in under the covers, or between the sheets, to be more precise.

Miranda came back. She was wearing a small ribbon, which held her shiny hair in place on the back of her neck. Aurèle noticed her firm flat stomach, her cheeky breasts and, at the junction of her thighs, a stylish, well-maintained triangle of astrakhan fur.

Aurèle became worried when he felt his friend starting to play tent poles with the top sheet, and started thinking of *The Satin Slipper*.

It worked a charm and the appendage relaxed.

Miranda slid in next to Aurèle.

Unfortunately for him, it was like coming in contact with an electric current. He never dreamed the girl would have such soft skin. He let out a moan.

"Kiss me," Miranda said. "We don't risk anything by kissing and I don't want to go to sleep straight away."

Keeping his distance as best he could, Aurèle kissed her timidly on the cheek. She took his head in her two hands and planted her mouth on his. Aurèle felt a lively demon prise apart his lips and began to recite to himself the beginning of *The Tidings Brought to Mary.*

It was a soothing ice bath for his burning loins. He was daring enough to return Miranda's kisses and found that, from an intellectual point of view, this was even better. His body remained calm, as his mind was now taking full advantage of the situation.

Miranda, however, was trying to move closer and closer and Aurèle could already feel the hard points of her breasts lightly brush his chest.

Aurèle reprimanded himself severely for the intense pleasure derived from the contact and, as punishment, recalled the opening lines of *Strait is the Gate*.

This time the effect produced felt almost too brutal. Nonetheless, there was a sequence that had to be followed. He went back to Claudel, and then summoned Hervé Bazin, keeping Gide in reserve.

But when Miranda slipped one of her long thighs between Aurèle's knees, he thought he was going to die. Unforgiving, his second-in-command awoke from his slumber.

Dosing the mix of Gide and Claudel was decidedly the most difficult operation that Aurèle had yet undertaken. With great difficulty, he invoked *Nathanaël* and *Fruits of the Earth*, but could only gain temporary relief.

Miranda was whispering sweet things to him.

"It's crazy how much I love sleeping with an impotent man," she said passionately, as she delicately nibbled and kissed the poor fellow's ear.

Aurèle, overwhelmed by so much passion, would have liked to prove that he was up to the task at hand by remaining as sexless as a tree stump, but the sudden contact between Miranda's delightful body and his own reduced to nought the devastating effect of a wonderful quotation from *The Counterfeiters*. From now on, there would be no stopping his noble steed, which was adamantly heading to its rightful destination.

Miranda noticed and protested.

"Listen Aurèle, I took you to be a man of your word."

"But," Aurèle stammered, "Miranda, my friend, I swear I'm doing my best."

"For goodness sake, my dear man, take some bromide!"

Having said that, she disentangled herself and turned her back on the poor renegade. One last hope... Aurèle recalled Monsieur Bernstein's *Thirst*. Instantly put on ice, he was able to plead his cause with some semblance of good faith. He moved closer to Miranda. Unfortunately, at the very moment his thighs brushed against her two sweet globes, whose purpose in life is to allay the cruelty of sitting down, which is not a natural position for man, designed as he is to live on his back because of his elongated shape, the rebel mutinied again.

Feeling like a fool, Aurèle threw off the covers and stood up. Miranda wouldn't talk to him.

"Miranda, my dear," Aurèle said with the greatest sincerity, "I know how appalling my behaviour has been, and I swear it was not premeditated. After experiencing recent sadness, I was entitled to think that my body, like my mind, would easily resist the baseness of ordinary physical love. Tonight, after meeting you, I believed, and still do believe, that the purest form of passion is that which can unite an impotent man and a frigid woman. You are frigid; this is seemingly less creditable for a woman than for a man, who has to contend with the whims of the nervous system that are difficult for him to conceal effectively. But from now on, all of my efforts will be devoted to the pursuit of that inactivity that will make me worthy of your affection. I'm leaving. I don't want this evening, that began so virtuously, to end in the ignominy and disgusting promiscuity of the sexes. Miranda, adieu. I'm acting in the interest of our love."

He got dressed with dignity. Miranda didn't move, but as he was about to leave, she sat up in bed. The lamp on the bedside table was casting warm shadows on her dishevelled hair and on her breasts which, in her guilelessness, she never dreamed of covering, and whose rosy tips irresistibly called to be touched, as lightning rods attract electricity. Two tears rolled down her smooth cheeks and she tried to smile.

"Aurèle, my darling," she said, "I have faith in you."

Inflamed by the words of his beloved, Aurèle rushed from the room and fell flat on his face in the darkened stairwell, because it was four o'clock in the morning and the automatic timer had already been long switched off.

III

The surgeon scratched his nose. He had some reservations. In his opinion, the operation was a little out of the ordinary.

"My dear sir," he said to Aurèle, "I must admit that what you're asking me to do is hardly standard procedure. You're extremely well-endowed," he added, feeling the weight of the two objects in question, "and with those things, you could have lots of children."

"Doctor," Aurèle said simply with a sob in his voice, "my happiness is at stake."

"But can I ask you why?" the surgeon said, regretfully letting go of the items on which he was refusing to operate.

Aurèle pulled up his underpants and trousers.

"The woman I love wants to be loved by an impotent man", he said.

The doctor scratched his head.

"Oh!" he said. "Well, if I cut it all off for you, of course you won't be able to reproduce, but it won't stop you from displaying all the outward characteristics of virility, including… how should I say this… your potency."

"Oh!" Aurèle said, heartbroken.

"Listen," the doctor said, "with the right medication…"

"Nothing calms me down, doctor," Aurèle said. "Not even Bernstein."

"Oh," the doctor said, "a good elastic band, you know…"

"H'mm…" Aurèle said.

"I've got it," the doctor said. "I have the solution in my hands. Before going to see your true love, find some normal girl and work out with her for an hour."

Aurèle gave it some thought.

"Yes!" he said. "I'll do it… for Miranda!"

IV

Miranda greeted him dressed like Botticelli's Venus. The sea shell was missing and her hair was shorter, but the effect was still the same.

Aurèle had just gone three rounds on the body of a sweet friend whose animalistic nature required common lovemaking. He was exhausted.

"Darling!" Miranda said when she saw him. "So, you're ready!"

Aurèle fell into bed and snuggled up in Miranda's arms. She gave him one of those artful kisses that almost made him melt.

V

He awoke at around eleven o'clock in the morning, aching all over beyond description. He was alone in bed.

Almost immediately, he saw her emerge from the bathroom. She was covered in bruises. She rushed over to him.

"My love…" she said. "You've shown me true happiness. Come, let's get married."

"I… what?…" Aurèle said.

"I love you," Miranda said. "Do you know…" She blushed. "Do you know how many times you made love to me last night?" she went on.

Aurèle shook his head. Miranda held out two hands with both thumbs tucked in.

"One, two, three… four…" Aurèle counted.

At eight, he fainted retrospectively. Before losing consciousness, he had time to hear Miranda exclaim: "Finally, I'm realising my dream… to marry an impotent man!"

Which is not difficult when it's all said and done, because they abound in Saint-Germain-des-Prés, as this true story goes to show.

MOTHERHOOD

I

When René Lantulé fell in love with Claude Bédale, his correspondent of several weeks through the columns of the *Revue du ciné*, he was still unaware that Claude was a man. They wrote very tender letters to each other. They loved the same stars, played the same sports, both loved dance… True romance with no clouds on the horizon. Claude lived in the country and only very rarely came to Paris. He had of course sent his photo to René, but because Claude wore his hair quite long, René, misled by fashion, thought that he had been writing to a somewhat liberated girl (by provincial standards) who had had her hair cut behind her parents' back. You would have thought that the spelling of the letters might have given it away, but since spelling wasn't one of René's strong points, he didn't venture to notice anything at all. Their epistolary passion lasted a long time. Then it so happened that the matter of a small inheritance required Claude to spend some time in the capital. Overcome with joy, René took himself off to the station with a bunch of flowers. Of course, since he was expecting to see a young girl, he didn't recognise Claude, but Claude knew what he wanted and that is how, quite naturally, the two friends moved in together, a common everyday occurrence in our era of great open-mindedness. At first René experienced a few misgivings, but Claude, guided by his conscience, drew his attention to the fact that, according to *Samedi-Soir*, the only people you ever saw in Saint-Germain-des-Prés at cafés such as Le Florette, La Tante Blanche and Le Montata were homosexuals, and that a lifestyle adopted on such a large scale by a whole group of intellectual and artistic young people could not possibly exist unless it was based on something solid. René gradually became used to the idea and he and Claude soon formed one of those happy little homosexual households, honouring the French traditions of loyalty and conformity.

II

Their life passed by uneventfully. The days unfolded sweetly for René Lantulé who, pampered by Claude, kept his house in meticulous order. He had a natural talent for cooking and carried out even the most menial household chores with the utmost care. Claude had cleverly invested his inheritance in a trust company. During the day, he went to his office and steered his ship as skilfully as he could for a man who drove a Renault 4CV. Around 6 pm, he filed his papers, closed the drawers and cheerfully headed home, sweet home, where René was waiting for him, knitting. Then by the light, they made plans for the future and Claude sometimes felt his heart melt as he thought about the *Revue du ciné*, which they read each week with a semblance of gratitude.

III

However, as their relationship wore on, René's mood became more and more peculiar. On several occasions when Claude arrived home, he noticed his friend's sadness. René would mope around and hardly even bother to respond to Claude's thoughtfulness as he humorously recounted the thousand and one events that had occurred during the day. Sometimes René would even stand up, leave the room without looking at Claude and go and shut himself away in his bedroom. At first Claude didn't say anything, but one evening René seemed more upset than usual. Claude waited until his friend had gone to his room and then went and joined him a few minutes later. He found him stretched out on the bed, his head buried in the pillow. When he placed his hand on his shoulder to console him, he noticed that René was crying.

"What's wrong, precious?" Claude asked.

"Nothing," René said between two huge sobs.

"What is it, my joy, my love, my one and only?"

"I don't want to say," René whispered.

"Tell me, my darling," Claude insisted.

"I don't dare," René said.

"Come on, my beautiful blue boy, tell me..."

"I'm ashamed to say," René said very quietly.

"Come on, pet, you can tell me."

"I want to have a child," René said.

And then he started crying again in the pillow. There was great surprise written all over Claude's face. You might have even said that he was a little annoyed. He didn't answer and left the room to hide his sadness from René.

IV

Obviously, from that point on, life became difficult. Claude was downcast and blew several business deals. Their relationship remained strained and neither he nor René were as gay as before. Claude was in two minds, and then one night he came to a decision.

"Listen, my one and only," he said. "Since you can't have children, we'll adopt one."

"Oh!" René said, his face beaming with joy. "Would you do that?"

Moved by his friend's joy, Claude nodded in agreement.

"What would you like?" he asked. "A boy or a girl?"

"A little girl," René said in raptures. "They're so sweet! And besides, they love their mothers more."

"Good," Claude said. "Then you shall have a little girl."

René flew into his arms and they spent a very pleasant evening together, the first in a long time. Claude was happy and the next day he signed off on a major deal. As soon as the afternoon came around, he treated himself to a half-day off and set out to see what he could find.

He soon realised that it was not going to be easy to find a little girl to adopt. All the ones on offer were too young and he was afraid that René wouldn't be able to feed them, and a child not fed by its mother is weak, as everyone knows. Furthermore, the children of refugees had already been placed. Large numbers were cruelly killed. In short, there was a shortage. That night, he returned home empty-handed and mentioned nothing to René about his fruitless search. For a good week he pounded the pavement in the hope of a discovery. His advertisements produced no result and finally, in a police station in the fourteenth arrondissement, something came up. It was a skinny little teenager with beautiful blue eyes and bedraggled black hair.

"That's all I have," the superintendent said.

"How old is she?" Claude asked.

"Seventeen," the superintendent said. "But she only looks fourteen."

"It's not exactly what I had in mind," Claude said, "but too bad. I'll take her."

On the way back to the house, he asked her name. It was Andrée. He told her to tell René that she was fourteen. He felt somewhat disgusted at finding himself so close to a person of this sex, but when he thought of the joy she would bring to René, he pushed these thoughts aside. Anyway, as thin and as nervous as she was, Andrée looked like a boy. But even so, you could clearly see two small breasts under her blouse.

"You'd better hide those," Claude said pointing to them.

"How?" Andrée asked.

"Put a Velpeau bandage over them," Claude suggested.

"They're not very big," Andrée protested.

"That's true," Claude admitted. "You don't have a lot to hide, but all the same, it is a bit disgusting."

"Why did you adopt me then if I disgust you?" Andrée asked angrily. "No-one is forcing you!"

"Come on," Claude said. "Don't be angry. I didn't mean to say anything offensive. René will spoil you, you'll see."

"Is that my mum?" Andrée asked.

"Yes," Claude said. "And she's very sweet."

As they passed a big hairdressing salon with brightly lit windows, Claude wondered if he should take Andrée inside so she would be more presentable on arrival, but he thought it would be depriving René of the pleasure of grooming his daughter himself, in his own way.

As they approached, he once again advised Andrée not to reveal her true age.

"René wanted a little girl," he explained. "It makes no difference to you if you say you're only fourteen, and it will make her so happy."

"You really like my mum," Andrée said, full of admiration. "You only think of her."

Claude brushed aside a sweet tear of joy at the thought of those that René had shed. The small car stopped outside the building where they lived.

"This is it," he said.

"It's a beautiful house!" Andrée said admiringly.

Up until then the poor child had only ever lived in the lower end of town.

"You'll see," Claude said, somewhat moved in spite of himself by the young girl's display of emotion. "You'll be fine with us. And there's even a lift."

"Oh! Great! One that works!" Andrée said. "And I'll have dresses to wear."

"Yes," Claude said, "but don't forget… you're fourteen… and you'll play with dollies."

"Okay," Andrée said, "I'll look like an idiot… but it doesn't matter. After all, I have to make some sacrifices."

She had all the innate good sense of a child of Paris.

V

It is difficult to describe René's joy when Claude and Andrée walked through the door of the small apartment. He gave Andrée a big hug and then, jumping into Claude's arms, kissed him passionately on the mouth. Andrée watched the scene unfold with some astonishment.

"They must be that way inclined," she thought. And then out loud, she added: "Where's my mum?"

"That would be me, my dear," René said. He let go of Claude, took her in his arms and smothered her with kisses.

"Oh right," Andrée said, not too surprised. "Is there any pork?"

"Anything you want my darling, my joy, my one and only," René said.

Claude, slightly put out by the display of affection René was showering on his new daughter, tried to make light of things to hide his pain.

"Pork?" he said. "Haven't you had enough pig?"

He was making an amusing reference to the police station. Andrée laughed and explained it to René, who in turn laughed when he learned that "pig" was another name for the police. Claude, somewhat heavy-hearted, felt nevertheless a certain melancholic joy on seeing René's beaming face.

VI

The three of them slipped easily into their new way of life. It was decided that Andrée would sleep in René's room, separate from Claude's, because it was more appropriate. Now when Claude came home from the office, he would find René and his daughter always busily engaged in some new activity. Andrée adored her adopted mother, and with the shyness you would expect from a young girl her age, called him "Auntie René". As for René, when it came to the subject of Andrée, he never tired of singing her praises. It would be fair to say that with Claude and René's love and affection, Andrée had developed into a beautiful young lady, full-figured with a keen eye and quick wit. Claude hadn't been able to hide the true age of their protégée for very long, but far from upsetting René, this revelation seemed to put him more at ease. Every day there would be new gifts — nail polish, a hat, a fine pair of shoes, nylon stockings. Andrée's life had become one long party. Whenever she went shopping on René's arm in the stylish boutiques of the Rue Royale and the Rue du Faubourg Saint-Honoré, rare were the passers-by who didn't turn around to look at her, drawn by her grace and the fire in her eye. Her education, neglected for so long, had been completed in the most appropriate fashion, and interacting with her two friends had polished her slightly uncouth manner of speaking. What's more, she loved the cinema, and this formed another special bond between these three affectionate human beings.

Now that he knew the real age of his daughter, René no longer hesitated to take her along to the great fashion designers, in particular Pierre Balpogne, whom he had known at the Club Saint-Germain-des-Pieds. While attending these fitting sessions, René discovered his penchant for haute couture. Several times, under the watchful eye of Balpogne, he himself draped the precious material over the curved hips of his adopted daughter, who seemed to take great pleasure in seeing herself adorned like an idol, as she stood in a short lace slip surrounded by the assistants. Balpogne encouraged René as much as possible, and René felt strongly drawn to this charming line of work to which he was naturally predestined. At home in the evening, they would entertain Claude with stories of their sessions with Balpogne. René managed to obtain some off-cuts and several good handbooks and often, instead of going out, he would undress Andrée in his room and have her try on his new creations. In the beginning, Andrée appeared very enthusiastic, but over time, she became almost shy. Now when René carefully removed her dress and undergarments to arrange a heavy piece of satin or watered silk on her, she would lower her head, cover her breasts with her hands and modestly squeeze her thighs together. It is true that René now derived great pleasure in fitting these dresses, and that his hands lingered as they smoothed out the creases in the material covering the shapely contours of his adopted daughter's body. One fine day, unable to hold back any longer, he kissed her on the mouth in such a way that the young girl became flustered, and recalling who knows what memories from her sad past, returned the kiss so passionately, that René almost passed out. No longer able to contain themselves, they lost control as their hands became bolder, so much so that half an hour later they emerged from a state of euphoria, arms (and legs) entwined, the dark rings under Andrée's eyes testimony to the pleasure she had experienced. As for René, he only wanted one thing — to do it all again, and he clearly demonstrated this to her in the two hours that followed.

After this, it was going to be difficult to continue with their previous way of life. René now went and joined Claude more and more rarely in the evenings, reserving all of his fervour for Andrée. The living arrangements and the fact that she was sleeping in the same room favoured the development of their reprehensible relationship. Meanwhile, René was now working with Balpogne who, still believing him to be batting for his team, was divulging the secrets of the industry and paying him on a regular basis. Andrée, for her part, had been taken on as a model with Diargent, a famous fashion designer, and René was taking full advantage of the information she was gathering daily.

René was unable to hide for very long from Claude the complete and utter transformation that had taken place in him. Claude suffered greatly from this incomprehensible situation and naturally neither his pleas nor his threats could make René go back on his decision to live on the earnings from his work with Andrée. They went their separate ways in the spring of the following year. One shocking thing came out of all of this. The action brought against René by Claude in the matter of deserting the family home was pronounced in favour of René who was, furthermore, granted full custody of the child. Only in France, country of declining moral standards, can such injustices be played out in the public arena.

A FUNNY OLD GAME

Trounaille was leaning on the bar in the Klub Sane-Germaine drinking his latest concoction, an authentic Slow-Burn which, as everyone knows, is made up of six parts vodka to one part Cointreau and one of crème de cacao — a tonic mixture, the veritable mother's milk of Russia. It also revealed his dislike for Anglo-Saxon gin, that diabolical but widely used base of so many infamous mixed drinks, which are the scourge of Western democracies. In actual fact, it was mainly because gin made him feel sick that he had switched to vodka, a product not too dissimilar to rubbing alcohol, whose wholesome effects and medicinal value have been recognised by government agencies.

In came his good friend Folubert Sansonnet, who had just come back from a tour. Folubert, a very talented saxofornist, had just spent several weeks using the sweet sound of his instrument to charm the Teuton hordes, a people deprived for years of the denazifying effect of bebop.

"Hello, Trounaille," Folubert said.

"Hello, Folubert," Trounaille said.

They both had broad grins on their faces because they were happy to see each other.

"What are you drinking?" Folubert asked.

"Something I invented," Trounaille said, rather pleased with himself.

"Is it good?" Folubert asked.

"Try it!"

So Folubert tried it, and Louis the barman, who was growing his moustache, had to make two more.

Meanwhile, Folubert cast a searching glance over the crowd.

"There are no women!" he said indignantly.

And in fact, apart from the few who were obviously paid to be there, there were hardly any members of the female sex.

"Why do you think I'm drinking?" Trounaille asked sarcastically.

"Oh! This is no good," Folubert said. "I've had a lean spell lately, and now it's time to lash out."

"Drink up," Trounaille said, "and let's see what we can find."

They finished their drinks and set off on their quest.

* * *

In Rue Saint-Benoît, the air was fresh and invigorating.

"It's a good thing you came along when you did," Trounaille said. "I was so bored!"

"Tonight's our lucky night. You'll see," Folubert assured him. "Let's start at the Vieux-Co."

They took the Rue de Rennes and turned right towards the Vieux-Co. The man on the door and the brunette in the cloakroom both recognised them, and smiled.

In Luter's cellar there was a crowd, but hardly any members of the female sex.

"This is no good," Folubert said after a few minutes.

"You know, they wait until the band has finished playing and then go off with the musicians," Trounaille informed him. "With Luter's boys, that's the rule."

"Oh!" Folubert said. "That's disgusting."

"Drink up," Trounaille said. "Let's go and see what we can find somewhere else."

Which is what they did.

* * *

It's only a short step from the Vieux-Colombier to the Rose Rouge. They managed to take it and went downstairs.

Inside, everything was dark, and the Frères Jacques were singing *Les Nombrils*. Folubert straight away spotted a blonde with short hair sitting close to the bar. He started to give her the come-on look, and was sorry he wasn't a cat with eyes that glowed in the dark.

However, after *Les Nombrils*, the Frères launched into *Barbara*, a heart-rending piece that seemed to send shivers through the blonde. So Folubert and Trounaille started shivering too, and when the line "Barbara, war is a load of bullshit" came around, they loudly voiced their approval.

Thereupon, they were discreetly ejected from the premises, because the crowd had actually come to listen to the Frères Jacques.

* * *

Moving into a different part of town, they went all the way to Caroll's Bar on foot, because taxis are expensive and because they also had a sneaking suspicion that this would not be their final port of call.

They went downstairs. The young lady in the cloakroom drew Trounaille's attention to his regrettable lack of a tie, to which he replied that this didn't seem the place to be wearing a knot around your neck. This innocent remark put them both back in good spirits.

The first face they saw was that of the girl from the Rose Rouge.

Folubert recognised her, turned pale, and said to Trounaille: "The bitch."

She was dancing with another girl and as soon as she saw Folubert, she deliberately rubbed up against her partner.

"Let's go," Trounaille said.

* * *

They went to the Lido, the Night-Club, the Bœuf sur le toit and the Club de Paris. They went back to the Saint-Yves, dropped into the Tabou, and headed back up towards Montmartre. They went into the Tabarin, and the Florence, into so many places that their eyes began to fail them. Finally, at six o'clock in the morning, two lovely ladies accepted their advances.

* * *

It was eleven o'clock. Folubert came out of his room and knocked on Trounaille's door. He was still asleep.

"So?" Folubert said.

"Well," grumbled Trounaille, who was sporting a huge shiner.

Folubert was wearing his on the other eye.

"Hey, I fell asleep," he said.

"Me too," Trounaille said. "And she didn't like it."

"Neither did mine," Folubert said.

"Women don't understand anything about men," Trounaille concluded.

And off they went to buy two pieces of steak from the butcher. The horse butcher.

THE MOTIVE

Odon du Mouillet, certified Justice of the Peace, was carefully cleaning the inside of his ear with the tip of a retractable pen, an uncouth old habit acquired years ago when he was wearing out the seat of his pants on the park benches of the Cours la Reine gardens.

"How many divorces this morning?" he asked his assistant, Léonce Tiercelin, a tall young man fifty-four years old.

"Only nineteen," Léonce replied.

"Good, good, good, good, good, good, good," the judge said, satisfied.

He would now have more time than usual to finish, refine, shine and polish his closing argument that he hoped would convince lost sheep to return to the path of married life when they presented themselves before him for a possible reconciliation.

So with his feet up and his head in his hands, he started to think, while Léonce Tiercelin went about rearranging the office in order to impress the impending arrivals. Léonce thus activated the small hydraulic jacks housed in the legs of the judicial table and armchair, raising everything by thirty centimetres. He placed artificial flowers in a vase to make the room look cosy, replaced the light globe in the ceiling with a straight-beam balance to represent Justice, and draped himself in a long length of bright red curtain material, as if it were a Roman toga. In general, people appeared responsive to this display of pomp and pageantry, and left the office either patched up or passed out. Judge Odon du Mouillet had a higher success rate than his other five colleagues put together. He put it down to his eloquent way with words, but Léonce thought that his own preparations might also have had something to do with it.

After the judge had sufficiently cogitated, he scratched his backside with great dexterity and said to Léonce, "Guard, bring in the applicants."

Léonce strode ceremoniously to the door and opened it. Jean Biquet and his wife (née Zizine Poivre) entered.

"Take a seat!" said Léonce in a mechanic fashion — that is, with a vast, sonorous and oily voice.

Jean Biquet sat on the right and Zizine Poivre on the left. Jean Biquet was blonde, weak, pale and insipid, yet dignified. Zizine Poivre, a passionate, busty brunette, gave all the indications of having a fiery personality.

At first, Odon du Mouillet was not surprised when he saw this mismatched couple, but then, remembering the terms of the divorce petition, he raised his eyebrows, for it was in fact Zizine Poivre who was asking for the divorce and, according to the file, it was because her husband was cheating on her.

"Sir," Odon said, "the first thing I have to say is that I'm surprised you could give up this lady to pursue the person whose name appears on the file, a person described by my sources as being rather plain."

"That's none of your business," Jean Biquet said.

"This filthy swine has been cheating on me, and with a complete idiot," Zizine proclaimed emotionally.

Odon du Mouillet continued.

"Madam, I must say in all honesty that I'm willing to find grounds in your filing for divorce. However, perhaps it's still not too late. An attempt to understand each other's position would surely help to reconcile your differences."

Zizine looked at Jean hopefully and licked her lips.

"My little Jeannot," she whispered in a husky voice.

Jean Biquet shuddered, as did the judge.

"Madam," he said, "the question I have to ask you is very personal. Was your husband cheating on you because you… um… you refused him your favours?"

"Oh, no!" Jean protested. "In fact, that's the reason why…"

He stopped mid-sentence.

"Please continue, sir," Odon insisted. "I'm sorry, but your case seems so unusual that I can't help thinking that it will be highly instructive."

"To put it simply, judge," Zizine interrupted, "I can't get enough."

"Not enough! Oh, please!" Jean Biquet sighed.

Dumbfounded, Léonce Tiercelin blew his nose, which made everyone jump.

"In short, sir, if I follow you correctly," Odon du Mouillet said, "you cheated on Madam because she… um… was demanding more love than you were able to provide."

"Exactly!" the husband and wife both answered together.

"And you didn't… um… do anything with the other one?" the judge continued, throwing caution to the wind.

"No way!" Zizine squealed, earnestly.

Completely at a loss, the judge looked to Léonce.

"What am I to do?" he said. "I don't understand. Why are you cheating on her then?"

"But it's really quite simple, your honour," Jean Biquet explained in a calm and steady voice. "The reason I have to get a divorce is that I can't live without women."

DANGER FROM THE CLASSICS

The electronic timer on the clock buzzed twice. I jumped, and tried to tear myself from the whirlwind of images that were spinning around in my head. With some surprise, I noticed that my heart was starting to beat a little faster as well. Blushing, I quickly closed my book. It was *You and Me*, a dusty old volume written prior to the last two wars, which I had hesitated to pick up until now, because I was aware of the bold realism of the theme. It was then I noticed that the cause of my distress lay as much in the time and date as in my book. Today was Friday 27 April 1982 and as usual, I was waiting for my intern, Florence Lorre.

The realisation hit me harder than I care to admit. I consider myself to be open-minded, but the man should not be the first one smitten; we need to maintain the dignity that befits our sex at all times. Nevertheless, after the initial shock, I began thinking, and found some justification for my behaviour.

There is a preconceived idea about scientists, and about women scientists in particular, that they are severe-looking and very unattractive. Certainly, women, more so than men, have a talent for research. And in certain professions where physical appearance is part of the selection criteria, in acting for example, there is a fairly large number of women who look like goddesses. However, if you take the problem one step further, you soon notice that a pretty mathematician is not, on the whole, harder to find than an intelligent actress, even though there are more female mathematicians than actresses. In any case, when it came time to draw lots for the allocation of interns, luck was on my side. Although not a single bad thought had crossed my mind to that point, I had already recognised, quite objectively of course, that my intern had an obvious charm. And therein lies the reason for my current state of confusion.

Right on time again. She arrived as usual, at five past two.

"You look awfully smart," I said, a little surprised at my own audacity.

She was wearing a tight-fitting pair of overalls made from shimmering pale green material, very simple, but they must have come from a factory that produced luxury lines.

"Do you like it, Bob?"

"I like it a lot."

I am not one of those people who find colour out of place, not even when it comes to something as traditional as women's laboratory overalls, and at the risk of causing a scandal, I have to admit that even a woman wearing a skirt doesn't shock me.

"I'm pleased about that," Florence answered mockingly.

Although I am ten years older, Florence assures me that we look the same age. For this reason, our relationship is a little different from most normal student-teacher relationships. She treats me as a friend, and that bothers me a little. Of course, I could always shave off my beard and cut my hair to look like an old scholar from the 1940s, but she insists that it would make me look effeminate and would do nothing to earn her respect.

"And how is your project coming along?" she asked.

She was referring to a rather tricky electronics problem that the Central Bureau had entrusted to me, and which I had only just resolved that very morning, much to my great satisfaction.

"It's finished," I said.

"Bravo! Does it work?"

"I'll know tomorrow," I said. "Friday afternoons are set aside for your education."

She hesitated and lowered her eyes. Nothing makes me feel more uncomfortable than a bashful woman, and she knew it.

"Bob… I want to ask you something."

I was feeling very ill at ease. A woman really must avoid this sort of charming affectation around a man.

She continued, "Explain to me what you're working on."

It was my turn to hesitate.

"Listen, Florence… this work is highly confidential…"

She placed her hand on my arm.

"Bob… even the cleaners in the lab know as much about all these secrets as… er… Antares' best spy."

"Ah, now that would surprise me," I said, feeling depressed.

For weeks, the radio had been bombarding us with songs from *The Grand Duchess of Antares*, the internationally acclaimed operetta by Francis Lopez. I hate all that popular music. I only like the classics, like Schoenberg, Duke Ellington or Vincent Scotto.

"Bob! Please explain it to me. I want to know what you're doing…"

Another interruption.

"What now, Florence?" I said.

"Bob, I like you… a lot. So you have to tell me what you're working on. I want to help."

So there you have it. For years you read about it in novels, the description of the emotions you feel when you hear your first declaration of love. And it was finally happening to me. To me! And it was more disturbing, more delightful, than anything I had ever imagined. I looked at Florence, with her bright eyes, and red hair cut into a crew-cut that was all the rage in that year of '82. I think that there is no doubt she could have taken me in her arms then and there without a struggle on my part. And to think I used to laugh at love stories! My heart was pounding and I felt my hands shake. I had a lump in my throat.

"Florence… you shouldn't say things like that to a man. Let's talk about something else."

She came up to me, and before I could do anything, she threw her arms around me and gave me a kiss. I felt the ground give way beneath my feet, and I found myself sitting on a chair. At the same time, I was experiencing a state of euphoria that was as indescribable as it was unexpected. I blushed at my own depravity and noticed, with renewed astonishment, that Florence was on my knee. That's when the cat let go of my tongue.

"Florence, this isn't right. Stand up. If someone were to come in… my reputation would be ruined. Stand up."

"Will you show me your experiments?"

"I… Oh!…"

I had to give in.

"I'll explain everything to you. Everything. But stand up."

"I always knew that you were a nice man," she said as she stood up.

"All the same," I said, "you've taken advantage of the situation. Admit it."

My voice was trembling. She patted me affectionately on the shoulder.

"Come on, Bob, dear. Don't be so old-fashioned."

I didn't waste any time launching into the technical details.

"Do you remember the first electronic brains?" I asked.

"The ones from 1950?"

"Slightly earlier," I corrected. "They were calculating machines. Quite clever, actually. You remember that, very quickly, they were fitted with special tubes which allowed them to store various pieces of information that could be drawn on when needed? Memory tubes?"

"You learn that in primary school," Florence said.

"Do you remember that this type of machine was being perfected up until around 1964, when Rossler discovered that a real human brain, properly set up in a nutrient bath, could, under certain conditions, accomplish the same tasks taking up much less space?"

"And I also know that in '68 this process was, in turn, replaced by Brenn and Renaud's super-circuit," Florence said.

"Fine," I answered. "Gradually, these various devices were fitted and tested with all the different types of "effectors" that were available, the effectors themselves having been derived from the thousand and one gadgets developed by man over time, to make up the class of machines we call robots. All these machines have one thing in common. Can you tell me what it is?"

The teacher in me couldn't help himself.

"You have lovely eyes," Florence answered. "They're a greeny-yellow colour, with a kind of star on the iris…"

I stepped back.

"Florence! Are you listening to me?"

"I'm listening very carefully. The one thing all of these machines have in common is that they only act on the data provided to their internal operating systems by the users. A machine that is not given a specific problem to solve remains incapable of any initiative."

"And why hasn't anyone tried to provide them with awareness and reason? Because it was noted that, with only a few elementary reflex functions, their behaviour was worse than that of the old scientists. Go to any old shop and buy a small electronic toy tortoise, and you'll soon see what the first electro-reflex machines were like: irritable, unpredictable… In short, endowed with a personality. We rather quickly lost interest in these kinds of automatons, which were created solely to provide a simple illustration of certain mental processes, but were far too difficult to live with."

"Dear old Bob," Florence said. "I love hearing you talk. Do you know how boring you are? I learned all that in the eleventh grade."

"And you're insufferable," I said seriously.

She was looking at me. I do believe she was making fun of me. I am ashamed to say it, but I would have liked her to kiss me again. I took up where I left off, very quickly, to hide my confusion.

"We're striving increasingly to introduce into these machines sustainable reflex circuits capable of interacting with a wide range of effectors. But we haven't yet tried to supply them with a broad-based education. To tell the truth, up till now there's been no point. But it so happens that the work the Central Bureau has asked me to do should allow the machine to retain a number of higher-level concepts in its memory bank. In fact, the model you see here is intended to assimilate the entire collection of knowledge contained in the sixteen volumes of the 1978 *Larousse Encyclopaedia*. Its purpose is almost purely intellectual, and it's fitted with simple effectors to allow it to move around by itself and to take hold of objects for identification and analysis, if need be."

"And what will be done with it?"

"It's an administrative device, Florence. The Flor-Fiña ambassador, who's taking up his post in Paris next month following the Mexico City Convention, is going to use it for advice on matters of protocol. Each time there's a request for information on his part, the machine will provide the ambassador with the kind of response that someone with an extensive knowledge of French culture would give. In each instance, it will tell him the steps to follow, and explain to him the nature of the problem and how to conduct himself, whether it be on the occasion of the naming of a new polymegatron or dinner with the Emperor of Eurasia. Since French has been adopted by world decree as the most prestigious language of diplomacy, everyone wants to be able to boast that they're highly cultivated. And so this machine will be invaluable to an ambassador who doesn't have time to educate himself."

"So!" Florence said. "You're going to cram sixteen fat volumes of the *Larousse* into that poor little machine! You're a sadist."

"It has to be done!" I said. "It has to absorb everything. If we only feed it bits and pieces of information, it'll more than likely acquire a personality like one of those unresponsive old tortoises. And what will that personality be like? Impossible to know in advance. The only chance it has of being well balanced is if it knows *everything*. That's the only way it can remain objective and impartial."

"But it can't know *everything*," Florence said.

"If it knows something *about* everything, in equal proportions, that will be enough," I explained. "The *Larousse* is reasonably objective. It's a fairly good example of a piece of work written without emotion. According to my reckoning, we should end up with a machine that's polite, sensible and well-behaved."

"That's wonderful," Florence said.

It seemed like she was making fun of me. Obviously, some of my colleagues solve more complex problems, but nevertheless, I had drawn some good conclusions from some rather imperfect data, and I think that deserved something better than the trite, "that's wonderful". Women don't seem to understand just how disheartening and thankless these mundane tasks can be.

"How does it work?" she asked.

"Oh, a run-of-the-mill system," I said, feeling a little dejected. "A basic lectoscope. All you do is insert the book into the tube and the apparatus reads and records everything. There's nothing very fancy about it. Naturally, once the material has been assimilated, the lectoscope will be dismantled."

"Start it up, Bob! Please!"

"I'd really like to show you how it works," I said, "but I don't have my volumes of the *Larousse*. They arrive tomorrow night. I can't get it to learn anything beforehand because that will upset its balance."

I went over to the machine and plugged it in. Small red, green and blue lights flashed randomly on the control panel. A gentle humming sound was coming from the electrical supply. Despite everything, I felt rather pleased with myself.

"The book goes in there," I said. "You push this lever and that's all there is to it. Florence! What are you doing? Oh no…"

I tried to switch it off but Florence held me back.

"I'm just trying it out, Bob. We can always delete it…"

"Florence! You're impossible! You can't delete it!"

She had thrown my copy of *You and Me* into the tube and had pulled the lever. I could now hear the rapid clicking of the lectoscope as it scanned the pages. In fifteen seconds it was done. The book came out, assimilated, digested and intact.

Florence was watching with interest. Suddenly she jumped. The speaker started cooing gently, almost tenderly:

I need to explain, convey, confess
That we can only feel what we can express…

"Bob! What's happening?"

"Oh my God," I said, exasperated. "It doesn't know anything else… It's now going to recite Géraldy non-stop."

"But Bob, why is it talking to itself?"

"All lovers talk to themselves!"

"What if I were to ask it something?"

"Oh no!" I said. "Not that. Leave it alone. You've already done enough damage!"

"What a grouch you are!"

The machine was making a soothing humming sound. It made a noise as if to clear its throat.

"Machine," Florence said, "how do you feel?"

This time it was an impassioned declaration that came from the machine.

Oh! I love you! I love you!
Do you hear? I'm crazy about you… Crazy!…

"Oh!" Florence said. "What a cheek!"

"It was like that back then," I said. "Men spoke to women first and I can assure you, young Florence, that they weren't afraid to do so…"

"Florence!" the machine said, deep in thought. "Her name is Florence!"

"That's not in Géraldy!" Florence protested.

"So, you haven't understood a single word I've said," I observed somewhat annoyed. "I haven't built a device that simply reproduces sounds. I'm telling you that inside there are lots of new reflex circuits and a complete supply of phonetics which allow it to formulate adequate responses to the sounds it accumulates… The difficult thing was to maintain its balance, and you've just ruined that by filling it with passion. It's like giving a piece of steak to a two-year-old child. This machine *is* still a child… and you've just fed it bear meat…"

"I'm old enough to take care of Florence," the machine remarked drily.

"It can hear!" Florence said.

"Of course it can hear!"

I was becoming more and more exasperated.

"It can hear. It can see. It can speak..."

"And I can also move around!" the machine said. "But kissing? I can see what it is, but I don't know how I'm supposed to do it," it continued with a pensive air.

"You won't be doing anything," I said. "I'm going to turn you off, and tomorrow I'm going to change your tubes and we'll start all over again."

"You, with that awful beard," the machine said. "You don't interest me. And you'll leave my switch alone."

"His beard is lovely," Florence said. "You're very rude."

"Maybe so," the machine said with a lecherous laugh that made my hair stand on end, "but in matters of love, I know a thing or two... Florence, come closer..."

For the things to you I have to say
Are things, you see, that can be said each day
With words, looks, deeds and smiles...

"Try to lighten up a little," I said mockingly.

"I *am* able to laugh!" the machine said.

It repeated its obscene laugh.

"In any case," I said furiously, "you should stop reciting Géraldy parrot-fashion."

"I'm not reciting anything parrot-fashion!" the machine said. "And the proof is that I can call you a fool, an idiot, a blockhead, a nag, a moron, a bumpkin, a loser, a deadbeat, a twit, a nutter..."

"Okay! That's enough!" I objected.

"Anyway, if I recite Géraldy," the machine continued, "it's because nobody speaks the language of love any better. And besides, I like it. When *you* can talk to women the way this guy can, let me know. Until then, stay out of it. It's Florence I'm talking to."

"Be nice," Florence said to the machine. "I like nice people."

"You can tell me to be gentlemanly," the machine pointed out, "because I'm feeling rather masculine. Be quiet and listen."

The things that you would say, my dear,
Are things I already know.
Come close. Draw near!
Allow me to undo your blouse.
Quickly now, let us begin.
To feel this way is not a sin.
Take off your clothes. Do not hide,
Lie down here, right by my side.
Remove your skirt do not be shy,
The time to be as one is nigh.

"Oh, will you be quiet!" I protested, outraged.

"Bob!" Florence said. "Is that what you've been reading? Oh dear!"

"I'm going to disconnect it," I said. "I can't bear to hear it speak to you that way. There are some things you read that you just don't repeat."

The machine became silent. And then a growling sound came from deep within.

"Don't touch my switch!"

I strode up to it and, without a word of warning, the machine launched itself at me. I threw myself to the side at the last minute but its steel housing struck my shoulder. Its wicked voice continued:

"So, you're in love with Florence, eh?"

I had taken up refuge behind the metal desk and was rubbing my shoulder.

"Run, Florence," I said. "Go on. Get out of here."

"Bob! I don't want to leave you alone… It… He … is going to hurt you."

"It's okay. It's okay," I said. "Get out quickly."

"She'll leave when I tell her to!" the machine said.

It made a movement towards Florence.

"Run, Florence," I said again. "Hurry."

"I'm afraid, Bob," Florence said.

In two bounds she had joined me behind the desk.

"I want to stay with you."

"You won't come to any harm," the machine said. "It's the bearded one who's going to get it. Oh, so you're jealous! So you want to turn me off!"

"I don't want anything to do with you!" Florence said. "You disgust me."

The machine backed up slowly, preparing to launch itself. Suddenly it charged at me with the full force of its engines. Florence screamed.

"Bob! Bob! I'm scared!"

Pulling her into my arms, I got nimbly onto the desk. The machine collided full on with the desk, which sent it careering towards the wall, which it struck with irresistible force. The room shook and a lump of plaster fell from the ceiling. If we had stayed between the wall and the desk, we would have been cut in two.

"It's lucky I didn't fit more powerful effectors," I said under my breath. "Stay here."

I sat Florence on the desk. She was more or less out of harm's way. I stood up.

"Bob, what are you going to do?"

"I mustn't say it out loud," I answered.

"You don't need to," the machine said. "I dare you again to try to flick my switch."

I watched it back up, and waited.

"Chicken!" I taunted.

The machine growled furiously.

"Oh yeah? We'll see."

It charged towards the desk, which is what I had been hoping for. Just as it was about to demolish that piece of furniture to get to me, I leaped forward and landed on top of it. With my left hand, I grabbed hold of the feeder cables sticking out of the top and tried to reach the contact switch with the other. I received a violent blow to the back of the skull. The machine, using the lever of the lectoscope against me as a weapon, was trying to beat my brains out. I groaned with pain as I tried to wrench the lever back. The machine screamed. But before I could tighten my grip, it began to shake itself like an enraged bull and I shot off the top. I collapsed in a heap on the ground. I felt a sharp pain in my leg and, through blurry eyes, I saw the machine backing up, getting ready to finish me off. And then there was darkness.

When I regained consciousness, I was stretched out, eyes closed, my head resting on Florence's lap. I was experiencing a range of complex sensations. My leg was hurting but something very soft was pressing against my lips and an extraordinary feeling swept through me. The first thing I saw was Florence's eyes two centimetres from mine. She was kissing me and I passed out a second time. This time, she slapped me and I immediately came to.

"You saved me, Florence..."

"Bob," she said, "will you marry me?"

"It wasn't my place to propose to you, Florence darling," I answered blushing. "But I accept with pleasure."

"I managed to turn it off," she said. "No-one will hear us now. Bob... would you like to... I don't dare ask..."

She had lost her confidence. The light on the ceiling in the laboratory was hurting my eyes.

"Florence, my angel, speak to me..."

"Bob... recite some Géraldy for me..."

I felt the blood flow more quickly through my veins. I took her pretty, close-cropped head between my hands and boldly went in search of her lips.

"*Dim the lights...*" I whispered.

THE WEREWOLF

In the Fausses-Reposes Woods at the bottom of the Picardy hill, there lived a very handsome adult wolf with a black coat and big red eyes. His name was Denis, and his favourite pastime was watching the cars from Ville-d'Avray accelerate as they approached the glistening climb on which, after rain, shimmering puddles sometimes formed, reflecting the olive green of the tall trees that lined the road. On summer evenings he also liked to roam the forest in order to catch impatient lovers in the act of struggling with the complicated elastic clasps that, unfortunately, are fitted to most undergarments these days. He philosophically observed the outcome of these occasionally successful attempts and modestly withdrew, shaking his head whenever it appeared that a willing victim, as you say, got laid. Descended from a long line of civilised wolves, Denis lived on grass and blue hyacinths, pepped up in autumn with a few select mushrooms, and in winter, much to his disgust, with bottles of milk taken from the large yellow truck that belonged to the Co-operative. He loathed milk because it tasted of animal, and from November to February he cursed the inclemency of a season that forced his stomach to endure such unpleasant things.

Denis was on good terms with his neighbours because, due to his discreet nature, they were unaware that he existed. He lived in a small cave that had been dug out many years earlier by a disillusioned gold prospector. The miner, having known bad luck all of his life, was sure he was never going to strike it rich and find the pile of gold nuggets that Louis Boussenard had described as a "basket of oranges". Towards the end, he had decided he might as well carry out his excavations, which were as frenetic as they were futile, in a warmer climate. Denis had created a comfortable retreat for himself in the cave, furnishing it over the years with hubcaps, nuts and other car parts that he had collected from the road where accidents frequently occurred. Being passionate about mechanics, he loved to survey his spoils, and dreamed of the workshop that one day he would own. Four light alloy connecting rods supported the car boot lid that served as a table. The bed was made from leather seats from an old Amilcar that had had a brief encounter with a big sturdy plane tree, and two tyres formed gorgeous picture frames for the portraits of dearly beloved parents. Everything blended in tastefully with the more ordinary pieces previously collected by the miner.

One beautiful August evening, Denis was out on his usual after-dinner stroll. The light of the full moon was filtering through the leaves, creating a lacework pattern of shadows, and under the bright moonlight, Denis's eyes had assumed the mellow ruby red colour of the wine from Arbois. Denis was approaching an oak tree, the usual end to his walk, when fate intervened and he stumbled upon the Magus of Siam, whose real name was Étienne Pample, and young Lisette Cachou, the dark-haired waitress from the Gronœil Restaurant, who had been led to Fausses-Reposes by the magus under false pretences. The Magus of Siam had spent hours trying to tear apart the brand new "Obsession" girdle that Lisette was wearing for the first time, and it was to that particular circumstance that Denis owed this late encounter.

Unfortunately for Denis, his arrival turned out to be badly timed. It was right on the stroke of midnight and the Magus of Siam was on edge. All around there abounded forgive-me-nots, lycopus bugleweed and white lupins, which in recent years have become the mandatory accompaniments to lycanthropy, or rather anthropolicy, that we are about to read. Enraged by Denis's arrival — although, discreet as ever, Denis was already withdrawing, mumbling an excuse — the Magus of Siam, disappointed with Lisette, and with a surplus of energy demanding to be released one way or another, threw himself on the innocent creature and savagely bit him below the shoulder blade. With a yelp of anguish, Denis took off like a shot. Once back home, he was overcome with an unusual feeling of fatigue, and fell into a deep sleep broken by troubled dreams.

Over time he forgot the incident, and things returned to the way they were, with some days being the same and others different. Autumn was approaching, as were the September tides, which have the funny effect of turning the leaves on the trees red. Denis stuffed himself with field mushrooms and boletus, and occasionally plucked a scarcely visible peziza off a piece of bark, but he avoided the indigestible ox-tongue like the plague. The woods were now emptying of walkers more quickly in the evening, and Denis was going to bed earlier. However, it seemed that this hardly made him feel any less tired and, after nights troubled by nightmares, he would wake up with a heavy head and aching limbs. He even lost his passion for mechanics, and at midday you would sometimes catch him daydreaming, clutching in his limp paw the rag with which he was to polish a piece of brass coated in verdigris. His sleep was becoming increasingly disturbed and he was surprised not to have found out why.

On the night of the next full moon, he emerged with a start from his slumber, gripped with fever, shivering, overcome by an intense sensation of cold. Rubbing his eyes, he was surprised at how strange he felt, and he looked around for a light. He had soon hooked up the superb headlight that he had inherited from a wayward Mercedes a few months earlier, and the dazzling light from the device lit up all the nooks and crannies of his cave. He made his way unsteadily to the rear-view mirror mounted above the washstand. He was amazed to find himself standing upright on his back legs, but he was even more surprised when his eyes fell upon his reflection in the small round mirror. A strange face stared back at him — whitish, devoid of hair, with only two beautiful ruby red eyes to remind him of his former appearance. Letting out an inarticulate cry, he looked at his body, and understood the reason for this icy cold feeling that gripped him all over. His splendid black coat had disappeared, and before his eyes stood the deformed body of one of those men whose awkwardness he usually ridiculed as they attempted to make love.

Time was of the essence. Denis sprang to the car-boot crammed with articles of discarded clothing gathered at random from accident scenes. Instinctively, he selected an elegant grey suit with white stripes, and chose a plain rosewood-tinged shirt and burgundy tie to go with it. As soon as he had put on these clothes, he felt better and his teeth stopped chattering. He was surprised at how he had managed to maintain his balance. It was then that his troubled gaze fell upon the small pile of black fur scattered around his bed, and he lamented his lost looks.

Nevertheless, through sheer determination, he regained his composure and tried to size up the situation. His books had taught him many things and the matter seemed clear. The Magus of Siam was a werewolf and, conversely, he, Denis, having been bitten by the beast, had just turned into a man.

At first he was filled with great terror at the thought of having to live in an unfamiliar world. Living as a man amongst men, what dangers would he not face! He recalled the futile struggles that the Picardy hill drivers were involved in day and night, and this provided him with a small insight into the atrocious existence that, whether he liked it or not, he would have to adapt to. Then he thought it over. In all likelihood, and if his information was correct, the transformation would probably not last long. So why not take advantage of the situation and venture into the town? It must be admitted that, at that moment, certain scenes he had glimpsed in the woods sprang to mind without making him feel the same way about them as he had before. He found himself licking his lips and noticed that, despite all the other changes, his tongue had remained just as pointy as before. He went over to the rear-view mirror and took a closer look at himself. His features didn't displease him as much as he had feared. When he opened his mouth, he saw that his palate had retained its beautiful black colour. Also, he still had control of his ears, that were perhaps a touch too long and hairy. In the small spherical mirror, he contemplated his oval face, with its matt complexion and white teeth, which seemed to compare quite well to the other faces he was familiar with. After all, why not make the most of the inevitable and learn some valuable lessons for the future? Before going out, however, a lingering sense of caution prompted him to reach for a pair of dark glasses to cover the erubescent flash of his eyes, if the need arose. He also grabbed a raincoat, which he threw over his arm, and he strode to the door with determination. A few moments later, equipped with a light suitcase and breathing in the morning air that seemed strangely devoid of odours, he found himself standing by the side of the road, turning his thumb confidently towards the first car he saw. He had decided to head for Paris, having learned from everyday experience that cars rarely stop as they go up the hill. They are more inclined to stop on the descent, because the downward slope makes it easier for them to take off again.

Due to his stylish appearance, he was soon picked up by someone who wasn't in too much of a hurry. Comfortably ensconced on the right-hand side of the driver, Denis gazed for the first time with his fiery eyes at the big wide world. Twenty minutes later, he got out at the Place de l'Opéra. The weather was cool, the sky was clear, and the traffic was still within the limits of decency. Denis boldly dashed across the pedestrian crossing and headed along the boulevard in the direction of the Scribe Hotel, where he took a suite with a bathroom and living room. Leaving his bag in the care of the hotel staff, he immediately went out again to buy a bicycle.

The morning passed by as if it were a dream. Overwhelmed, Denis didn't know where to pedal next. From deep within, he felt the burning desire to look for a wolf to bite, but he didn't think it would be very easy to find a victim, and he wanted to avoid being overly influenced by what he'd read in all the books. He knew that, with a bit of luck, he could get close to the animals in the Jardin des Plantes, but he reserved this possibility for a time when he might be overcome by a more powerful urge. The new bicycle occupied all his thoughts. This nickel-plated thing fascinated him and, what is more, it would be very useful for when the time came to return home to his cave.

At midday, Denis parked his bike in front of the hotel under the somewhat astonished eye of the porter. But Denis's elegant appearance, and especially his ruby red eyes, seemed to prevent people from saying anything to him. Carefree, he set off in search of a restaurant. He chose one that looked nice and quiet, because he still felt uncomfortable around large groups of people and, despite the level of his overall refinement, he was afraid that his manners were still a little countrified. He asked to be seated somewhere out of the way and to be served promptly. However, Denis was unaware that, in this place that seemed so peaceful, on that very day, the monthly meeting of the Rambolitain Fresh Water Amateur Fishing Club was being held, and it so happened that, in the middle of his meal, he witnessed a procession of jolly gentlemen with ruddy complexions stream in, who, in one fell swoop, occupied seven tables with four diners at each. Denis frowned at this sudden intrusion and, as expected, the head waiter politely came over to his table.

"I'm very sorry, sir," the smooth-talking, clean-shaven man said. "But would you do us the favour of sharing your table with this young lady?"

Denis took one look at the kid and immediately wiped the scowl from his face.

"I'd be delighted," he said, getting to his feet.

"Thank you, sir," said the creature in a musical voice. A musical saw, to be exact.

"If you're thanking me," Denis continued, "what must I…?" Thank, he was implying.

"Probably divine intervention," the beauty opined.

And she immediately dropped her handbag, which Denis caught in mid-air.

"Oh!" she exclaimed. "What extraordinary reflexes you have!"

"Y-e-e-e-s," Denis agreed.

"And what unusual eyes you have as well," she added five minutes later. "They remind me of… of…"

"Of?" Denis queried.

"Garnets," she concluded.

"It's the war," Denis said.

"I don't follow you…"

"I meant," Denis clarified, "that I was expecting you to allude to rubies and, hearing you mention only garnets, I thought of restrictions, which immediately led me to the war, through a relationship of cause and effect."

"Are you a Political Sciences man?" asked the brown-eyed doe.

"Never to return."

"I find you rather fascinating," obsequiously asserted the young maiden, who, just between us, had lost her virginity more than most.

"I would gladly return the compliment," Denis said, gallantly.

They left the restaurant together and the strumpet confided to the wolf-cum-man that she was staying nearby in a beautiful room at the Hotel Silver Potato-Masher.

"Come and see my etchings," she whispered in Denis's ear.

"Is that wise?" Denis enquired. "What about your husband, or your brother, or some other member of your family? Won't they be worried?"

"I'm a kind of orphan," she moaned, delicately flicking away a tear with the tip of her slender forefinger.

"What a pity!" her elegant companion politely remarked.

Following her into the hotel, Denis was sure he noticed that the receptionist seemed to be strangely absent and that all that faded red shagpile carpet was the one major difference between her hotel and the one where he was staying. But, on the staircase, the stockings and then the calves of the beauty were revealed to him and, wanting to learn more, he let her mount another six steps. Enlightened, he hurried after her.

He was somewhat revolted at the thought of fornicating in the company of a woman, because it was so comical. But when he recalled past events in Fausses-Reposes, it helped him to pick up the pace. As a result, he soon found himself in a position to put into practice what he had observed. The beauty tried to express her complete satisfaction and the theatrics she used to declare her arrival in seventh heaven were lost on good old Denis, who had little experience in these matters.

He was just beginning to emerge from some kind of unconscious state, quite different from any he had previously experienced, when he heard the hour sound. "All stifling and pale, when…" he sat up and was stunned to discover his lady friend — her bare backside in full view, if you don't mind — busily rummaging through the pocket of his jacket.

"Would you like a photo of me!" he said suddenly, thinking he understood what was going on.

He felt flattered, but understood the error of this assumption from the sudden shudder that ran through her twin hemispheres.

"But… er… yes, my darling," the dear lady said, without really knowing whether he was making fun of her or *nyet*.

Denis scowled. He got up and went to check his wallet.

"So you're one of those females whose turpitudes one reads about in the literature of Monsieur Mauriac!" Denis concluded. "A whore, in other words."

She was about to reply, and how, that he was a pain in the arse and that she couldn't give a stuff about him and that she wasn't going to screw some guy just for the fun of it when, instead, a glow in the eye of the anthropised wolf shut her up. Two thin red rays of light emanated from Denis's eye sockets and zoomed in on the brunette's eyeballs, plunging her into a strange state of disarray.

"Kindly cover yourself and clear off this instant!" Denis suggested.

It suddenly occurred to him to let out a howl in order to intensify the effect. Never before had such a thought entered his head but, despite his lack of experience, he produced a long, frightful noise.

Terrified, the maiden got dressed without saying a word, in less time than it takes for a clock to strike twelve. When he was alone, Denis began to laugh. He was experiencing a sense of depravity, which was rather stimulating.

"That's the sweet taste of revenge," he mused out loud.

He adjusted his attire, cleaned himself wherever necessary and went out. It was dark and the boulevard was sparkling in a wonderful way. Before he had taken two steps, three men approached. Dressed somewhat gaudily in suits that were too light-coloured, hats that were too new and shoes that were too polished, they boxed him in.

"Can we have a word with you?" said the thinnest of the three, a sallow man with a pencil moustache.

"What about?" said Denis in astonishment.

"Don't be a dickhead," uttered one of the other two, a red-haired man built like a brick.

"Let's step inside here," the sallow chap suggested, as they walked past a bar.

Denis entered, rather curious. Up until then he had found the incident rather amusing.

"Do you play bridge?" he asked the three men.

"You're going to need one," the red-haired brick remarked obscurely. He seemed angry.

"My dear fellow," the sallow chap said once inside, "you have just behaved somewhat inappropriately with a young lady."

Denis burst out laughing.

"The bugger thinks it's funny," the brick observed. "We'll soon wipe that smile off his face."

"It so happens," the sallow chap continued, "that we have a vested interest in that girl."

Denis suddenly understood.

"I see," he said. "You're pimps."

All three of them stood up at once.

"Don't push it!" the brick threatened.

Denis looked at them.

"I'm going to get angry," he said calmly. "It will be the first time in my life, but I recognise the feeling. It's just like it says in the books."

The three men seemed thrown off guard.

"Don't think you scare us, you mug!" Red said.

The third one didn't have much to say. He clenched his fist and lunged. Denis evaded the fist just as it was about to land on his chin; he grabbed the wrist and squeezed it. It made a noise. Denis was hit over the back of the head with a bottle. He blinked and took a step back.

"We're going to hang you out to dry," the sallow chap said.

The bar had emptied. Denis leaped over the table and the brick. The latter, his mouth wide open in surprise, was nevertheless quick enough to grab hold of the suede-shod foot of the lone wolf of Fausses-Reposes.

A brief scuffle followed. After it was over, Denis, whose shirt collar was torn, looked at himself in a mirror. A gash ran across his cheek and one eye was turning indigo. With alacrity, he lined up the three motionless bodies under the bench seats. His heart was pounding furiously inside his ribcage. He tidied himself up a little and suddenly noticed the time. Eleven o'clock.

"Great Scott!" he thought, "I have to fly!"

He quickly put on his dark glasses and raced back to his hotel. He was filled with a deep hatred, but he was aware that he had to be gone urgently.

He paid his bill, picked up his suitcase, jumped on his bicycle and took off like Fausto Coppi.

***

He had just reached Saint-Cloud Bridge when he was pulled over by a policeman.

"Don't you have a light, then?" said this human, who seemed to be the same as any other.

"What?" Denis asked. "Why? I can see!"

"It's not so you can see," the policeman said. "It's so you can be seen. What happens if you have an accident, eh?"

"Ah!" Denis said. "Yes, I see what you mean. But how does this light work?"

"Are you taking the piss?" the cop asked.

"Listen," Denis said, "I'm really pushed for time. I don't have time to take the piss."

"Do you want a fine?" the loathsome copper said.

"You're extremely annoying," answered the wayward wolf on wheels.

"Right, that's it," the vile flatfoot said.

He started to take a fine notebook and a ballpoint pen out of his pocket and lowered his head for a moment.

"Name?" he said, raising his head.

Then he blew his whistle, for, in the distance, he spotted Denis speeding away, launching his bike into an assault on the hill.

Denis gave it everything he had. The astonished asphalt yielded to his furious pace. He made short work of Saint-Cloud Hill. He crossed the part of town that borders the exposed protuberance that is Montretout, a subtle reminder of the perverts wandering Saint-Cloud Park, and turned left towards Pont Noir and Ville-d'Avray. As he was leaving that fine town, just in front of the Cabassud Restaurant, he became aware of a commotion behind him. He quickened his pace and veered sharply off onto a forest trail. Time was of the essence. Suddenly, in the distance, a clock was chiming midnight.

From the very first stroke, Denis noticed that something was wrong. He was having difficulty reaching the pedals. It seemed to him that his legs were becoming shorter. In the moonlight, however, his momentum was still carrying him over the stones on the dirt track when he caught a glimpse of his shadow — long muzzle, pointed ears. And so he suddenly took a tumble, for a wolf on a bike has no balance.

This proved to be lucky for him. Scarcely had he hit the ground than, in a single bound, he leaped into a clump of bushes and the police motorcycle crashed noisily into the discarded bike. The motorcycle cop lost a testicle in the accident and his sense of hearing subsequently diminished by thirty-nine per cent.

Scarcely had Denis turned back into a wolf than he began wondering about the strange fit of anger that had gripped him while he was in man's clothing. He, who was usually so mild-mannered and so calm, had seen his high moral standards and indulgence fly like butterflies out the window. His fit of vengeful rage — the full impact of which had been felt by the three pimps of La Madeleine, one of whom, let us hasten to say in the defence of real pimps, was working undercover for the vice squad attached to the Paris Police Department — seemed to him to be both unthinkable and fascinating. He shook his head. What a terrible piece of bad luck the bite from the Magus of Siam had turned out to be. Luckily, he thought, this difficult transformation is going to be confined to the days when there's a full moon. However, there was still something there deep inside of him. And this vague feeling of simmering anger, this desire for revenge, was more than a little worrying.

THE SNOWMAN

I

Happy Valley seemed a sleepy, lethargic little place. Despite repeated attempts, nobody had ever been able to make this secluded spot work as a fashionable ski resort; it just hadn't taken off. A few advertising billboards, remnants of past attempts at glory, had temporarily littered the magnificent rugged countryside, from the Deer's Leap vista to the grandiose Three Sisters Ridge. But the relentless attack of the mountain winds and of the cold that eventually causes even the toughest rock to crack had turned the advertising billboards into moss-covered planks which had gradually been reclaimed by the wild landscape of the valley. The altitude of the place, in any event, discouraged even the hardiest skiers, and, as for the others, the one hotel — a tiny, red, wooden chalet — denied the most basic comforts such as the chairlifts and cable cars you find in luxury resorts that are carefully designed to lighten the weight of wallets.

The hamlet itself consisted of a few houses scattered over an area up to six kilometres from the chalet, on a more sheltered part of the mountain; as a result, travellers who stopped at the hotel could be forgiven for thinking that they had landed in a foreign country at the end of the earth. The welcome they received from the hotelier, a taciturn mountain man whose face was weathered from long walks in the snow, was, moreover, so diffident, and his lack of enthusiasm so obvious to anyone who tried to stay at his establishment, that the almost total absence of guests was understandable. Only true devotees could put up with such a cool reception. But on the other hand, the dizzying slopes that looked as though they had been custom made for speed were a just reward for those thrill-seekers determined to steer clear of the beaten track.

II

Jean saw the hotel from the top of the steep slope he had just climbed, puffing under the weight of his skis and heavy suitcase. It was exactly what he had been promised: a unique outlook, solitude and crisp clean air that had a bite to it even though the sun was streaming down.

He stopped, wiped his brow. Without giving a thought to the wind, he had stripped to the waist, and his skin was turning bronze under the bright rays of the sun. On seeing his destination within reach, he set off again, quickening his pace. The yellow rubber soles of his boots left deep jagged imprints in the snow. The indentations thus created took on a pale blue watery colour. Jean was bursting with joy, the joy experienced from contact with a pristine environment, the joy of all these silver-coated slopes, of these fir trees heavy with a dusting of sugar, of the red timber chalet that he imagined to be warm and cosy, with a blackened fireplace where a log fire would be burning with a thick smokeless orange flame…

A few metres from the hotel, Jean stopped for a second time. Undoing the sleeves of the thick pullover he had tied around his waist, he put it back on. He then leaned his skis up against the wall and dropped his suitcase next to them. In three bounds, he climbed the timber steps that provided access to the chalet via a kind of verandah, a metre above the ground, that stretched all the way around the squat building. Without knocking, he lifted the metal latch and went in. He found himself in a narrow entrance-hall, at the end of which was a stairway. The communal living area was on the right. Its windows allowed just enough light into the room to produce red flashes when the rays happened to fall on the copperware hanging on the walls. At first, you screwed up your eyes, blinded by this shaft of light bursting through the blackness of the wall. Then you gradually became accustomed to the half-light and you began to discern the slightly eerie calm of the hotel.

A pleasant warmth pervaded the building. A feeling of lethargy crept up on you, inviting you to stretch out in one of those split wicker armchairs, to take down one of those books that lined the shelves rising halfway up the wall, to doze off to the sound of the creaking of the varnished red pine panels beneath the solid beams of the low ceiling. In front of one of the windows, there was a long table, blackened by years of use, and some sturdy chairs; there was a tall cupboard in one corner and, on the floor, some coarse rugs.

From the floor above there came the sound of footsteps, that then tumbled noisily down the stairs. Three girls in ski gear flashed past so quickly, he hardly had time to see them. Under the hoods of their black anoraks, they all had the same healthy sparkle in their eye. Their skin, glowing from the sun, made you want to sink your teeth into it. All three were wearing black ski pants, the same colour as their anoraks, and seemed to be as fit and agile as young animals in the wild. They disappeared through the door that closed again as quickly as it had opened, leaving Jean momentarily blinded by the sun-drenched snow.

Shaking himself, he looked at the staircase and walked towards it. Somewhere, in another room, a kettle was whistling on a stove.

"Is anyone there?"

His voice echoed throughout the building, and nobody answered. Unsurprised, he called out again.

This time, slow footsteps answered his call. A man came down the stairs. Blond-haired, rather tall, in his forties, he had the complexion of someone who had spent his entire life in the mountains. His eyes shone with astonishing brightness.

"Hello there!" Jean said. "Can I have a room?"

"Of course," the man said.

"What are your terms and conditions?"

"That's not important."

"It's just that I don't have a lot of money."

"Neither do I," the man said. "That's why I'm here. Six hundred francs a day?"

"That's not enough," Jean said.

"Well," the man replied, "you won't be very comfortable. Breakfast at eight, lunch at one, dinner at seven. Go upstairs and take your pick. They're all free, except five and six."

"The three girls?" Jean asked.

"Yes," said the man. "Excuse me, I must get on."

"Please do," said Jean, as the man went up the stairs.

Going back outside to fetch his suitcase, Jean noticed that it was badly dented, as though someone had kicked it with a steel-capped boot. The leather gaped, its fluffy lining appearing through the tear. Jean shrugged his shoulders and, picking up his suitcase, he climbed the worm-eaten steps. Happy all the same because of the snow, he bounded up the stairs that led to the first floor.

III

He soon learned their names, but nothing further. Leni was the fairest. Tall, with slender hips and enticing breasts, she had a short, straight nose that seemed to be an extension of her forehead. She had a round face with high cheekbones. Laurence, dark and with rings under her eyes, and Luce, sophisticated all the way down to her pointy fingernails, were also just as tantalising in their own way. One strange thing — they all seemed to have been modelled on the muscular young goddess Diana. At first they looked rather like tomboys, but a second, longer, look revealed the enticing round shapes whose tips were straining against the light material of the silk anoraks.

Jean didn't know why, but right from day one, they refused to have anything to do with him, and decided to make his life unbearable. Contemptuous, scornful, they ignored all of his attempts to be friendly, going so far as refusing to acknowledge even simple gestures, such as when he offered them bread or passed them the salt at the table. This upset Jean for the first few days, but he could get no explanation for their behaviour from the hotelier. The latter lived on his own, in an office on the first floor, and only ever ventured out for one of those interminable walks of his in the mountains. An elderly couple made sure the residence and guests were looked after. Apart from those seven individuals, no-one else was to be seen at the chalet.

The three girls would rise early, get ready quickly and head off armed with their skis. They would return in the evening ready to drop and spend an hour before going back up to their rooms, coating their skis with a rough and ready wax of their own concoction ready for the next day's skiing.

Jean, for his part, avoided them as far as possible. He would go off on his own, generally in the opposite direction to the one they had taken. There were plenty of slopes, so he had no problem choosing. He would make his way up the curved slopes of the mountain alone, take the steep descents in an explosion of snow and a gentle whooshing of hickory, zigzagging his way across the edge of sheer cliffs, and return to the hotel hours later, on a natural high, heart pounding, tired but happy. Since his arrival, he had got his feel back and was beginning to make progress, gaining more control in the launch and in the turns, refining his technique and strengthening his muscles, while at the same time remaining supple. Time was passing quickly, clearly, uneventfully. He was on holidays.

IV

He had set out very early that morning, hoping to reach by midday the Three Sisters Ridge, whose extraordinary silhouette stretched out on the horizon. Alone on the mountain, he struggled from one ridge to the next, threading his way between the lifeless fir trees, their branches frozen with crystals. One particularly difficult slope tempted him. Throwing all caution to the wind, he took off, knees bent, weight forward. He descended, leaving behind him a pair of gossamer thin lines, the wind whipping his cheeks and ears. Here and there, the slightly sticky snow slowed his run, but he soon regained his speed. There was a rise in the ground before him and, instead of slowing down, he pushed on, a little concerned despite himself. On the other side of the rise, there was a slope so steep that, in places, the snow gave way to dark patches of young fir trees. Trusting his instincts, he tried to get through, slaloming around the rigid tree-trunks. At full speed, he collided with a low-hanging branch. He made a desperate attempt to avoid the next tree, shifting his weight, but the exposed ground stopped one of his skis dead and he fell, losing consciousness under the force of the impact.

When he came to, Jean saw that the trail he had intended to take ended there. The tips of both skis were shattered, making them unusable.

What's more, one of his ankles was causing him a great deal of pain, certainly sprained, perhaps broken. With great difficulty, he undid the straps from their bindings. He used some shards of wood to make a splint for his aching ankle. He picked up his poles ten metres from where he had landed and slowly started to hobble home, the blinding light causing him to screw up his eyes in pain. His sunglasses had disappeared in the snow.

Using his poles for support to take the weight off his ankle, he was making slow progress. Every hundred metres he stopped to catch his breath. Bent double, he kept going, worried about being so far from the hotel. The cold snow was beginning to stab at his aching leg.

He reached the top of a ridge that two hours earlier he had climbed without stopping and stopped, his attention caught by the movement of three dark shapes skiing past, following the floor of the valley. Without knowing why, he tried to stay out of sight — as the crow flies, it was about two hundred metres between him and them — it was the three girls from the hotel. He turned as he watched them go by. They disappeared behind some fir trees. They were hidden from view by a small rise and Jean did not see them reappear.

He crept quietly towards them. He had forgotten about his leg.

V

Despite everything, he was not prepared for the shock he received when he cautiously raised his head to look over to where they were frolicking about. He tucked himself deeper into the thick polar blanket to avoid being seen. Leni, Luce and Laurence were alone, naked in the snow. Like a proud golden statue, Leni stood before her friends who were picking up handfuls of frozen powder to rub over her tanned body. Jean felt the blood flowing through his veins and his heart started beating more quickly. The three girls were running around, dancing and playing, agile as cats, occasionally pairing off for a brief wrestle. They seemed to be becoming more and more worked up as the game went on. Their touches lingered, their embraces endured. Suddenly, from behind, Luce grabbed Laurence around the waist, causing her to stumble, and then to fall flat on her back. Leni dropped to her knees next to her. Laurence's body remained motionless, her arms outstretched in the snow. Luce in turn lay down next to her… A short moment later, Jean, stunned, was no longer able to distinguish one body from another in that tangled mass. Breathing heavily, he briefly turned away, then turned around again, eager to view the scene that was unfolding before him, unable to resist the pull of these writhing bodies.

Leni now lay over the intertwined bodies of her two friends, her long agile hands seeming to send a thrill through their limbs and hardening breasts. Jean felt his heart beat slowly and dully in his chest, and his mouth dried. Spellbound, he did not dare move. Leni, Laurence, Luce, were they women? Mysterious spirits, perhaps, who had come to make him forget time and reality, filling his veins with a heady and potent elixir.

Leni stood up at last, the two tired bodies of her friends still rolling about. She moved away and, her eyes half-closed, lay down herself, allowing Jean's misty gaze to follow the enticing movement of the others' hips, which snow and hands had marked with their tender caress…

Suddenly, a small snowflake landed on Jean's hand, causing him to shiver. The sky had gradually clouded over. The three girls, completely sated, lay motionless. Reluctantly, they disentangled themselves and ran to fetch their clothes. Aware of his perilous position, Jean held his breath. He went to step back, but the movement reawakened the pain in his ankle with such intensity that he could not help letting out a groan.

Like lionesses smelling prey, Luce and Leni turned in his direction and sniffed the air, nostrils flaring. Their dishevelled hair and brusque movements made them look like bacchanalian revellers caught in flagrante. They rushed towards him. Jean stood up, grimacing in pain.

They recognised him and turned pale with rage. Leni's dark lips tightened and she shouted insults at him.

"It was just an accident," Jean said simply. "I didn't mean to."

Leni drew her arm back and her fist struck Jean in the mouth. His lower lip split open. Warm blood flowed down onto his chin. He stumbled and pain shot through his ankle.

"I wouldn't have said anything," he murmured simply. "It was wonderful."

Leni was holding a ski pole around the aluminium disc near the tip. Her hand tightened around the hard shaft. She swung the pole like a golf club and the heavy leather grip struck Jean hard on the temple. He fell to his knees, stunned, and his body sank into the snow.

Laurence had joined them. They took Jean's poles, tied them into a Saint Andrew's Cross, and stuck them in the snow. Then, slowly and deliberately, they undressed the lifeless body and raised it back to its knees, its back leaning against the cross. They tied his wrists to the centre of the X shape. Jean's head fell forward onto his chest and a drop of dark blood ran from his left nostril, joining up with the wound on his lip. Luce and Leni had already begun piling large handfuls of snow around the body.

When the snowman was finished, snow began to fall like a thick mist. Where Jean's face had been, a rough round shape protruded, forming a large grotesque nose. Derisively, Leni placed a black woollen bonnet on top. They put a gold cigarette holder in his mouth. Then, under the cover of whiteness, the three girls hurried back to Happy Valley.

ONE LICENCE FOR LOVE

By Joëlle Bausset

Marthe and Jean got out of the car. Marthe prised open her bag, took out a hundred franc note and furtively slipped it into the hand of the driving instructor, a solidly built and slightly clumsy looking forty-year-old.

"Thank you, madam," he said in a low voice. "Have no fear, you'll both pass." As if the modest sum she'd handed him would in some round-about way lead to certain success.

Marthe and Jean looked at each other.

"Touch wood," he said.

This was the last of the ten lessons that they had been taking together and, in three days' time, they were both scheduled to appear before "the engineer", a much-feared examiner, in a small grey street near the Jardin des Plantes. Marthe felt a shiver of anxiety. She loved Jean with all her youth, with all her senses. She would have liked a strong and adventurous companion. She would have liked him to be the best, the strongest. But her husband's love, which was too friendly and too affectionate, reflected his timid and discreet personality. Faced with such a lukewarm attitude, would she continue to pay no heed to the constant attention and advances of all Jean's friends, who were so daring, sporty and intrepid?

They headed off towards the nearest metro station.

"What a relief it will be," said Marthe, "when we no longer have to go down into these corridors. I can't wait to get our car!"

"Licence first," Jean said.

"It would be really silly if we managed to save enough money for a car," Marthe said, "only to fail the test. If one of us fails, you for example, the other can always drive."

"Why do you say 'me for example'?" Jean said. "What if you were the one to fail?..."

Laughing, they went down the stairs.

Marthe would have really liked to take this same cheerfulness with her when, three days later, the stony-faced examiner told her in a flat voice to do a U-turn in a narrow dead-end street. Marthe breathed deeply, took her time and, remembering all her instructor's advice, correctly performed a hill start and the U-turn. She may have lacked flair but the man seemed satisfied. After a few questions about the road rules, he handed her licence to her.

"But," stammered Marthe, "is it already over?"

She got out, feeling a little dazed; it had been so easy! The next candidate took the wheel and she heard him take off with a crunch of gears. She looked around for Jean.

"Your husband has the other examiner in the second car," said her driving instructor, who always accompanied his students to their tests.

Marthe now felt horribly worried. Oh, please let Jean pass as well! She even found herself wishing, stupidly, that she herself had not passed. She was afraid that her good luck might harm Jean's chances, that fate might refuse to smile on them both.

"Come on! Cheer up! Don't make such a drama out of it, my little Marthe. Take a look!"

Jean waved his licence in the air. Marthe had never before seen him like this, triumphant, sure of himself.

"Come on, you can sit for it again. There's nothing to it! It's easy!"

Marthe pulled herself together. He had it! That was the main thing.

"I got mine too," she said in a soft, shy voice.

"So why that face?" he asked, slightly irritated. "You had me worried."

Should she tell him that she had been anxious for him? No, not this

Jean, not this new Jean who was emerging. She made up an excuse.

"I'm emotional..."

The car completely changed Jean. The unassuming, almost timid, boy whom Marthe had practically dragged from the clutches of a perpetually worried mother gradually gave way to a driver who knew no inhibitions, who was sometimes almost too intrepid. Marthe no longer dared ask to drive. The way Jean carried on when this happened, his sighing, discouraged her from pushing the issue. She soon got out of the habit of driving when they were together. But she felt amply rewarded. Calmer, stronger, more affectionate, Jean had become a new man; it was as though the sense of control over the brute force of a machine and the ability to bend it to his will were enough to make him forget his nervousness and his former hesitancy. Even at work, he was more assured than before, panicking less over little things, no longer overawed by his responsibilities. Easter was approaching and Jean plucked up enough courage to ask for four days off. Marthe began preparing for their first big trip.

"Did you see how I overtook that guy!" Jean exclaimed.

Marthe, lost in the spectacle of the apple trees in bloom unfolding to her right, gave a start.

"And he won't be the last," her husband said. "When you can outdo an average size car with a small one, you can overtake anyone."

Marthe almost commented that, in her opinion, overtaking on a bend on a rather narrow road with no visibility did not qualify as masterful driving; she refrained. It was too nice a day, the air was clean and crisp, and the beautiful deeply ploughed black soil was beginning to boast a light green cover. Marthe would have liked to take a stroll along a country lane beneath fresh green leaves. But it was pointless asking Jean to stop, even for a moment.

"A car," he would answer, "is made for driving."

"A car," Marthe thought, "is above all made for taking you where you want, when you want."

But how could you be cross with Jean? Once again, she remembered how he had been a few months earlier, so sensitive, so timid. Let him do what he liked. Let him even drive too fast, so long as he stayed, as he was now, stronger and more stable. She loved this confidence she now had in her husband's future, this poise that allowed her to sleep untroubled next to him at night. All those annoying little habits of the wide-eyed convert would pass and time would make of him the Jean that she alone could sense.

A huge car roared past without warning. He hit the accelerator. The silhouette of the other car was already fading into the distance.

"Just wait until there are a few bends," said Jean, "and then watch me get him."

The small car's engine howled. The needle on the speedometer was creeping slowly towards the edge of the dial.

"I'll get him," Jean said.

In a screeching of tyres, the car careered around a bend then righted itself.

"There he is," Jean said.

Suddenly, a hundred metres ahead, a cyclist emerged from a side-track. A boy, head down, started to cross the road. The sound of the horn froze the boy in his tracks. Jean hit the brake pedal hard, the tyres skidded on the road, a tug on the wheel sent the car veering onto the verge, collecting the back wheel of the bike along the way. A scream. And the car, vanquished, was brought to a halt by a pile of gravel.

"I've killed him," Jean said flatly, in the sudden silence.

Marthe hardly heard him. "I should have warned him!" she thought. "It's my fault." She ran to where the child lay sprawled out a few metres from his bike. He was deathly white. His eyes were closed. She picked him up and carried him carefully over to the grass.

"Jean, come and help me!"

He got out of the car, more pale than his victim.

She knelt down beside the injured child and took his pulse.

"He's alive," she said. "He's alive."

"I've killed him!" Jean repeated in the same flat tone.

The boy opened his eyes. The colour returned to his round cheeks.

"My bike..." he sighed. He tried to stand up, let out a cry and fell down again.

"My leg..."

A steady droning sound could be heard. Two police motorcycles appeared in the distance.

"Stay by his side," Marthe said to Jean. "He has a broken leg. Put a cushion under his head. And don't say anything. Not a word! You hear me!"

The motorbikes stopped and two men wearing leather helmets dismounted. Marthe stole a glance at Jean. Poor fellow! He was pale; all that wonderful confidence had deserted him. What a blow it would be if they took his licence! Gone was that young man full of confidence, that husband who was impulsive, admittedly, but so alive...

"It's my fault," Marthe said, "I was driving too fast. I couldn't stop in time."

"Give me your licence," one of the policemen asked.

She handed him the pink card.

"You've had it for six months. I'm going to have to keep this. There are too many accidents. I don't know if you'll get it back."

Jean and the other policeman were putting the boy in the car.

"He has to be taken to hospital," the policeman said to his colleague. "You stay here with the bikes. I'll drive him."

"That's not necessary," said Marthe very calmly. "Get back on your bike. My husband will take him. He has his licence."

A SAD STORY

The yellowish glow from the street light illuminated the black square of the window pane. It was six o'clock at night. Ouen looked up and sighed. He was making little to no progress with the word trap he was building.

He hated these windows without curtains, but he hated curtains even more. And he loathed the nondescript architecture of buildings designed for human habitation that had been pierced with holes for thousands of years. With a heavy heart he went back to his work. He quickly had to finish aligning the cogs on the decomposer, which broke sentences down into words so that these could then be captured. He had made things more difficult for himself almost on purpose by refusing to treat conjunctions as real words. Because he thought them dry, he was denying them the right to noble status and was eliminating them and collecting them in the shuddering compartments where full stops, commas and the other punctuation marks were piling up before being filtered out and eliminated. It was a routine operation, standard mechanics, but it was difficult to get right. Ouen was working his fingers to the bone.

But he was taking it too far. He put down the pair of fine gold tweezers, popped the magnifying glass from his eye with a flex of his cheek bone, and stood up. He suddenly needed to stretch his legs. He felt energetic and restless. Being outside would do him good.

The footpath of the deserted alley stole along beneath his feet. Despite the fact that Ouen had been down this path before, such furtive and cunning behaviour on its part never ceased to irritate him. He stepped off it onto the side of the road where the oily residue of a recently dried up drain was glimmering under the halogen lights.

The walk did him good and, as the air flowed up through his nasal passages to wash back over the convolutions of his brain, it gradually decongested that large, weighty bihemispheric organ. This is standard biology, but still, it amazed him every time.

Being in a state of perpetual naïvety, he was more alive to the present than other people.

He reached the end of the short dead-end street and hesitated, because he wasn't sure which way to go next. Unable to make up his mind, he kept going straight ahead, port and starboard offering no viable alternative. The road led straight on to the bridge. He could look down on the water of the day, which was probably not much different from that of the day before, but then again, the appearance of water is only one of its many features.

Like the alley he had just left, the road was also deserted and was speckled with liquid yellow light, creating a salamander-like effect on the asphalt. The road rose slightly to the hump of the stone arch that spanned the river and tirelessly devoured its waters. Ouen would only stop and lean on the wall of the bridge if there was nobody upstream or downstream to see him. If there were already others looking up and down the river, it would be rather pointless to add one more gaze to the collective visual apparatus of the leering throng. He would simply continue on to the next bridge, which was always deserted because that was where you caught impetigo.

Two young priests passed furtively by, reducing the nothingness of the street to blackness. From time to time they would stop to kiss in the shadow of a doorway. Ouen was moved. Leaving the house had certainly been the right thing to do. Out on the street, you could see all sorts of things to cheer you up. He now had a spring in his step and immediately thought of a solution to the remaining problems associated with the assembly of his word trap. It was so childish really. With a little care, he would definitely be able to take control of them, flatten them, strike them down, dismember them and tear them apart. In a word, he would make those words disappear.

A general passed by next. He was holding a leather leash attached to a prisoner who was frothing at the mouth. So that there would be no danger to the general, the prisoner had been put in shackles and his hands tied behind his head. At the first sign of any trouble, the general would tug on the leash, which would then cause the prisoner to fall back into line. The general was walking quickly, because his day was over. He was on his way home to eat his alphabet soup. As he did every night, he would spell out his name on the rim of the bowl three times faster than the prisoner and, as the prisoner looked on furiously, he would then devour both bowls of soup. The prisoner was unlucky: his name was Joseph Ulrich de Saxakrammerigothensburg, while the general's name was Pol. But Ouen couldn't be expected to know this. He was nonetheless interested in the small polished boots the general was wearing and thought that he wouldn't feel comfortable in the prisoner's shoes, or in those of the general for that matter. The prisoner hadn't chosen to be a prisoner, while this was not the case with the general. You can't always find someone who wants to be a prisoner, but there is never a shortage of applicants who want to be sewerage workers, cops, judges and generals — proof that even the dirtiest jobs must have something going for them. Ouen lost himself in thought, wondering about all those occupations nobody wanted to do. Certainly, you were ten times better off building word traps than you were being a general. In fact, ten times didn't seem to be enough. Doesn't matter. Same principle.

The abutment piers of the bridge bristled with beacons. This created a very nice effect and, moreover, they were very useful to navigation. Ouen appreciated it for what it was and walked past without even looking. His destination was in sight and he hurried towards it. However, something caught his eye. On one side of the bridge, an unusually short silhouette could be seen above the parapet. He started running. There was a young girl standing above the river on a small moulded stone ledge with a dripstone that had been built to allow water to drain away after heavy rain. She seemed to be contemplating throwing herself in the river. Ouen leaned on the wall behind her.

"I'm ready," he said. "You can jump now."

She looked at him, not knowing what to do. She was a pretty young girl, with a beige complexion.

"I'm wondering which side of the bridge I should jump from," she said. "If I throw myself in upstream, there's a good chance I'll be caught in the current and dashed onto a pier. Downstream, there are the whirlpools. But then again, I might become disorientated when I hit the water and try to grab hold of the pier if I take the upstream option, and if I go in downstream there's a good chance someone will see me and jump into the river to try to rescue me."

"The problem is worthy of consideration," Ouen said. "And I cannot but agree that you're right to take it so seriously. Naturally, I am entirely at your disposal to help you make the right decision."

"You're very kind," the young girl said with her red mouth. "It's been bothering me so much that I just don't know what to think any more."

"We could always go and find a café and discuss it further," Ouen said. "I don't talk very well without a drink in front of me. Can I buy you one? You might even have a stroke."

"I'd love to," the young girl said.

Ouen helped her climb back down onto the bridge and, as he did, he noticed that she had curves in all the prominent and vulnerable places. He complimented her on her attributes.

"I know I should be blushing," she said, "but I know deep down you're absolutely right. I do have a nice figure. And you should see my legs."

She lifted her flannel skirt and Ouen cast an admiring glance over her legs, and noticed that she was a natural blonde.

"I see what you mean," he answered, his eyes almost bulging out of his head. "So! Let's go and have a drink and when we've sorted out your problem we'll come back here so you can jump off the right side."

They set off together, arm in arm, both feeling very happy. She told him her name was Flavie and this sign of trust only served to heighten the interest he already had in her.

When they were comfortably seated in the warmth of a modest establishment frequented by barge operators and their barges, she resumed her story.

"I shouldn't like you to think me silly," she began, "but this uncertainty, which I felt when deciding from which side of the bridge I should jump, has always been with me. The time had thus come to be decisive, just for once. Otherwise, I'll always be remembered as being foolish and faint-hearted."

"The problem," Ouen conceded, "comes from the fact that you always have to make a choice. In your case, neither upstream nor downstream seems to be satisfactory. However, you have to choose one or the other. Wherever the bridge is situated on a river, there is always an upstream and a downstream."

"Except at the source," Flavie observed.

"Exactly," Ouen said, charmed by such presence of mind. "But generally, the sources of rivers are not very deep."

"And therein lies the problem," Flavie said.

"Well," Ouen said, "there's still the possibility of resorting to a suspension bridge."

"I wonder if that wouldn't be cheating just a little."

"Going back to sources for a minute, that of the Touvre in particular has a sufficient flow of water for most run-of-the-mill suicide attempts."

"It's too far away," she said.

"It's near the Charente," Ouen noted.

"If it becomes a chore," Flavie said, "if you have to devote as much time and effort to trying to drown yourself as you have to do for everything else in life, it becomes disheartening. It's enough to make you want to go and commit suicide."

"By the way, why such a definitive gesture?" Ouen said. The question had only just occurred to him.

"It's a really sad story," Flavie answered, wiping from her eye a single tear. This, appropriately enough, produced a disturbing lack of symmetry.

"I'm dying to hear it," Ouen revealed, warming to the occasion.

"All right then."

He liked Flavie's straightforward approach. She didn't have to be asked twice to tell her story. She was undoubtedly aware of the greater ramifications of revealing this type of secret. He was expecting her story to be quite long and drawn out: under normal circumstances, there is never a shortage of opportunities for a pretty girl to be surrounded by people her own age. In the same way, a jam sandwich has more chance of gathering information on the anatomy and morals of dipterans than a worthless, spotty piece of flint. So, undoubtedly, Flavie's life story would be full of facts and events from which a useful moral could be drawn. Useful to Ouen, that is: the lessons of one person's life are useful only for others, because the teller knows all too well the reasons why he is telling his tale in a selective, false and truncated manner.

"I was born," Flavie began, "twenty-two and two-thirds years ago in a small castle in Normandy near Quettehou. My father, a former teacher of deportment at Mademoiselle Désir's Institute, had retired there with lots of money, to enjoy in peace his chambermaid and the fruits of his persistent labour. My mother, one of his former students who had been quite difficult to seduce because my father was very ugly, had not gone there with him and instead was living in Paris, the mistress, alternately, of an archbishop and a police commissioner. My father, fiercely opposed to anything to do with the church, was unaware of the relationship between my mother and the archbishop, otherwise he would have asked for a divorce. But, he was delighted with the vicarious family connection to the sleuth, because it provided him with the opportunity to humiliate that fine public servant publicly by ridiculing him for contenting himself with leftovers. My father also had a considerable fortune tied up in a plot of land (that was left to him by his grandfather) located in Paris, at the Place de l'Opéra. He liked to go there on Sundays to tend his artichokes right under the very noses of the bus drivers. As you can see, my father despised uniforms of all shapes and sizes."

"But where do you fit into the picture?" Ouen said, thinking she might have wandered off the track.

"Yes, indeed."

She swallowed a mouthful of green drink. And, all of a sudden, she began to cry silently, like an Ideal tap. She seemed despondent. She must have been. Moved, Ouen took her hand. He let go of it immediately, because he didn't know what to do with it. Flavie had started to settle down.

"I'm a silly sausage," she said.

"No you're not," Ouen protested. He thought she was being too hard on herself. "Go on. I shouldn't have interrupted you."

"I've told you a pack of lies," she said, "because I was ashamed. The archbishop was, in fact, a simple bishop, and the police commissioner, a traffic policeman. As for me, I'm a dressmaker who has trouble making ends meet. Customers are scarce, and those I have are so mean. More trouble than they're worth. You'd think it amuses them to see me work myself into the ground. I don't have any money, I'm hungry and I'm unhappy. And my friend is in prison. He sold secrets to a foreign power, but the price he got for them was higher than that set by the government, so he was arrested. The taxman is always asking me for more money. He's my uncle. If he doesn't pay off his gambling debts, my aunt and her six children will be ruined. Do you realise that the oldest is thirty-five? If only you knew how much a boy that age eats!"

She broke down sobbing.

"Day and night I work away with my needle, but all to no avail because I no longer have enough money to buy a spool of thread."

Ouen didn't know what to say. He patted her on the shoulder and thought he should try to make her feel better. But how? You can't just blow these problems away. At least… come to think of it, has anyone ever tried?

He breathed on her.

"What's wrong with you?" the young girl asked.

"Nothing," he said. "I was sighing. Your story makes me sad."

"Oh," she continued. "That? That's nothing. I hardly dare tell you this, but it gets worse."

He stroked her thigh affectionately.

"Get it off your chest. It'll make you feel better."

"Is that making you feel better?"

"My goodness," he said, "that's what people say. As a general rule, of course."

"But what does it matter?" she said.

"But what does it matter?" he repeated.

"There's another thing that's contributed to making my already miserable life hell," Flavie continued, "and that's my good-for-nothing brother. He sleeps with his dog, spits on the floor as soon as he wakes up, kicks the poor cat up the backside and repeatedly belches in front of the caretaker's wife."

Ouen remained silent. When a person's behaviour becomes so crude and unorthodox, you find yourself lost for words.

"You have to wonder," Flavie said, "that if he's like this now at eighteen months, what will he be like when he's older?"

At that point, she broke down again. The sobbing was less frequent but more intense. Ouen patted her cheek, which was hot with tears, but quickly withdrew his scalded fingers.

"Oh, my poor girl," he said.

That was her cue.

"As I said, I've saved the worst for last," she added.

"Go on," Ouen insisted. He was ready for anything now.

She told him, and he quickly stuck something in his ears so he didn't have to listen. The little he did hear sent an unhealthy shiver down his spine, which made him wet his underpants.

"Is that everything?" he asked in the loud voice of someone who has recently become deaf.

"That's everything," Flavie said. "I feel better now."

She drank her glass in one gulp, leaving the contents on the table. This childish prank didn't manage to cheer Ouen up.

"Poor thing!" he finally sighed.

He hauled his wallet out into broad daylight and summoned the waiter, who came over despite his obvious disgust.

"Did you want something, sir?"

"Yes," Ouen said. "How much do I owe you?"

"Plenty," the waiter said.

"Here you are," Ouen said, giving him more.

"I'm not going to thank you," the waiter pointed out, "service is included."

"That's fine," Ouen said. "Go away, you smell."

The waiter was offended, which served him right, and went away. Flavie looked at Ouen with admiration.

"You have money!"

"Take it all," Ouen said. "You need it more than I do."

She was overwhelmed, like she had just met Father Christmas. The look on her face was hard to describe, because no-one has ever met Father Christmas.

He was returning home, alone. It was late. Only one in every two street lamps was still lit. The others were out on their feet. Ouen was walking, head down, thinking about Flavie, thinking about how happy she had been when she had taken all of his money. He felt quite moved. Not a penny left in his wallet. Poor girl. At her age, you can feel lost with no means of support. Now that's strange. He remembered that they were both exactly the same age. She was so destitute. Now that she had taken everything, he was starting to realise the effect it can have. He looked around. The street was bathed in pale light. The moon was directly over the bridge. No money, and that word trap to finish. The empty street filled with a sleepwalker's slow-moving wedding procession. But not even this could cheer Ouen up. He cast his mind back to the prisoner. For him, things were simple. For himself as well, really. The bridge was approaching. No money. Poor, poor Flavie. No, that's right, she had some now. What a heart-wrenching tale all the same. No-one should have to endure such misfortune. It was lucky he had been there. For her, that is. Does someone always arrive just in time?

He climbed over the wall and took up his position on the ledge. The sounds from the wedding party were tapering off in the distance. He looked right, then left. It had indeed been lucky for her that he had passed by. Not a soul in sight. He shrugged his shoulders and felt his empty pockets. Obviously, it was pointless to go on living under these conditions. But what's all this fuss about upstream and downstream?

He let himself fall into the river, giving no further thought to the matter. It was just as he thought: you go straight to the bottom. The side didn't matter.

THE WALTZ

Unpublished short story by Joëlle Bausset

Olivier was bored with this ball. Claude was there, Lise and Gisèle as well, but the ball was too modern and Olivier didn't like dancing to the rhythm of the band. The salons with their polished timber floors opened out onto a rectangular terrace decorated with climbing roses, blue and white hydrangeas and coarse-leafed dwarf bamboo in tubs filled with bark and freshly cut straw that had been dragged into place. Olivier was wearing a romantic costume — a pair of dark blue pants with satin braid, a blue spencer jacket open over a shirt front with rows of white stitching and a very small starched lace ruffle. The girls looked beautiful with their bright eyes and summer tans, their short thick hair, slim waists and high spirits. Olivier was dreaming of a waltz, one great endless waltz, of soft light violins. Olivier was dreaming that he could hear that waltz. It was in a big castle near a wood and there was a large open fire on a huge solid bronze grid. On the walls, a few tapestries, paintings and draperies, and on the floor, alternate slats of rosewood and ebony stretching as far as the eye could see.

Claude came and took his hand. She was in a tight-fitting dress of watered silk slit over tulle flounces, like a big upside down carnation. Her yellow eyes were shining from the pleasure of the dance.

"Olivier, you've abandoned us. Are you bored?"

"Yes," said Olivier with perfect simplicity.

"What's the matter?"

"I must be getting old."

"Come and dance with me."

"Gladly."

He took her in his arms. The band was playing a popular tune, something that was supposed to sound like jazz, but it was poorly executed, with fake improvised solos. It was sloppy, grating and ugly, and had no soul.

"I don't like this music," Olivier said.

"You're a purist. They don't have the means to bring a big name band over from America."

"That's not what I'm talking about," Olivier said. "A waltz is so much better for dancing."

"Is that you talking?" Claude asked.

She stopped, dumbfounded.

"You want to dance a waltz? You? Olivier?"

"Oh, leave me alone," he said.

"No," Claude said. "We're leaving. You're clearly not having a good time here. Come on. Gisèle, Lise and Marc will come with us. You want to dance a waltz! That's insane!"

"Yes," Olivier said.

The car came to a halt outside one of those clubs which, in a few short years, had caused more harm to the younger generation than two world wars and twenty currency devaluations combined. The secretary, a rather tall young man with a patchy beard, allowed them to enter after the usual act of extortion, forcing them to take passes they would never use and that would be out of date before the next visit. The band was playing a furious foxtrot. The low-pitched sound of a saxophone could be heard above the other instruments. Olivier, disgusted, stopped at the foot of the stairs. Smoke and laughter filled the packed cellar.

"I'm not going in," he said.

Claude looked at him, really worried.

"What's the matter, Olivier?" she repeated. "Please tell me what's wrong."

"I don't feel like listening to that."

"But you used to like that," Claude insisted.

The others were growing impatient.

"So, are we going in or not?" Marc said. "I don't care one way or the other, but make up your minds."

"I'm not going in," Olivier said. "You do what you want."

He could see the big hall with the polished floor stretching off into the distance, the mirrors reflecting the soft lights and the light material billowing in the gentle breeze. He could hear the waltz. He could feel the soft abandon of another being's body against his own… and his eyes were open. However, all around, it was smoke and noise and laughter and cold hard jazz that you could not escape. Marc, Gisèle and Lise were standing nearby.

"I'm spoiling everything for you," Olivier said. "Go in without me. For a start, I feel ridiculous here in this jacket."

"Listen Olivier," Gisèle said, "we're staying with you, and if you don't feel like going in, let's go somewhere else. I thought it would do you good."

They went back up the stairs. Out in the street, it was mild. The lights from the local cafés were casting an unusual yellowy-green reflection on the trees that lined the boulevard. At regular intervals you could hear gunshots. It was the King of Saint-Germain, Flor Polboubal, chasing young people from his terrace. They had been drawn there by the American cars in Rue Saint-Benoît and he didn't want annoying young people at his place.

"Do you want to go and listen to Luter?" Lise asked.

Lise had a weakness for Luter. A lot of girls have a weakness for Luter. But others have the hots, and they are the ones who win his heart.

"Not Luter," Olivier said. "I want a waltz."

"But there are no waltzes," Marc said. "Do you want to go to a gypsy nightclub?"

"No," Olivier said. "I want a grand old-fashioned waltz like they have in England, a Boston waltz with lots of violins and beautiful rising melodies."

He hummed one and started to cry.

"There aren't any in Paris," he said.

"So, what do you want us to do for you?" Claude said.

She felt like crying too. Olivier was so strange tonight. He hadn't even noticed her lovely dress.

"Let's go and have a drink," Olivier said, after having finally calmed down. "Come on."

Claude felt better. Olivier didn't drink much and usually one drink was enough to set him straight again. They climbed back into the car and ended up in another part of town.

They went into a bar and had a drink. When they came out, Olivier took the wheel.

"We've been here long enough," he said. "I'm going to take you to another place."

"Is it far?" Lise asked.

"Far enough," Olivier said vaguely.

"Just a minute then," Marc said. "Don't go yet."

He got back out, raced into the bar and returned with a bottle of liqueur brandy and a large package.

"There," he said. "Brandy and sandwiches. That should keep us going."

"Pass them here," Gisèle said.

"No. Not now," Marc said. "They're for the trip."

"Great," Claude said. "A mystery tour, just like in the movie."

She hadn't seen the movie.

"Nothing like the movie," Olivier said.

AND OTHER SHORT STORIES... BORIS VIAN AND SHORT FICTION

Christelle Gonzalo and François Roulmann

Boris Vian is better known as a novelist than as a writer of short stories. And yet, no less than three collections of his short stories are available today in France in paperback: *Les Fourmis* (1949),[1] which was the only collection put together in Vian's lifetime; *Le Loup-garou*,[2] first published by Christian Bourgois in 1970; and finally *Le Ratichon baigneur*,[3] also published by Bourgois, which came out in 1981. Add to these volumes a number of stories published in different short story collections, not to mention the chronicle pieces written for various reviews and magazines of the time (especially, those he wrote on his specialist subject, jazz), and you have a rather different image of Boris Vian, who was incontestably a great writer of short fiction. It is our intention here to reveal how his predilection for this narrative form, as distinct from his poems and the hundreds of songs that he produced, was the result of a network of influences that came to the fore over a period of time which, although limited (1945-1952), was sufficiently productive to warrant a re-evaluation of the way in which his output is generally categorised.

---

1 Translated as *Blues for a Black Cat and Other Stories* by Julia Older (Lincoln: University of Nebraska Press, 1992).

2 This translates as *The Werewolf.*

3 "The Swimming Priest" is the title given in the present volume to the story of the same name.

Influences

"SHORT Stories: Divers." This was the heading Vian used in his personal reading list for the entry corresponding to his deep fascination with short stories, be it stories originally written in French or, as his use of the English term suggests, translated stories.[4] Indeed, the use of English in the heading seems odd in this French context, almost as if he had read various texts by a famous author called "Stories Short". Fortunately, the rest of the list looks like a standard bibliography, with each title listed next to the author's surname and first name. Thanks to this document, which had remained unknown until only recently, we can see which writers and short stories Vian enjoyed reading; and from this we can attempt to judge whether his wide reading in the genre might have influenced his personal style and his imaginary when he came to write his own short stories.

We already know that Marcel Aymé's short stories were greatly admired by Vian, notably for the way they used classic French as a vehicle for an unbridled imagination.[5] As far as Anglo-Saxon literature is concerned, it has become clear that William Faulkner's collection of short stories, *These 13*, translated into French as *Treize histoires*, contributed to the construction of Vian's own *Les Fourmis*, which, as mentioned above, was the only collection of his short stories that Vian compiled entirely himself. Less expected, perhaps, are the many references to fairy tales included on Vian's reading list. These include the classic forty-one volume *Cabinet des fées*, which included tales by Madame d'Aulnoy, Charles Perrault and other eighteenth-century authors, as well as, less surprisingly, works by Hoffmann, Andersen and Wilde. More surprising are the references to the *Contes du vieux Japon* (*Tales of Old Japan*, first translated into French in 1913) and to the unusual *Contes des mille et deux nuits* (*Tales of a Thousand and Two Nights*), a rare pastiche of *The Arabian*

---

[4] The word "divers" ("various" or "miscellaneous") is obviously a French term. Vian's list is set out in purple ink in a notebook with alphabetical tabs; it was filled out as he and his first wife Michelle Léglise read. From the beginning of the 1940s the stories read by Michelle were also included.

[5] For further details on this, see Boris Vian, *Œuvres romanesques complètes*, edited by Marc Lapprand, with Christelle Gonzalo and François Roulmann (Paris: Gallimard, Bibliothèque de la Pléiade, 2 vols, 2010), vol. II, p. 1203.

Nights dating back to the nineteenth century. But then again, we should not forget that Vian's very first short story, which was written during the winter of 1942-1943 and which opens the 2010 Pléiade edition of his collected works, was none other than a fairy tale — *Conte de fées à l'usage des moyennes personnes* (*Fairy Tale for Middle-Sized People*).

Vian's wide reading encompasses the works of Edgar Allan Poe, Herman Melville, Robert Louis Stevenson (including his *New Arabian Nights*) and, more contemporaneously, Rudyard Kipling, Jack London, Ernest Hemingway and Henry Miller. This immersion in the world of short fiction, in the original English or in French translation, must have had an impact on the budding writer. It is, however, from the collections or short texts of Lewis Carroll, H.G. Wells and Franz Kafka, each of whom is well represented on Vian's list, that he seems to have drawn the most inspiration for his short stories, which are almost always a mix of linguistic inventiveness, an often morbid sense of fantasy and parodies of science fiction.

Vian's affinity with short fiction is reflected in the translations that he carried out, especially in the 1950s. His French adaptations of some of the great short works of science fiction, including stories by Lewis Padgett, Frank M. Robinson and Ray Bradbury, remain as landmarks of the introduction of Sci-Fi into France, often appearing in periodicals that ostensibly had nothing to do with the genre, such as the very serious *Mercure de France* and *Les Temps modernes*, or even the rather colourful *France-Dimanche*.[6] And yet, for all this, Vian's short stories are remarkable for their lively, cutting and very "French" style — the very style, in fact, for which Paul Morand, Pierre Mac Orlan (both of whom are well represented on Vian's bookshelves) and, of course, Marcel Aymé himself had become famous in the 1920s.[7] His contemporaries and

6 This high-circulation weekly publication had only months previously serialised the first episodes of *Et on tuera tous les affreux* (*Let's Kill All the Ugly Ones*), one of the novels that Vian wrote under the pseudonym of Vernon Sullivan and which was itself a somewhat racy parody of the science fiction short story.

7 The works listed by Vian include: Morand's *Ouvert la nuit* (1922, *Open All Night*) and *Fermé la nuit* (1923, *Closed All Night*); Mac Orlan's collection *Les Poissons morts* (1917, *Dead Fish*), whose title is used by Vian for one of the short stories of *Les Fourmis*, and Aymé's *Derrière chez Martin* (1938, *Behind Martin's Place*).

contacts at Gallimard, Jean-Paul Sartre and Jean Paulhan, were also masterful short story writers. Naturally, Vian knew their work, but, perhaps out of a desire not to imitate them, he chose another path, inspired in part by his passion for American writers. Like his friend Raymond Queneau, he would create a style that accommodated his love of linguistic inventiveness, and it was a style that would see him transcend his French predecessors.

The Golden Years: 1945-1952

In the Pléiade edition of Vian's collected fiction, we included forty-five short stories under the heading "*nouvelles*". With the exception of two of these, "Drencula" and "Paris, le 15 décembre 1999…", which are fantastic or science fiction tales, all were written between 1945 and 1952.[8] This period corresponds exactly to the years when Vian was writing his novels, and it is interesting to note the numerous connections between the different genres of fiction in which he was engaged.[9] A prime example is "Le Rappel" ("Recall"), which was probably written in 1946 and revised in 1949. Its storyline is something of a mirror image of the novel *L'Herbe rouge* (*Red Grass*), which was also completed in 1949.[10] Indeed, "Le Rappel" relates the last moments of a man who commits suicide by throwing himself off the Empire State Building. As he falls, he pauses at various floors to remember key episodes in his life. In *L'Herbe rouge*, on the other hand, the protagonist Wolf builds a machine to go beyond the skies and relive his memories with a view to destroying them. The idea of associating movement — be it upwards or downwards — with memory thus produced parallel texts of short-story and novel length.[11] Other examples tend to show that Vian's short stories often served as a testing-ground for drafts of his novels. But the opposite is also true: "Surprise-partie chez Léobille"

8 "Drencula" remained unpublished in Vian's lifetime; we estimate that it dates from 1955. "Paris, le 15 décembre 1999…" was published in *Actualité littéraire*, 50, 1958.

9 Vian's last novel, *L'Arrache-cœur* (*Heartsnatcher*), was published in 1953. It was written in 1951 and reworked in 1952 to take on board suggestions made by Raymond Queneau.

10 *Red Grass*, translated by Paul Knobloch, was released in 2013 by TamTam Books.

11 Vian's ideas were taken up again by the cinema as recently as 2004 in Michel Gondry's film *Eternal Sunshine of the Spotless Mind.* For a comparative analysis, see Alistair Rolls, "Boris Vian's Eternal Sunshine, Or the Truth about Mother's Textuality", *Forum for Modern Language Studies*, 43, 7, 2011, pp. 289-303.

("Léobille's Party"), for example, draws directly on passages from the novel *Vercoquin et le plancton* (*Vercoquin and the Plankton*).

Even a cursory reading of the eleven short stories published as *Les Fourmis*, all of which were written between 1946 and 1947, and of other short stories written during the same period reveals a striking similarity in tone and themes between these and Vian's first novels; indeed, it is often impossible to determine with any degree of certainty which came first, the novels or the short stories. The latter are set against a variety of backdrops such as war-time and post-Liberation politics ("Les Fourmis" — "Pins and Needles") or music ("Blues pour un chat noir" — "Blues for a Black Cat"), all of which were a source of inspiration for Vian's early novels. And then there is that disturbing strangeness that marks "Le Voyage à Khonostrov" ("Journey to Khonostrov") and "Les Poissons morts" ("Dead Fish"), a strangeness which is taken to new heights in certain famous scenes in *L'Écume des jours* (*Foam of the Daze*) and *L'Automne à Pékin* (*Autumn in Peking*).[12] Finally, there are characters, some entirely fictional and others taken from real life, that appear in both the short stories and the novels. These include "the Major", hero of *Vercoquin et le plancton*, who crops up in any number of short stories — at times fleetingly, and at others taking over the whole story. There is also Claude Léon, who was, like the Major, a friend of Vian's in real life, and who plays a secondary role in several stories, including "Martin m'a téléphoné" ("Martin called...") and "Surprise-partie chez Léobille" ("Léobille's Party"), but is an important character in *L'Automne à Pékin*.[13]

If we extend our analysis to the short stories written after 1947, we see this same thematic and stylistic correspondence, this same mix of the fantastic, of transposed anecdotes, humour and word play, throughout Vian's

---

[12] As noted in the introductory essay to this volume, *L'Écume des jours* was translated twice into English in the 1960s — by Stanley Chapman as *Froth on the Daydream* (London: Rapp & Carroll, 1967), and by John Sturrock as *Mood Indigo* (New York: Grove Press, 1968). Brian Harper's translation, *Foam of the Daze*, was published by Tosh Berman's Californian publishing house TamTam Books in 2003. *Autumn in Peking* was translated by Paul Knobloch (TamTam Books, 2005).

[13] The original manuscript of this novel reveals that the episode in which Claude Léon appears for the first time was initially conceived of as a short story in itself. See the Pléiade edition of Vian's *Œuvres romanesques complètes*, vol. I, p. 1221.

wider corpus, including in his poems and plays. From 1950, Vian's fictional production lost some of its verve. Of course, he still went on to write *L'Arrache-cœur* (*Heartsnatcher*),[14] but when he ceased writing for the magazine *Dans le train*, in February 1950, his short story output slowed greatly (he wrote no more than half a dozen stories between 1950 and 1952). From that point, his writing focus shifted to other short formats: jazz reviews, chronicles and, above all, songs.

Writing/Publishing

Before he had any urge to publish in magazines, Vian's first thought was to publish his short stories as a collection. Indeed, in April 1946 he signed a contract with Gallimard for a collection entitled *Les Lurettes fourrées*, which was due to contain a number of the texts that would in fact make up *Les Fourmis*, three years later. At that point in time, Vian was still unpublished, although *Vercoquin et le plancton* had been accepted by Gallimard and *L'Écume des jours* was about to be entered for the literary prize *Le Prix de la Pléiade*, with publication in Gallimard's prestigious "Collection Blanche" up for grabs. The theme running through this first planned collection was jazz, with the short stories all initially beginning with an epigraph referring to a jazz musician or theme; their plots drew largely on the author's lived experiences, which necessarily included jazz. Other short stories of this early period, which Vian intended for publication in magazines and which were not therefore included in *Les Fourmis*, were also predominantly about jazz, especially "Martin m'a téléphoné" ("Martin called…"), "Surprise-partie chez Léobille" ("Léobille's Party") and "Méfie-toi de l'orchestre" ("Don't Trust the Band"). If, in 1946, he ultimately published some of the stories that he had planned to include in *Les Lurettes fourrées* in magazines, he nonetheless still had a collection of short stories in mind.[15] However, the initial project was soon in tatters. In the first

[14] Boris Vian, *Heartsnatcher*, translated by Stanley Chapman (Champaign, Urbana: Dalkey Archive Press, 2003).

[15] The stories published in magazines include: "Les Fourmis" ("Pins and Needles") in *Les Temps modernes* in June 1946; "L'Oie bleue" ("Blue Fairy Tale") in *La Rue* in July 1946; "Les Poissons morts" ("Dead Fish") in *L'Arbalète* in spring 1947; then in 1948, "Le Voyage à Khonostrov" ("Journey to Khonostrov") in *Pan* and "La Route déserte" ("One-Way Street") in *Nyza*.

place, the two novels published by Gallimard struggled to sell. Second, the eruption of the Vernon Sullivan scandal did seemingly irreparable damage to Vian's reputation.[16] Certainly, he was never again to publish with Gallimard (not in his lifetime at least). It was his friend Jean d'Halluin, from the Éditions du Scorpion, the publishing house responsible for *J'irai cracher sur vos tombes*, who took over from Gallimard and, finally, published the collection. In the end, the title chosen was that of the opening short story, "Les Fourmis", which had been praised three years earlier by Jean-Paul Sartre when it had appeared in *Les Temps modernes*. Most of the stories found their way into the published volume, but *Les Fourmis* only met with limited success — any book bearing the name of Boris Vian was by this stage undoubtedly less marketable than one signed "Vernon Sullivan".

If we look at Vian's short stories in the context of the various publication outlets in which they appeared, it is clear that the author was careful to adapt his style to the particular magazine for which each story was written. This explains, for example, the striking difference in style between the stories bound for prestigious reviews or journals — *Les Temps modernes* for "Les Fourmis" ("Pins and Needles"), *L'Arbalète* for "Les Poissons morts" ("Dead Fish") and *Combat* for "Les Pompiers" (The Firemen) — and those that he literally churned out for the magazine *Dans le train*, which, as its name suggests, was designed to help passengers while away the time on train trips. The twelve stories that Vian published in *Dans le train* between 1948 and 1950, which include "Les Pas vernis" ("The Slip-up"), "Un test" ("The Test"), "Un drôle de sport" ("A Funny Old Game") and "Le Motif" ("The Motive"), are generally shorter in format and have a simpler plot favouring realism over the fantastic. To meet demand (he was publishing in this magazine on almost a monthly basis), Vian at times had to fall back on work produced previously.[17] He also

16 *J'irai cracher sur vos tombes* (*I Spit on Your Graves*), which was a novel supposedly in the style of the American hard-boiled thriller, appeared in November 1946. The name Vernon Sullivan that it bore on the cover was a pseudonym for none other than Vian himself. Three months later, news of the deception broke and the author was attacked by a public morals group. The affair caused quite a commotion and Vian's name quickly became associated with a project said to amount to "pornographic literature".

17 Four short stories that appeared in *Dans le train* had been written in 1946 and bear the marks of that period, at which time Vian was very much a part of the Saint-Germain-des-

dipped back into his writings from 1946 in order to supply four stories for the short-lived and quite literally under-dressed review *Paris-Tabou*. While three of these had already been published in *Les Fourmis*, it is worth noting that it was to this Saint-Germain-des-Prés based review that Vian first sent one of his best short stories, one combining eroticism and science fiction: "L'Amour est aveugle" ("Love is Blind").

Reading/Classifying

Boris Vian was, and remains, difficult to categorise. This is as true of his work as of his personality and career path. He belonged to no literary movement. His short fiction is no different in this respect. Indeed, Vian scholars and biographers have gone to great, and often frustrating, lengths to establish the best working classification for his writing within traditionally recognised genres.

The difficulty with any attempt to classify Vian's short fiction lies in the fact that he did not always set out to write "short stories" as such; rather, he produced narratives for all manner of publications. One of his earliest short stories is a good case in point: "Le Ratichon baigneur" ("The Swimming Priest") looks very much like a chronicle in terms of the tone Vian has adopted and the outlet in which it appeared.[18] Perversely, on the other hand, some of the actual chronicles assembled by Noël Arnaud under the heading "Chroniques du menteur" (which translates as "The Liar's Column") could just as easily be classified as short stories. "Impressions d'Amérique" ("Impressions of America") is a prime example. It was scheduled to be published in number 11-12 of *Les Temps modernes* in the summer of 1946 as one of Vian's famous "chronicles" but was ultimately rejected by the review. It presents a fantasy in which Vian and his off-sider Alexandre Astruc arrive in New York in a submarine. There,

---

Prés set: "Divertissements culturels" ("A Cultural Experience"), "Un test" ("The Test") "Une grande vedette" ("A Big Star") and "Un métier de chien" ("A Dog of a Job").

[18] Indeed, as early as the opening line we discover that the narrator — and the author — are referring directly to a humoristic piece in an earlier number of the same review, *La Rue*, by journalist Louis Pauwels, in which the latter had analysed the fauna of the Parisian swimming pool: "Mœurs et coutumes aux bains Deligny" ("The Life and Times of the Deligny Baths"). Vian's text thus offers a response to Pauwel's article, with just enough distance for the text to be able to be read outside the context of the era.

the two tourists meet Henry Miller, André Breton and various native New Yorkers. This is a well-crafted narrative, full of farce and imagination. As such, it is a typical Vian short story.

Of the forty-five short stories written by Vian, only ten went unpublished in his lifetime. He had no trouble getting his texts published because, as a journalist, he was on the editorial board of several reviews. This was the case for *La Rue*, which took "Le Ratichon baigneur" for its July 1946 edition, *Les Temps modernes*, as previously mentioned, *Samedi-Soir*, which dedicated a full page to "Surprise-partie chez Léobille", and, later, *Constellation*, to which Vian was a regular contributor of chronicles, essentially, but in which he nonetheless published the short story "Un seul permis pour leur amour" ("One Licence for Love").[19] The chronicles that Vian wrote for *Constellation*, a French version of the American *Reader's Digest*, are not easy to classify. In fact, they fall somewhere between the chronicle and the short story, presenting (often only slightly) fictionalised accounts of the author and his friends in scenarios inspired by real life. The chronicle "Mes vacances comme en 1900" ("My Holidays as in 1900") tells the story of a person who leaves Paris in an old-fashioned car for a road trip around France planned by consulting a Michelin guide dating from 1905. This guide was on Vian's bookshelves, and at the time of writing this story he was the proud owner, and driver, of a 1911 Richard-Brasier Torpédo. Texts such as this ended up being classified by Gilbert Pestureau as "chroniques romancées" (fictionalised chronicles), which is to say not quite chronicles and not quite short stories either. When we came to edit the Pléiade edition of Vian's complete fictional works, we opted for a clearer definition by categorising these ten or so texts as chronicles — a decision based on the fact that they predominantly feature real-life events (the sole exception being "One Licence for Love", which appeared to be totally fictional in origin and which is therefore included amongst the short stories).

The Order of the Short Stories

At the time of Vian's death on 23 June 1959, the collection *Les Fourmis*, along with most of his other published work, was no longer available in bookshops.

[19] This short story was renamed "Marthe et Jean" by Noël Arnaud when he included it in the collection *Le Ratichon baigneur*.

But in 1960, at a time when only the Collège de 'Pataphysique was publishing Vian,[20] Éric Losfeld decided to publish two titles from the Éditions du Scorpion's publishing catalogue, *Les Fourmis* and *Et on tuera tous les affreux* (*Let's Kill all the Ugly Ones*).[21] Spurred on by the growing success of Vian's works in the French market during the early 1960s, 'Pataphysician Noël Arnaud, with the help of Ursula Vian Kübler, Vian's second wife, undertook the enormous task of working through the archives left by the author. With Arnaud's assistance, Jean-Jacques Pauvert and Christian Bourgois began to publish Vian's forgotten works on a wider scale. And the rest, as they say, is history. From amongst these new publications and re-publications, Arnaud compiled the first of two new short story collections: *Le Loup-garou* (*The Werewolf*), which appeared in 1970. Then, in 1981, he published *Le Ratichon baigneur*,[22] which brought together all the stories written for *Dans le train* and those that had remained unpublished during the author's lifetime. Still other short texts found their way into various other collections, such as *La Belle Époque*, *Cinéma/science-fiction*, *Écrits sur le jazz* and *Écrits pornographiques*. But, most importantly, three of Vian's best short stories, three texts that can certainly be considered amongst his most striking and original, almost got left behind in this (re-)publication process, in what has since become quite a famous publishing oversight. The stories in question are "Le Rappel" ("Recall"), "Le Retraité" ("The Retiree") and "Les Pompiers" ("The Firemen"). When, in 1962, Pauvert decided to publish a small set of short stories to go with *L'Herbe rouge* (*Red Grass*) and *L'Arrache-cœur* (*Heartsnatcher*), he inadvertently locked these three previously unknown short stories together in a triad to be known henceforth as *Les Lurettes fourrées*. Initially designed to give new Vian readers a taste of his skills as a writer of short fiction, these three stories have since that time been

---

20 The College of 'Pataphysics published Vian's play *Les Bâtisseurs d'empire* (*The Empire Builders*) in 1959; it also dedicated volume 12 of its *Dossiers* to him the following year.

21 *Les Fourmis* was thus published two years before Vian's major novels were republished (those he published under his own name) and also two years before his first volume of poetry was posthumously published as *Je voudrais pas crever*, at which point there was something of a Vian renaissance.

22 This is the English title given in this present volume to the short story that lends its name to the collection.

systematically included in every reprint of *L'Herbe rouge*. The last, and by no means the least, of the unclassified short stories is "Les Chiens, le désir et la mort" ("Dogs, Death and Desire"). Unlike the case of *Les Lurettes fourrées*, it was Vian's choice to publish this text alongside the second Vernon Sullivan novel, *Les Morts ont tous la même peau* (*The Dead All Have the Same Skin*) in 1947.[23] From that point on it was annexed inside this book and thus failed to appear in the later collections. It is, however, one of the most powerful short stories, and the only one to be passed off as "American".

It was not until 1999, when work began on editing Vian's collected works,[24] that the short stories were put back into chronological order. Only then were we able to get our first look at the evolution of Vian's writing in the short story format. And so now, in the present volume, we are finally able to present what we believe is an exclusive, world-first reclassification of Boris Vian's short stories.

Boris Vian's Short Stories

The following classification is by chronological order of publication. When the short story was not published during the author's lifetime, the estimated date of composition is used instead. The list gives information in the following order:

- "Title" (date of composition), *Publication outlet* (date of publication) — *Collection*.[25]

The title of the translation, as given either by Peter Hodges in the present volume or Julia Older in *Blues for a Black Cat and Other Stories*, is given at the end in brackets. There is obviously no publication outlet indicated for stories that remained unpublished.

---

23 The English translation, *The Dead All Have the Same Skin*, translated by Paul Knobloch (California: TamTam Books, 2008), also includes "Dogs, Desire and Death". The story is retranslated in the present volume by Peter Hodges under the reconfigured title "Dogs, Death and Desire".

24 *Boris Vian, Œuvres complètes* (Paris: Fayard, 15 vols, 1999-2003).

25 Until 1997, the collection titles given in italics here were all available in the famous 10/18 paperback collection. Since then, Livre de Poche has taken over the paperback arm of Vian sales.

1. "Martin m'a téléphoné" (25 October 1945) — *Le Loup-garou.* ("Martin called…")
2. "Le Figurant" (n.d. [2nd semester 1945]) — *Les Fourmis.*
3. "Les Fourmis" (n.d.), *Les Temps modernes*, 10 (June 1946) — *Les Fourmis.* ("Pins and Needles")
4. "L'Oie bleue" (n.d.), *La Rue* (5 July 1946), then *Paris-Tabou* (November 1949) — *Les Fourmis.* ("Blue Fairy Tale")
5. "Le Ratichon baigneur" (n.d.), *La Rue* (26 July 1946) — *Le Ratichon baigneur.* ("The Swimming Priest")
6. "La Bourse ou la vie" (n.d. [1946]) — *La Belle Époque.*
7. "Blues pour un chat noir" (n.d. [1946]) — *Les Fourmis.* ("Blues for a Black Cat")
8. "Le Brouillard" (n.d. [1946]) — *Les Fourmis.* ("Fog")
9. "Le Rappel" (n.d. [1946], reworked in 1949 with a view to include it in *Les Fourmis*) — *L'Herbe rouge.*
10. "Marseille commençait à s'éveiller" (n.d. [2nd semester 1946]) — *Le Loup-garou.* ("Another Day in Marseille")
11. "Le Plombier" (n.d. [1946-1947]) — *Les Fourmis.* ("The Plumber")
12. "Les Chiens, le désir et la mort" (n.d. [1st semester 1947]), *Les Morts ont tous la même peau* (10 September 1947). ("Dogs, Death and Desire")
13. "Méfie-toi de l'orchestre" (n.d.), *America/Jazz 47* (March 1947) — *Le Ratichon baigneur.* ("Don't Trust the Band")
14. "Les Poissons morts" (10 March 1947), *L'Arbalète*, 12 (spring 1947) — *Les Fourmis.* ("Dead Fish")
15. "Les Remparts du sud" (n.d. [1946], reworked for *Samedi-Soir*, 7 May 1947) — *Le Loup-garou.* ("Ramparts of the South")
16. "Surprise-partie chez Léobille" (June 1947), *Samedi-Soir* (12 July 1947) — *Le Loup-garou.* ("Léobille's Party")
17. "Les Pas vernis" (7 June 1948), *Dans le train* (July 1948) — *Le Loup-garou* ("The Slip-up")
18. "Les Pompiers" (June 1948), *Combat* (15 August 1948) — *L'Herbe rouge.*
19. "En rond autour de minuit" (n.d.), *Jazz-Hot* (December 1948) — *Écrits sur le jazz.*

20. "Le Voyage à Khonostrov" (February 1947), *Pan* (1948) — *Les Fourmis.* ("Journey to Khonostrov")
21. "La Route déserte" (n.d. [1947]), *Nyza* (1948) — *Les Fourmis.* ("One-Way Street")
22. "Francfort-sous-la-main" (n.d. [2nd semester 1948]), *Dans le train* (April 1949) — *Le Ratichon baigneur.* ("Frankfurt on Tap").
23. "Le Retraité" (22 March 1949), *Dans le train* (May 1949) — *L'Herbe rouge.*
24. "Divertissements culturels" (10 January 1946), *Dans le train* (June 1949) — *Le Ratichon baigneur* ("A Cultural Experience")
25. "Un test" (n.d. [1946], then 29 June 1949), *Dans le train* (July 1949) — *Le Ratichon baigneur.* ("The Test")
26. "Une grande vedette" (5 March 1946), *Dans le train* (August 1949) — *Le Ratichon baigneur.* ("A Big Star")
27. "Les Filles d'avril" (n.d.), *Dans le train* (September 1949) — *Le Ratichon baigneur.* ("April's Daughters")
28. "L'Amour est aveugle" (n.d.), *Paris-Tabou* (September 1949) — *Le Loup-garou.* ("Love is Blind")
29. "L'Écrevisse" (June 1946), *Paris-Tabou* (October 1949) — *Les Fourmis.* ("Cancer")
30. "Un métier de chien" (2 January 1946), *Dans le train* (October 1949) — *Le Ratichon baigneur.* ("A Dog of a Job")
31. "Le Penseur" (n.d.), *Dans le train* (November 1949) — *Le Loup-garou.* ("The Thinker")
32. "L'Assassin" (n.d.), *Dans le train* (December 1949) — *Le Ratichon baigneur.* ("The Killer")
33. "Un cœur d'or" (April then June 1949), *La Bouteille à la mer* (4th term 1949) — *Le Loup-garou.* ("A Heart of Gold")
34. "L'Impuissant" (n.d. [1949]) — *Le Ratichon baigneur.* ("Impotence")
35. "Maternité" (n.d. [1949]) — *Le Ratichon baigneur.* ("Motherhood")
36. "Un drôle de sport" (n.d. [1949]), *Dans le train* (January 1950) — *Le Ratichon baigneur.* ("A Funny Game")
37. "Les Bons Élèves" (July 1946), *Paris-Tabou* (January 1950) — *Les Fourmis.* ("Good Students")

38. "Le Motif" (n.d. [1949]), *Dans le train* (February 1950) — *Le Ratichon baigneur.* ("The Motive")
39. "Le Danger des classiques" (n.d. [1950]) — *Le Loup-garou.* ("Danger from the Classics")
40. "Le Loup-garou" (n.d. [1950]) — *Le Loup-garou.* ("The Werewolf")
41. "Le Bonhomme de neige" (n.d.), *Sensations* (April 1951) — *Le Loup-garou.* ("The Snowman")
42. "Un seul permis pour leur amour" (n.d.), *Constellation* (March 1952) — *Le Ratichon baigneur.* ("One Licence for Love")
43. "Une pénible histoire" (n.d. [c. 1949]), *La Bouteille à la mer* (1st term 1952) — *Le Loup-garou.* ("A Sad Story")
44. "Drencula" (n.d. [c. 1955]) — *Écrits pornographiques.*
45. "Paris, le 15 décembre 1999…" (n.d.), *Actualité littéraire* (1958) — *Cinéma/Science-fiction.*

VIAN, IN SHORT: AN IRONIC TAKE ON THE ART OF THE SHORT STORY

Audrey Camus

Of the many literary and artistic activities practised by Boris Vian, his production of short fiction is one of the least discussed, and this in spite of the success that many of his stories appear to have had at the time of their publication.[1]

The occasion of this reconnection with the posthumously published short stories of *Le Loup-garou* (1970) and *Le Ratichon baigneur* (1981), in translation and thus for the first time for most English-speaking readers, is an opportune moment to analyse what is so often undervalued — Vian's skill as a short story writer.[2]

---

1 Michel Fauré includes a discussion of Vian's short stories in his monograph *Les Vies posthumes de Boris Vian* (Paris: UGE, 10/18, 1975), especially p. 155. As this work came out before the collection *Le Ratichon baigneur* was itself posthumously published, the account that Fauré provides of the success of Vian's short stories is necessarily incomplete. However, Marc Lapprand mentions the positive reviews of *Le Ratichon baigneur* that appeared in *Le Monde* and *La Quinzaine Littéraire* following its publication in 1981. For Lapprand's commentary, see the Pléiade edition of Vian's complete prose fiction: Boris Vian, *Œuvres romanesques complètes* (Paris: Gallimard, 2 vols, 2010), vol. II, pp. 1312-1313.

2 These collections were both edited by the famous Vian scholar Noël Arnaud and first published in French by Parisian publisher Christian Bourgois under the following titles: *Le Loup-garou, suivi de douze autres nouvelles* and *Le Ratichon baigneur et autres nouvelles*. The French titles of these collections will be referred to throughout this essay in abbreviated form as *LG* and *RB*.

Boris Vian as Short Story Writer

If this aspect of Vian's writing has been scarcely touched upon until now, it is probably because it was just one element of a broad-ranging literary output. As René Godenne has observed, the French short story of the twentieth century is not only less widely read than its nineteenth-century counterpart but, since it no longer corresponds to such a tightly defined genre, it is often considered almost a bastardised version of the novel. In fact, if the work of certain specialist short story writers of the last century is reasonably well known (we might think of Paul Morand, Marcel Arland, Marcel Aymé or Pierre Gripari), we are generally far less familiar with the short stories of those writers for whom this was not the principal format (such as François Mauriac, Louis Aragon, Romain Gary and, we might add, Boris Vian).[3] This is all the more true in Vian's case because only one collection of his short stories, *Les Fourmis*, was published in his lifetime.[4] Indeed, while he published a number of stories in magazines, it was only after his death that most of them were assembled into collections. It was quite legitimate, therefore, to state in 1976 that, "until recentlyVian's novels were not well known by the general public, but his short stories have been readily available, whereas now that the novels are gaining recognition, the short stories are becoming more or less neglected".[5] We might reasonably expect the recent publication of Vian's complete fiction in

[3] With the exception of Boris Vian, these authors are discussed by René Godenne in his chapter "Fortune/Infortunes, permanence/avatars d'un genre", in Vincent Engel and Michel Guissard (eds), *La Nouvelle de langue française aux frontières des autres genres, du Moyen Âge à nos jours* (Ottignies: Éditions Quorum, 1997), vol. I, pp. 396-409, especially pp. 406 and 408. In the same way, scholars of the short story tend to focus on specialist short story writers, thus, on the whole, ignoring Vian.

[4] With the exception of "Le Figurant" (meaning "The Extra"), the short stories of *Les Fourmis* have been translated into English by Julia Older and published under the title *Blues for a Black Cat and Other Stories* (Lincoln: University of Nebraska Press, 1992). The French edition was originally published by Bourgois in 1949 (reprinted in 1972). This collection will henceforth be designated in the body of the text by the abbreviation *F*.

[5] Herbert Dickhoff, "Approche discrète des nouvelles de Boris Vian", in Noël Arnaud and Henri Baudin (eds), *Boris Vian: Colloque de Cerisy* (Paris: UGE, 10/18, 1977), vol. I, p. 334 (editors' translation). All subsequent quotations from French critical sources are likewise translated by the editors of the present volume.

Gallimard's prestigious Pléiade collection, which includes the short stories, to broaden their French readership to some extent, as was the case when Gilbert Pestureau edited the Pochothèque collected works in 1991.[6] It is the aim of the present volume to extend this audience still further, this time to an Anglophone public.

The status of Vian the writer cannot now be divorced from his legendary status as impresario-polymath-genius, and in all likelihood this Vian legend has had its part to play in the indifference shown by critics to his short stories, all the more so since these stories have not benefited from the same scandal factor as the *noir* novels that he wrote as Vernon Sullivan, the jazz adventures of the "Prince of Saint-Germain-des-Prés" or the anti-war songs and plays that have become synonymous with the name of Boris Vian. Versatility, of course, is typically associated with dilettantism, and the dilettante is but a stone's throw from the amateur. People as a result tend to cite the many areas in which Vian excelled as an author, expressing their admiration at this remarkable diversity, but then fail to take the time to look more closely.

Yet, there is probably a more fundamental reason for the neglect of Vian's short stories: rather like his "Chroniques du Menteur" (the chronicles from his "Liar's Column"), which appeared in *Les Temps modernes*, and which similarly attracted little commentary, these texts are often light, of their day and thus ephemeral — the thumbnail sketch, by its nature, not only undermines its own posterity but also requires no explanation. Written for reviews or magazines, these short stories bear the mark of their target publication: famously spontaneous in tone and written at breakneck speed, they defy analysis. Furthermore, their use of humour tends to detract from their legitimacy as literary texts. Indeed, the extent to which this rejection of seriousness on Vian's part has affected the reception of his work cannot be overstated.[7]

As a consequence, more or less the only critical work that has been conducted to date on the short stories has been undertaken by those who have

---

6 Boris Vian, *Romans, Nouvelles, Œuvres diverses* (Paris: Le Livre de Poche, 1991).

7 For more details, see the special edition of *Europe* dedicated to Boris Vian, 967-968, 2009 (guest editor: Audrey Camus).

edited and published them, that is to say Noël Arnaud for Christian Bourgois, Gilbert Pestureau for the Livre de Poche and Fayard, Marc Lapprand for Fayard and Gallimard's Pléiade collection, and François Caradec for the three stories published in 1962 by Jean-Jacques Pauvert as *Les Lurettes fourrées*.[8] In his paper on the subject at the Cerisy colloquium in 1976, Herbert Dickhoff did some preliminary work, principally outlining the contents of the texts that were still unpublished at that stage. One of the first questions that he was asked after his presentation was about the possible evolution of the short stories over time. Unanswered at the time, this question is all the more pertinent because it is complicated by the varying status of the short stories within Vian's *œuvre*. Posthumous collections, made up of texts that had been either previously unpublished or which had appeared in magazines, are necessarily less accomplished than collections published by the author himself. Indeed, in 1969 Michel Rybalka noted the relative weakness of certain texts written for the periodical *Dans le train*.[9] While the attention given to the dates of composition and publication of the stories initially appears to reveal little in the way of change in Vian's themes or praxis between 1945 and 1952, it does, on the other hand, confirm the importance of the selection process.[10] It is therefore essential to re-examine these texts in their context, taking into account their specific place within Vian's fiction; but it is also important to reintroduce distinctions into the short story corpus itself, that is to say, between the stories in *Les Fourmis*, whose cover blurb quite rightly signals the collection's key place among Vian's major works, and the later collections, which for their part can be categorised as minor works, as Arnaud points out in his preface to *Le Ratichon baigneur*.

---

8 See also the entry under "Lurettes" in Marc Lapprand, *V comme Vian* (Québec: Les Presses Universitaires de Laval, 2006), pp. 115-122.

9 Michel Rybalka, *Boris Vian, essai d'interprétation et de documentation* (Paris: Minard, 1969), p. 223.

10 For Noël Arnaud, the three short stories about the cinema in *Le Ratichon baigneur* are among the first fictional works Vian wrote. Interestingly, however, these texts are not included in *Les Fourmis* but in the final posthumous collection. Neither does the author produce the same texts when writing for *Samedi-Soir* as he does when writing for *Jazz-hot, La Rue, Combat* or *Dans le train* and so on. For more on these variations, see Lapprand's note in the *Œuvres romanesques complètes*, vol. I, p. 1270.

Clearly, it would be possible to trace the development of Vian's short-story praxis over time, from an early phase that saw him transform the daily events of his own life into tales of high farce, as he did in longer form in the adolescent novels *Trouble dans les Andains* and *Vercoquin et le plancton*, to a second, apparently more highly developed phase that is more the realm of the imaginary. Yet, it can also be seen how this second phase lost ground as Vian succumbed to an increasing pressure to sell books, and as his hopes of being recognised as an author began to fade. Despite the particular constraints that shaped them, these two categories of praxis seem in fact to coexist throughout Vian's career as a short story writer, always jointly present but with one by turn dominating the other and with each illustrating a particular aspect of his writing.[11] My intention here is therefore to study both in more detail in order to determine on what literary necessity they are predicated.

The Reflexive and the Ludic Short Story

The fact of the matter is that, between the humorous sketch at one end of the scale — those texts "written in haste" and produced primarily for publication in magazines[12] — and, at the other extremity, the more fully developed short stories, many of which feature in the collection put together by the author himself, the difference is not simply one of degree of accomplishment but also one of type. The short story that we shall refer to here as "ludic" is essentially funny and entertaining: its consistent abuse of logic and its preposterous story lines function principally around word play and are compensated by meaning at the macro level or find resolution in the story's ending. The complex short story, which will be called "reflexive" for our purposes here, tends on the other hand to depart from rules that are more fundamental, calling into question

[11] It is difficult to go past Daniel Sangsue's argument that any typology of the short story is made impossible by virtue of the genre's inherent tendency towards variety and individuality. See Daniel Sangsue, "Formes brèves. Le Conte et la nouvelle au XIXe siècle", in Patrick Berthier and Michel Jarrety (eds), *Histoire de la France littéraire* (Paris: PUF, 3 vols, 2006), vol. III, p. 107. It seems to me, nonetheless, that a typological approach that is conscious of its own limitations remains a useful one for assessing this variety and this individuality, especially within the corpus of a particular author.

[12] See Noël Arnaud's preface to the 1981 Bourgois edition of *Le Ratichon baigneur*, p. 12.

the way in which we understand the world, and thereby convey a sense of anguish. In the first instance, readers can form a figurative interpretation; in the second, we come up against literal meanings whose incongruity brings to light impossible realities.[13]

Of course, the line of demarcation separating the ludic from the reflexive short story is open to some debate. Nevertheless, this argument itself at least has the merit of highlighting the fact that there are differences within this complex collection of texts and of identifying tendencies, even if it fails to bring into play the mischievous intelligence of a "discrete approach to the object".[14] Indeed, these preliminary remarks raise an important point: when one considers the evolution of the short story in France, it can be seen that the ludic variety is closer to older examples of the genre, with their emphasis on an entertaining tale often turning on clever word play, whereas the reflexive type belongs to the tradition of the serious story, which is more prevalent in the modern era with its preference for "fragmented, enigmatic and predominantly elliptical" writing over wit.[15] The predominance of the former, in terms of sheer numbers, may in part explain why Vian's short fiction has not really found its niche in the history of the genre in the twentieth century; this distinction nonetheless gives us some clues as to its genealogy.

Chronicles and Fabliaux: Signs of the Times

If, keeping the above caveats in mind, we accept this initial classification, we can next move to subdivide the ludic category into two types. The first includes short stories that are anecdotal in character and that bear a certain resemblance to the chronicles that Vian was publishing at around the same

---

[13] For a more detailed analysis along these lines, see my article "Les Contrées étranges de l'insignifiant: Retour sur la notion de fantastique moderne", *Études françaises*, 45, 1, 2009, special issue on "Écritures de l'insignifiant" (guest editor Audrey Camus), pp. 89-107.

[14] "Approche discrète de l'objet" was the title of a conference paper given by Vian in 1948. It is reproduced in the first volume of the Pléiade edition of his *Œuvres romanesques complètes*, pp. 1089-1103. As Lapprand *et al.* note, the title reflects the "discrete function" and is thus testament to Vian's background as a mathematician, p. 1300.

[15] Aron Kibédi Varga, "Le Temps de la nouvelle", in Engel and Guissard, *La Nouvelle de langue française*, p. 13. On the movement from the comic to the serious in the seventeenth century, see Godenne's previously cited chapter, also in Engel and Guissard.

time. These include such stories as "Francfort sous-la-main" ("Frankfurt on Tap") and "Divertissements culturels" ("A Cultural Experience") (both *RB*). These texts, which for the most part date back to the early part of the author's career, and which we shall call "chronicle short stories", relate or are inspired by aspects of Vian's life at that time and generally bear the marks of that period of history. They characteristically end in a reversal of circumstances, typically affecting the protagonist. We should note that the editors of the complete works published by Fayard also elected to distinguish between what they call "intimate and picturesque *reportages*", similar to chronicles, and "short stories proper, which are genuine fictional texts in terms of their distance from 'reality', their poetic transmutation of real life or their creation of an imaginary universe".[16] However, they only include in the first category "Martin m'a téléphoné" ("Martin called...") (*LG*) "Méfie-toi de l'orchestre" ("Don't Trust the Band") (*RB*) and "Francfort sous-la-main" ("Frankfurt on Tap") (*RB*), which is to say the texts with a jazz-related theme. The three texts about the cinema — "Une grande vedette" ("A Big Star"), "Divertissements culturels" ("A Cultural Experience") and "Un métier de chien" ("A Dog of a Job") (all *RB*) — are nonetheless of the same type, notwithstanding their greater emphasis on narrative construction than linearity and the greater distancing of the narrator (first or second person in the first series and third person in the second). A comparison of the two series reveals the progressive transition from the chronicle short story to the next type.

This second type of text, which similarly builds towards a punch line but which is shorter in format, is made up of little stories prepared for publication in magazines. They have a pseudo-moralising dimension that is more general in nature and that takes us beyond the anecdotal framework of the real-life incident. This sub-category includes stories such as "L'Impuissant" ("Impotence") or "Le Motif" ("The Motive") (both *RB*).[17] Bearing in mind

---

[16] Gilbert Pestureau and Marc Lapprand in *Boris Vian, Œuvres complètes* (Paris: Fayard, 1999), vol. 5, p. 255.

[17] Mixed types are clearly imaginable: the conclusion of "Un test" ("The Test") (*RB*) makes it a good example of a fabliau short story while its setting (the Deligny swimming pool) and the inclusion of little Bison in the plot tend to ground it in the biographical tradition (Vian occasionally includes family members in his stories, typically using derivations of anagrams of his own name, such as "Bison ravi", which explains the presence of bisons in Vian's fiction).

this particularity and the odd marriage of licentiousness and triviality that is their hallmark, we shall call this type "fabliaux short stories" in reference to the fabliau tradition, which influenced the beginnings of the short story genre in the fifteenth and sixteenth centuries.[18]

Furthermore, the short stories related to the chronicle tradition can also be shown to reflect the origins of the short story genre itself, which Goethe defined as relating an incredible event that has taken place. Michel Viegnes recalls that the etymology of the now standard French term for the short story, *nouvelle*, "links the concept of the genre to the oral tradition since the short story designated by this term is supposed to provide news [or *nouvelles*] of existing people".[19] And indeed, the stories that Vian likes to tell are directly linked to current events, as demonstrated in particular by their extensive use of polyphony.[20] Even when written in the first person singular, they represent a mine of information on their era, and it is this that seems to interest the author, more so than the psychology of his characters. Thus, we (re)discover, some sixty years later, for the infatuation of the times with parties, jazz, the cinema and all that the USA had to offer — all delivered with a heady and perverse mix of high energy and disillusionment. Such texts in fact represent an important vector of Anglo-Saxon culture, which Vian helped to introduce into France with his own brand of critical enthusiasm.[21] This is all the more

---

18 Again, for more on this, see Godenne's chapter in Engel and Guissard, *La Nouvelle de langue française*. Elsewhere, Godenne uses this same term (*nouvelle-fabliau*) in a stricter sense to refer to the short forms of the fifteenth and sixteenth centuries. In so doing, he points to a direct influence rather than a distant relationship. See René Godenne, *La Nouvelle française* (Paris: PUF, 1974), especially the first chapter.

19 Michel Viegnes, *L'Esthétique de la nouvelle française au vingtième siècle* (New York: Peter Lang, 1989), p. 3.

20 Much work remains to be done on the oral tradition in Vian's short stories. Whether it is in the rather colourful retorts that the lady in "Le Loup-garou" ("The Werewolf") imagines saying to Denis or the cursory exchanges with the Americans in a short story like "Martin m'a téléphoné" ("Martin called..."), in which the protagonist curiously ends up changing into a duck, as much, we might imagine, as a result of mimicking the accent of his interlocutors as of blowing into his trumpet. (This phrase is translated in the present volume as "let out an enormous quack" — an attempt to capture both the image of the duck and the musical allusion to a false note or discordant sound that can be read into the word "canard" in French).

21 For a more detailed analysis of Vian's role in this process, see Gilbert Pestureau, *Boris Vian,*

interesting when one considers the short story's fall from grace in France in the twentieth century and its relative prosperity in the United States. As Arnaud notes in his preface to *Le Ratichon baigneur*, Vian was a great reader of short stories in English, and it is probably no coincidence that he was one of the few French authors of the period to have worked in the genre. Through his chronicle short stories, therefore, he appears as a smuggler of culture as well as the voice of his time. Form and content are in harmony here.

Vian's trademark black humour arguably conveys better than any history book the electric atmosphere of Liberation Paris, with its new generation of young people torn between disillusionment and a thirst for new beginnings. The fact is that these short stories, assembled though they may be around a key moment in history, are never entirely sacrificed to realism. Here, then, as in all of Vian's work, we witness the "projection of reality, in a biased and heated atmosphere, onto an irregularly undulating reference plane, resulting in some distortion" evoked in the author's preface to *L'Écume des jours* (*Foam of the Daze*).[22] But whereas in the novels and reflexive short stories this praxis gives rise to a poetics that is essentially visual, based on a reliteralising of the figurative and a refusal of allegory, in both the chronicle and fabliaux short stories the aforementioned projection is used to drive a satire-based comedy that amplifies historical detail by caricaturing it. Examples include the opening of "Les Remparts du Sud" ("Ramparts of the South") (*LG*), in which the three-year-old Little Bison,[23] who has just inopportunely shattered the marble top of a table on the terrace of the Deux Mâghos café, embarks on a literary debate of the utmost seriousness with the waiter, lampooning the authors whom those in his entourage clearly dislike, including, unsurprisingly, Vian's favourite targets. In this case, the comedy hinges on several techniques, which, when combined, induce a figurative interpretation of the text. The first technique is that of exaggeration: in Saint-Germain-des-Prés, literature is so essential that it even

les Amerlauds et les Godons (Paris: UGE, 10/18, 1978), in which the short stories are dealt with, although not as a specific case study.

22 The quotation here is taken from Brian Harper's translation of *L'Écume des jours*, published as *Foam of the Daze* by Californian publishing house TamTam Books in 2003 (p. 3).

23 In French, *le Bisonnot...*, signifying the son of Boris Vian himself, also known as *le Bison ravi* (the delighted Bison).

preoccupies waiters and young children. Then there is repetition, including, in Little Bison's case, the repetition of phrases that are beyond his years and that furthermore belong to a rhetoric specific to Saint-Germain-des-Prés, which is satirised here. Actions are also repeated: not content with destroying the furniture, this *enfant terrible* next causes an innocent customer to fall when he accidentally seizes his chair, at which point he once more demonstrates his incredible sense of repartee: "'Who's responsible for this?' the waiter asked. 'It was the Major,' Little Bison said." It is interesting to note, too, how these short scenes that send up (although not entirely without affection, of course, as is further illustrated by the inimitable "pasta scene" at the beginning of the story) the bohemian tendencies of the Parisian literary intelligentsia, of which Vian was himself a part, are echoed in their non-fictional counterpart, the *Manual of Saint-Germain-des-Prés*.[24]

As in his songs, such as "La Complainte du progrès" ("A Lament on Progress"), for example, the author looks at his contemporaries as might a mocking sociologist, first drawing on insider knowledge of the Latin Quarter, jazz or the cinema, before turning to subjects with more universal applicability, such as seduction or the use of the automobile, and even the relationship between the two. If the choice of driving as the backdrop for a story like "Un seul permis pour leur amour" ("One Licence for Love")[25] (*RB*) has particular resonance when one considers the recent securing of women's right to vote, the insight into the way in which driving arouses the power dynamics in a relationship, which is provided in this story, is as valid today as it was then. In the same way, readers may well be surprised to see the question of parenting by homosexual couples, so topical in recent years, raised as early as this by Vian in "Maternité" ("Motherhood") (*RB*), albeit in burlesque mode. Surprisingly, too, a short story like "Le Danger des classiques" ("Danger from the Classics")

---

24 Vian's *Manuel de Saint-Germain-des-Prés* was first published in French in Paris by the Éditions du Chêne in 1974. An English translation by Paul Knobloch, co-edited by Tosh Berman and Eva Prinz, was published by Rizzoli Books in 2005 as *Manual of Saint-Germain-des-Prés*.

25 As Lapprand, Gonzalo and Roulmann note (*Œuvres romanesques complètes*, vol. II, p. 1320), this short story was first published under a pseudonym in the magazine *Constellation* in 1952. Its title was changed to "Marthe et Jean" for publication in *Le Ratichon baigneur*.

(*LG*) not only anticipates in its own way the questioning of the evolution of romantic relationships that will be typical of a twenty-first-century writer like Michel Houellebecq[26] but invents for the purpose a "lectoscope" that proleptically signals the editorial revolution that we are experiencing even as this present book goes to print.

While this satirical dimension is also present in the fabliaux short stories, the dependency on real, current events is less pronounced than in the chronicle variety. A tighter plot construction than in the chronicle short story leads to a greater unity of effect, reminiscent of what Kibédi Varga insightfully calls the "narrativised maxim".[27] However, unlike authors of the classical period, who used this form when writing in, and for, closed societies "whose members subscribed officially to the same value system",[28] Vian systematically introduces irony, thereby making the moral of the tale undecidable. Parody thus represents the fabliau's vector of modernisation, and the apparently obvious moral is always obscured. Despite the distancing effect and the lighter touch deployed here, the satire remains caustic. Vian's critical vision is every bit as effective in the fabliau short story as it is, for example, in the famous Jean-Sol Partre lecture scene from *L'Écume de jours*.

The chronicle short stories and many of the fabliau ones thus appear to offer snapshots of life in Paris, which when read as a whole constitute a kaleidoscopic, satirical picture of social change in the period immediately following the end of the Second World War. Yet this critical perspective should not make us forget the vivacity and boldness of the stories. Their humour, incisive word play and, of course, the resultant reading pleasure, all attest to Vian's skill as a short-story writer. Importantly, too, as we have shown here, they invite us to change our perspective when we engage with these texts. Indeed, in order to gain a fuller understanding of Vian's praxis, one must reinscribe it within a tradition beginning with the ancient forms of the short story, with their quasi-journalistic function, and extending into the moralising

---

26 Michel Houellebecq, *La Possibilité d'une île* (Paris: Livre de Poche, 2005).

27 In French, *la maxime narrativisée.* The concept of unity of effect was first theorised by Edgar Allan Poe and was introduced into the French short story via Baudelaire's famous translations.

28 Kibédi Varga, in Engel and Guissard, *La Nouvelle de langue française*, p. 12.

farce of the fabliaux, the ironic art of the end of the nineteenth century, and the work of Alphonse Allais.[29]

Reflexive Short Stories: The Art of Ellipsis

We turn our attention now to those texts belonging to the reflexive category. These are relatively long in comparison and closer in terms of the richness of the text to what we normally understand by the literary short story.[30] While they also have a comic dimension, they resemble fairy tales insofar as a strong fantasy element dominates the story, giving them a strong sense of angst. Examples include "Les Poissons morts" ("Dead Fish") (*F*), "Un cœur d'or" ("A Heart of Gold") or "Une pénible histoire" ("A Sad Story") (both *LG*).[31] Here again, the categories are porous. For example, "Blues pour un chat noir" ("Blues for a Black Cat") (*F*), whose content is suggestive of fantasy, can be counted among the chronicle short stories in terms of its depiction of urban night life; "Les Remparts du sud" ("Ramparts of the South") (*LG*), for its part,

---

[29] Corinne Noirot-Maguire's article positioning Vian's poetry in a lineage that includes the grotesque, the medieval *fatrasies* and the *Grands Rhétoriqueurs* of the fifteenth and sixteenth centuries is groundbreaking in this respect. See Corinne Noirot-Maguire, "Vian et le vers coquin: Le Coup d'essai des *Cent Sonnets*", *Europe*, 967-968, 2009, pp. 144-155. And while Vian has often been compared to Alphonse Allais, including by Arnaud in his cover blurb for *Le Ratichon baigneur*, no detailed analysis of this filiation has been conducted. Jean-Marc Defays's article "Alphonse Allais nouvelliste!?! Ou quelques réflexions sur la nouvelle moderne et le comique" invites us to undertake just such an analysis, given that his approach could be applied to many aspects of Vian's short stories. See Engel and Guissard, *La Nouvelle de langue française*, vol. II, pp. 184-192.

[30] If we compare the short stories from *Le Ratichon baigneur* with those published as *Les Fourmis* (*Blues for a Black Cat*), they are on average half the length: nine pages on average as compared to 18, even excluding the short story "Le Figurant" ("The Extra"), which makes up 67 pages of the 10/18 edition of *Les Fourmis* and which Julia Older excludes, primarily but not exclusively on this basis, from *Blues for a Black Cat*.

[31] We have used "fairy tale" here as the equivalent of the French word *conte*. In the nineteenth century this term was synonymous with the short story (*nouvelle*). Many scholars and practitioners, however, prefer to reserve the term *conte* for imaginary tales while *nouvelle* covers more realist stories (see Viegnes, *L'Esthétique de la nouvelle française au vingtième siècle*, especially chapter one). Vian's short stories always avoid *mimesis*, but along a sliding scale: there is a distinction between stories that are simply funny and others that are more reminiscent of the *conte*, including some that can be considered deliberate parodies of it, as in the case of "Le Loup-garou" ("The Werewolf").

is clearly inspired by elements of Vian's life but abandons realism completely when the protagonist's car begins "grazing on the grass at the base of an apple tree". So, provided that we accept the caveat that such classifications can never be set in stone, it remains possible to discuss the short stories in terms of dominant tendencies and to establish a working taxonomy of the corpus.

Serious and enigmatic, the reflexive short stories are the closest to what one would expect from the modern *nouvelle*. Here, as in all Vian's fiction, a deep, disconcerting strangeness abounds, even if humour pervades the text. Clearly, this is because the world constructed by the author teems with improbable events, but especially because nothing steps in to make sense of them. "Adepts of *Alice in Wonderland* will not be put off by Boris Vian", wrote Jacqueline Piatier for *Le Monde* in 1963. "He is rather like our own Lewis Carroll, an angry, insolent Lewis Carroll, writing for adults rather than children".[32] For, whereas Alice ultimately wakes up, no-one ever really emerges from Vian's nightmares. If we follow Kibédi Varga's model and consider the way the short stories resist analysis in terms of ellipsis, we discover that what we are looking at are oneiric ellipses that defy logic because the key to unlocking the dream is missing. But we are also confronted by phenomenological ellipses where the elimination of motivation breaks the causal chain and leads to a vertiginous disquiet. Examples of this breakdown include the cynical portrayal of heroic wartime butchery in "Les Fourmis" ("Pins and Needles") (*F*) and the seemingly gratuitous cruelty of Brise-Bonbon in "Un cœur d'or" ("A Heart of Gold") and of the three skiers in "Le Voyeur" ("The Voyeur") (both *LG*),[33] and to a lesser extent the fate of the pathetic hero of "Une pénible histoire" ("A Sad Story") (*LG*).

Thus far, we have observed a sliding scale in the narrative distance — from the texts on jazz to those on the cinema within the chronicle short stories, then from these to the fabliaux short stories, which are more general in theme. But in the ludic short stories, either the protagonist remains an ironic

[32] Jacqueline Piatier, *Le Monde*, 24 August 1963, cited in David Noakes, *Boris Vian* (Paris: Éditions universitaires, "Classiques du XXe siècle", 1963), p. 118.

[33] The manuscript version of "Le Voyeur" was entitled "Le Bonhomme de neige" ("The Snowman"). It is this manuscript text that is translated in the present volume, with its original title.

"I", sometimes masquerading as the third person singular, or the plot is driven by two-dimensional puppets who serve as mere props for the demonstration and contribute to the supposed illustration of the maxim of which they are themselves the victims. There is nothing of the kind in the reflexive short stories, which lead us into the dark thoughts of a character who makes us forget his creator. While we cannot talk of psychology as such, since the motivations of these characters are not usually revealed, what we have here are nonetheless complex beings, and it is in this absence of motivation that the enigma of Vian's best short stories lies. Although the plot is generally predicated on either a phrase, a proverb or a word play — even the title of a jazz piece, as is the case of many of the texts of *Les Fourmis* (*Blues for a Black Cat*) — we are no longer dealing with a narrativised maxim but instead with a narrative born of a literal understanding of the opening formula, which is a technique characteristic of Vian's writing. While texts such as "Une grande vedette" ("A Big Star"), "Un drôle de sport" ("A Funny Old Game"), "Un test" ("The Test") (all *RB*) or "Surprise-partie chez Léobille" ("Léobille's Party") (*LG*), for example, all give their own twist to the story of the unlikely romantic hero, old man Mimile's heart of gold does not explain the short story to which it gives its name; and in the same way, the adage according to which man is a wolf for man cannot by itself explain "Le Loup-garou" ("The Werewolf") (*LG*). That is to say that, whereas in the ludic short stories everything points to a resolution of the would-be narrativised maxim on which the story appears to be predicated, in the reflexive short stories the implicit formula drives a fantastic narrative designed to bring about its own undoing. In the remainder of this essay I shall briefly analyse the way in which this type of text functions in two short stories: "Un cœur d'or" ("A Heart of Gold") and "Le Loup-garou" ("The Werewolf").

"A Heart of Gold" ("Un cœur d'or", 1949, *LG*)

What happens when an expression like "to have a heart of gold" is taken literally? The reference to a person's "good-heartedness" is superseded by an image of a vital organ made of precious metal, notably in this case a heart that is both heavy and dear in value. The "dear heart" calls out to the thief; the "heavy heart" throws impediments in his way. First, one must find a way of getting hold of it. Aulne uses some of the least inconspicuous tools to do this:

a bludgeon and a sickle. Whatever tools he uses, however, one cannot help but be reminded of the heart-snatcher (*l'arrache-cœur*) used by Alise in *L'Écume des jours* (1946), which later gives its name to the story of Jacquemort and the triplets Joël, Noël and Citroën (*L'Arrache-cœur*, 1951).[34] We need to be able to explain this link. A heavy heart can, of course, be difficult to carry; and indeed, the weight of old man Mimile's heart drags Aulne down to such an extent that, at the end of the story, he is left struggling to maintain his grip on the window ledge which is his escape route. The whole plot turns on the re-literalisation of popular adages. Thus, it is the weight of his sin that brings about the villain's downfall, but in Vian's world both the weight and the fall are quite real.

And yet, revealing the word plays on which the story is predicated does not tell the whole story of Vian's praxis here. For some rather odd reason, Aulne goes to great lengths to get himself caught: "he conspicuously tore off the thief's cap he was wearing, threw it into a drain and swapped it for a gentleman's floppy hat". He then gets rid of the murder weapons, with their tell-tale fingerprints, in full view of everybody while keeping "his clothes that were sticky with blood, because after all passers-by don't expect a killer to be dressed like everybody else", before taking the most conspicuous taxi he can find and asking the driver to go around the block "[a]s many times as it takes to get spotted by the cops". And so it goes on. Two things can be said about this (un)characteristic behaviour, with its references to the burlesque chase scenes of early cinema. First, it is clear that in this story, in keeping with the theme of literalised expressions, *one can in fact judge a book by its cover*. Second, Aulne reflexively sets a scenario in motion: like Chick will do in equally dire circumstances in *L'Écume des jours*, he plays at *cops and robbers*. His concern for his clothes is therefore driven by his wish to conform to the right code. As for the behaviour of those pursuing him, this is codified, too, in this case by the traditional need to have them pass for fools: "Up on the roof, the cops were running around in circles, making a racket with their boots, so as to comply with the local government ordinance established for the acceptable minimum noise level in the conduct of police pursuits."

---

34 Completed in 1951, *L'Arrache-cœur* was first published by Vrille in Paris in 1953. Translated as *Heartsnatcher* by Stanley Chapman, it was published in English by Dalkey Archive Press in 2003.

While the adults are playing children's games, taking care to avoid "running over some kid", the six-year-old Brise-Bonbon is for his part taking his role very seriously. Apparently given the task of "looking after the house" in his parents' absence, he prevents Aulne from getting in by slicing off his fingers with his father's razor. This a clear reversal of roles, which is designed to conform with the strange logic of Vian's world rather than to convey some kind of moral message. For, in this world, children are astonishingly mature and everybody else plays, especially adults in serious professions — policemen in this case, but also doctors, clergymen, pharmacists, archaeologists, and the list goes on. Indeed, this list includes the writer, who, in "A Heart of Gold", cannot resist having his characters perform tricks of consummate untranslatability. To give just one example, as "Aulne was edging his way raspingly across the face of the wall", he was doing so, in French, *à sec*, or "dry"; this is because the expression "to keep close to a wall" uses the verb *raser*, "to shave". (We might therefore be tempted to say that, for Aulne, this is more of a dry shave than a close one...) This is a world shaped by childhood because it is forever conscious of what is at its foundation, namely that moment of original sin when the child first enters the realm of language.[35]

"The Werewolf" ("Le Loup-garou", 1947, *LG*)

Things get even more complicated in a short story such as "The Werewolf", which is playful like the short stories of the ludic category but which is close to the reflexive short story in terms of the internal focalisation used for its protagonist. The first thing to note, of course, is the reversal of the Latin maxim *homo homini lupus est*. The wolf of Fausses-Reposes Woods, whose name is Denis,[36] is the very model of civilised behaviour: he eats blue flowers,[37] likes nothing more than watching passing cars and is bashful when he stumbles

---

35 For more on this, see Audrey Camus, "L'Enfance de l'écriture", *Europe*, 967-968, 2009, pp. 87-99.

36 He would appear to be related, in an inverted fashion, to Vian's other Wolf, the hero of *L'Herbe rouge* (*The Red Grass*). Instead of being a man with a wolf's name, Denis is a wolf with a man's name.

37 In French, *fleur bleue*, or blue flower, connotes sentimentality.

across examples of human courtship, especially when "a willing victim, as you say, got laid". Through these images, especially the last one, which in the original French has carnivorous overtones,[38] the roles of man and wolf are reversed. In fact, when, during a bout of "anthropolicy", Denis finds himself in a man's skin, he experiences with horror the base instincts of which he had previously been unaware: "Living as a man amongst men, what dangers would he not face!" If man is portrayed in this text as a veritable wolf for man, poor Denis, who is as gentle as a lamb, demonstrates just how unjust this saying is to his species. The reversal is effected through the figure of the werewolf, whose civilised-savage polarity is reversed; but upon closer inspection, it can be seen that the intertextuality at play is much more complicated.

"In the Fausses-Reposes Woods at the bottom of the Picardy hill, there lived a very handsome adult wolf with a black coat and big red eyes." Thus begins the short story. This impersonal *once-upon-a-time* opening gambit leads us inevitably to Charles Perrault and Little Red Riding-Hood:

> Once upon a time there lived in a certain village a little country girl, the prettiest creature who was ever seen. Her mother was excessively fond of her; and her grandmother doted on her still more. This good woman had made for her a little red riding-hood; which became the girl so extremely well that everybody called her Little Red Riding-Hood.[39]

His ruby-coloured eyes, which Denis retains after his metamorphosis, are mentioned regularly in the text and evoke the riding-hood of the same colour. They are, moreover, *big*, which prepares us for the fact that "his tongue had remained just as pointy as before" and that his ears "were perhaps a touch too long and hairy" — both of which characteristics point to the true nature of

[38] The French expression employed by Vian here, *passer à la casserole* — literally, "to be put in a cooking pot" — has the meaning that a woman is forced have sex against her will. However, not only is the victim presented as consenting (an oxymoron which echoes that of the wolf-man), but the original French expression also picks up what wolves usually do to female humans in fairy stories, which is to eat them (as suggested by Vian through the reference to the cooking pot).

[39] This transcription of Perrault's famous opening is taken from the second of two versions available on the following website http://www.ifyoulovetoread.com/book/chtwo_storiesfullred.htm (accessed 8 May 2013).

the metamorphosed wolf. As in Perrault's tale, they give away his disguise. Clearly, this is no coincidence. What we have here is a parodic rewriting, which is further reinforced by allusions to *Beauty and the Beast* (the mirror scene) and *Cinderella* (the twelve strokes of midnight). On the one hand, Vian is reappropriating the old form of the fairy tale, as he famously did in an early text, *Conte de fées à l'usage des moyennes personnes*, which he wrote for his wife Michelle.[40] On the other hand, much like the adventures of Little Red Riding-Hood, whom Perrault takes the trouble of undressing before putting her into bed with a big bad wolf who is himself dressed up as grandma, Denis's story is one of sexual initiation. At the beginning of the short story, the wolf observes the mating rituals of couples in the bushes and walks away discreetly. Once he has changed into a man and has been approached by "one of those females whose turpitudes one reads about in the literature of Monsieur Mauriac", he quickly overcomes his disgust for such behaviour and begins to practise it himself. He thereby discovers not only human sexuality but at the same time the venal ruses that sometimes give it that little extra spice. Ironically, then, this is a cautionary tale much in the vein of Perrault.

Another intertext that comes into play here is Tex Avery's animation, *Red Hot Riding Hood*, which was first shown in cinemas in the United States in 1943.[41] In this famous cartoon, the wolf displays a sartorial elegance every bit as refined as that of Denis. Indeed, when the latter loses his fur his instincts are to choose "an elegant grey suit with white stripes, and [...] a plain rosewood-tinged shirt and burgundy tie", complete with dark glasses and a raincoat. In Tex Avery's version, Little Red Riding-Hood is an attractive pin-up girl singing in a cabaret, and she snubs the wolf on whom she nonetheless has quite an effect (his eyes bulge out of his head and his tongue extends down to the floor). As for grandma, who looks every inch the madam of a brothel, she gets her revenge for having once been eaten by incessantly pursuing the wolf with her own advances. The cartoon's original ending, which saw the wolf

[40] Boris Vian, *Conte de fées à l'usage des moyennes personnes* (Paris: Pauvert, 1997 [1943]). In French, adults are "big people" (*grandes personnes*) while children are "little people" (*petits*). Vian's fairy tale is designed for middle-sized people (*moyennes personnes*).

[41] Much has already been written on the fundamental influence of the cinematic gag, and more particularly of cartoons, on Vian's fiction.

forced into marriage with grandma, followed by the birth of their children, was censored by MGM because it was too evocative of bestiality.[42]

In "The Werewolf", therefore, we have a rewriting of more than one version of the tale of Little Red Riding-Hood: from the Latin maxim through to Tex Avery, Vian's text is entirely interwoven with other texts. And, as in "A Heart of Gold", no-one is more conscious of this than the protagonist himself. Much like Emma Bovary, Denis decodes the new world with which he is confronted through books, which "had taught him many things". Transformed into a man, he draws on studies of lycanthropy (or perhaps anthropolicy) in order to come to terms with his metamorphosis. Later, when he catches a woman in the act of going through his pockets after they have made love, his first thought is that she is looking for a photo of him (this is perhaps the influence of sentimental fiction *à la* Paul Géraldy); and it is thanks to Mauriac (of all people) that he realises that she is in fact a "whore, in other words", whereupon he throws her out and gets what he supposes is the "sweet taste of revenge". When three men dressed in loud suits later accost him and invite him to go into a bar with them, he asks them whether they play bridge before realising his mistake: "'I see,' he said. 'You're pimps.'" The wolf-made-man gives them fair warning — "'I'm going to get angry,' he said calmly. 'It will be the first time in my life, but I recognise the feeling. It's just like it says in the books.'" — before taking care of the men and coming to terms with the resultant feelings: "He was filled with a deep hatred". The contrast between the hard-boiled vocabulary that Denis picks up from such bad company and the trite, gushy expressions that he has derived from books in an attempt to understand what he is feeling increases our pleasure as readers when the tale is contorted.

***

Our reading of these texts demonstrates the underlying intertextuality of the reflexive short stories. What one discovers is no longer a narrativised maxim but literary scenarios, tales already told, sentences read and reread, inventions

---

42 See Michael Barrier, *Hollywood Cartoons: American Animation in its Golden Age* (Oxford/ New York: Oxford University Press, 1999), pp. 413-414.

and characters passing from novels into short stories, and vice versa. The interrogation of language, which pervades Vian's *œuvre*, is accompanied here by an interrogation of the fabric of literature. Ultimately, the intertextuality and intratextuality that are key to his novels are just as important in the short stories.[43]

Therefore, despite the techniques specific to its genre, the short story coexists productively with the author's longer fiction. Across the range of short stories, from the ludic to the reflexive, two dimensions of Vian's creative process — farce and tragedy — are articulated separately here, whereas in the rest of Vian's fictional production they are often indissociable. In the short stories, it becomes possible to study these two forms, as it were, *in vitro*. Yet we can also see the considerable work involved in transforming such raw material, as greater distance is placed between us and the narrator, and as the influence of real-life events is replaced by the products of an unbridled imagination. This is pure Vian. And it is not the case that the short story simply serves as a testing-ground for the novel; rather, across the variety of its forms, it develops its own singular style and responds to a particular need. Between the ludic short story, which records the spirit of the times and gives free rein to the author's satirical verve, and the reflexive short story, where the unusual is allowed to blossom, engendering images that find in this literary fomat the ideal temporal space for their deployment, Boris Vian is, "in short", a writer worthy of rediscovery.

---

[43] On this subject, see Alistair Rolls, *The Flight of the Angels: Intertextuality in Four Novels by Boris Vian* (Amsterdam/Atlanta: Rodopi, 1999).

PART III

ON TRANSLATING BORIS VIAN

ON NOT WANTING TO DIE: TRANSLATION AS RESURRECTION

Maria Freij

Even though Vian did not himself choose the title *Je voudrais pas crever* for the volume of his collected poetry — it was published posthumously in 1962 — it is a title that most fittingly captures the core premise of the book. *Je voudrais pas crever* (*I wouldn't wanna die*) encompasses, firstly, the two great contrasts in Vian's all too short existence: his passion for life and the *memento mori* with which he lived and which permeates this little volume of poetry. I say "little" because the book is small: the French 1972 edition contains only twenty-three poems, and in addition some writings on the Collège de 'Pataphysique, not included here. Little, also, because it appears, deceptively, to be a light read. Certainly, it is easy to be fooled by Vian's playfulness and jocularity, by his pun and word play, and by his own reiterated assertions that he is "no great poet". But Vian's work is anything but slight. The complexities at play are manifold and full of contrasts: his boyish charm, childishness and penchant for vulgarity coexist with a genuine despair and with that other side of childishness that is marked by sincerity — a way of looking at the world with awe and through the lens of a wonderful imagination.

With the notable exception of some of Vian's songs, disappointingly few of his poems have been translated into English. This is a shame, because Vian's poetry, though not easy to translate, has that special something that translates well: subject matter that, although extremely personal, survives both the passing of time and its expatriation from one linguistic home to another. It has a cheekiness that brands the poems as unmistakably "Vian" and a playfulness that invites the reader to become a co-creator, a playmate. Translating him requires the translator to engage fully in that process: co-creating, reinventing, resurrecting.

The often competing demands of, on the one hand, poetic features such as rhyme and metre, and, on the other, meaning and allusion, make translating poetry a particularly difficult and fraught task at any time. These difficulties are compounded in Vian's case by a number of other semantic and stylistic challenges: playful sonorities, onomatopoeia, pun, clever alliteration, intratextual allusions — the list is long.

To illustrate the extent of the difficulty, it is useful here to provide some examples. Vian's plays on words are arguably the most difficult but also the most enjoyable to translate (especially when combined with a rhyme scheme). In "Quand j'aurai du vent dans mon crâne" ("When the wind's blowing through my skull"), we find the phrase "ça sera une impression fosse", where the word "fausse" (false) has been replaced with the homophone "fosse" (tomb). Instead of a "false impression" we therefore have a "tomb-like impression". The translation adopted here — "gravely at a loss" — is aimed at keeping the joke while at the same time retaining the "-oss" sound. Similarly, in the same poem, the use of the terms "duchesses", "popesses", and "she-asses" is designed to respect the iconoclastic nature of the original French words ("duchesses", "papesses", and "ânesses") and the political comment implicit in them, while at the same time retaining their playful assonance. Other poems, such as "Un homme tout nu marchait" ("A stark naked man was walking") and "J'ai mal à ma rapière" ("My rapier hurts") — or, as one could think of them, the "penis poems" — display a childish humour. In "A stark naked man was walking", the phrase "l'habit à la main" (his clothes in his hand) invites the pronunciation "la bite à la main" (dick or cock in hand) if the liaison is made. The English version proposed in this volume — "his gear in his hand" — is aimed at creating an equivalence through the (perhaps less obvious) *double entendre* created by the word "gear". In "My rapier hurts", Vian's nouns — "rapière", "bédane", "cardans", "graisseurs", "badiole", "sacoche" — are all inanimate objects; they are also words that could be used to describe the male anatomy. In the translation proposed here, they are rendered as "rapier", "chisel", "couplings", "lubricators", "ball-bearings" and "tool bag", respectively — words that all sustain allusions to the male genitalia and sexuality. (Some liberty has admittedly been taken in translating "ma badiole" as "ball-bearings", but the shift from a wild cherry to an object of mechanical engineering seemed warranted in terms of the unity of the imagery, and also because "badiole" conjures up "babiole" — a worthless object.) Another feature crucial to keep here was the nursery-rhyme quality of the poem, a recurring characteristic in Vian's poetry and one that often functions to soften the blow of his subtext. Naturally, the voice is lighter in the nursery rhyme and lends itself to a childlike perspective.[1]

In a number of the poems, rhyme serves a central purpose in establishing the poetic voice and in providing a counterweight to the darkness of the themes. In those cases, every attempt has been made to keep the rhyming structure in the translated version — a challenging task, given the syntactical differences between French and English. French, for example, favours the placement of the adjective after the noun, and to complicate matters further, Vian tends to break his lines after adjectives; however, the different syntactic patterns of French and English also open up interesting new possibilities for rhyme. In order to maintain the end-rhyme pattern, it may, for instance, be possible to change the syntax so as to draw from a different word group. This can nevertheless be a perilous exercise, as modifying the syntax can risk compromising the meaning. A good example of the necessity of this kind of change is provided by the following lines from "Ils cassent le monde" ("They are breaking the world"):

Il suffit que j'aime	I need just to love
Une plume bleue	A feather shimmering blue
Un chemin de sable	A sandy path
Un oiseau peureux	A frightened bird or two

Here, "bleue" and "peureux" are both adjectives; consequently, the English version could not remain faithful to both the syntax of the original and the

[1] "J'ai acheté du pain dur" ("I bought some bread, stale and all") is the most obvious example of Vian alluding to a nursery rhyme, or "comptine" — in this case "Une poule sur un mur".

parameters of idiomatic English. Thus, instead of "a blue feather" (or "a feather blue"), we have proposed "a feather shimmering blue", and instead of simply "a frightened bird" (or "a bird frightened"), we have instead "a frightened bird *or two*". Some additional meaning has been introduced in both of these lines, but this was seen as less of a transgression than losing the rhyme.

Similarly, "Un poète" ("A poet") is complicated to translate due mainly to the competing demands of form and content:

Un poète	A poet
C'est un être unique	Is someone heaven sent
A des tas d'exemplaires	You can meet any time
Qui ne pense qu'en vers	Who thinks only in rhyme
Et n'écrit qu'en musique	Writes with musical bent
Sur des sujets divers	On most any paradigm
Des rouges ou des verts	Be it crude or sublime
Mais toujours magnifiques.	But always magnificent.

While the rhyme-scheme here (ABCCBCCB) has been kept, some modifications had to be made to the content. The "unique being" of line 2, for example, becomes "someone heaven sent", with the result that the oxymoron in lines 2-3 (a unique being of which there are many to be found) is less obvious in the English version. The translation of the line "Des rouges ou des verts" is also difficult, given that "verts" (green) is a homophone of "vers" (verse, poetry). The word "vert" in French can also mean "crude" or "saucy". The proposed translation, while no doubt less rich in allusion than the original, represents at least an attempt to maintain the contrast created by the opposing colours (red and green) while at the same time maintaining the rhyme and capturing at least one of the possible meanings of "vert".

Vian often changes the pronunciation of words in order to create the desired metre or rhyme. In "Je n'ai plus très envie" ("I'm no longer at ease"), for example, the adjective "paresseux" ("lazy") becomes "parressieux" so as to rhyme with "vieux" ("old"), "sérieux" ("serious") and "consciencieux" ("conscientious") in the three preceding lines. In keeping with that spirit, the translated version proposed here takes similar licence in order to reproduce a comparable rhyme pattern, through the combination of real and modified or invented words: "senescentious", "serious", "conscientious" and "indolentious".

There are, of course, occasions on which the decision has been made that a rhyming translation would mean too significant a corruption of the content. In such cases, an attempt has been made to compensate for this loss through the use, for example, of consonance. To take one example, in "Il y a du soleil dans la rue" ("There is sunshine in the street"), there is a couplet that includes three rhyming words: "sèche" ("dry"), "rêche" ("harsh") and "fraîche" ("cool", "fresh"). These words have been translated as "awash", "harsh" and "fresh", respectively. Here, the consonance atones to a degree for the lack of rhyme, and these words importantly also keep the onomatopoeia and evoke the sound of running water. (It should be noted that "dry", the most obvious translation of the French term "sèche", is shifted to the second part of that particular line of verse, thereby offering further lexical compensation.)

Metre is also important in most of Vian's poems — he was, after all, a musician — and every attempt has been made either to retain the original cadence or to create a comparable one in the translation. The rhythms of English and French are different, and it is not always possible to keep the same syllable count in translation. The aim, though, has been to stay as close as possible to the original, both in terms of scansion and visual presentation, and as few syllables as possible have been added or taken away. This sometimes requires making adjustments, particularly where rhyme is also a feature. This is illustrated by the following lines from "I wouldn't wanna die":

La terre qui craquelle	The crunch of the soil
L'odeur des conifères	The smell of the pine
Et les baisers de celle	And the kisses so fine
Que ceci que cela	Of what's her name — ah!
La belle que voilà	This beauty — voilà

The rhymes have been maintained here, although their position has shifted slightly, and the six-syllable lines of the original have become five-syllable lines in English (with the exception of the middle line). But overall, the regularity of the metre and the rhymes remain strong features of the translated version.

While we have focused here on rhyme and metre, there are other recurring features that pose problems for the translator. Many factors come into play in Vian's technique, and most of them result from his creative use of language. His word play, in particular, is as intelligent as it is frequent. In addition to the use of homophones, which has been discussed above, there are numerous uses of alliteration, repetition and, of course, pun. Sometimes Vian's word play works on several levels, such as in "Donnez le si" ("If I say *if*"), one of the most multi-layered and complicated poems in the collection, in which Vian plays with the fact that some French words are pronounced like English words and, conversely, some English words can be found in French, with or without the same meaning. The "si" of the French title corresponds to the English "ti" in the musical scale but is also the French word for "if", which features in the following line. However, the French word "if" means a "yew" — which throws to the word "tri" in the next line ("le tri" in French actually means "selection" or "sorting"). And so it continues. Vian engages in bilingual humour, here, while maintaining the inter- and intratextuality at which he excels. The subtext nevertheless remains dark, as the card game of bridge reveals itself to be a metaphor for duplicity.

Two poems introduce a very specific set of complications. In "Si les poètes étaient moins bêtes" ("If poets weren't such fools"), Vian invents a whole range of words, some of which are based, more or less loosely, on actual words. In one section, he announces that he is introducing a list of fishes, but the ensuing list contains a number of invented words:

Il y aurait deux cents poissons	There would be two hundred fishes
Depuis le croûsque au ramusson	From crustoceans to antlishes
De la libelle au pépamule	From lampdragoons to pepaflies
De l'orphie au rara curule	From needlefish to rare curuleyes
Et de l'avoile au canisson	And from bowsprats to poodlefishes

Some of these words are more or less identifiable. The "orphie" of the third line is the French term for a garfish or needlefish. The "libelle" ("lampoon") of the third line becomes "libellule" ("dragonfly") if we add the final syllable of the following word to it. In similar fashion, the words "avoile" and "canisson" from the fourth line become "avoine" ("oats") and "calisson" (a type of sweet made from ground almonds) if we swap two of their consonants around. But of course, "l'avoile" can also be read as "la voile" ("the sail") and "canisson" is not too distant from "caniche" ("poodle"). It is clearly not possible in translation to capture all of the possible allusions and lexical connections that are present in the original French, but the version proposed here aims at least to convey something of that inventive word play.

We similarly find invented words in "Un jour" ("One day"). The term "volutin", for instance, evokes both "volute" ("spiral") and "lutin" ("elf") — hence "spirelf" in our translation. The word "ivrunini" is reminiscent of "ivrogne", or "drunkard", whereas "analognes" is close to "analogues" or "analogies". The solutions proposed here — "drunkaninny" and "anahologies" — hopefully respect the inventiveness and spirit of the original text.

Trying to decipher Vian's language and solve mysteries such as these involves trying to unearth original meanings, including what two (sometimes invented) words he has used to make a third. This is forensic work that requires some lateral thinking as well as the close examination of meaning, imagery and linguistics. But unlike the forensic scientist, whose task it is to determine the cause of death, the translator is aiming to resurrect the text. In that sense, it is highly desirable for the translated texts to stand alone and be judged in their own right. Nevertheless, it may be useful for readers to have at their disposal some commentary that explains this behind-the-scenes work. That is the function of the notes that are provided on the various poems at the end of this volume. Here, specific points of interest may be clarified or given their due attention: intertextual nods may be acknowledged, puns highlighted and cultural specificities clarified. If a translator's commentary cannot be as specific as to explain all individual choices, it can at least introduce the reader to the grid of ideas that have been applied during the translation process and provide a sense of the philosophy that has guided the translator.

For monolingual and bilingual readers alike, translation offers new ways of approaching a text. More than this, though, what translation ultimately does is allow the text to keep being recreated — it gives it new life. It is, in other words, a sort of resurrection of a text into a different linguistic, cultural and temporal context. And a text that is read, recreated and read again is saved from the oblivion that Vian, in his title poem, wanted so much to avoid.

DETERMINING A STRATEGY FOR THE TRANSLATION OF BORIS VIAN

Peter Hodges

An author such as Boris Vian, who is renowned for his non-conformism, poses a set of problems for the translator that are rarely encountered in the work of any one single author. François Roulmann has indeed described Vian as an "anarchist when it comes to writing", an author who is "so creative that he is difficult to categorise".[1] Nevertheless, numerous academic studies have sought to put order into this apparent disorder. His creative use of language has attracted particular attention. As Marina Yaguello noted in her article of 1984, "Vian's word plays have been listed and classified for some time: neologisms, use of polysemy and homophones, puns, syntactical ambiguity, metaphors".[2] Ten years earlier, Lydie Jeannette Haenlin had produced a systematic study of Vian's literary language, inspired by the work of the Liège School of *rhétorique générale*.[3] This group of linguists developed a system in which linguistic operations were considered in terms of five categories:

1 Tristan Savin interview with François Roulmann, April 2009. Available online as "La Comète Vian" at http://www.lexpress.fr/culture/livre/la-comete-vian_815677.html (accessed 24 January 2012) (my translation).

2 Marina Yaguello, "Linguiste malgré lui?", *L'Arc*, 90, 1984, p. 30 (my translation).

3 Lydie Jeannette Haenlin, Analyse rhétorique du discours romanesque de Boris Vian, PhD Thesis, University of Buffalo, 1973.

1. *Metagraphs*: alterations at the level of spelling, which affect acronyms, foreign expressions and syntagmas.
2. *Metaplasms*: alterations at the level of morphology, which are found in allophones, phonemes, morphemes, lexemes and syntagmas.
3. *Metataxes*: alterations at the syntactic level, which are found in archaic poetry or in anglicised or popular syntax.
4. *Metasememes*: alterations at the semantic level, in metaphors and similes.
5. *Metalogisms*: alterations at the level of logic and referentiality.

While such studies are certainly relevant to the present volume insofar as they shed light on any number of textual problems, the aim here is to offer an alternative system of classification specifically designed to take into account the problems presented by the translation of Vian's short stories. This classification can be divided into three parts, building from individual lexical items to phrases and sentences, and finally to the level of the text itself.

1. Problems and Operations at the Level of the Word

The principal among these are as follows:

- *Presupposition*, or implied knowledge, which is inherent in the proper nouns relating to the biographical detail of the author (presupposition refers to both source-text author intent and to source-text audience knowledge and applies to the names of real-life people and places, which may be left unchanged or altered slightly).
- *Socionyms*: the names of societies, businesses, government departments, institutions or products that are bound to the source culture. These raise the possibility of using translation techniques such as the hyponym/superordinate relationship and the addition of descriptors.[4]
- *Charactonyms*: proper nouns used by authors to suggest the personality of a character. These raise the question of how to transfer connotative meaning.

[4] Magdalena Mitura defines socionyms as "the name given to the names of companies, businesses, brands". Magdalena Mitura, *Écriture vianesque: traduction de la prose* (Bern/Berlin...: Peter Lang, Publications Universitaires Européennes, 2006), p. 206 (my translation).

- *Anagrams* and the subsequent derivations of names of characters, the significance of which may be lost on a target-text reader.
- *Phonetic spelling* of the names of characters and places, which involves homophony, already identified by Marina Yaguello.
- *Spoonerisms*: the inversion of initial letters or syllables in names and words.
- *Modification* of a word by the addition or subtraction of a syllable (these words are recognisable as potentially being French because of groupings of letters and sounds).
- *Neologisms*: the creation of a totally new word, often in relation to the infinitive form of a verb.
- *Portmanteau words*, created by the blending of sounds and combining the meanings of two words into a single word.
- The use of *specialist terminologies*, such as linguistic, mechanical and scientific jargon, expressions related to skiing, and homosexual terms of affection and denigration.
- *Intrusion* of non-source language words into the source text.
- *Ambiguity* as to whether a word is archaic or a word play.
- *Bilingual word plays* between French and English.
- *Collocation*: the juxtaposition of seemingly unrelated words, usually as image association.
- *Repetition* or *overuse* of a particular word, which invites the question as to whether the translator should intervene.
- *Interchange* of noun and pronoun to avoid ambiguity in the target text where there is none in the source text, or of definite article and indefinite article to avoid ambiguity in the target text where there is none in the source text.
- *Vocalic suffix addition; grammatical gender change* with the use of *paronymy*, or words with the same derivation (extremely difficult to capture in English, which has no grammatical gender).
- The *formation of new words* when changes in the sound of the last letter of a word and the first letter of the following word create a liaison.
- *Different varieties of French*, including Belgian French.

2. Problems and Operations at the Level of the Phrase and Sentence

These include:

- *Literal use of language*, according to which the words on the page are taken at face value, even if the result is nonsensical (this absurd logic is suggestive of Surrealism).
- *Disguised expressions* and *hidden references*.
- The *literary use of spoken language*, where the spoken language of Post-War France is replicated and incorporated into the text.
- The *poetic use* of language.
- *Complex syntactical structures*, which sometimes cause the reader to stop and ask what exactly is being said (from a translation perspective, this raises the question as to whether phrases, sentences and even paragraphs should be re-sequenced for target-text orientation).
- The question of *repair* of the author's use of English in the source text (when a character whose native language is supposed to be English does not actually seem to be a native speaker).
- *Verb tense interchange*.
- *Lack of equivalence* in the target language of certain grammatical and cultural features described in the source text (where a compromise is not always readily available).

Some of the above devices may lead to a brand of humour which is firmly entrenched in a specific time and place, sometimes making cross-cultural transposition difficult.

3. Problems and Operations at the Level of the Text

Intertextuality is an important factor at this more general level, as is *register*, which affects translation choices regarding how to capture the "feel" of the text (the juxtaposition of minimalist language and expansive style sometimes involves different registers within the same story). Various facets of Vian's own life are also inextricably linked to the text and woven into it, making it almost impossible to separate the life of the author from the motifs and themes in the stories under translation. This brings into play the following pragmatic fields:

- *Coherence*, where the understanding of the world may be somewhat different for the source audience compared to that of the target audience.[5]
- *Presupposition*: the assumption that the receiver has certain knowledge and that a statement has to be true in order for something else to be true.
- *Implicature*, which may incorporate sociolinguistic factors, and which implies that the words alone may not be enough to convey the true meaning.[6]

These are all important features in Vian's texts. Extensive background knowledge is thus required of the translator.

Theoretical Considerations

The field of translation studies has been shaped by a number of influential theories, such as Justa Holz-Mänttäri's theory of translational action, Hans Vermeer's skopos theory, Christian Nord's translation-oriented text analysis and Itamar Even-Zohar's polysystems theory. Each of these theories has contributed in some way to the present translation of Boris Vian's short stories. It is therefore useful to give a brief overview of them in order to explain some of the translation choices that have been made.

Translational Action

Translational action is very heavily target text oriented, placing the target audience's needs to the fore in any translation assignment. As a result, there may be clarification in the target text where there was none in the source text. Translational action operates on a number of levels. On the textual level, the form and genre may vary between source text and target text if the source text format is deemed to be unsuitable or if it hinders communication in the target culture. Therefore it does not promote the strict replication of source

[5] Mona Baker describes coherence as "decontextualized […] language". *In Other Words* (London & New York: Routledge, 2009), p. 222.

[6] Baker (*In Other Words*, p. 223) defines implicature as "what the speaker means or implies rather than what s/he says".

text format. On the cultural level, it is the role of the translator to facilitate communication across borders: "it is not about translating words, sentences or texts but is in every case about guiding the intended co-operation over cultural barriers enabling functionally oriented communication."[7] Intercultural transfer deals with determining strategies for the translation of specific features of the source culture that are different from, or have no equivalent in, the target culture. Many of Boris Vian's short stories are time- and culture-specific, so transferring this detail in a manner that is comprehensible to a target audience is an important consideration if full understanding of the source text is to be achieved. Specific features include plays on words, such as the pig joke in "Motherhood",[8] or the names of characters and geographical locations. If the purpose of translational action is to produce a target text that is target audience oriented, then textually integrated solutions, a preface, footnotes or endnotes may be required, and this leads to a variation in form between the source text and target text. As a genre, the short story exists in both the French source and English target cultures, but the presentation of the stories is different in the present volume. Instead of forming part of Vian's entire prose œuvre, and being spread, according to their chronology, across two volumes, the twenty-eight stories have been pooled and combined here within one larger volume, with a quite different critical apparatus.[9]

Skopos Theory

Skopos, like translational action, is target text oriented. It states that the purpose (or *skopos*, in Greek) of the translation needs to be clarified at the

---

7 Justa Holz-Mänttäri, *Translatorisches Handeln: Theorie und Methode* (Helsinki: Suomalainen Tiedeakatemia, 1984), translated in Jeremy Munday, *Introducing Translation Studies: Theory and Applications* (London & New York: Routledge, 2004), p. 77.

8 Our translation changes the French "poulet" (chicken) to "pig" in order to preserve the joke regarding policemen (see Secion V of "Motherhood").

9 As noted elsewhere in this volume, the short stories were originally gathered and published posthumously by Noël Arnaud in book form in two separate collections: *Le Loup-garou* (Paris: Bourgois, 10/18, 1970) and *Le Ratichon baigneur* (Paris: Bourgois, 10/18, 1981). In the 2010 Pléaide edition of Vian's collected prose works, edited by Marc Lapprand with Christelle Gonzalo and François Roulmann, the short stories are spread chronologically over two volumes, because of their intermittent composition over a period of thirteen years.

beginning of the assignment so that a target text can be produced that will meet target audience expectations. As Reiss and Vermeer themselves say, the target text "must be interpretable as coherent with the target text receiver's situation."[10] Skopos theory, which predates translational action, downplays the importance of the source text according to a series of hierarchical rules. The rules state that the intratextual coherence of the target text is more important than intertextual coherence with the source text — in other words, the readability of the target text is more important than its relationship with the source text.

Having said that, it is important to see how the skopos of the source text compares to that of the target text when determining a translation strategy. Between 1942 and 1943, one of the important features of Vian's writing was its ludic quality. He often wrote to amuse his friends by recreating the atmosphere of their milieu.[11] However, in the late 1940s and the early 1950s, when most of these short stories were composed, he was writing in a wide range of genres, from pastiches of the American thriller to the philosophical or moral fable. Some stories appeared in magazines and reviews such as *Dans le train*, *La Rue*, *Samedi-Soir* and *Paris-Tabou*; others remained unpublished. They did not appear in edited collections until many years later when Noël Arnaud gathered the manuscripts together from Vian's desk. Vian longed to be taken seriously as a writer, as is demonstrated by his bitter disappointment at not winning the Pléiade Prize for his first major novel, *L'Écume des jours* (published in 1947). This bitterness was compounded by the fact that the only public recognition he achieved was through the writings he published under the pseudonym Vernon Sullivan. It would therefore be reasonable to assume that he considered these short stories — which were usually composed spontaneously, late at night, for experimentation and his own pleasure — to be of secondary importance. If the spirit of Vian is to be recreated, then some replication of his experimentation is needed in order to produce target texts that reflect the diverse registers and the playfulness of the original French texts.

---

10 Katharina Reiss and Hans Vermeer, *Groundwork for a General Theory of Translation* (Tübingen: Niemeyer, 1984), p. 113.

11 Michel Le Bris, "Une stratégie de disparition", *Les Collections du Magazine Littéraire*, 6, 2004-2005, p. 47.

Translation-oriented Text Analysis

Christiane Nord is critical of the prominence given to the target text by Holz-Mänttäri and Vermeer because in her view it allows the translator too much licence. Before translation begins, she proposes that the translator should conduct a detailed analysis of the source text to see where divergence with the target text is likely to occur, and to see which elements of the source text should be retained. Her "analysis in translation" distinguishes between two types of translation: documentary and instrumental. Documentary or exoticising translation retains certain culture-specific lexical items of the source text so that the target audience is aware that what they are reading is a translation, or at the very least a text that is based in a different culture. More extreme features of documentary translation are strict word-for-word or literal translations, which highlight the foreign through structure and syntax. This branch, which calls for source text features to be retained once the purpose has been stated, has sometimes been called "function-preserving translation".[12] Instrumental translation is where the target audience is unaware that what they are reading is a translation, because they believe that the text before them is the original. Culture-specific items of the source text are replaced and target language conventions such as structure, syntax, punctuation and rhythm are adopted.

These two types of translation somewhat mirror Juliane House's "overt" and "covert" classification, Lawrence Venuti's "foreignisation" and "domestication" strategies, and Basil Hatim and Ian Mason's "dynamic" and "stable" text types, with the terms "covert", "dynamic" and "domestication" roughly corresponding to "instrumental", and "overt", "stable" and "foreignisation" roughly corresponding to "documentary" translation.[13] It could be argued that the translation of Boris Vian's short stories should incorporate features of both documentary and instrumental translation.

[12] Christiane Nord, *Text Analysis in Translation: Theory, Methodology and Didactic Application of a Model for Translation-Oriented Text Analysis* (Amsterdam: Rodopi, 1997), p. 73.

[13] See, for example, Juliane House, *A Model for Translation Quality Assessment* (Tübingen: Gunter Narr, 1977); Lawrence Venuti, *Translation: Theory in Practice* (Oxford & New York: Routledge, 2004); Basil Hatim and Ian Mason, *The Translator as Communicator* (Oxford & New York: Routledge, 1997).

Because most of the stories are time and place specific, and autobiographical in nature, with many of the characters centred around the author himself or based on family and friends, they are strictly culture bound. Thus, any attempt to reposition them will inevitably result in significant loss of authorial intent.

Culture-specific items include socionyms such as "SNCF", "préfecture" and "TCRP";[14] magazines and reviews such as *Les Temps modernes* and *La Rue*;[15] consumer items such as the "stylobic" or "Vivaquatre";[16] the geographical place names "Montmartre" and "Deligny";[17] and (coyly misspelt) iconic establishments such as the Café de Flore and the Deux Magots,[18] to name but a few. There are also the names of real people, Charles de Gaulle, Yvon Pétra and Claude Luter,[19] all of whom help to accentuate the "Frenchness" of the work.

The question could be asked, however, as to whether the retention of every culture-specific lexical item might have a negative impact on the target text reader by creating a sense of isolation, which is a possibility if the text sounds "too foreign". Since the reader will more than likely be aware that the text in question is a translation, because of the retention of certain culture-specific items or because of other, paratextual indicators, one potential strategy is to reduce the number of source culture references in instances where it will not negatively impact on the text. This may lead to devices such as superordinate substitution (e.g. "SNCF" becoming "rail company") or cultural substitution, whereby, for example, in "A Heart of Gold", "je roule à gauche" ("I drive on the left") becomes "I drive on the wrong side of the road" (for an Australian or UK readership).[20]

Having said this, there are a number of stories that, with only a few minor alterations, could actually be perceived as belonging to the literature

---

14 "Ramparts of the South" (for "SNCF" and "préfecture"); "Martin called…" (for "TRCP").

15 "Love is Blind" and "The Swimming Priest", respectively.

16 "The Werewolf" and "Another day in Marseille", respectively.

17 "The Killer" and "The Test", respectively.

18 "Ramparts of the South".

19 "Don't Trust the Band (for De Gaulle and Pétra); "The Waltz" (for Luter).

20 "A Heart of Gold".

of the target culture, in which case they would firmly be placed in the realm of instrumental translation. "One Licence for Love" is a case in point: if the names of the two characters, Marthe and Jean, were anglicised to "Martha" and "John", and if the "billet de cent francs" were converted to target currency, then a target text would be produced that could easily be mistaken for an original in almost any English-speaking country where motor vehicles are driven on the right-hand side of the road.[21] Other stories that readily lend themselves to this form of adaptation are "The Werewolf", "Love is Blind" and "The Killer". "The Snowman" presents a different case, on the other hand, because the proper nouns in the story need to be anglicised in order to provide the target text reader with the same opportunity as the source text reader to glean the hidden significance encoded within the names "Vallyeuse" ("Happy Valley"), "Saut de l'Elfe" ("Elf's Leap") and "Cirque des Trois-Sœurs" ("Three Sisters Ridge").[22]

Up until this point, only cultural references and culture-specific lexis have been discussed. Documentary and instrumental translations also operate on the textual level in relation to structure and syntax. In the early stages of the strategy development for this project, *Blues for a Black Cat* and *Froth on the Daydream* were distributed to a number of individuals who had expressed an interest in Vian in order to gauge their reaction to a range of features. While a number of the comments echoed those of some French readers of the original with regards to their contrasting attitudes towards the content, "flow" was the predominant criticism. One reader's observation that "[i]t just doesn't sound like English" perhaps best summarises the consensus. Despite the use of complex syntactical structures in a number of Vian's stories, his texts are fundamentally easy to read in French, so this criticism indicated an immediate discrepancy in target text reception with respect to those particular translations.

As a result, and in accordance with the skopos of recreating Vian in English, consideration has been given in the translations presented here to the adoption of the target language conventions of structure, syntax, punctuation

21 "One Licence for Love".

22 "The Snowman".

and rhythm, with the aim of facilitating readability for the target audience, in keeping with the textual principles of instrumental translation. At the same time, certain cultural and lexical items of the source text have been retained, in accordance with the tenets of documentary translation.

Polysystems

Itamar Even-Zohar notes that the position of translated literature within any given literary "polysystem" is not fixed. Translated literature may occupy a primary or secondary position, and the translation strategy should be adjusted accordingly. When a translated work occupies the central position — in countries for example where people read a lot of literature in translation, perhaps over and above works originally written in the native language — then that work is generally strong in itself and does not need to conform to target culture conventions. The translator does not have to adopt target language models and can adhere more closely to source text format. If the position of translated literature is weak, because it does not have a widespread readership, then it occupies a peripheral position and the reverse trend occurs. In this latter case, the translator aims for target text "acceptability"[23] by creating a text that adopts target culture norms and target language conventions.

The works of Boris Vian are already deemed to be marginal or within the French literary system, having been kept outside the French canon and largely excluded from university study by a system that is more stable and conservative than that to be found in Anglo-Saxon countries. It may therefore be that translations of Vian in English will occupy a similar position within the target system.[24] This assumption appears to be justified by the fact that a number of English versions of Vian texts are no longer available in print, *Froth on the Daydream*, *Mood Indigo* and the 1992 hardcover edition of *Blues for a Black Cat* being cases in point. The following statement from Mark Thwaite provides further confirmation of this marginal status:

---

[23] Nam Fung Chang, "Itamar Even-Zohar's Culture Theory and Translation Studies", Paper presented to the 1st Athens International Conference on Translation and Interpretation: "Translation: Between Art and Social Science", Athens, 13-14 October 2006.

[24] The perception of Vian as an anarchic author is likely to erode quite quickly following the release of the 2010 Pléiade edition of his prose works.

> Boris Vian seems, here in the UK at least, to be rather forgotten. The redoubtable Scottish publishers *Canongate* brought out an edition of the stark, bitter *I Spit on Your Graves* (*J'irai cracher sur vos tombes*) a year or so ago and that remains the only other one of his works [the other being *Heartsnatcher*] readily available in English translation. [...] For those of us whose schooldays' French is barely up to the job this dearth of translations could not be more frustrating.[25]

Add to this the fact that the English publications of Vian's works tend to mirror the early publication process in France, with only relatively minor players involved, such as the commercial TamTam Books and the non-profit Dalkey Archive Press, and Vian in the English-speaking world could certainly not be touted — yet — as mainstream.

This could lead to the conclusion that an increase in the degree of target text orientation might be required in order to move his work closer to the centre of the English literary polysystem, although perhaps not quite so far as the 2010 American horror movie remake of *I Spit on Your Graves*, which bears only a slight resemblance to the original.

External Factors

The four main theoretical considerations in determining a translation strategy are text type, text function, text orientation and external factors. Since text type, text function and text orientation have been examined in the above presentation of some of the main translation theories or approaches, it now remains to be seen how external factors impact on target text production.

The nature and role of these external factors have been theorised by André Lefevere, whose approach evolved out of polysystems and the Manipulation School.[26] Lefevere considers factors that may determine the acceptance or rejection of texts, moving away from universal norms to culturally dependent ones. This may then have a direct impact on translation decisions. He believes

25 Mark Thwaite, "Some Thoughts on the Work of Boris Vian", *Ready Steady Book for literature*, 2003. Available online at http://www.readysteadybook.com/Article.aspx?page=borisvian (accessed 7 October 2011).

26 See, for example, André Lefevere, *Translating Literature: Practice and Theory in a Comparative Literature Framework* (New York: MLA, 1992).

that the first major factor to determine the success or otherwise of a text involves the influence of professionals within the system, such as reviewers, critics, teachers or even other translators. The second factor includes other people such as publishers, or institutions such as schools and universities or academic journals. Lawrence Venuti is also of the opinion that the publishing industry, by controlling finances and often basing text selection on potential profitability, dictates current Western translation methodology by calling for fluent translations that can be easily consumed by a target audience. The third factor in Lefevere's approach is the dominant poetics of the target culture, which may include the relationship between literature and the social system. Some literature will be more acceptable because it is already operating within a system that recognises it. This is very reminiscent of polysystems.

Let us take an example of how this cultural approach may influence translation decisions. In "The Slip-up", Vian situates his characters on the "Avenue Merdozart", a partially disguised reference to Vian's well-known loathing of the music of Mozart. While most French readers and some non-French readers of the source text will probably recognise the word *merde* in this name, the translator should be aware of the implications and any possible repercussions of the choice taken to translate it. A literal translation, for example, may upset some people, including reviewers and critics who may condemn the target text on the grounds that it is offensive, regardless of the status of the source text in the source culture. Any criticism may then have a negative impact on the reception of the text and subsequently on sales. If the text is destined for study in schools, teachers or review panels may deem the content to be inappropriate for some students, leading to its exclusion from the curriculum. One solution — which has been adopted in this present volume — is to leave the term as it is and to rely on the probability that a reasonable proportion of readers will be familiar with the word *merde* and make the appropriate inference (with the back-up of an explanatory note). This of course may be seen by some as a non-solution that does not attempt to deal with an important stylistic and thematic issue. Another potential solution arose at an international translation conference when a paper on Vian's proper nouns adopted the euphemistic "awful" in an attempt to avoid offending some members of the culturally diverse audience.[27] In the world of economic reality, if it were considered that a particular translation choice might have a detrimental effect on potential readership, it is possible that the publisher or editor could intervene and assume the role of censor, which might then force the translator to use an inadequate alternative.

At this point in time, the translation of the stories in *Le Loup-garou* and *Le Ratichon baigneur* has not been subjected to any external forces. There have been no commercial publishing houses trying to dictate schedules and trends, and academic journals such as *The AALITRA Review* have been prepared to accept unadulterated work on several occasions.[28] Realistically, in the modern English-speaking world, it is likely that only a small minority of readers would be offended by the literal translation of "*merde*". Its English equivalent is in common usage across the social spectrum; it can sometimes be heard on television and in movies; it appears as an entry in a number of dictionaries; and it is perhaps less confrontational these days than a number of other words bandied around in the mass media. With the possible thematic exceptions of female subservience and homosexual denigration, which tend to be era-specific, and some humorous sexual innuendos,[29] Vian may be judged to be fairly inoffensive by modern standards. As such, any self-imposed or editorial censorship dictated by cultural norms should not impact on translation decisions.

Conclusion

Theoretical considerations in the formulation of a translation strategy lead to the production of a target text that has both target audience and source text orientation. Translational action, skopos, polysystems and instrumental translation favour target orientation, whereas documentary translation, with its retention of culture-specific lexical items, and André Lefevere's cultural

[27] Peter Hodges, unpublished conference paper, "What's in a Name? The Translator as Facilitator", "Writing Past Each Other" Conference, University of Wellington, New Zealand, 11-13 December 2010.

[28] *AALITRA Newsletter*, April 2008; *The AALITRA Review*, September 2008; *The AALITRA Review*, March 2010.

[29] Respectively, "One Licence for Love", "The Killer", "April's Daughters" and "Impotence".

approach, which centres on external factors such as the publishing industry and social systems, ensure that the target text is endowed with a certain degree of source text orientation.

Following careful consideration of the implications of these theoretical positions, a combination of source and target strategies has been adopted for the translation of the short stories presented in this volume. Target orientation requires a certain degree of creativity in order to reproduce Vian's elusive word plays, stylistic anomalies, rhymes and rhythms. It nevertheless allows an ease of expression through the adoption of target language structures, syntax, idiomatic expressions and punctuation. It is an approach designed to facilitate the readability of the text while allowing for cultural exchange by means of textually integrated solutions — such as substitution, borrowing, contraction and annotation — that do not override the primary text but that aim to transfer assumed source audience knowledge to the target audience. Source orientation, on the other hand, involves the retention of lexical items and cultural references that situate the text in a specific time and place, maintaining the register of potentially offensive words and expressions, and instilling in the target audience an awareness of intertextuality. This provides more direct access to the source culture, but at the risk of alienating the reader. Finding the balance is a delicate exercise. It is hoped that the hybrid solution adopted in this volume has been successful in producing texts that will meet the skopos outlined at the beginning of this project — namely to recreate Vian in English.

NOTES TO THE POEMS

I WOULDN'T WANNA DIE

Page 17

This is the title poem of the collection. The French title, "Je voudrais pas crever", has a distinctly familiar tone created by the absence of the "ne" in the negation and the use of the slang verb "crever". The translation proposed here is intended to capture that spoken tone, though the more neutral English verb "die" has been preferred to other possibilities such as "to cark it", "to kick the bucket", "to croak", and so on, as these have a slightly old-fashioned flavour and even a degree of flippancy that is inappropriate as a translation of the French.

Those black dogs of Mexico

Black dogs with incandescent eyes are frequently represented in Latin American folklore as incarnations of the devil. In Mexico, they are also seen as the incarnation of a sorcerer who changes form.

The silver spiders

The poet may be referring here to water spiders, which fill their underwater homes with air, thus creating bell-shaped "bubbles". The air trapped around this spider when it is in the water gives it a silvery appearance.

Without having eyed/The eye of the sewer

This translation is designed as a means of picking up the word play in the original French: "Sans avoir regardé/Dans un regard d'égout", where the verb "regarder" (to look) throws to the "regard d'égout" (sewer access hole cover).

Or the seven diseases

Vaccination has, of course, allowed modern medicine to control seven serious human diseases: smallpox, diphtheria, tetanus, yellow fever, whooping cough, poliomyelitis and measles. However, given that the reference here is to maladies that are caught "over there", Vian is likely to have had more exotic diseases in mind, such as the tropical diseases that still prevail in parts of Africa: river blindness, elephantiasis, trachoma, snail fever (schistosomiasis) and other parasitic diseases.

And there is too as well

The French line here is: "Et il y a z aussi". The "z" is meant to capture the sound produced when an "s" is followed by a vowel in French, as in "les oiseaux" (the birds). However, there is no "s" at the end of the expression "il y a" so the "z" sound is extraneous. It is a sign of lower register, familiar French, as spoken by a child or by someone whose grasp of spelling is not entirely certain. The translation has attempted to capture the spirit of this through the redundant expression: "too as well". The letter "z" is used on several occasions in Vian's poetry to insist on a pronunciation feature (liaison) that does not exist in standard, "correct" French. Further on in this same poem, for example, we find the line "À voir et à z-entendre" (translated here as "To see and contemplate"), and in the following poem, "Why do I live", Vian writes "Comme zoiseaux lents/Comme zoiseaux bleus" (translated as "Like slow-moving birds/ Like blue-moving birds"). In both cases the "z" sound is extraneous, though in "Why do I live", it serves a practical purpose by adding an extra syllable to the original lines. More significantly, this forced "z" sound gives a certain childlike quality to some of Vian's verse and can perhaps be seen as an expression of his love of childhood and nostalgia for its loss.

My bear cub, Ursula

Ursula was arguably Vian's true love. She was not, however, his first. This role fell to Michelle Léglise whom he met in 1940, at the age of 20, and whom he married the following year. This relationship had been floundering for some time when, in 1950, Vian met Ursula Kübler, whom he would marry in 1954. They would be the love of each other's lives, with Ursula continuing to support Vian's legacy through her generous patronage of *la Fond'action Boris Vian* until her death on 18 January 2010. The similarity between her name and the French word for "bear", "ours" (of the Ursidae family), explains the affectionate nickname Vian used for her.

Before having consumed

Ursula is quite literally "worn away" here. The French noun "usure" (wear and tear, wearing down) and the corresponding verb "user" (employed here) form something of a leitmotiv in Vian's longer fiction. The theme of erosion or wearing away is particularly dominant in *L'Automne à Pékin* (*Autumn in Peking*), where the hero, Angel, wishes to die alongside the woman he loves, Rochelle, but is prevented from doing so. In the present poem, the desire to "erode" Ursula or "wear her away" is quite unmistakably a sign of love. Death, love and life become inextricably entwined. The English translation hints at the sexual connotations through the use of the verb "consumed".

Such a wait to await

This picks up on the alliteration and assonance of the original French: "Tant de temps à attendre".

WHY DO I LIVE

Page 20

The original French title of this poem, "Pourquoi que je vis", has a familiar, colloquial feel due to the use of "que" as a device suggesting an interrogative form. A more straightforward rendering has been given here, however, as it would sound forced to create a similarly colloquial tone in the English translation. The poem consists of lines of five syllables. The use of the "que" in the title and in the first two lines also serves to establish that particular rhythm.

For the golden leg

The alliteration in the original French, "jambe jaune", could not be retained without transforming the meaning. It was also important to stay faithful to the colours evoked in order to retain the "jaune/blonde" pairing ("Pour la jambe jaune/D'une femme blonde"). Attractive legs of various colours (but often greys or tans because of the more common shades of silk and nylon stockings of the period) are regularly commented on in close up as women pass by in Vian's novels. This is most obviously the case in *L'Écume des jours* (*Foam of the Daze*) when the legs of three women passing by (first a deceptively old woman and, just a few pages later, two young women) usher the novel from a moment of prelapsarian bliss into its entropic decline. The colour scheme picked up in the "yellow leg" of the original French poem here recalls the colour of Colin's handkerchief, which blows into the story of *L'Écume des jours* and picks up, even as it summons, the colour scheme of the outfit worn by Alise when the couple first meet. Although her legs are smoke-grey (stockings) and white (ankle-socks), Alise is otherwise the yellow of Colin's desire. The legs of the women passing by later flesh out this desire further as they lead Colin to his first encounter with Chloé, who represents desire-become-woman and, as such, the simultaneous accomplishment and death of desire. For more on this theme, see Alistair Rolls, "'In Olden Days a Glimpse of Stocking': Fashion, Fetishism and Modernity in Boris Vian's *L'Écume des jours*", *French Cultural Studies,* 15, 2, 2004, pp. 99-113.

Like blue-moving birds

A strictly literal translation of this and the previous line would produce two lines of three syllables: "Like slow birds/Like blue birds". Vian has introduced an extraneous "z" sound to force these lines to five syllables ("Comme zoiseaux lents/Comme zoiseaux bleus"). The translation given here attempts to achieve something analagous.

LIFE IS LIKE A TOOTH

Page 21

Once again, the French title, "La vie c'est comme une dent", has something of a colloquial tone due to the emphasis created by the use of "c'est". In contrast to the previous poems, there is a more systematic use of rhyme here, which the translation has sought to reproduce.

THERE WAS A BRASS LAMP

Page 22

The ellipsis of the pronoun "il" in the original title, "Y avait une lampe de cuivre", places this poem, like those that precede it, firmly within the context of familiar, spoken French.

Closing it for evermore

The resonance with Edgar Allan Poe's "The Raven" in the English wording given here is not accidental, nor should such intertextuality surprise Vian's contemporary readers. Vian was famous for having "read everything", and, as Nicole Bertolt, who looks after his estate, is quick to remind us, this is meant quite literally: on the one hand, there were fewer books printed then than now, and the frames of reference for what reading matter counted would have been set by the Parisian smart set of whom Vian was a part; on the other hand, in the particular case of Poe, his translations into French by Charles Baudelaire have arguably made him a more important literary figure in France than in his native America. As such, Vian would certainly have been familiar with his works, all the more so indeed given his own role (as translator and pseudonymous author) in the development of the *noir* tradition in France after World War II. Poe, we should remember, is widely considered the father of crime fiction, and his importance in this role cannot be overstated in this post-war context.

And wound around the tower's stone

The original reads as follows: "Tout autour de la tour de pierre". The translation provided here takes some liberties with respect to the sentence structure of the French, but is designed to reflect the original in terms of cadence, alliteration, and imagery.

WHEN THE WIND'S BLOWING THROUGH MY SKULL

Page 23

The original French title of this poem includes the familiar use of the word "crâne" to designate the poet's head: "Quand j'aurai du vent dans mon crâne".

But then you'll be gravely at a loss

The expression "gravely at a loss" is designed to capture the meaning and humour of the original ("Mais ça sera une impression fosse"), where the word "fosse" (pit, grave) is a homophone for "fausse" (false).

My thighs my derrière

In the original French text, Vian adds an "e" to the word "cul" (arse) to invent a word — "cule" — that rhymes with the last words of the two preceding lines of verse ("bidule", "rotule") and with the three lines that follow the next one ("fistules", "cérules", "mandibules"). The word "derrière" is clearly a more polite term than "cul" but its use in the English translation provides an analogous sense of intrusion, and also allows the rhyme scheme to be retained.

With dukes and duchesses/With popes and popesses/With abbots and she-asses

Vian's iconoclasm is in evidence here: in addition to "popesses", we have she-asses that are coupled with abbots, thus making the latter the male equivalent of the female donkey — or simply "asses", in the American idiom.

the wind in this mould

The word "mould" has been used here for the sake of maintaining the rhyming scheme, though it is something of a departure from the original term "crâne" (skull). The evocation of the wind in this line nevertheless reminds the reader of the poem's title and allows the connection to be made. The pathos of these last two lines is all the more striking given the playful and light-hearted quality of what precedes.

I'M NO LONGER AT EASE

Page 24

The original title of this poem is "Je n'ai plus très envie". Vian has taken some liberties in order to create a poem with a particular rhyme scheme and regular metre. A degree of creativity is therefore required in order to produce an equivalent English version. The English title offered here, for example, is a somewhat free rendering of the original French. The term "poetries" likewise helps to respect the rhythm and rhyme, while at the same time capturing something of the whimsy of the French "pohésies" (for "poésies"). Playfulness in the service of rhyme is also evident in the final line, where Vian has added an "i" to the adjective "paresseux" (lazy) to create the new word "paressieux". In the English version, this same spirit has inspired the addition of the suffix "-ious" to produce the words "senescentious" and "indolentious".

IF I WERE A POET-O

Page 25

Original title: "Si j'étais pohéteû". The final word in the title and in each of the first four lines of this poem ends in a mute "e", but Vian has written these words in such a way as to insist on the pronunciation of that final vowel sound: "pohéteû", "ivrogneû", "rougeû", "boîteû". This, together with the six syllable metre, gives the first section of the poem a rollicking feel. The translation, which adds an "o" to each of the first four lines, produces a sea shanty effect that is intended to capture the form and rhythm of the original.

sonnects/complect

In the second section of the poem, Vian has changed the spelling of "sonnets" to "sonnais" and of "complet" to "complait" to make these words end in the same way as the verb "j'empilerais". The translation has adopted the same principle in changing "sonnets" to "sonnects" and "complete" to "complect".

A hundred or more sonnects

This is a reference to another collection of Vian's poems, *Cent sonnets* (*100 Sonnets*), the title of which is a homophone of the French word "sansonnet" (starling).

I BOUGHT SOME BREAD, STALE AND ALL

Page 26

Original title: "J'ai acheté du pain dur". Some liberty has been taken in the translation of the title to replicate the rhyming scheme of the French version.

By old man Thyme's beard

The French text here reads: "Par la barbe Farigoule". As Gilbert Pestureau points out in the Fayard edition of Vian's *Œuvres complètes* (Paris: Fayard, vol. V, 1999, p. 237), the kinship of this poem with French nursery rhymes is obvious, but the relationship to the French novelist Louis Farigoule, who wrote under the pseudonym Jules Romains, is not. The word "farigoule" is a common noun used in the Provence region of southern France to designate thyme, hence the translation given here.

THERE IS SUNSHINE IN THE STREET

Page 27

Original title: "Y a du soleil dans la rue". The tension between Vian's multiple worlds and their interdependence are obvious in this poem. The childlike withdrawal from the world (suggested by the narratorial voicc — "I like it; I don't like it") and the preference for fantasy and the imaginary over the reality of the world are a trademark of Vian's. For him, writing and the life of the imagination complement living, or are a substitute for it. Not that he did not do an ample amount of living; indeed, his lust for life and ability to work around the clock at tasks that he both loved and hated were matched only by his efforts to find time to ponder and to let life wash over him.

With its golden towers/And its white waterfalls

The sunshine in the street in this poem is a rather prosaic version of the sublime illumination of Arthur Rimbaud's famous "Aube" ("Dawn"). In Rimbaud's poem, the waterfall is neither white nor golden but is silver at its top, like the cascading hair of a goddess. We might further note that Rimbaud's waterfall-goddess is not described as "une cascade" but as a "wasserfall". She is therefore more Teutonic than French, much like Vian's own favourite blonde, Ursula.

And I walk awash with dry water/In the harsh water of the fresh night

The assonance created by the terms "awash", "harsh" and "fresh" is an approximation of the rhyme produced by the equivalent French words "sèche", "rêche" and "fraîche", whose use can be seen to mimic the sound of water.

A STARK NAKED MAN WAS WALKING

Page 28

Original title: "Un homme tout nu marchait".

His gear in his hand

The French reads: "L'habit à la main" — his clothes in his hand. But this line can also be read phonetically as "la bite à la main" — his cock in his hand. This no doubt explains the poet's mirth. To retain the *double entendre*, the word "gear" has been adopted here, though it is clearly far less crude than the French version. The schoolboy joke is deflated by the final line, where we learn it was indeed a suit ("costume") the man was holding in his hand.

MY RAPIER HURTS

Page 29

Original title: “J’ai mal à ma rapière”. As Marco Valdo points out, there is a resemblance between this poem and a song by the Italian writer and political activist Ivan della Mea (1940-2009) entitled “Ho male all’orologio” — translated into French as “J’ai mal à ma tocante” (http://www.antiwarsongs.org/canzone.php?id=10558&lang=it — accessed 10 October 2013). Phallic imagery is evident in both texts: in Mea’s song his “balls” (“coglioni”) go wandering while in Vian’s poem his “toolbag” (“sacoche”) hurts. This is also reminiscent of Vian’s “When the wind’s blowing through my skull”, where the poet evokes his missing pair of “playthings” (“bidules”). In that poem, the rats feed off his “surrounding plastic”, “tick tick”. And here lies perhaps the most important similarity between Mea’s song and Vian’s poem (“When the wind’s blowing through my skull”): the sound of the ticking clock — or heart — the metronome that counts out the beat of the poems and the lives of the poets, both of their “tocantes” or “tickers” ultimately failing.

THEY ARE BREAKING THE WORLD

Page 30

Original title: “Ils cassent le monde”. This poem, perhaps more powerfully than any other, expresses the paradoxical connection for the poet between two opposing drives. The strength of the life force in him is evident in his repeated assertion that he needs only the smallest signs of existence to keep him going, and could even find reason to live (and love) if he were put into prison. This translates, however, into a death wish as he emerges from his putative incarceration and embraces the prospect of his execution with a sense of eternal love.

I love these two tall posts/This triangular blade

This is, of course, the guillotine, below which lies a basket filled with straw to catch the poet’s head and soak up his blood.

YET ANOTHER

Page 32

Original title: "Un de plus". This poem highlights Vian's preoccupation with words and writing. In particular, the tension between the reality of writing and the idea of what it is to be a "real" writer, is a constant thread in his work. It is the main focus in several of the poems that follow, such as "I should like", "A poet" and "If poets weren't such fools". Comparisons can also be made to the poems of Vian's contemporary and neighbour Jacques Prévert (they lived in adjoining flats overlooking the roof of the Moulin Rouge). Prévert's famous post-war collection of poems, *Paroles*, is predicated on the pain of forcing beauty out of words and contains striking images of poets struggling to translate the muse onto the page.

And hesitate/Reiterate, etc.

The verbs in this series of six lines are all in the infinitive form and therefore rhyme because of the "-er" ending they share. As English verbs do not have such a pattern, other, more resourceful, strategies need to be adopted by the translator if the rhyme is to be maintained.

It's full of blood and full of sex

We see here the intimate link between the erotic and the violent, sex and death, Eros and Thanatos.

To the sodomite in my pocket

Vian has made a noun from the slang French verb "papaouter". As Pestureau points out (*Œuvres complètes* [Paris: Fayard, vol. V, 1999]), p. 242), this word is derived from "empapaouter" (to sodomise) and has the same meaning. It should be noted that it is also similar to "papoter" (to chat, talk) and that it contains the word "papa" (as in *il Papa*, the Pope). Considering the clergyman in the next line, it is not unlikely that Vian is, again, being critical of the (Catholic) Church. The mention of "Pegasuses" later on in the poem may be seen as providing further evidence for this reading given that "Pégase" is the name of one of the two homosexual page boys (or "pédérastes d'honneur") at Colin and Chloé's wedding in *L'Écume des jours* (*The Foam of Daze*). This conflation of the parallel themes of anti-clericalism and homosexuality is not uncommon in Vian's work. The image in the following lines of a "nun" who "grabs you by the dick" is clearly a variation on this anticlerical theme.

With pedal lyres, etc.

The lyre obviously represents the art of the poet, but Vian is ironically placing on a pedestal those poets whose "craft" is based on mechanical and unimaginative means such as pedals, steam and motors. The "Pegasuses" are likewise jet-powered rather than self-propelled. Unlike himself, the poets who churn out verse in this mechanical way never suffer from a lack of inspiration. Hence his bitterness: "they've taken all the easy words", leaving him only the "dullest" and the "dumbest" (such as personal pronouns, interrogative pronouns and the like).

Oh well, whatever, I will not.

Vian's anti-establishment tone and resentment are strong here, and the childlike obstinacy is nicely contrasted with both the message of the poem and its cadence and rhyme. We should also note that the concluding sentiment recalls the rather flippantly beautiful poems of Jacques Prévert, who, as noted above, had a similar obsession with writing and who likewise dwelt on the poet's inability to write a poem. Poetic non-expression and expression are thus conjoined, as are, again, the simultaneous life and death of the texts. This is also picked up in the desire for literary success expressed by Vian in the following poem, "I should like".

I SHOULD LIKE

Page 34

Original title: "J'aimerais".

And I think about people in excess

A more literal translation ("I think about people too much") would throw more obviously to the following line. However, the rhyme scheme in lines 7-13 is strongly marked in the French version so some creativity is required if that pattern is to be maintained.

Writing air and emptiness

In the end, all is air (cf. especially "When the wind's blowing through my skull"). As we have already noted, wind often blows through Vian's novels as well, ushering in death but also effecting a transition into the following novel. Such is the case at the end of *L'Herbe rouge* (*Red Grass*) when Wolf falls to his death, the wind rushing through the bars of his cage. At the very end of the novel a glimpse of another cage suggests Wolf's reincarnation, as a psychoanalyst, in the last of Vian's four major novels, *L'Arrache-cœur* (*Heartsnatcher*). For more on this, see Alistair Rolls, "Boris Vian's Eternal Sunshine, Or the Truth about Mother's Textuality", *Forum for Modern Language Studies*, 47, 3, 2011, pp. 289-303.

IF I SAY *IF*

Page 35

Original title: "Donnez le si". As noted in Maria Freij's translator's comments, this is a particularly challenging poem to render in English because of the bilingual word play on which it is based. (It is largely for this reason that we have considered this poem to be metonymic of the translation project undertaken for this volume, hence its use in the title.) The "si" of the French title translates into English as "if", which in turn is the French word for a "yew". The third line of the French poem — "Faites le tri" — is an injunction to sort or to sift, but of course the word "tri" is a homonym for the English word "tree", which leads us back to the "if"/"yew". In similar vein, line 5 of the French poem suggests that by playing "bridge" — "Jouez au bridge" — a "pont" ("bridge") will open. In line 7, the French word "fond" meaning the "bottom" (of the river) also doubles as an English adjective with a totally different meaning, which leads Vian to write, by association: "Au fond, au fond affectionné" ("to the bottom, to the affectionate bottom"). Some creative licence has been taken in order to capture that same spirit. In line 7, for example, the "Culled, sacked" is intended to evoke a French expression — "cul de sac" — that also happens to be used in English and that appropriately suggests the end or bottom of something (a road). The conclusion to the French poem is that "les Anglais sont bien dangereux". The obvious transposition has been made in the translation proposed here.

A POET

Page 36

Original title: "Un poète". In order to maintain the ABBCBBC rhyme scheme of the French poem, some liberty has been taken in the translation. Lines 2 and 3 of the original French, for example, read as follows: "C'est un être unique/À des tas d'exemplaires" ("Is a unique being/Of which there are many copies/specimens"). The oxymoron is perhaps less obvious in the translation than in the French poem, though the spirit of the original has been maintained. Lines 6 and 7 likewise require a creative approach in order to respect the rhyme pattern. In the original French, they read: "Sur des sujets divers/Des rouges ou des verts" (literally, "On various subjects/Red or green"). The colours here suggest a contrast between the ripe and the unripe, the mature and the crude.

IF POETS WEREN'T SUCH FOOLS

Page 37

The original title, "Si les poètes étaient moins bêtes", translates literally as "If poets were less foolish/stupid". In this poem, as in "One day" further on, we find a number of words that are combinations of existing words or derivations of combinations of existing words; some are invented altogether.

Of nasal flutes and lizirds", etc.

This group of three lines contains several examples of words that have been made up by combining existing words or that are pure inventions on Vian's part. The "nasal flute" is a rendering of the word "mirliflûte", which can be read as a combination of "mirliton" ("kazoo") and "flûte". The "lizeaux" is an invented word designed to rhyme with the "zoiseaux" of the previous line. It has sonorities that are reminiscent of "lézards" ("lizards"). In the following line, we find the word "mésongres", which suggests both "mésanges" ("tits" of the feathered variety) and "congres" ("conger eels"). The word "feuvertes" might be seen as a variation of "fauvettes" ("warblers"). The French words for "feather" ("plume") and "budgerigar" ("perruche") appear to be combined in the third of these lines to give "plumuches". And the word "picassiettes" in that same line is a homonym of "pique-assiettes" ("gatecrashers" or "spongers").

From crustoceans to antlishes

The French reads: "Depuis le croûsque au ramusson". The sonorities of the word "croûsque" are reminiscent of words such as "croustade" (a form of pie crust that is often filled with seafood) and "crustacée" ("crustacean"). The word "ramusson" similarly calls to mind "ramures" ("antlers", in this zoological context).

From lampdragoons to pepaflies

The French here reads: "De la libelle au pépamule". A "libelle" is a text that lampoons, but if we add to it the last syllable of "pépamule" we get "libellule" — "dragonfly". "Pépamule" is more obscure. It does contain the word "mule", of course, but in the context of the poem we are invited to imagine insects or fish. The prefix "pépa-" is not used in French, but the "pép" might suggest a number of words, such as "pépé" ("grandpa", "old-timer"), "pépée" ("doll", "chick"), or, more appropriately in this context, "pépier" and "pépiement" ("to twitter", "twittering").

From needlefish to rare curuleyes

The French reads: "De l'orphie au rara curule". An "orphie" is indeed a kind of fish, such as the garfish, with elongated, needle-shaped jaws. As for "rara curule", the "rara" perhaps suggests something rare, while the "curule" is a type of seat reserved for high-ranking Roman dignitaries. It came into fashion in France during the Napoleonic period.

And from bowsprats to poodlefishes

In French: "Et de l'avoile au canisson". As noted in Maria Freij's translator's comments, swapping consonants in these two invented words produces "avoine" ("oats") and "calisson" (a type of French candy traditionally made in the town of Aix-en-Provence). But "l'avoile" is also a homonym for "la voile" ("the sail") and "canisson" invites the word "caniche" ("poodle").

It would take two — that's evident.

A literal translation here would give: "We would only forget them after two", so some licence has been taken to preserve the rhyme. The extra day of being remembered is obviously a small gain, and little consolation, for the more industrious poets.

IT WOULD BE THERE, SO HEAVY

Page 39

Original title: "Elle serait là, si lourde". The French title contains the personal pronoun "elle", which has a certain ambiguity: does it refer to a woman, a "she", or to an object that has a grammatical feminine gender, an "it"? It is of course more likely that an object rather than a woman would be described as "heavy", and the first lines of the poem confirm this. The "it" in question, as we learn further on, is a locomotive (a feminine noun in French). Nevertheless, Vian's renowned use of word play and his tendency towards unusual and unexpected comparisons perhaps help that ambivalence linger to a certain extent. Interestingly, Émile Zola, in his classic nineteenth-century novel *La Bête humaine*, famously conflated woman and steam engine in the feminine curves of an engine or locomotive named la Lison. At the end of the novel, a common love (of the same woman and the same engine) drives the engine-driver protagonist, Lantier, and his fireman colleague, Pecqueux, to their deaths as the train speeds out of control.

As befits a coniroster

As its name suggests, a coniroster is a small bird, such as a finch, with a cone-shaped beak.

The birdie or the choo-choo

Vian has written "comotive" for "locomotive" and "zoizillon" for "oisillon". The translation is similarly child-like. The two terms have been swapped, to maintain the rhyme with the previous line. ("Un unique échantillon", in French).

If I leave the machine

In 1947, Vian gave up his career as an engineer to devote greater time to his diverse artistic pursuits; other than its larger-scale significance, this poem also evokes his personal struggle regarding which path to choose.

THERE ARE THOSE WHO HAVE DEAR LITTLE TRUMPETS

Page 41

Original title: "Y en a qui ont des trompinettes". Vian is famous for his musicianship and many iconic images of him feature his trumpet, which he always referred to as his "trompinette". This is a diminutive version of the standard French word for the instrument, "une trompette", and is clearly a term of affection.

And wooden serpents

The wooden serpent is a wind instrument made of brass-coated wood. Its name comes from its serpentine form. The serpent was commonly used up till the nineteenth century for church and military music. Given Vian's hostility towards those two institutions — the Church and the army — we might surmise that he is writing here with ironic intent about those who possess such instruments.

And ophicleides of giant form

An ophicleide is a wind instrument consisting of a conical metal tube that is bent double. It is a development of the wooden serpent.

And I kazoom

The French verb "mirlitonner" means "to play the kazoo" ("mirliton"). No equivalent simple verb exists in English, so in true Vian spirit one has been invented here. It is important to note that the verb "mirlitonner" can also mean in the figurative sense "to write bad poetry". When the poet asks us at the end of the poem if we like the way he plays, he is essentially wondering out loud whether he writes well. The self-doubt in this final, isolated, line is extremely moving, especially in contrast to the bravado of the preceding line. Compared to the poetic instruments other poets have at their disposal, his may be modest and even ridiculously trivial, but none of that would matter if he were able to play it well. He has doubts even about that, however.

I WANT A LIFE SHAPED LIKE A FISHBONE

Page 42

Original title: "Je veux une vie en forme d'arête". This is the only poem in the collection that Vian dated (5 December 1952). However, as Noël Arnaud notes in his edition of *Je voudrais pas crever* (Paris: 10/18, 1972, p. 5), all of the poems in the collection, with the exception of "I shall die of a cancer of the spine", were written between 1951 and 1952. In this particular text, Vian evokes living the cessation of living, as it were, by expressing his wish for a life like bones stripped bare. The first line — "Je veux une vie en forme d'arête" — presents life and death neatly before the reader on "une assiette bleue" ("a blue plate"), if not a silver platter. In typically complex and contradictory fashion, Vian desires something that will bring about its own end. Noteworthy, too, is the homophony of "arête" ("fishbone") and "arrête", from the verb "arrêter" ("to stop").

In the shape of green bread or a pitcher

Green bread — "pain vert" — is a type of bread made from equal parts of flour and green rice.

ONE DAY

Page 43

Original title: "Un jour". As in one of the previous poems, "If poets weren't such fools", Vian has sprinkled this poem with invented words, many of which appear to be made up using combinations of existing words. The "goldenear" of line 6, for example, is a rendering of Vian's "auraille", which sounds similar to "oreille" ("ear") and which begins with three letters evoking gold. The "spirelf" of line 7 is an equivalent term to the French "volutin", which can be read as a combination of "volute" ("spiral") and "lutin" ("elf", "imp"). The "hot impro" in line 9 is inspired by the resemblance between Vian's "baouf" and the word "bœuf", which means "ox" in French but is also the word used by musicians to refer to a jam session. The sonorities of the French "chalamondre" have been retained in the following line (perhaps suggesting a kind of salamander?), whereas the "drunkaninny" of line 11 comes from the French "ivrunini" (formed from "ivre" — "drunk"). The word "heroi-baroque" translates "baroïque", which suggests a combination of "baroque" and "héroïque". And finally, "anahologies" is a rendering of "analognes", which looks very much like "analogue" ("analagous"). It is clearly impossible to capture all the possible allusions in these nonsensical terms, but the whimsy of the original nevertheless comes through in the translation proposed here.

EVERYTHING HAS BEEN SAID A HUNDRED TIMES

Page 44

Original title: "Tout a été dit cent fois". This is yet another poem about writing poetry, but here the poet's attitude is irreverently defiant throughout, despite his acknowledgement that others have been more successful at it than he has.

I SHALL DIE OF A CANCER OF THE SPINE

Page 45

Original title: "Je mourrai d'un cancer de la colonne vertébrale". This is very much the terminal poem of the collection. Indeed, as Noël Arnaud notes (*Je voudrais pas crever*, p. 5), it was the only one written in the final years of Vian's life.

My hands fastened under a waterfall

It seems appropriate that, in this concluding poetic expression of the instant of death itself, the image of the waterfall should re-emerge, referring back, via the earlier poem "There is sunshine in the street", to Rimbaud's Teutonic waterfall-goddess who must now be seen as standing for the love of Vian's life, Ursula.

NOTES TO THE SHORT STORIES

MARTIN CALLED...

Page 65

- French title: "Martin m'a téléphoné..." First published in the collection of short stories entitled *Le Loup-garou*, edited by Christian Bourgois (Paris: 10/18, 1970), pp. 91-117. The manuscript, dated 25 October 1945, was untitled. The story obtained its title from the opening words of the first paragraph, which explains the suspension points.

- This is a difficult story to translate primarily because of the punctuation. Reading it out loud is perhaps the best method for determining comma and full stop breaks, since French and English punctuation do not always correspond. It is important to retain the ambiguity that surrounds the fast-paced action of the evening. This means resisting the temptation to "over translate".

- Rue Notoire-du-Vidame is in all probability a playful allusion to rue Notre-Dame des Victoires where Vian worked as an engineer for Afnor — the Association française de normalisation (the French national organisation for standardisation) — from 1942 to 1946. This organisation is heavily satirised in Vian's novel *Vercoquin et le plancton* (*Vercoquin and the Plankton*), which was published in 1947 by Gallimard.

- The sections of dialogue in italics here and elsewhere are in English in the original text. Although the English is of a very high standard, it is clear in a number of instances that it is not quite the language of a native speaker. Nevertheless, apart from correcting "february" to "February" and making a couple of minor adjustments to the punctuation, we have retained Vian's original English text in such instances.

- Doddy refers to Claude Léon, a drummer and friend of Vian who lived in the rue Lamarck during the period when this story was written. Roby is Roby Savin, one of the various anagrams of his own name that Vian invented. The brother refers to Alain Vian, who sometimes played the drums in the group Abadie-Vian. During the 1940s, Boris played trumpet in this orchestra, which was led by clarinettist Claude Abadie. Miqueut is a character from the novel *Vercoquin et le plancton* who works as an engineer for the Consortium national de l'unification (a fictionalisation of Afnor). The conversation over the telephone with Martin is in English in the original text.

Page 66

- Heinz's French is not quite correct: "Je voudrais vous reverrer" should be "Je voudrais vous revoir" (meaning "I'd like to see you again"). "C'est comme ça qu'on dit?" means "Is that how you say it?"

- Vian's first wife Michelle frequented the bar at the Hôtel Normandie, in the 1st arrondissement of Paris, when she was preparing for her baccalauréat. Freddy, the owner, experienced problems as a Nazi collaborator.

- Weegee is the pseudonym of Arthur Fellig (1899-1968), who was a New York photographer famous for his work with that city as subject. He was a regular contributor to *Photography* and published his first photographic book, *Naked City*, in 1945. He earned his nickname, a rendering of Ouija, because of his uncanny knack of turning up at the scene of major crimes and accidents only minutes after the authorities had been notified of them.

- The rue de Trévise, like the rue de Caumartin, is in the 9th arrondissement of Paris.

Page 67

- The number "seventy-three" is written in English in the original text. Temsey is Taymour Nawab, a guitarist and singer who was fond of the bottle.
- A "black 11" is an eleven horsepower car. Several such models were produced from the 1920s to the 1940s by companies such as Delage, De Bazelaire and, most notably, Citroën, with its famous front-wheel drive vehicle (the "traction avant") that features in many films of the Second World War.
- The TCRP (Transports en commun de la région parisienne) was the Paris region's public transport operator. In 1948, this would become the RATP (Régie autonome des transports parisiens).

Page 69

- The phase value refers to the time shift of a sinusoid and is a significant feature of the way in which car engines function. We should not be surprised to find Vian using such technical language, as he had studied mathematics to a high level and worked as an engineer for Afnor.
- Saint-Lazare is one of the six main train stations in Paris. It is situated in the 8th arrondissement.
- The Matford company, a collaborative venture between Mathis and Ford, produced cars and trucks in France from 1934 to 1940.
- The outer boulevards ("boulevards extérieurs") are those boulevards that correspond more or less to the Paris wall known as the "mur des Fermiers généraux" (the Wall of the Farmers-General), which was constructed just prior to the French Revolution in order to levy taxes on goods entering the city, much to the displeasure of its inhabitants. It was demolished in 1860 in order to expand the city,

under the major renovation programme undertaken by the Prefect of Paris, Baron Haussmann. These outer boulevards now form part of Paris proper.

- The Air Transport Command was established by the US Air Force to provide urgently needed supplies to American military bases during World War II. After the Liberation of France, its French headquarters were indeed located at 7 Place Vendôme.

Page 71

- The Fête Foraine is a carnival or fun fair.
- Suresnes is a commune in the western suburbs of Paris, across the Seine from the Bois de Boulogne.
- Maxence Van der Meersch (1907-1951) was a well-known writer of the time. *Corps et âmes* (1943) was perhaps his best-known work.

Page 72

- Buescher is a famous brand of oil in music circles.
- Aubusson, in the upper valley of the Creuse in central France, is famous for the manufacture of tapestries and carpets.
- Pierre Mac Orlan is one of the pseudonyms used by Pierre Dumarchey (1882-1970), a French novelist and songwriter. His novel *Quai des brumes* (*Port of Shadows*) was adapted for the cinema by Marcel Carné in 1938. The film starred Jean Gabin, Michel Simon and Michèle Morgan.

Page 73

- Johnny Mercer (1909-1976) was an American composer and singer who sometimes worked with Duke Ellington. He also co-founded Capitol Records in 1942.
- The *zazous* were young jazz fans who constituted a subculture in France, and especially in Paris, during World War II. In addition

to their love of swing and bebop, they were identifiable by their distinctive and outlandish clothing. The name "zazous" probably derives from a Cab Calloway song featuring the line "zah zuh zah".

- Dittishausen and Unadingen are localities in Germany's Black Forest.

Page 74

- American Beauty is a type of rose which is vibrant red in colour. The term is used metonymically for the colour itself.
- Johnny Mercer wrote the lyrics for "Laura", which achieved popularity in 1945 thanks to the 1944 movie of the same name in which it was featured. "Sentimental Journey" was Doris Day's first number 1 hit. It was composed by Les Brown and Ben Horner, with lyrics by Bud Green.

Page 75

- "I Dream of You (More Than You Dream I Do)" was a popular song recorded by Tommy Dorsey and his orchestra in 1944. "There! I've Said It Again" (its correct title) was written by Redd Evans and David Mann and popularised by Vaughn Monroe in 1945. Bobby Vinton revived its popularity when he recorded it in late 1963.
- A musette is a traditional form of popular French music that came into fashion in Paris in the 1880s. "Ah! Le Petit vin blanc" was a very popular French song written in 1943 by Jean Dréjac and Charles Borel-Clerc.

Page 76

- As previously noted, speech written in italics denotes English text in the original version of the story. The signs mentioned further on in the same paragraph are also in English.
- *Yank* was a weekly publication released and edited by the American War Ministry between 1942 and 1945.

Page 77

- "I condole" is a translation of "Je condoulois", from the verb "condouloir". This is an archaic word that is rarely used today, and only in its infinitive form. Vian's creative use of language is once again in evidence here.
- The Gare du Nord is another of the major train stations in Paris. Neuilly-sur-Seine is a suburb adjacent to the western end of the city of Paris, sitting north of the Bois de Boulogne.
- The last sentence is extremely difficult to translate, because the meaning is so obscure. The original text, "Je me suis changé en canard", literally means "I turned into a duck". In musical terms, the word "canard" can refer to a false note struck when playing an instrument. The context of the story perhaps invites this reading. The translation given here is an attempt to retain the dual reference to the duck and an unpleasant noise, while remaining similarly obscure.

THE SWIMMING PRIEST

Page 78

- French title: "Le Ratichon baigneur". First published in the weekly journal *La Rue*, n° 8, 26 July 1946, p. 9. Republished in the collection of short stories edited by Christian Bourgois, who chose this title as the title of the volume (*Le Ratichon baigneur*, Paris: 10/18, 1981, pp. 49-55). The manuscript, which is not dated, is signed "Révérend B Vian de la Compagnie de Jésus". The title makes clear the author's ironic intent: "ratichon" is a pejorative familiar term for a priest. In similarly irreverent vein, the title suggests a play on words with "raton laveur" (the French term for a "raccoon"). The word "laveur" comes from the French verb "laver" ("to wash"). The raccoon's preference for small aquatic animals and its habit of rubbing its prey between its paws led to the popular belief that it washes its food before eating it. The word "baigneur" generally pertains to swimming (a bather, a swimming-pool attendant or swimming instructor, etc), but the verb "baigner", like "laver", also means to wash. Vian is well known for juxtaposing seemingly unrelated words and expressions. This title is a good example of that tendency. It is worth noting that, in addition to the sense of swimming or bathing it most commonly connotes, the word "baigneur" is used more specifically to designate a child's doll made from plastic and that can therefore be washed.

- Louis Pauwels (1920-1997) was born in Belgium. He was a writer and journalist for a number of different publications, including *Variété*, *Esprit* and *Le Journal du dimanche*. In issue 7 of *La Rue*, Pauwels published an article entitled "Mœurs et coutumes aux bains Deligny" ("Life and Customs at the Deligny Baths"). It has been said that "Le Ratichon baigneur" was written in response to that article.
- Deligny was a floating swimming pool moored on the left bank of the Seine, near the French National Assembly. Its origins date back to 1785. In more recent times, it comprised a pool, a solarium and a bar-restaurant. It met its demise when it sank in 1993.
- *La Rue* was a weekly publication to which Vian contributed.

Page 79

- The "Prix de la Pléaide" was awarded annually to the writer deemed best young author by the publishing house Gallimard. In 1947, one year after the publication of this short story, Vian would experience deep disappointment at not being awarded this prize for his novel *L'Écume des jours*.
- *Le Pèlerin* (*Pilgrim*) was a weekly journal founded in 1873 by the Assumptionists. *Témoignage chrétien* (*Christian Witness*) was a weekly news publication of Christian inspiration, but with Leftist tendencies. It was founded in 1941 during the German Occupation of France and was linked to the French Resistance movement.

- Pelota is a sport, originating in the Basque country, played on a court with a ball and either a racket, a bat or the hand.

- Rimbaud (1854-1891) was a symbolist poet. Kierkegaard (1813-1855) was a profound and prolific writer in the Danish "golden era" of intellectual and artistic activity. He is sometimes known as the "father of existentialism." The *Hundred and Twenty Days of Sodom* was the infamous book written by the Marquis de Sade during his imprisonment in the Bastille in 1785. In it, he graphically describes varieties of sexual perversion.

- Cremona is a town in the Lombardy region of northern Italy. It is famous for the manufacture of musical instruments. "Le violon de Crémone" is also the title of a painting completed in 1860 by French artist Charles-Louis Müller (1815-1892). The "Géricault Trumpet" likewise evokes both music and painting. As a feminine noun, the word "trompette" designates the musical instrument, but it also exists as a masculine noun meaning "the trumpet player". The figure of the (military) trumpetist was the subject of several paintings by Théodore Géricault (1791-1824). There may also be a play on words here, given that the trumpet was the musical instrument that brought down the walls of Jericho.

ANOTHER DAY IN MARSEILLE

Page 81

- The manuscript for this story is undated but it is known to have been composed in the second half of 1946. It was first published in 1970 in the collection *Le Loup-garou* (pp. 119-130) with the title "Marseille commençait à s'éveiller" (literally, "Marseille was starting to awaken"). The translation of the title offered here is an example of Vinay and Darbelnet's theory of modulation: the transfer of a message through a change in point of view.

- Palavas is a seaside resort in the south of France, near Montpellier.

Havas is an advertising group. It is currently the second largest communications group in France, and the sixth largest in the world.

- Nogent is located in the well-to-do eastern suburbs of Paris.

Page 82

- Mr Mackinley could be based on Ray McKinley, a singer and drummer with Glenn Miller.
- The battle of Iwo Jima was fought between the US and Japan in February and March 1945.
- ASS alludes to the OSS (Office of Strategic Services), which was later to become the CIA. The change of first letter is clearly aimed at mocking the US.

Page 83

- Hirohito was the Emperor of Japan from 1926 until 1989. He approved the attack on Pearl Harbour that led to the war between the US and Japan.
- According to the note in the Pléiade edition of Vian's *Œuvres romanesques complètes* (vol. I, p. 1276), Jules M. could be Jules Moch, who was Minister for Public Transport and reinstated trans-Atlantic flights for Air France in July 1946. The Gromiline Report may be a reference to the Gromyko Plan, which was presented to the United Nations in June 1946 and which aimed to prevent the military use of atomic energy.
- Marthe Richard (1889-1982) was a French prostitute and spy during both World Wars. She later led the campaign for the closing of brothels, which earned her the Légion d'honneur.

Page 84

- The Vivaquatre was an eleven-horsepower Renault produced between 1932 and 1939.

- Casimir Pulaski (1745-1779) was a Polish nobleman and military officer who fought unsuccessfully against Russian domination of the Polish-Lithuanian Commonwealth. He was exiled because of the role he played in that uprising, and emigrated to North America where he espoused the cause of the American colonists against the British in the American Revolutionary War, notably saving the life of George Washington.

Page 85

- As noted in the Pléiade edition of Vian's *Œuvres romanesques complètes* (vol. I, p. 1276), Goloubtchik is an affectionate diminutive form of "goloub", meaning "my little dove" in Russian.

- Harbin is the capital of the Songjiang province of China, which was merged in 1954 with the neighbouring province of Heilongjiang (the present-day name of the merged province). Heilongjiang province is located in China's north-east corner, in relative proximity to the Korean peninsula.

Page 87

- NRF, or Non-Remember Fluid, was a serum developed by the American Secret Service during the Second World War. It is also a play on the French literary magazine, *La Nouvelle Revue française*, which was founded in 1909. The note is Vian's.

DOGS, DEATH AND DESIRE

Page 88

- This story, entitled "Les Chiens, le désir et la mort", was included in *Les Morts ont tous la même peau*, which Vian published in 1947 under the pseudonym of Vernon Sullivan. Vian wrote the story during the first half of that year (though the manuscript itself is undated). It was subsequently republished in 1970, in *Le Loup-garou*. The word order of the original title has been changed here, primarily for reasons of euphony and rhythm.

- The clubs on New York's 52nd Street were in full flight in the 1940s. Veterans of the swing era could be heard playing there, and bebop also began to make its mark during that period. This particular music scene would prove to be a major influence on the development of modern jazz. The Three Deuces was one of those clubs.

DON'T TRUST THE BAND

Page 96

- The manuscript of this story, entitled "Méfie-toi de l'orchestre", is undated. It first appeared in March 1947 in a special edition of the review *America*. That issue, entitled "Jazz 47", contained contributions from such influential figures as Jean Cocteau, Charles Delauney, Hugues Panassié and Jean-Paul Sartre, who had only just returned from the United States. This story was subsequently included in *Le Ratichon baigneur* (pp. 57-62). An earlier version of this translation was published in the March 2010 number of *The AALITRA Review*. It is reproduced here, with a number of minor modifications, with the kind permission of the editor of that journal, Brian Nelson.
- A convolution is a sinous fold in the surface of the brain.
- Paul Pierre Broca (1824-1880) was a famous neurologist. He was the first to describe in detail a particular form of aphasia, in 1861. In the 13th arrondissement of Paris, there is a hospital specialising in gerontology named after him. Captain Pamphile is a fictitious sea-faring character created by Alexandre Dumas (senior). As noted in the Pléiade edition of Vian's *Œuvres romanesques complètes* (vol. I, p. 1276), both Broca and Dumas advanced scientific theories in the 1860s regarding the influence of the brain's weight on the intelligence of women and native peoples.

Page 97

- The Avenue du Bois is the Avenue du Bois-de-Boulogne, which runs from the Place de l'Étoile south-west to the Bois de Boulogne. Its name was changed to Avenue Foch in 1929. It is today one of the most exclusive and expensive streets in Paris.

- Charles de Gaulle (1890-1970) was a general and statesman. He was the leader of the Free French during World War II, and the architect of the Fifth Republic. Yvon Pétra (1916-1984) was a tennis player who won Wimbledon in 1946. Both men were exceptionally tall, de Gaulle standing at 1.96 metres and Pétra at 1.93 metres. There is a play on words in the original French, with "Double-Maître" and "Double-Mètre" pronounced exactly the same.

- Apollo is the Greek god of prophecy, music, healing and the sun. He is also considered to be the ideal of male beauty.

RAMPARTS OF THE SOUTH

Page 99

- This story, titled in French "Les Ramparts du sud", was written in 1946. It was re-worked on 7 May 1947 for publication in the review *Samedi-Soir*. This did not eventuate, however, and the story remained unpublished during Vian's lifetime. Its inclusion in *Le Loup-garou* (pp. 35-74) thus represented its first publication, in 1970.

Page 100

- The "Major" is a recurring character in Vian's prose fiction. It is the nickname by which he referred to his friend, Jacques Loustalot, who died in 1949 after falling from a building. He was trying to enter an apartment in the building by a window, in response to a dare.

- From the Liberation until 1949, permission had to be obtained to take a car on the road, due to the scarcity of petrol.

- "Bison ravi" ("Delighted Bison") is an anagram of Boris Vian's name. He consequently referred to his son, Patrick, as "Little Bison" ("Petit Bison" or "Bisonnot").

- Wine was in limited supply during and just after the war and had to be rationed. One of the sections of Afnor, where Vian worked, was responsible for managing supplies and standardising wine bottles. The meal described here needs to be understood in that context of post-war rationing.

Page 101

- Saint-Jean-de-Luz is a seaside resort and fishing village on France's Atlantic coast, near the Spanish border.

Page 102

- Cheramy was a brand of American perfume created in 1921 by Robert Bienamé, working for the French perfume house Houbigant. It was designed as a means of combating the American protectionists in the intense competition at the time between French and American perfumers. Jules Gouffé (1807-1877) was a renowned French chef and pâtissier. He was nicknamed the "apostle of decorative cooking" ("l'apôtre de la cuisine décorative").

- The Café Duflor is a play on the Café de Flore on the Boulevard Saint-Germain. Like its rival café, Les Deux Magots (referred to a little further on in a similarly transparent manner as the Deux Mâghos), it has a long-established reputation for attracting intellectuals and other famous figures.

Page 103

- The SNCF (Société Nationale des Chemins de fer Français) is the French National Railway Company.

Page 104

- François Mauriac (1885-1970) was a celebrated French Catholic writer who was awarded the Nobel Prize for literature in 1952. His novels are generally austere psychological studies of religious characters attempting to come to terms with sin and salvation.

- Georges Duhamel (1884-1966) was a doctor and writer who examined in his fiction various moral and social issues.

Page 106

- The city of Nuremberg in the German state of Bavaria is famous, among other things, for manufacturing toys since the Middle Ages.

Page 110

- The Rue Cœur-de-Lion is a reference to the place of residence of Jacques Loustalot (the Major), who lived in the villa Cœur-de-Rey near the Place Denfert-Rochereau, in the 14th arrondissement of Paris, which features the statue of the Lion of Belfort.
- The N306 leads south-west from Paris to Rambouillet. The Montlhéry Tower is located 26 kilometres south-west of Paris.

Page 111

- The N152 links Briare, south of Paris, to Angers around 300 kilometres south-west of Paris. The N751 runs from the central French département of Cher to the Atlantic coast just south of Nantes.
- The Houdan chicken is an old and distinctive breed. The town of Houdan, after which it was named, served as an important poultry market for Paris. It is some 60 kilometres to the west of the capital.

Page 112

- The N764 linked the town of Tivoli, near Blois, and the town of Loches, on the Indre River near Tours. It was downgraded to a departmental road in 1972. Pontlevoy is a small town about 20 kilometres to the south-west of Blois. Montrichard is a further 5 kilometres to the south-west, and Le Liège is another 10-12 kilometres to the south-west of Montrichard. The intersection of the N764 (now the D764) and the D10 is about 4 kilometres to the south-west of Le Liège.

- Julien Da Rui (1916-1987) was a legendary goalkeeper for the French national team during the 1940s.

Page 115

- In the original text, Verge places a piece of "charbon du Sérail" on top of the mound. This is a transformation of "pastilles du Sérail" — sweet smelling air fresheners sold in France and presented as coming from Constantinople. The word "sérail" means "harem", hence the "sweet harem smelling smoke".

Page 118

- Montmoreau is about 30 kilometres south of Angoulême in the Charente department in south-western France. The N709 (now the D709) links it with Ribérac, a small town in the Dordogne department, some 25 kilometres to the south-east of Montmoreau. Chalais is about 10 kilometres south-west of Montmoreau and 25 kilometres west of Ribérac, so the Major has taken a circuitous route to get there. Boresse-et-Martron is 10-12 kilometres west of Chalais and Montlieu-la-Garde is another 10 kilometres further west. There, the N10 leads directly down towards Bordeaux, through Cavignac.

Page119

- Saint-André-de-Cubzac is halfway between Cavignac and Bordeaux. By travelling through Branne, Targon and Langoiran, the Major has bypassed Bordeaux, following an arc to the east. Hostens is 50 kilometres south of Bordeaux by road, in the Landes de Gascogne Regional Natural Park. It is another 160 kilometres from there to Saint-Jean-de-Luz.

Page 120

- A chadburn is a communications device on a ship that allows the bridge to send orders to the engineers in the engine room regarding speed settings.

Page 121

- Jules Romains (1885-1972) was a novelist, dramatist and poet.

Page 122

- La Négresse and Guéthary are localities on the road from Bayonne to Saint-Jean-de-Luz.

LÉOBILLE'S PARTY

Page 123

- Written in June 1947, this story was initially entitled "Les paupières de Folubert" ("Folubert's Eyelids"). It was published in *Samedi-Soir* on 12 July of that same year with the title "Surprise-partie chez Léobille". It was subsequently published in *La Revue de poche* in June 1965 and again in 1970, in *Le Loup-garou* (pp. 181-197). The events of a "surprise-partie", popular among Vian's circle of friends, are recounted here and exaggerated in a burlesque tone. The story features the Major, Jacques Loustalot, as the villain.

- Folubert is a play on the name of Hubert Fol, a saxophone player in Claude Abadie's band. The surname "Sansonnet" is the French word for "starling", but is also a homonym for *Cent sonnets* (*100 Sonnets*), which was the title of a collection of poetry by Vian.

- The Hesperides were named after the daughters of Hesperus. They were the guardians of a tree of golden apples belonging to Hera in a garden located beyond the Atlas Mountains, at the western border of Oceanus, or the known world.

Page 124

- Doddy is the drummer Claude Léon, Rémonfol is Raymond Fol, a pianist and the brother of Hubert, and chief Abadibada is Claude Abadie, clarinettist and orchestra leader. The Lorientais Club, in the 5th arrondissement of Paris, was host to a group of well-known musicians led by Claude Luter.

- A "barbette" can be either a kind of wimple worn by nuns or a form of military fortification. Here, however, it is almost certainly a reference to Barbette (1898-1973), an American female impersonator and high-wire performer who was immensely popular in France during the 1920s and 1930s, and who inspired artists such as Man Ray and Jean Cocteau. In an essay published in 1926 ("Le Numéro Barbette"), Cocteau describes the "shuffling little street urchin dance" performed by Barbette during his curtain call.

Page 125

- The Major, who also featured in the preceding story, "The Ramparts of the South", is Jacques Loustalot. He was almost like a brother to Vian.

- The Prévert brothers, Jacques and Pierre, were well known to Vian. Jacques was Vian's neighbour at Cité Véron, while Pierre was a filmmaker (a commemorative plaque to Boris Vian and Jacques Prévert was officially unveiled at 6 bis, or "6A", Cité Véron in November 2013, just as this volume was being completed). The original French contains a play on words: an "anicroche", which is a hitch or a snag, is grazing in the "frères prés-verts" (literally, the "brothers green fields"). The "stupid ass" in the translation offered here is inspired by the first syllable of "anicroche", an "âne" being a donkey or ass.

- *Ivan the Terrible* is Sergei Eisenstein's film, the first part of which was released in 1944 (Part 2 was not released until 1958 because of political censorship). The actor's surname is a reference to Ivan Papanine, a Russian explorer who visited the North Pole in 1940. His middle name could be inspired by Boris Fyodorovich Andreyev, an actor noted for his role in the renowned Soviet film *Two Soldiers* (1943).

Page 126

- Azyme is an unusual choice of name. It is a type of unleavened bread eaten by the Jews at Passover.

Page 127

- Judo was widely practised after the Liberation and remains a strong sport in France.

Page 128

- The "crepuscular dance move" is a rendering of "un entre-chien-et-loup", which is a play on words. After the verb "esquisser" (translated here as to "execute"), a French reader would expect the word "entrechat", which is a ballet move. However, the second part of the word, "chat", if taken on its own means "cat". This has inspired Vian to use instead the expression "entre chien et loup" (literally, "between dog and wolf") — a familiar expression used to designate dusk, when it can be difficult to distinguish objects, or animals, clearly.

Page 129

- "Ma-jor-i-ty" is a rendering of yet another play on words, this time between "Major" and "majoration". The French sentence reads: "Pour chaque parole de trop, il y aura une Majoration." A "majoration" is an extra charge or an increase in price.

Page 130

- Jean Berdin was a jazz drummer with Bolling, Abadie, Vian and others. Berdindin is a playful rendering of his name.

Page 132

- As already noted (see above, the notes to "The Ramparts of the South"), Jacques Loustalot (the Major), lived in the Villa Cœur-de-Rey, near the Place Denfert-Rochereau, in the middle of which is the large statue of the Lion of Belfort.

THE SLIP-UP

Page 133

- French title: "Les Pas vernis". First published in the review *Dans le train* (July 1948). Subsequently published in 1970 in *Le Loup-garou* (pp. 147-156). The story revolves around an eccentric family based on Vian's own, and includes good friend and drummer Claude Léon as Léon Dodiléon (referred to as Doddy in "Martin called…"). The names of Clams and Gaviale are clearly inspired by marine animals, a "gavial" being a crocodilian (also called a gharial) native to India. The name Jorjobert is a phonetic rendering of Georges Aubert, an actor who played in a theatrical adaptation of *J'irai cracher sur vos tombes* in 1948. An earlier version of this translation was published in the September 2008 number of *The AALITRA Review*. It is reproduced here, with a number of minor modifications, with the kind permission of the editor of that journal, Brian Nelson.
- Boris Vian's son Patrick was born on 12 April 1942.

Page 134

- The name Caroline Lampion is an oblique reference to the Belgian actress Anne Campion. She played the role of Jean Asquith in the 1948 theatrical adaptation of *J'irai cracher sur vos tombes*. The name of the street in which Caroline Lampion lives is a contraction of "merde" ("shit") and Mozart. Vian was not a fan of Mozart's music, needless to say. The number of her building is given in the original text as "cent septante", which is the Belgian equivalent of the French "cent soixante-dix". In order to retain the slightly quaint feel (for a French reader) of the Belgian number, the translation has, ironically, drawn on the standard French version. André-Charles Boulle (1642-1732) was a renowned cabinet-maker who worked for many years for Louis XIV. Bonnichon Brothers and Mape were two noted makers of luxury prams. The names of the two "illustrious" families that own these prams are clearly pastiches of the upper class.

Page 136

- Heidsieck is a brand of French champagne.
- "High-speed cushion" is a rendering of "coussin berzingué". Vian has invented the adjective "berzingué", drawing from the familiar expression "à tout(e) berzingue", meaning "at full speed".

Page 137

- "Léonging to be let out" is a rendering of "trouvait le temps léong", where Vian has changed the adjective "long" to make it sound like the character's name.

FRANKFURT ON TAP

Page 139

- First published in April 1949 in the review *Dans le train*. Subsequently included by Christian Bourgois in *Le Ratichon baigneur*, published in 1981 (pp. 63-74). The French title, "Francfort-sous-la-main", is a play on words on "Francfort-sur-le-Main". The Main (masculine noun) is the river on which the city of Frankfurt sits, whereas "la main" (feminine noun) is French for "the hand". To have something "sous la main" is to have it at hand or within easy reach. Jef is Jean-François Devay (1925-1971), a journalist who travelled with Vian to Frankfurt in 1948. Pralin is Vian's friend Pralon, who also accompanied him to Germany. The "delighted Jason" ("Jason ravi") is a reference to Vian himself, "Bison ravi" ("delighted bison") being an anagram of his name. Jason and the Argonauts, and the quest for the Golden Fleece, are taken from Greek mythology. Knokke is a seaside resort in Belgium renowned for its jazz festivals.
- The Bretton Woods Conference took place in the United States in July 1944. Its aim was to regulate international money and finances after World War II. The final agreements led, among other outcomes, to the establishment of the International Monetary Fund.
- Steatopygia is excess fat on the buttocks.

Page 141

- PX is an abbrevation for Post Exchange, a kind of retail outlet operating in US military bases.

Page 142

- The MPs are the Military Police.
- Morpheus is the god of dreams.

A CULTURAL EXPERIENCE

Page 145

- French title: "Divertissements culturels". First published in *Dans le train* in June 1949. Included by Christian Bourgois in *Le Ratichon baigneur*, in 1981 (pp. 29-38). Charlie, the young cinephile, and the Admiral, who is based on the engineer Roger Lamoral, will also figure in "A Big Star" and "A Dog of a Job". Paul Boubal was the owner of the Café de Flore during the 1940s. Ops, who also features in "The Test", is the name of the Roman goddess of fertility. Gréco and Anne-Marie refer, respectively, to Juliette Gréco, the French actress and singer, and Anne-Marie Cazalis, a journalist and writer who was a close friend of Vian and who won the Prix Paul-Valéry in 1943 for her poetry.

Page 146

- Alexandre Astruc was a French cinematographer and writer, and a friend of Vian. *Gone With the Christmas Spirit* is clearly a play on *Gone With the Wind.* Edward G. Robinson (1893-1973), an American actor of Romanian descent, was famous for his gangster roles.

Page 147

- Salicylate is a bitter chemical used as a fungicide and in the manufacture of aspirin and dyes. Beeman's is a brand of chewing gum created in the 1880s by the physicist Dr Edward Beeman.

- Marliche Dihêtrenne is an obvious play on the name of the actress Marlene Dietrich who starred in the movie *The Blue Angel* (1930), directed by Josef von Sternberg.

Page 148

- *Storm Over Oustoupinski* may be a reference to the 1928 Russian film, *Storm Over Asia*, directed by Vsevolod Pudovkin. It may also refer to a 1938 French film of the same name, directed by Richard Oswald.

THE TEST

Page 149

- French title: "Un test". First published in *Dans le train* in July 1949. Republished in 1981 in *Le Ratichon baigneur* (pp. 75-84). According to a note in the Pléiade edition of Vian's prose works (vol. II, p. 1315), this story must have been written in 1946, given the similarity, in terms of characters and settings, to other stories composed at that time. The Deligny baths, for example, also figured in "The Swimming Priest" (for details about these baths, see the notes to that story, above). Certain characters are recognisable as being members of Claude Luter's jazz group: Maxime Saury the clarinet player, Roland Bianchini the bass player, Moustache (François Galepides) the drummer. Christian Castapioche may be based on Christian Casadesus, a movie actor and a familiar figure in Saint-Germain-des-Prés.

Page 150

- Little Bison is Vian's son, Patrick.

Page 151

- Don Byas (1912-1972) was a black American saxophone player who spent most of his career in France after World War II.

A BIG STAR

Page 154

- French title: "Une grande vedette". First published in *Dans le train* in August 1949. Republished in 1981 in *Le Ratichon baigneur* (pp. 39-48). Vian will include the character of a talking dog in another story, "A Dog of a Job", and also in his 1950 novel, *L'Herbe rouge*.

Page 155

- Louella Bing is most likely a reference to the American movie columnist, Louella Parsons (1881-1972). Her columns were read in some 400 newspapers around the world.

- Calambar is possibly derived from Calabar, an international seaport in south-east Nigeria. The film title is of course purely invented.

- The names are, as always, playful. A "muguet" is a small white spring flower, the lily of the valley. A "mouillette" is a finger of bread or toast (a "soldier") used for dunking.

- The Abbaye is presumably a cinema club in Saint-Germain-des-Prés. The Club des Stars designates the Club des Vedettes and the Cygne-Ecran is the Cinécran. These two theatres in the 9th arrondissement of Paris were popular during the 1940s.

Page 156

- Michelle Meringue is most probably a reference to the famous French film actress, Michèle Morgan.

APRIL'S DAUGHTERS

Page 159

- French title: "Les Filles d'avril". First published in *Dans le train* in September 1949. Republished in 1981 in *Le Ratichon baigneur* (pp. 85-93).

Page 160

- The Gare de Lyon is one of the eight major train stations in Paris. It serves the south and the south-east of France.

Page 161

- The Place des Ternes is in the north-west of Paris, on the border between the 8th and the 17th arrondissements.

LOVE IS BLIND

Page 164

- French title: "L'Amour est aveugle". First published in the inaugural number of *Paris-Tabou* in September 1949. Republished in 1970 in *Le Loup-garou* (pp. 75-90). This story has something of a surreal and even a science-fiction feel to it, and combines the burlesque with the erotic.

- The woman lives in the Rue Saint-Braquemart, "braquemart" being a slang term for the male member.

Page 165

- The tower in question is undoubtedly the Eiffel Tower.

- The Book of Genesis recounts that Noah, wandering drunk and naked through a campsite, was covered with a cloak by his sons as they walked backwards towards him, to avoid seeing his nudity. Salammbô is the heroine of Gustave Flaubert's novel of the same name. At the end of the story, she is poisoned as punishment for having touched Tanit's sacred veil. Tanit was a Phoenician lunar goddess worshipped as the patron goddess of Carthage.

Page 166

- The noises made by the stairs are mostly invented words: "criquement", "crainquement", "croquement", "brruiquement", "gyyment" and "zouinguement", for example.

Page 168

- "Fucoholic aresole" is a rendering of "aréosole aphrobaisiaque", an expression that is a pure invention on the part of Vian. The first word looks like a deformation of "aérosol" and has a happy resemblance to the English word "arsehole"; the second is a combination of "aphrodisiaque" and "baiser", the verb "to screw".

Page 169

- The Valkyrie, in Scandinavian mythology, were the maidens who carried out the will of Odin in determining the victors in battle, and in determining the warriors whose souls were deserving of the afterlife in Valhalla.
- Mr Curepipe's name is again a joke. A "curepipe" is a pipe cleaner (for pipes that are smoked, however, not organ pipes).

Page 170

- *Quo vadis?* ("Where are you going?") was the question Peter is said to have asked Jesus while fleeing persecution in Rome. Fabiola was a Roman woman who had an unfaithful husband. She became a patron to those experiencing difficult marriages, adultery and loss. *Fabiola* was also the title of a 1949 French epic film with Michèle Morgan in the leading role. *Et cum spirituo tuo* means "and with your spirit".

Page 172

- *Les Temps modernes* was a literary review founded in 1945 by Sartre, Merleau-Ponty and Simone de Beauvoir. Vian was a contributor. The woman's observation that she is no longer afraid of Orvert's gaze is a clear reference to existentialist philosophy, one of the tenets of which is that we are defined by how others see us.

A DOG OF A JOB

Page 173

- French title: "Un métier de chien". This story was first published in *Dans le train* in October 1949, though it is thought to have been written in January 1946. The story is listed in various bibliographies with the title "Cinéma et amateurs", which is the title given to it on a typescript of the story, which has now disappeared. It was republished in 1981 in *Le Ratichon baigneur* (pp. 21-28). The Admiral, who also featured in "A Cultural Experience", may well be another incarnation of the Major (Jacques Loustalot), who collaborated with Vian on a number of film projects, although according to Vian's wife Michelle, the character was based on Roger Lamoral, a cousin of the Major. The character of the talking dog also featured in "A Big Star".

THE THINKER

Page 177

- French title: "Le Penseur". First published in *Dans le train* in November 1949. Republished in 1970 in *Le Loup-garou* (pp. 173-179). Vian once again displays an adolescent sense of humour here in the choice of people and place names. Urodonal Carrier owes his first name, for example, to a brand of medication for kidney problems. There is a similar sense of the ridiculous in the name of the town of La-Houspignole-sur-Côtés (interestingly, one of the characters in Vian's 1946 novel *Vercoquin et le plancton* is the Baron Piniouf de la Houspignole). And the "nouille" in "Marinouille", Urodonal's girlfriend, is the French word for "noodle".

Page 178

- Epictetus (55-135) was a Greek philosopher.

Page179

- Babylon, in ancient Mesopotamia, was a rich and powerful city, but it earned a reputation as being full of corruption. Unsurprisingly, perhaps, it is also the name by which the French commonly refer to Paris, or indeed to any large city whose citizens are perceived to be corrupt and immoral.

- The figure of the young hopeful leaving home to seek success in Paris was a common trope in the nineteenth-century French novel.

THE KILLER

Page 181

- French title: "L'Assassin". First published in *Dans le train* in December 1949. Republished in 1981 in *Le Ratichon baigneur* (pp. 95-103).
- The contrast between the ammonites and trilobites, which are real, and the "stalagpites" and "salpingites", which are both fanciful, is for comic effect. A stalagpite is clearly a variation on the stalagmite and stalagtite; salpingitis is an inflammation of the Fallopian tubes.

Page 182

- Yvan Audouard (1914-2004) was a writer and journalist who frequented Saint-Germain-des-Prés and who was well known for his maxims. "Eye-van Audouard" is a rendering of "Audouard et à l'œil", which is a word play on the French idiomatic expression "au doigt et à l'œil" (used to describe someone who commands with authority or who obeys submissively). As noted in the Pléiade edition of Vian's *Œuvres romanesques complètes* (vol. II, pp. 1316-1317), the question asked by the narrator regarding the story about the eye is most likely a reference to the final line of Victor Hugo's poem "La Conscience": "The eye was in the grave and was watching Cain". There may also be an allusion here to the title of Georges Bataille's first novel, *Histoire de l'œil,* published under the pseudonym Lord Auch ("auch" being an abbreviation of "aux chiottes" — to the shithouse). Finally, given the context, it is hard not to be reminded here of the expression "an eye for an eye".

- Cain's description of Abel as a "dirty bitch" is in keeping with the intention of the original French, where Abel is called "une sale dégueulasse". This highlights the problems that can be posed when translating grammatical gender. The word "bitch" has been used as an equivalent to the derogatory female expression of the French text. The use of a feminine form is in fact unusual in the French, hence the first-person narrator's question: "Une?" (translated here as "Bitch?").

- Paul Claudel (1868-1955), the younger brother of the sculptor Camille Claudel, was a French writer and a devout Catholic. He was often a target of Vian's derision. André Gide (1869-1951) also found himself the subject of Vian's contempt, partly because of his homosexuality, but also because he was well regarded by the publishing house Gallimard. Gide won the Nobel Prize for literature in 1947. The "Nabel Prize" is an obvious play on this. Claudel and Gide corresponded with one another over a long period of time.

A HEART OF GOLD

Page 185

- French title: "Un cœur d'or". First published in the review *La Bouteille à la mer*, in its fourth trimestrial number of 1949. Republished in 1970 in *Le Loup-garou* (pp. 27-33). Vian wrote the first part of this story on 8-10 April 1949 and gave it the title "Le Rasoir" ("The Razor"). This title was inspired by the first sentence, in which Aulne "rasait les murs à sec" — a play on words, since "raser… à sec" means to have a dry shave, whereas the expression "raser les murs" means to hug the walls (to avoid being seen). The story contains many such word plays, often based on combinations of idiomatic expressions. It was intended to be read to the Vian family on Christmas day.

- The "Bernazizi" is obviously an invented make of car. It ends with "zizi", which is a child's word for a penis.

Page 187

- The "sheet-house" is a rendering of "les va-te-faire closette", which is meant to sound like "water-closet" (toilet), but which also contains the expression "va te faire…" (go and get…), after which one would normally expect to find a verb (of a rather vulgar nature).

- The "stepladder to heaven" is a rendering of "escabeau comme un astre", which conflates "escabeau" (stool) and the expression "beau comme un astre" (beautiful as a star).

- A mansard roof has two slopes on each of the four sides, with the lower slope being steeper than the upper slope. This style of roof was made popular in the seventeenth century by François Mansart (hence its name). It returned to fashion in the nineteenth century, under Napoleon III.

- The name "Brise-Bonbon" is derived from the verb "briser" (to break) and the word "bonbon", which is a sweet. The name is also a play on words with the expression "casser les bonbons à quelqu'un" — "to break someone's balls".

Page 188

- Alphonse Bertillon (1853-1914) was a police officer who was interested in biometrics, applying anthropometry to assist in the identification of criminals.

IMPOTENCE

Page 189

- French title: "L'Impuissant". This story is thought to have been composed in 1949. It was first published in 1981, in *Le Ratichon baigneur* (pp. 163-181).

- Vian is having fun in describing Aurèle as an "invert" (an "inverti" in French). The reader expects the word "introverti" (an "introvert"), but is surprised to find instead a term for a homosexual.

- Louis Barucq and his sister, Lisette, are real-life characters. Louis was a barman at the bookshop, and Lisette was a hairdresser.

Page 190

- "Strawberry Sutra" is a rendering of "foutralafraise" (literally, strawberry-flavoured come), which was also called "Sperme de flamant rose" (Pink Flamingo Sperm). The cocktail was invented by Boris Vian and Louis Barucq. The recipe given here is authentic.

Page 192

- As already noted, Claudel was often a target for Vian's derision. Gide does not fare particularly well either, in these stories.

Page 193

- Astrakhan is the fleece of the newborn karakul lamb. It is expensive and highly sought after. It takes its name from the Russian city of Astrakhan which sits on the Volga Delta.

- *The Satin Slipper* (*Le Soulier de satin*) and *The Tidings Brought to Mary* (*L'Annonce faite à Marie*) are two plays by Paul Claudel. *Strait is the Gate* (*La Porte étroite*) is a novel by André Gide. Like Claudel's plays, Gide's novel is an austere work with religious underpinnings ("strait is the gate" is a quotation from the Bible — Matthew 7:14). Hervé Bazin published his first novel, the autobiographical *Vipère au poing* (*Viper in the Fist*) in 1948. In it, he portrays a family characterised by hypocrisy, strictly observing Catholic rituals while failing to show true love and compassion. *Nathanaël* and *Fruits of the Earth* (*Les Nourritures terrestres*) are novels by André Gide, as is *The Counterfeiters* (*Les Faux-monnayeurs*).

Page 195

- Bromide compounds were commonly used as sedatives and headache remedies in the nineteenth and twentieth centuries.

- The play *La Soif* (*The Thirst*) by Henri Bernstein (1876-1953) was created in February 1949.

MOTHERHOOD

Page 198

- French title: "Maternité". This story is thought to have been composed in 1949. It was first published in 1981, in *Le Ratichon baigneur* (pp. 145-161). It tackles the delicate topic of adoption by a same sex couple. Considering he wrote this story in 1949, Vian might be considered to have been well ahead of his time. The final twist to the story, however, gives pause for thought. It is worth noting that the names of the main characters are deliberately ambiguous in gender terms: René sounds the same as Renée, Claude can be both a masculine and a feminine name, and Andrée sounds the same as André. Vian being Vian, he could not resist some word play in creating the surnames of the two main characters: Lantulé sounds suspiciously like "l'enculé" (someone who is "buggered"), and Bédale sounds very much like "pédale", which is a vulgar term for a homosexual.
- Adjectives have masculine and feminine forms in French, so the spelling in the letters would certainly have revealed the gender of the writer — provided, of course, that the reader had a good control of French grammar and spelling and was attentive to such detail (which is not the case with René).

Page 199

- Le Florette, La Tante Blanche and Le Montata refer, respectively, to the well-known Parisian cafés Le Flore, La Reine-Blanche and Le Montana. In changing the names, Vian has introduced playful references to homosexuality: "tante" and "tata" both mean "aunt" or "auntie", but are also used in familiar French to refer to effeminate homosexuals.
- The Renault 4CV was a four-horsepower small sedan that was designed as an economy vehicle. The first model was produced in 1947.

Page 201

- Velpeau bandages were commonly used to strap injured shoulders.

Page 203

- In French, the police are disparagingly referred to as "poulets" (chickens). "Pig" is a ready English equivalent.

Page 204

- Pierre Balpogne is the famous French couturier Pierre Balmain (1914-1982), "pogne" being a slang word for "main" (hand). The Club Saint-Germain-des-Pieds is obviously the Club Saint-Germain-des-Prés ("pied" means "foot", whereas "pré" means "field").

Page 205

- Diargent is a play on words with the name of the fashion designer Christian Dior ("argent", meaning "silver", replaces "or", meaning "gold"). A similar play on words is found in the first words of two lines of Arthur Rimbaud's famous poem "Le Dormeur du val" ("The Sleeper in the Valley"), in which "d'argent" is echoed by "dort", which means"sleeps", but which is also homophonous with "d'or".

A FUNNY OLD GAME

Page 206

- French title: "Un drôle de sport". First published in *Dans le train* in January 1950. Republished in 1981 in *Le Ratichon baigneur* (pp. 105-112). The story was most likely written towards the end of 1949, when Vian was experiencing marital problems (his wife Michelle had become Jean-Paul Sartre's mistress that year). This story may be a reaction to those difficulties.
- The "Klub Sane-Germaine" is a phonetic approximation of the "Club Saint-Germain", as pronounced in English. (The original French is "Klub Singer-Main", which is a phonetic equivalent of the French pronunciation.) The Slow-Burn was invented by the barman

at the Club Saint-Germain, Louis Barucq. The recipe is authentic. "Mother's milk of Russia" is a translation of "lait du Volga".

- Folubert Sansonnet also featured in "Léobille's Party". As explained in the notes to that story, this name derives from Hubert Fol, who played saxophone in Abadie's orchestra, and the word for a "starling", which is a homonym for "cent sonnets", the title of a collection of poems by Vian. Folubert is presented here as a "saxofornist" — an obvious play on "fornication".

Page 207

- The Vieux-Co is the Club du Vieux-Colombier, a jazz club during the war in the basement of the Théâtre du Vieux-Colombier in the Saint-Germain quarter of Paris. It is just around the corner from the Rue de Rennes, on the Rue du Vieux Colombier.
- Claude Luter was a trumpeter, clarinettist and orchestra leader. Vian played with him at various times during the 1940s.

Page 208

- The Rose Rouge was another jazz club in Saint-Germain-des-Prés, in the Rue de Rennes. It was founded in 1947 and helped launch the careers of artists such as the Frères Jacques, Nicole Louvier and Juliette Gréco. The Frères Jacques were a French vocal quartet that combined song and mime. In June 1949 they released a single entitled *Son nombril* (*His Navel* — the song featured on both sides of the disc). The well-known song *Barbara*, written by Jacques Prévert and Joseph Kosma, was released as a single in October 1949. This helps to date the composition of the story during the final months of that year. The line that Folubert and Trounaille loudly approve is: "Quelle connerie, la guerre".
- Le Caroll's was a cabaret in Paris made famous in the 1950s by the French singer and actress Dany Dauberson, who co-owned it. It had a largely female clientele at that time.

- The Lido, the Night-Club, the Bœuf sur le toit and so on are all authentic Parisian nightclubs, clubs and cabarets.

THE MOTIVE

Page 210

- French title: "Le Motif". First published in *Dans le train* in February 1950. Republished in 1981 in *Le Ratichon baigneur* (pp. 113-119). Like "A Funny Old Game", this story was most probably written towards the latter part of 1949 and may also bear the traces of the marital problems Vian was experiencing at the time.

- The Cours la Reine is a garden promenade situated on the right bank of the Seine in the 8th arrondissement of Paris, between the Place de la Concorde and the Place du Canada. It was created in 1616 by the then queen, Marie de Médicis.

Page 211

- "In a mechanic fashion" is a rendering of "d'une voix de garage" (literally, in a garage-like voice) — hence the oiliness. The French word play of the original text is difficult to capture fully in English: "une voie de garage" is a railway siding and it can be used metaphorically to mean "to shunt someone aside".

DANGER FROM THE CLASSICS

Page 213

- French title: "Le Danger des classiques". First published in the review *Bizarre* in the first trimestrial number of 1964. It was then republished in 1970 in *Le Loup-garou* (pp. 213-233). It was initially given the title "Les Vieux Classiques" ("The Old Classics") and is thought to have been written in 1950. Vian's love of science fiction, inspired by its success in the United States at the time, is evident in this tale, which is set in a futuristic 1982. Vian reverses here the role of the instigator in the male-female relationship and mocks sentimental verse.

- *Toi et moi* (*You and Me*) is a collection of poems by Paul Géraldy (1885-1983) (real name Paul Lefèvre). Published in 1912, it was immensely popular, especially with women.

Page 215

- Francis Lopez (1916-1955) was a well-known composer of operettas. *The Grand Duchess of Antares* may in fact be a reference to Jacques Offenbach's *The Grand Duchess of Gerolstein*, the conclusion of which contains the memorable line: "If you can't have what you love, you have to love what you have" ("quand on n'a pas ce que l'on aime, il faut aimer ce que l'on a"). Antares is a giant star in the Milky Way. Arnold Schoenberg (1874-1951) was an Austrian-American composer. Duke Ellington (1899-1974) was a friend of Vian. In 1939, Vian helped to organise the Duke's second concert in France. Vincent Scotto (1874-1952) was a French composer of popular songs and operettas.

Page 216

- Rossler, Brenn and Renaud appear to be fictitious names, although it is possible they were based on real people.

Page 218

- Flor-Fiña is obviously a fictitious country, though it is not clear what inspired Vian here. Flor Fina ("Fine Flower") is a type of cigar made under the Arturo Fuente brand (established in Florida in 1912).

Page 219

- The two lines of verse are from Géraldy's poem "Expansions": "J'ai besoin d'exprimer, d'expliquer, de traduire/On ne sent tout à fait que ce qu'on a su dire".

Page 220

- These are the opening lines of Géraldy's poem "Expansions": "Ah! je vous aime! Je vous aime!/Vous entendez? je suis fou de vous, je suis fou..." (note the minor variation in punctuation).

Page 221

- These three lines come from Géraldy's poem "Lettre": "Car les choses que j'ai chaque jour à te dire/Sont de celles, vois-tu, que l'on ne se dit pas/Sans la voix, les regards, les gestes, les sourires".

Page 222

- These ten lines of verse are from Géraldy's erotic poem "Explications" ("Explanations"), though with some minor variations (a line omitted, some change in punctuation, replacement of "s'expliquer" with "s'exprimer"…). The original reads as follows:

  Tais-toi, tiens! Laisse-moi dégrafer ton corsage:
  cela vaudra beaucoup mieux.
  Les choses que tu veux me dire, ma petite,
  je les sais d'avance. Allons, viens.
  Déshabille-toi. Viens vite.
  Prenons-nous. Le meilleur moyen
  de s'expliquer sans être dupe,
  c'est de s'étreindre, corps à corps.
  Ne boude pas. Défais ta jupe.
  Nos corps, eux, seront d'accord.

Page 224

- The final line is the opening line of the ninth verse of Géraldy's poem "L'Abat-jour" ("The Lampshade": "Baisse un peu l'abat-jour".

THE WEREWOLF

Page 225

- French title: "Le Loup-garou". First published in 1970 in *Le Loup-garou* (pp. 7-26). The exact date of composition is unknown, but it is thought to have been written in 1950, which coincides with the commercial release of the Bic pen mentioned in the story. The plot reveals a classic reversal of roles: it is man who is depicted as the animal — dishonest, violent, angry and ugly — while the wolf is portrayed as handsome, calm, philosophical and refined. The setting of Ville-d'Avray, between Paris and Versailles, and the nearby Fausses-Reposes Woods was familiar to Vian and had special significance for him. Ville-d'Avray is where he was born and spent his early childhood. He is now buried there. The description he gives in the story of this area is accurate. The name "Fausses-Reposes" is a hunting term used to describe feints used by animals ("falsely resting") to throw hunters off the scent. It has special significance in relation to the story of Denis, the wolf.

- Louis Boussenard (1847-1910) was a traveller and author of adventure novels. The expression "basket of oranges" first appeared in his novel *Les Pirates des champs d'or* (1883). It refers to the basket of gold nuggets that Australian prospectors on the Victorian goldfields all hoped to find.

Page 226

- The Amilcar was a French car produced in Paris from 1921 to 1940.
- The area around the town of Arbois, in the Jura, produces both red and white wines.
- The Gronœil Restaurant is in all likelihood a reference to the restaurant in Saint-Germain-des-Prés that Vian frequented, La Grenouille.
- The "Obsession" girdle is fictitious but refers no doubt to the wonderfully named "Scandale" girdle that was popular at the time.
- A werewolf is known as a lycanthrope. Lycanthropy is the term to describe the transformation of a man into a werewolf. Anthropolicy ("anthropolycie") is a term that Vian has presumably coined to describe the reverse process.

Page 227

- Boletus, peziza and ox-tongue are varieties of mushroom.

Page 229

- The Scribe Hotel is situated a short distance to the west of the Paris Opera, in the Rue Scribe.

- The Jardin des Plantes, as its name suggests, is a botanical garden, but also serves as a zoo.

- Rambolitain is the adjective derived from Rambouillet, a town some 45 kilometres south-west of Paris. The fishing club is obviously an invention on Vian's part.

Page 230

- The "Hotel Silver Potato-Masher" is a literal translation of the "hôtel du Presse-Purée d'Argent" — yet another example of Vian's creativity and playfulness.

Page 231

- "All stifling and pale, when..." is a quotation from Verlaine's poem "Chanson d'automne" ("Autumn Song"): "Tout suffocant/Et blême, quand/Sonne l'heure".

- François Mauriac (1885-1970) was a novelist and member of the Académie Française.

Page 234

- Fausto Coppi (1919-1960) was a legendary Italian cyclist of the pre- and post-World War II era. His achievements include two victories in the Tour de France (in 1949 and 1952).

- Saint-Cloud is a commune on the western edge of Paris. Montretout is one of the quarters of Saint-Cloud. Its name means "show all" ("montre tout") — hence the reference to perverts. It was actually given this name because of the fine view of Paris that could be had from the top of its hill.

- The Cabassud Restaurant is an upmarket restaurant in Ville-d'Avray.

THE SNOWMAN

Page 236

- First published in the risqué review *Sensations* in April 1951 with no title but under a drawing of a snowman. Vian had initially given it the title "Les Filles de neige" ("The Snowgirls") but crossed that out on the manuscript. It was republished in 1970 by Christian Bourgois in *Le Loup-garou* (pp. 199-212), with the title "Le Voyeur". The opening of the story as it is given in *Le Loup-garou*, the text of which is based on the manuscript, is somewhat different from the version published in *Sensations*. It is this latter, published, version that is reproduced in the Pléiade edition of Vian's *Œuvres romanesques complètes* and that has served as the basis for the translation presented here. The first paragraph of the Bourgois edition reads as follows:

  > That year, it seemed visitors had deserted Happy Valley for more popular resorts. There were no footprints in the snow on the narrow track which provides the only access to the village, and the shutters of the "hotel", if that's what you can call the tiny red timber chalet overlooking Deer's Leap, looked as though they were stuck to the windows.

- The other differences are minor and relate mostly to style.
- The place names in this story have been invented by Vian, and have therefore been translated. "Vallyeuse" has become "Happy Valley", the "Saut de l'Elfe" is "Elf's Leap", and the "Cirque des Trois-Sœurs" is "Three Sisters Ridge". It is interesting to note that a "saut-de-loup" (literally, "wolf's leap") is an architectual feature of the formal garden, which consists of a ditch at the end of a path designed to prevent entry to outsiders but without impeding the view of those within. The name derives from the fact that this ditch is conceived to be so wide that only a wolf could leap across it. A ditch narrow enough for an elf to leap across it has a certain comical effect as well as a certain charm.

Page 239

- In Roman mythology, Diana is the virgin goddess associated with hunting, women and childbirth, and later with the moon.

ONE LICENCE FOR LOVE

Page 244

- This story was first published in the March 1952 number of the review *Constellation* with the title "Un seul permis pour leur amour". The author was given as "Joëlle Bausset", a pseudonym inspired by an acquaintance of Vian's from Saint-Tropez. The story was republished in 1981 by Christian Bourgois in *Le Ratichon baigneur* (pp. 121-135) with the title "Marthe et Jean" (the opening words of the story). The version published in *Le Ratichon baigneur* is based on the untitled manuscript, which is somewhat more developed than the text that appeared in *Constellation*. It is this latter version, reproduced in the Pléiade edition of Vian's *Œuvres romanesques complètes*, that is the basis of the translation presented here. The following translation of the first five pages of the Bourgois edition of the story provides a good illustration of the differences:

  > Marthe and Jean got out of the small car, and while Marthe searched around in her bag for a hundred-franc note to slip the driving instructor before saying goodbye, Jean was questioning him on their chances of success. Marthe couldn't hear what they were saying, the noise from the street was drowning out their conversation, but she did detect the optimism in the man's laugh and the note of confidence in his voice. She felt her heart beat a little faster. This was the last of the ten lessons that she and Jean had been taking together, and in three days' time, they were both scheduled to appear at the place indicated on the application form, a small street near the Jardin des Plantes, to undergo the ordeal of a driving test.

Jean said goodbye to the man, a solidly built forty-year-old with a ruddy complexion, who tipped his hat as he held out his hand to Marthe.

"Thank you madam," he said, when he felt the note in his hand. "And have no fear. It's in the bag, so to speak."

Marthe and Jean looked at each other.

"Touch wood," he said cautiously.

"Come on," Marthe said, "no childish superstitions, kind sir."

They headed off, arm in arm, towards the nearest metro station.

"It breaks my heart," Jean said, "to have to go down into these filthy, foul-smelling subways. I can't wait to get the car!"

"Licence first," Marthe pointed out.

"It's as if it's already ours," Jean said, falsely optimistic. "The main thing is not to panic."

"We'll soon see," Marthe said.

"Listen," Jean said, "it would be really silly to have managed to save enough money for the car and then not be able to drive it. Anyway, one of us is bound to pass, probably me!"

"Why you?" Marthe asked cheekily. "What if it was me?"

* * *

Three days later, however, Marthe felt a little nervous when the stony-faced examiner told her to do a U-turn in a narrow laneway. There was little traffic, but it was on a slope, and she had to make sure she didn't stall the car. It was a test of skill, combining a hill start with the actual manoeuvre itself. Remembering the driving instructor's advice, she took her time and correctly executed all of the requirements. Maybe it lacked a little polish, but the man seemed satisfied. He told her to pull over to the kerb, asked her a few questions that she easily answered, and then cut her off before she had finished.

"That's all," he said. "Thank you. Here is your licence."

"Is it over already?" Marthe asked, stunned, as she took the pink card.

"Why yes," he answered.

"Thank you sir," Marthe stammered.

She got out, feeling a little dazed. It had been so easy! The next candidate took the wheel, and she vaguely heard the car take off with a loud roar of the engine. She looked around for Jean. The driving instructor, who had accompanied them, informed her that he was sitting the test in a second car with the other examiner. Now she was really worried. As long as he passed too. It would be terrible if he missed out. How would she face him? She started to wish she had failed. She was afraid her luck might have impacted on Jean's, and that fate would not favour them both.

"Well! Have you got the sulks!"

Jean put his arm around her and gave her a kiss.

"Come on! Now, now! Don't make such a drama out of it, little Marthe, the one I love and adore! Take a look!"

He waved his licence in the air, triumphant, sure of himself.

"I told you that one of us was bound to pass. You can sit for it again, you'll see. There's nothing to it! It's easy!"

Marthe pulled herself together. He had his licence. That was the main thing.

"But… I got mine too," she said in a soft, shy voice.

"So why that face?" he asked, slightly irritated. "You had me worried."

Should she tell him that she had been anxious for him? She made up an excuse.

"I'm emotional," she stammered. "I almost failed my manoeuvring. I was so scared. You know, I didn't pass by very much. The examiner gave it to me almost as a favour."

"I'm sure you used your charm on him," he said, calming down again. "Come on. Let's go and celebrate. And don't worry, it will all fall into place eventually."

***

The car changed Jean. The shy, unassuming, almost fearful boy that Marthe had practically dragged away by force from the clutches of a perpetually worried mother hen gradually gave way to a person full of confidence, unleashing a driver who was always ready to react angrily to the rude remarks of taxi drivers, quick to worm his way into a better position in the long queue of vehicles brought to a standstill at a red light, one who hardly had any regard for road rules or the rights of other drivers angrily brought to a sudden halt by a well executed fishtail as they were driving along.

- It is worth noting that this story was published in 1952, only eight years after women achieved the right to vote in France. Old habits were slow to change, however, and anything to do with automobiles remained firmly in the male domain. The story is thus significant, among other reasons, because it tackles the question of equal rights (notwithstanding the sacrificial act of Marthe at the end). This may explain in part the choice of a female pseudonym.

A SAD STORY

Page 249

- Original title: "Une pénible histoire". First published in 1952, in the first trimestrial number of the review *La Bouteille à la mer*. Republished in 1970 by Christian Bourgois in *Le Loup-garou* (pp. 157-172). This story, conceived towards the end of 1949, is a reflection on society and involves two of Vian's pet hates: the

Church and the military. The story also focuses on issues such as the shortage of money and the contemplation of suicide, which can be traced back to facets of Vian's own life. His fascination with language and machines, and the possibilities of combining them, is also in evidence here, as in "Danger from the Classics".

Page 250

- Impetigo is a highly contagious bacterial infection of the skin. It is most common among pre-school children.
- In the Christian Bourgois edition of the text, the two priests kiss "langueoureusement" — a play on "langoureusement" ("langorously") and "langue" ("tongue"). Peter Hodges suggests that this might be translated as "tongloriously", which neatly captures the word play, though with a slight variation in meaning.

Page 251

- The Touvre is a tributary of the Charente at Angoulême, in the south-west of France, where Vian spent some time in 1940. It is a short river that is as wide at its source as at its mouth.

Page 253

- Dipterans are flies or other insects characterised by a single pair of wings.

Page 254

- Quettehou is in the north-east of the Normandy peninsula, some 20 kilometres to the east of Cherbourg and just south of Landemer, where the Vian family spent their post-war summer holidays.
- The *Cours Adeline Désir* was a private school for Catholic girls in Paris. Simone de Beauvoir was educated there.
- Ideal Standard is a brand of tap and plumbing supplies officially established in 1949, the year this story was written.

THE WALTZ

Page 258

- French title: "La Valse". First published in 1981 by Christian Bourgois in *Le Ratichon baigneur* (pp. 137-144). According to Noël Arnaud (*Le Ratichon baigneur*, p. 18), the story was most likely intended for publication in *Constellation* and might be considered to be unfinished. On his manuscript, Vian has once again used his feminine pseudonym, Joëlle du Beausset (written as Joëlle Bausset in the case of "One Licence for Love").

Page 260

- Flor Polboubal refers to Paul Boubal, the owner of the Café de Flore.
- Claude Luter, the trumpeter, clarinettist and band leader, features in a number of the earlier stories presented here.

BIBLIOGRAPHY OF WORKS CITED

1. Works by Boris Vian

Sullivan, Vernon (pseud.), *J'irai cracher sur vos tombes* (Paris: Éditions du Scorpion, 1946).

Sullivan, Vernon (pseud.), *Les Morts ont tous la même peau* (Paris: Éditions du Scorpion, 1947).

Sullivan, Vernon (pseud.), *Et on tuera tous les affreux* (Paris: Éditions du Scorpion, 1948).

Vian, Boris, *L'Écume des jours* (Paris: Gallimard, 1947).

Vian, Boris, *L'Automne à Pékin* (Paris: Éditions du Scorpion, 1947).

Vian, Boris, *Les Fourmis* (Paris: Éditions du Scorpion, 1949).

Vian, Boris, *L'Herbe rouge* (Paris: Toutain, 1950).

Vian, Boris, *L'Arrache-cœur* (Paris: Vrille, 1953).

Vian, Boris, *Les Bâtisseurs d'empire* (Paris: Collège de 'Pataphysique, 1959).

Vian, Boris, *Je voudrais pas crever*, edited by Jean-Jacques Pauver (Paris: Pauvert, 1962).

Vian, Boris, *Froth on the Daydream*, translation of *L'Écume des jours* by Stanley Chapman (London: Rapp & Carrol, 1967).

Vian, Boris, *Mood Indigo*, translation of *L'Écume des jours* by John Sturrock (New York: Grove Press, 1968).

Vian, Boris, *Le Loup-Garou*, edited by Christian Bourgois (Paris: 10/18, 1970).

Vian, Boris, *Je voudrais pas crever*, edited by Noël Arnaud (Paris: 10/18, 1972).

Vian, Boris, *Manuel de Saint-Germain-des-Prés* (Paris: Éditions du Chêne, 1974).

Vian, Boris, *Le Ratichon baigneur*, edited by Christian Bourgois (Paris: 10/18, 1981).

Vian, Boris, *Romans, Nouvelles, Œuvres diverses* (Paris: Le Livre de Poche, 1991).

Vian, Boris, *Blues for a Black Cat and Other Stories*, translation of *Les Fourmis* by Julia Older (Lincoln: University of Nebraska Press, 1992).

Vian, Boris, *Chansons* (Paris: Bourgois, 1994).

Vian, Boris, *Conte de fées à l'usage des moyennes personnes* (Paris: Pauvert, 1997 [1943]).

Vian, Boris, *Boris Vian, Œuvres complètes*, edited by Marc Lapprand and Gilbert Pestureau (Paris: Fayard, 15 vols, 1999-2003).

Vian, Boris, *Foam of the Daze*, translation of *L'Écume des jours* by Brian Harper (California: TamTam Books, 2003).

Vian, Boris, *Heartsnatcher*, translation of *L'Arrache-cœur* by Stanley Chapman (Champaign, Urbana: Dalkey Archive Press, 2003).

Vian, Boris, *Autumn in Peking*, translation of *L'Automne à Pékin* by Paul Knobloch (California: TamTam Books, 2005).

Vian, Boris, *Manual of Saint-Germain-des-Prés*, translation of *Manuel de Saint-Germain-des-Prés* by Paul Knobloch, edited by Tosh Berman and Eva Prinz (New York: Rizzoli Books, 2005).

Vian, Boris (Vernon Sullivan), *The Dead All have the Same Skin*, translation of *Les Morts ont tous la même peau* by Paul Knobloch (California: TamTam Books, 2008).

Vian, Boris, *Œuvres romanesques complètes*, edited by Marc Lapprand, with Christelle Gonzalo and François Roulmann (Paris: Gallimard, Bibliothèque de la Pléiade, 2 vols, 2010).

Vian, Boris, "Don't Trust the Band", translation of "Méfie-toi de l'orchestre" (from *Le Ratichon baigneur*) by Peter Hodges, *The AALITRA Review*, 1, 2010, pp. 27-30.

Vian, Boris, *Red Grass*, translation of *L'Herbe rouge* by Paul Knobloch (California: TamTam Books, 2013).

2. Studies of Boris Vian and his Work

Baus, Emma, *Boris Vian: 'Un jour il y aura autre chose que le jour'* (Paris: L'Esprit frappeur, 2002).

Boggio, Philippe, *Boris Vian* (Paris: Flammarion, 1993).

Camus, Audrey, "L'Enfance de l'écriture", *Europe*, 967-968, 2009, pp. 87-99.

Clouset, Jean, *Boris Vian* (Paris: Seghers, 1966).

Dickhoff, Herbert, "Approche discrète des nouvelles de Boris Vian", in Noël Arnaud and Henri Baudin (eds), *Boris Vian: Colloque de Cerisy* (Paris: UGE, 10/18, 1977), vol. I, pp. 333-345.

Fauré, Michel, *Les Vies posthumes de Boris Vian* (Paris: UGE, 10/18, 1975).

Haenlin, Lydie Jeannette, "Analyse rhétorique du discours romanesque de Boris Vian", PhD Thesis, University of Buffalo, 1973.

Hodges, Peter, "What's in a Name? The Translator as Facilitator", unpublished conference paper presented at the "Writing Past Each Other" Conference, University of Wellington, New Zealand, 11-13 December 2010.

Jones, Christopher, *Boris Vian Transatlantic: Sources, Myths, and Dreams* (New York/Bern: Peter Lang, 1998).

Julliard, Claire, *Boris Vian* (Paris: Gallimard, 2007).

Lapprand, Marc, *Boris Vian: La vie contre* (Ottawa: Presses de l'Université d'Ottawa, 1993).

Lapprand, Marc, "Lire Boris Vian", *Magazine littéraire*, 6, 2004-2005, pp. 97-98.

Lapprand, Marc, *V comme Vian* (Québec: Les Presses Universitaires de Laval, 2006).

Lapprand, Marc, "Relire Vian aujourd'hui", *Europe*, 967-968, 2009, pp. 38-49.

Le Bris, Michel, "Une stratégie de disparition", *Les Collections du Magazine Littéraire*, 6, 2004-2005.

Mitura, Magdalena, *Écriture vianesque: traduction de la prose* (Bern/Berlin...: Peter Lang, Publications Universitaires Européennes, 2006).

Noakes, David, *Boris Vian* (Paris: Éditions universitaires, "Classiques du XXe siècle", 1963).

Nodrest, Sophie de, "Re-Creation of a Recreation: A Comparative Study of Two English Translations of *L'Écume des jours*", MA Thesis excerpts of which are available online at http://rob.toadshow.com.au/01_cms/details.asp?ID=339 (accessed 8 February 2012).

Noirot-Maguire, Corinne, "Vian et le vers coquin: Le Coup d'essai des *Cent Sonnets*", *Europe*, 967-968, 2009, pp. 144-155.

Pestureau, Gilbert, *Boris Vian, les Amerlauds et les Godons* (Paris: UGE, 10/18, 1978).

Pestureau, Gilbert, *Dictionnaire des personnages de Vian* (Paris: Bourgois, 1985).

Piatier, Jacqueline, *Le Monde*, 24 August 1963.

Renaudot, Françoise, *Il était une fois Boris Vian* (Paris: Seghers, 1973).

Richaud, Frédéric, *Boris Vian. C'est joli de vivre* (Paris: Éditions du Chêne, 1999).

Rolls, Alistair, *The Flight of the Angels: Intertextuality in Four Novels by Boris Vian* (Amsterdam/Atlanta: Rodopi, 1999).

Rolls, Alistair, "Prière de relire *Je voudrais pas crever*", *Poésie*, 96, 2003, pp. 35-41.

Rolls, Alistair, "'In Olden Days a Glimpse of Stocking': Fashion, Fetishism and Modernity in Boris Vian's *L'Écume des jours*", *French Cultural Studies*, 15, 2, 2004, pp. 99-113.

Rolls, Alistair, "C'est en se déguisant qu'on devient Boris Vian: *J'irai cracher sur vos tombes* et la 'bonne littérature érotique latine'", *Europe*, 967-968, 2009, pp. 50-60.

Rolls, Alistair, "Boris Vian's Eternal Sunshine, Or the Truth about Mother's Textuality", *Forum for Modern Language Studies*, 43, 7, 2011, pp. 289-303.

Rybalka, Michel, *Boris Vian: Essai d'interprétation et de documentation* (Paris: Minard, 1969).

Savin, Tristan, "La Comète Vian" (interview with François Roulmann),

L'Express, 1er avril 2009. Available online at http://www.lexpress.fr/culture/livre/la-comete-vian_815677.html (accessed 24 January 2012).

Thwaite, Mark, "Some Thoughts on the Work of Boris Vian", *Ready Steady Book for literature*, 2003. Available online at http://www.readysteadybook.com/Article.aspx?page=borisvian (accessed 7 October 2011).

Valdo, Marco, "Ivan Della Mea: Ho male all'orologio", *Canzoni contra la guerra*, http://www.antiwarsongs.org/canzone.php?id=10558&lang=it (accessed 10 October 2013).

Yaguello, Marina, "Linguiste malgré lui?", *L'Arc*, 90, 1984, pp. 29-32.

3. Other Works

Baker, Mona, *In Other Words* (London & New York: Routledge, 2009).

Barrier, Michael, *Hollywood Cartoons: American Animation in its Golden Age* (Oxford/New York: Oxford University Press, 1999).

Barthes, Roland, *Le Plaisir du texte* (Paris: Seuil, 1973).

Barthes, Roland, *The Pleasure of the Text*, translation of *Le Plaisir du texte* by Richard Miller (New York: Hill and Wang, 1975).

Barthes, Roland, *S/Z* (Paris: Seuil, 1973).

Barthes, Roland, *S/Z*, translated by Richard Miller (Oxford: Blackwell, 1990).

Barthes, Roland, "La Mort de l'auteur", in *Le Bruissement de la langue* (Paris: Seuil, 1984), pp. 61-67.

Barthes, Roland, "The Death of the Author", translation of "La Mort de l'auteur" by Stephen Heath, in Roland Barthes, *Image, Music, Text* (New York: Hill and Wang, 1978), pp. 142-148.

Baudelaire, Charles, *Œuvres complètes*, edited by Claude Pichois (Paris: Gallimard, Bibliothèque de la Pléiade, 2 vols, 1976).

Bellos, David, *Is That a Fish in Your Ear? Translation and the Meaning of Everything* (London: Penguin, 2011).

Camus, Audrey, "Les Contrées étranges de l'insignifiant: Retour sur la notion de fantastique moderne", *Études françaises*, 45, 1, 2009, special issue on "Écritures de l'insignifiant" (guest editor Audrey Camus), pp. 89-107.

Chambers, Ross, *Loiterature* (Lincoln/London: University of Nebraska Press, 1999).

Chang, Nam Fung, "Itamar Even-Zohar's Culture Theory and Translation Studies", Paper presented to the 1st Athens International Conference on Translation and Interpretation: "Translation: Between Art and Social Science", Athens, 13-14 October 2006.

Covin, Michel, *L'Homme de la rue: Essai sur la poétique baudelairiennne* (Paris: L'Harmattan, 2000).

Defays, Jean-Marc, "Alphonse Allais nouvelliste!?! Ou quelques réflexions sur la nouvelle moderne et le comique", in Vincent Engel and Michel Guissard (eds), *La Nouvelle de langue française aux frontières des autres genres, du Moyen Âge à nos jours* (Ottignies: Éditions Quorum, 1997), vol. II, pp. 184-192.

Folkart, Barbara, *Second Finding: A Poetics of Translation* (Ottawa: University of Ottawa Press, 2007).

Godenne, René, *La Nouvelle française* (Paris: PUF, 1974).

Godenne, René, "Fortune/Infortunes, permanence/avatars d'un genre", in Vincent Engel and Michel Guissard (eds), *La Nouvelle de langue française aux frontières des autres genres, du Moyen Âge à nos jours* (Ottignies: Éditions Quorum, 1997), vol. I, pp. 396-409.

Hatim, Basil and Ian Mason, *The Translator as Communicator* (Oxford & New York: Routledge, 1997).

Holz-Mänttäri, Justa, *Translatorisches Handeln: Theorie und Methode* (Helsinki: Suomalainen Tiedeakatemia, 1984).

Houellebecq, Michel, *La Possibilité d'une île* (Paris: Livre de Poche, 2005).

House, Juliane, *A Model for Translation Quality Assessment* (Tübingen: Gunter Narr, 1977).

Johnson, Barbara, "The Critical Difference", in Diana Knight (ed.), *Critical Essays on Roland Barthes* (New York: G.K. Hall and Co., 2000), pp. 174-182.

Kibédi Varga, Aron, "Le Temps de la nouvelle", in Vincent Engel and Michel Guissard (eds), *La Nouvelle de langue française*, pp. 8-16.

Kristeva, Julia, *Séméiotikè. Recherches pour une sémanalyse* (Paris: Seuil, 1978).

Lefevere, André, *Translating Literature: Practice and Theory in a Comparative Literature Framework* (New York: MLA, 1992).

Machin, Richard and Christopher Norris (eds), *Post-structuralist Readings of English Poetry* (Cambridge: Cambridge University Press, 1987).

Munday, Jeremy, *Introducing Translation Studies: Theory and Applications* (London & New York: Routledge, 2004).

Nord, Christiane, *Text Analysis in Translation: Theory, Methodology and Didactic Application of a Model for Translation-Oriented Text Analysis* (Amsterdam: Rodopi, 1997).

Poujol, Jacques, "Jacques Prévert ou le langage en procès", *French Review*, 31, 5, 1958, pp. 387-395.

Prévert, Jacques, *Paroles* (Paris: Gallimard, 1949).

Prévert, Jacques, *Selections from 'Paroles'*, translated by Lawrence Ferlinghetti (London: Penguin, 1965).

Reiss Katharina, and Hans Vermeer, *Groundwork for a General Theory of Translation* (Tübingen: Niemeyer, 1984).

Rimbaud, Arthur, *Poésies complètes* (Paris: Vanier, 1895).

Rimbaud, Arthur, *Rimbaud. Complete Works, Selected Letters*, translated by Wallace Fowlie (Chicago/London: The University of Chicago Press, 1966).

Rolls, Alistair and Deborah Walker, *French and American Noir: Dark Crossings* (Houndmills: Palgrave Macmillan, 2009).

Rolls, Alistair, "L'Élégante de la rue Lepic: A New Look for *Une Passante*", *Contemporary French Civilization*, 34, 2, 2010, pp. 91-114.

Sangsue, Daniel, "Formes brèves. Le Conte et la nouvelle au XIXe siècle", in Patrick Berthier and Michel Jarrety (eds), *Histoire de la France littéraire* (Paris: PUF, 3 vols, 2006), vol. III.

Shapcott, Thomas, "Georges Perec in Brisbane", review section of the *Weekend Australian*, August 14-15 2010, p. 22.

Venuti, Lawrence, *Translation: Theory in Practice* (Oxford & New York: Routledge, 2004).

Viegnes, Michel, *L'Esthétique de la nouvelle française au vingtième siècle* (New York: Peter Lang, 1989).

Vinay, Jean-Paul and Jean Darbelnet, *Stylistique comparée du français et de l'anglais* (Paris: Didier, 1958).

This book is available as a free fully-searchable PDF from
www.adelaide.edu.au/press

www.ingramcontent.com/pod-product-compliance
Lightning Source LLC
Chambersburg PA
CBHW080850190726
48292CB00010B/2942

9781922064608